HOW TO
RECOGNIZE
FLOWERING
WILD
PLANTS

CASTLE BOOKS ★ NEW YORK

how to recognize flowering wild plants

Text and Illustrations by

William Carey Grimm

To

Garvin and Louise Hughes

Jay and Martha Shuler

This edition published by arrangement with
STACKPOLE BOOKS
This title formerly published as Recognizing Flowering Wild Plants

Library of Congress Catalog Card Number 68-30888. Printed in U.S.A.

CONTENTS

PAGE GUIDE
TO PLANT FAMILIES

INTRODUCTION

This book is intended to be a popular guide to the wild flowers found east of the Mississippi River, from the Canadian Provinces southward as far as northern Florida and the Gulf Coast region. It therefore covers a much larger area, and includes many more of the species found in the southeastern part of our country, than other popular books published thus far. An attempt has been made to include the flowering plants most apt to attract one's attention, both on trips afoot and while travelling along the highways. However, we have included some which, although local, are of more than casual interest.

No popular book could possibly include all of the flowering plants of such a vast area, or even a small part of it. That is the province of the more technical manuals, some of which are listed in the "Books to read for further information" at the end of this book. The choice of the species included here is the author's own, but it has been based upon more than forty years of field experience in various parts of the region covered. In general, only herbaceous plants have been admitted, the only exceptions being a few of the more or less woody vines which have particularly showy flowers. Many of our shrubby plants, such as the rhododendrons and azaleas, have truly spectacular flowers. The reader will find all of them treated in the author's book *Recognizing Native Shrubs*.

An annoying feature of many books has been the separation of illustrations and text on different pages, often without any cross-reference to each other. To remedy this fault, the illustrations of the plants and the text pertaining to them will be found on pages which face each other in this book. To accomplish this it was necessary to make the accounts of the species brief, yet they must include whatever information may be necessary to aid in identification.

The arrangement of the plants in the book follows that found in the technical manuals: by flower families and genera. This seemed to be the most logical arrangement. The illustrations are not all on the same scale for the plants differ greatly in size, and this is often true even among those of the same species. Information about the size of the plant, the size and color of its flowers, its habitat, general range, and other items of interest are given in the text. The time of blooming covers the entire range of the plant. Thus "blooming between April and July" may mean that it begins to bloom in April in the southern part of its range, but it may not bloom until July at the northern extremity or at higher elevations in the mountains.

Colored illustrations are beautiful but frequently they tend to be confusing. This is especially true in the case of photographs of the plant taken in its natural environment, where the leaves of surrounding plants are apt to be taken for those of the plant meant to be portrayed. More often than not, they fail to show points essential for identification. There is often considerable variation in the color of the flowers of many species; and all too often even the best color illustrations are so poorly reproduced that they tend to be very misleading.

The 140 pages of pencil drawings in this book portray 728 species of plants. In addition, some 200 species, similar to the ones illustrated, are mentioned, and the user should experience little if any difficulty in identifying them. The scientific names of many of the plants included in the book have been updated, following the *Guide to the Vascular Flora of the Carolinas* (1964); but otherwise they follow the 8th edition of *Grays Manual of Botany* (1950), or Small's *Manual of the Southeastern Flora*.

Because the book has been prepared for users without any special training in botany, botanical terms have been reduced to a minimum. Nevertheless the usage of some terms could not very well be avoided. These have been explained under *Getting acquainted with flowers* (pages 9 through 15) and in the glossary.

GETTING ACQUAINTED WITH FLOWERS

The parts of a flower

Many of us who would like to know more about the wild flowers and be able to recognize them have had little or no training in the subject of botany. For this reason it is well to present here a brief introduction to the structure and arrangement of flowers.

Most of the flowers that we ordinarily see are what the botanist would call a *complete flower*: one which has four sets of flower parts or organs— sepals, petals, stamens, and one or more pistils.

The outermost of these sets of organs are the *sepals*. Very often they are green in color and they cover the parts of the flower in the bud stage. Collectively the sepals are known as the *calyx* of the flower. In some flowers the sepals are more or less united and they may form a sort of cup or tube. In this case it is usually spoken of as the *calyx tube*. Usually it has lobes on its rim which represent the free tips of the individual sepals and they are called the *calyx lobes*. The number of calyx lobes therefore tells us how many sepals have been united to form the calyx tube.

The next series of flower parts is made up of the *petals*. They are usually the showy and brightly colored parts of the flower. Collectively the petals are known as the *corolla* of the flower. As in the case of the sepals, the petals may be joined to one another to form a *corolla tube*. The free ends of the individual petals which were united to form the corolla tube are usually seen as *corolla lobes* on its rim. Often at the bases of the petals there are glands which secrete a sweet substance called nectar, from which bees make their honey. The petals actually serve as billboards to attract bees or other insects to the flower.

Sepals and petals taken together are usually spoken of as the *floral envelopes* or the *perianth* of the flower. While the sepals and petals are quite distinct and differently shaped and colored in most flowers, this is not universally true. In most members of the Lily Family, the Amaryllis Family, and in many plants belonging to the Iris Family, the sepals and petals are very much alike in size and color. It is therefore quite convenient just to speak of them as the *perianth parts*. Some flowers actually have but one set or series of floral envelopes, the sepals. In many members of the Buttercup Family these sepals are white or variously colored and look very much like petals. The sepals, in this case, have taken over the usual role of the petals in attracting insects to the flowers.

9

FLOWER PARTS AND STRUCTURE

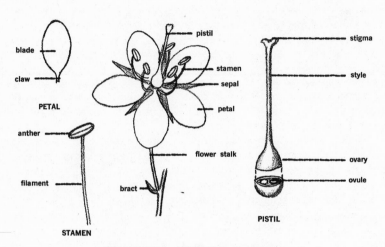

PETAL

STAMEN

PISTIL

blade, claw, anther, filament, bract, pistil, stamen, sepal, petal, flower stalk, stigma, style, ovary, ovule

PARTS OF A COMPLETE FLOWER

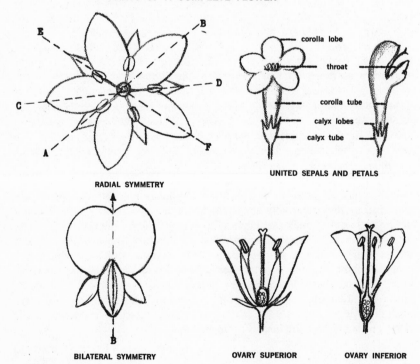

RADIAL SYMMETRY

UNITED SEPALS AND PETALS

corolla lobe, throat, corolla tube, calyx lobes, calyx tube

BILATERAL SYMMETRY

OVARY SUPERIOR

OVARY INFERIOR

Stamens and pistils are the only flower parts that are actually involved in the production of the fruits and seeds. They are the *sexual organs* of flowers. The *stamens* are the organs just inside of the petals when petals are present. They usually have a slender stalk which is called the *filament* and a box-like compartment at the summit which is known as the *anther*. The anthers contain the grain-like, powdery, and usually yellow or yellowish pollen. Stamens are the male organ of a flower.

In the center of the flower there is a *pistil* or sometimes several pistils. Usually the pistil has a somewhat swollen part at its base which is called the *ovary,* inside of which are one to many small bodies known as *ovules*. The summit of the pistil is commonly enlarged, often knob-like or branched, and usually quite sticky. This part of the pistil is the *stigma.* Between the stigma and the ovary there is usually a stalk-like portion called the *style.* Pistils are the female organs of a flower.

Several things must happen before the flower can produce seeds. First of all, some of the pollen must get from the stamens to the sticky stigma of the pistil. This transfer of the pollen is known as *pollination* and in plants with showy flowers bees or other insects usually perform the task. That is why their flowers have attractive petals, alluring odors, and produce the sweet nectar. Following pollination each pollen grain sends a tube down through the style and into the ovary. There it seeks out one of the ovules. A sperm from the pollen goes down this tube and unites with an egg cell within the ovule, a process which is called *fertilization.* Thereafter the egg cell develops into a tiny plant or *embryo* and the ovule becomes a *seed.* The ovary of the pistil (sometimes with other parts attached) matures into what botanists call a *fruit.*

Various devices are frequently employed to assure that pollen from the stamens will not pollinate the pistil of the same flower. In some flowers the anthers will have shed their pollen before the stigma of the pistil is ready to receive the pollen, or vice versa. In some plants the stamens and pistils are found in separate flowers, or the stamen-bearing and pistil-bearing flowers may even be on separate plants.

The forms of flowers

Flower structure is of primary importance in the identification of plants. In fact, botanists base the classification of plants into species, genera, and families on the basis of their flower structure. While color is sometimes useful in making an identification, it is by no means a reliable characteristic. The same species of plant may have flowers in two or more different colors, and the colors of flowers sometimes change with age. Size, too, is quite variable. A plant may vary considerably in size depending upon environmental factors, especially in the case of annuals.

In the simpler types of flowers all of the flower parts are attached to the *receptacle* or enlarged tip of the stem, and they are all separate and distinct. Good examples are seen in members of the Buttercup Family. A flower in which the ovary of the pistil is free from the surrounding parts is said to be a *superior ovary*. In many flowers the ovary is more or less surrounded by and united with the calyx tube or the receptacle. Such flowers are said to have an *inferior ovary*. The filaments of the stamens in many flowers are attached to the petals or the corolla tube rather than the receptacle.

In many flowers all of the flower parts radiate from the center of the flower and those in each series are more or less alike in size and shape. Like a pie, such a flower could be divided in any number of directions through the center into quite identical halves. Such a flower is said to have a *radial symmetry*. It is often called a *regular flower*.

It should take but one look at a flower of a pea, mint, violet, or orchid to see that it could be divided into two similar halves by cutting it in but one direction—vertically through the center. A flower of this type has a *bilateral symmetry*. It is often called an *irregular flower*. Often when the sepals or petals of a flower are joined together, the calyx or the corolla will be two-lipped. Such flowers are common among the members of the Mint Family but they also occur in many of the other flower families.

Flower clusters or inflorescences

Flowers may be solitary but more often they are arranged in various types of flower clusters or *inflorescences* as shown diagramatically on page 13. A *spike* is a simple inflorescence of stalkless flowers which are arranged along a stem. A *raceme* is similar except that the flowers are stalked. A *head* is a dense cluster of stalkless or very short-stalked flowers at the tip of a stem. In an *umbel* the flowers are on stalks which all arise from the summit of a stem. It is the typical inflorescence of the Parsley Family but it also occurs among the members of other flower families. A *panicle* is a branching flower cluster which may be likened to a compound raceme. The *cyme* is also a branching flower cluster, a more or less forking one in which the central flowers open first, and it tends to be flat-topped. Another flat-topped inflorescence is the *corymb* but in this one it is the outer or marginal flowers which open first.

It is very easy to be fooled unless one is very observant, and what is usually taken to be a flower may really be a flower cluster. In the Arum Family the flowers are quite small and seated on a thick and somewhat fleshy stem called a *spadix*. Usually the spadix is more or less surrounded by a large and often colorful bract called a *spathe*. The "flowers" of the familiar Jack-in-the-pulpit and the cultivated calla-lilies are good examples.

The sunflower or a daisy is not a flower in the ordinary sense, but rather a dense cluster—a head—of many small flowers. What may be mistaken for petals are the marginal *ray flowers* which have a strap-shaped corolla. In the center of the head is a prominent *disk* which contains a large number of small flowers (*disk flowers*) which have a tubular corolla. The entire head is surrounded by an *involucre* made up of greenish bracts which may

12

TYPES OF INFLORESCENCES

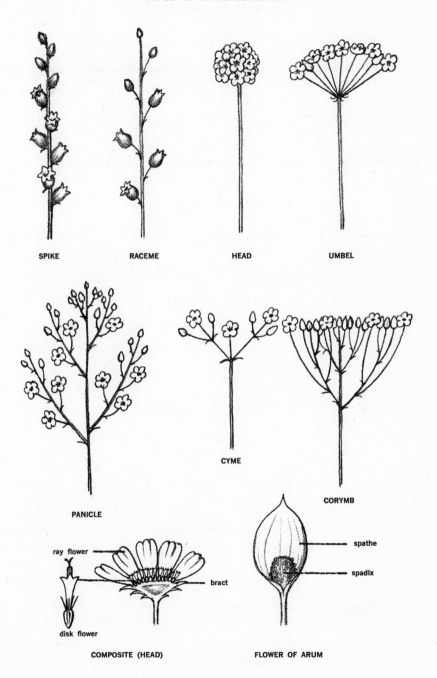

SPIKE   RACEME   HEAD   UMBEL

CYME

PANICLE

CORYMB

ray flower

bract

disk flower

spathe

spadix

COMPOSITE (HEAD)   FLOWER OF ARUM

LEAF PARTS AND TYPES OF LEAVES

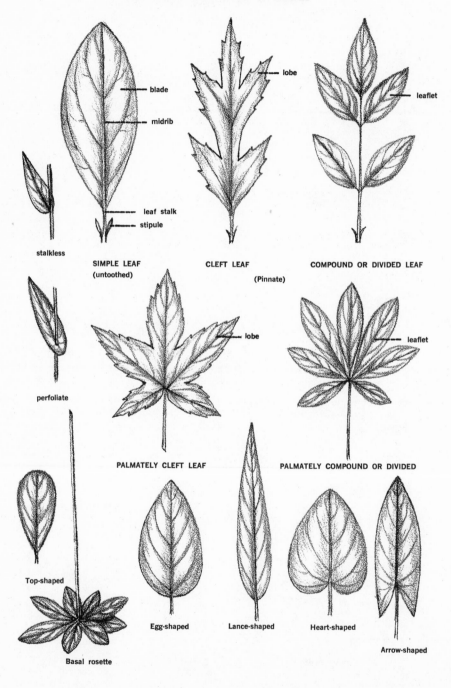

blade

midrib

lobe

leaflet

leaf stalk

stipule

stalkless

SIMPLE LEAF
(untoothed)

CLEFT LEAF

(Pinnate)

COMPOUND OR DIVIDED LEAF

perfoliate

lobe

leaflet

PALMATELY CLEFT LEAF

PALMATELY COMPOUND OR DIVIDED

Top-shaped

Egg-shaped

Lance-shaped

Heart-shaped

Arrow-shaped

Basal rosette

be mistaken for sepals. Sunflowers, daisies, asters, goldenrods, and many other common flowers are called *composites*. They are members of the very large Composite Family.

Types and arrangements of leaves

Leaves show a marked variation in size, shape, and arrangement on the stems. In a few cases plants have leaves which are so distinctive that they may be identified by the leaves alone. Many of the features of leaves are shown on page 14 and it would be well to become acquainted with them.

Most leaves have a flattened and more or less broad portion which is called the *blade*. In a great many there is a prominent central vein or *midrib* from which the veins branch off like the barbs from the shaft of a feather. Such a leaf is said to be *pinnately-veined,* or feather-veined. Other leaves have several main veins which radiate from the base or from the summit of a leaf stalk. This type of leaf is *palmately-veined.* The margin of the leaf blade may be untoothed or *entire*, or it may have teeth of various sizes or shapes. Sometimes a leaf blade is deeply cut or cleft, or it may be divided into smaller leaf-like parts which are called *leaflets.* A leaf in which the blade is in one piece is known as a *simple leaf.* One in which the blade is divided into leaflets is called a *compound leaf.* A leaf may be *pinnately* divided or pinnately compound or *palmately* divided or palmately compound. In many leaves there will be a pair of appendages or *stipules* at the base of the leaf stalk.

WHY PLANTS HAVE SCIENTIFIC NAMES

Have you ever wondered why plants have scientific names, or why common names are not good enough?

To begin with, and this may amaze you, most of our wild plants actually have no common names at all. They never have been given any. On the other hand, every known kind of plant does have a scientific name.

Common names are frequently very confusing. In some instances the same name is used for two or more entirely different plants. Button-snakeroot, for example, is used as a common name for plants in both the Parsley and Composite families. Samson's-snakeroot may be either a gentian or member of the Pea family. A fireweed may be a plant belonging to either the Evening-primrose or the Composite Familes; and a loosestrife could be either a true loosestrife or an entirely different plant of the Primrose Family.

To make things a bit more confusing, a plant may be known by more than one common name. Thus the little member of the Lily Family which bears the scientific name *Erythronium americanum* is variously known as the Trout-lily, Fawn-lily, Yellow Adder's-tongue, and even Dog's-tooth Violet. Often a plant is known by one common name in one part of its range and by other names elsewhere. It is obvious, too, that common names are often misleading in that they do not show the true relationship of a plant. The little lily-like plant just mentioned is most certainly not a violet, nor even remotely related to the true violets.

Scientific names have several advantages. First there can be but one plant known as *Erythronium americanum*. It cannot therefore be confused with any other plant. The first part of its scientific name tells us that it belongs to the genus *Erythronium*. It is the generic name of the plant and this particular genus is a member of the Lily Family. Its relationship is thus firmly established beyond a doubt. The second part of the name—*americanum*—is the Latin adjectival name, the two together comprising the name of the species. In this case it means "American". Scientific names are always in Latin and are the same throughout the world, regardless of language differences in the various countries.

In some cases two or more varieties of the same species of plant may be recognized. *Cypripedium calceolus* is the Yellow Lady's-slipper of the Old World. Botanists now recognize our American plants as a variety of this wide-ranging species. Thus our Yellow Lady's-slipper is known as *Cypripedium calceolus var.* (or variety) *pubescens*.

16

Naturally the question is going to arise as to why the scientific names do not always agree in even the technical manuals. The rule is that the first published name, accompanied by a valid description of the plant, becomes its scientific name. Thus a great many of the scientific names of our plants have remained the same for a long time, even for more than two centuries. Often, however, researchers find that a plant was given a valid scientific name before one in current usage was given; and in such a case it becomes necessary to make a change in its name. Research is constantly continuing in the taxonomy of plants and for other reasons a name may become invalid. As we learn more about the true relationship of species, a change often becomes necessary in the name. Thus botanists no longer accept *Ascyrum* and *Hypericum* as two distinctly different genera of plants. All species formerly placed in the genus *Ascyrum* are now regarded as species of *Hypericum*. Someday such matters will, of course, be definitely decided, but right now they are in a state of flux.

Scientific names are actually not as dreadful as they may at first seem. We use many of the generic names of plants—names such as *Trillium, Hepatica, Anemone,* and *Chrysanthemum*—without ever thinking, or perhaps even knowing, that they are scientific names. Others such as *Lilium* (lilies), *Viola* (violets), and *Rosa* (roses) come very close to the English equivalents of the generic names. With a little practice one could soon become adept at using scientific names of plants and appreciate their advantages.

GLOSSARY

ACHENE   A small, dry, 1-seeded fruit which does not split open at maturity.

ALTERNATE   Spaced singly along the stem.

ANTHER   The part of a stamen that produces pollen.

AQUATIC   Living in water.

ASCENDING   Rising obliquely upward or curving upward.

AXIL   The upper angle that a leaf makes with the stem.

AXILLARY   Borne in the axil of a leaf or bract.

BEAK   A long and prominent point.

BEARD   A group of long or stiff hairs.

BERRY   A fruit formed from a single ovary which is fleshy or pulpy throughout.

BILATERAL   A flower so constructed that it can be divided into two like halves only by dividing it vertically through the center.

BLADE   The expanded or flat part of a leaf or a petal.

BLOOM   A powdery or waxy substance which is easily rubbed off.

BRACT   A small or scale-like leaf associated with a flower cluster.

BRISTLE   A stiff hair.

BULB   A kind of underground bud with fleshy scales.

CALYX   The outer circle of floral organs; a term used for the sepals collectively.

CAPSULE   A dry pod formed from two or more carpels which splits open along two or more lines at maturity.

CARPEL   A simple pistil or one of the parts of a compound pistil.

CELL   A compartment or division of a compound ovary.

CHAFF   A small, thin, dry scale associated with the disk flowers in many composites.

CLAW   The narrow base or stalk of a petal.

CLEFT   Deeply cut but not divided.

COLUMN   The central structure of an orchid flower composed of one or two staments united with the style and stigma.

COMPOUND LEAF   A leaf in which the blade is divided into two or more leaf-like parts or leaflets.

CORM   The enlarged base of a stem which is bulb-like but solid.

18

COROLLA   A collective name for the petals of a flower, either separate or joined together.

CORYMB   A more or less flat-topped inflorescence in which the outer or marginal flowers open first.

CRESTED   Having elevated ridges or projections.

CYME   A more *or* less flat-topped inflorescence in which the central flowers open first.

DISK FLOWER   The tubular flowers in the center of the heads of some composites such as asters and daisies.

DISTINCT   Separate; not united.

DIVIDED   Separated to the base.

DOWNY   Possessing short, fine, and soft hairs.

ELLIPTIC (ELLIPTICAL)   Oval-shaped and about equally narrowed to both ends.

ENTIRE   A leaf margin which is untoothed.

EPIPHYTE   A plant growing upon another plant or other elevated support but not parasitic; an "air-plant".

EYE   A prominent mark in the center of a flower.

FEATHER-VEINED   A leaf in which the veins arise along the sides of a midrib.

FERTILE STAMEN   A stamen which produces pollen.

FILAMENT   The long and slender or stalk-like part of a stamen.

FLORET   A small flower, especially one in a dense cluster.

FREE   Not joined to other organs.

FRUIT   The seed-bearing body of a plant; botanically a ripened ovary together with parts united with it.

GLAND   A secreting surface or appendage.

HEAD   A dense cluster of stalkless or very short-stalked flowers on a stem end.

HOARY   Grayish-white with fine and close hairs.

INFERIOR OVARY   An ovary which is surrounded by and united with the calyx of a flower.

INFLATED   Seemingly blown up; bladdery.

INFLORESCENCE   A group or cluster of flowers.

INSERTED   Attached to or growing out of something.

INVOLUCRE   A circle (or circles) of bracts beneath a flower or a flower cluster.

IRREGULAR FLOWER   A flower in which the parts are not of the same size or shape; a bilaterally symmetric flower.

KEEL   The two lower petals of a pea-like or papilionaceous flower; with a central ridge like the keel of a boat.

LANCE-SHAPED   A leaf which is much longer than broad, widest near the base and gradually tapered to the tip.

LEAFLET   One of the leaf-like divisions of a compound leaf.

LINEAR   Long and narrow with the sides parallel or nearly so; like the leaves of grasses.

LIP   One of the parts of an unequally divided calyx or corolla; in orchids the petal, usually the lowest, which differs in size, shape, and often in color from the other petals.

LOBE   A more or less rounded or projecting part of a leaf, or the calyx or corolla of a flower.

MIDRIB   The central or main vein of a leaf, often appearing like an extension of the leaf stalk.

NODE   The point on a stem to which a leaf or leaves are attached.

NUTLET   A small, hard, dry fruit.

OBLONG   Longer than wide and with the sides nearly parallel.

OVAL   Broadly elliptical; broadest near the middle and rounded at both ends.

OVARY   The basal part of a pistil which contains the ovules.

OVULE   A small body (or bodies) within the ovary which develops into the seed.

PALMATE   Veins, lobes, or divisions of leaves which radiate from one central point like the spread fingers of a hand.

PANICLE   A branching and raceme-like flower cluster.

PAPILIONACEOUS   Butterfly-like; a term used for flowers of the Pea Family which have a standard, wings, and keel.

PAPPUS   Hairs, bristles, or scales that form the calyx limb in composites.

PARASITE   An organism which obtains its food directly from another living organism or host.

PARTED   Cleft nearly but not quite to the base.

PERIANTH   The parts of a flower (usually sepals and petals) surrounding the stamens and pistils.

PETAL   One of the separate divisions of the corolla; the part of the flower which is usually white or colored other than green.

PINNATE   Veins, lobes, or divisions of leaves which are arranged along the sides of a midrib.

PISTIL   The central organ of a flower, the ovary of which develops into a fruit.

POLLEN   The minute grains produced in the anthers and containing the male reproductive cells.

POLLINIUM   A mass of pollen grains which are shed as a unit from an anther.

RACEME   A simple long and narrow inflorescence of stalked flowers.

RADIALLY SYMMETRIC   A flower so constructed that all of its parts radiate from the center; it can be divided in any direction through the center into two similar halves.

RAY or RAY FLOWER   In composites the flowers with strap-shaped, petal-like corollas.

RECEPTACLE   The enlarged or expanded end of a stem to which the parts of a flower are attached; in composites, the enlarged stem end to which the flowers of the head are attached.

RECURVED   Curved backward or downward.

REFLEXED   Abruptly bent or turned downward.

REGULAR FLOWER   A flower in which the parts in each series of organs are alike in size and shape; a radially symmetric flower.

RIB   A primary or prominent vein of a leaf.

ROOTSTOCK   An underground stem which grows more or less horizontally.

ROSETTE   A circle of leaves which lies more or less flat on the ground.

RUNNER   A slender or trailing stem which takes root at the nodes, or points to which leaves are attached.

SEPAL   One of the separate parts of the calyx or outermost circle of flower parts.

SMOOTH   Without roughness or lacking hairs.

SPADIX   A thick stem bearing crowded, small, stalkless flowers; it is characteristic of the Arum Family.

SPATHE   A large bract surrounding or partially surrounding a flower or flower cluster.

SPIKE   A simple inflorescence of stalkless flowers arranged along a common stem.

SPUR   A hollow tubular or sac-like projection of a petal (or sepal).

STAMEN   The pollen-bearing part of a flower.

STANDARD   The broad upper petal in a pea-like or papilionaceous flower.

STERILE STAMEN   A stamen which lacks a pollen-producing anther.

STIGMA   The part of the pistil (usually at the summit) which receives the pollen.

STIPULE   An appendage, usually in pairs, at the base of the leaf stalk.

STOLONIFEROUS   Having stolons or runners.

STYLE   The part of the pistil above the ovary which bears the stigma.

SUPERIOR OVARY   An ovary that is free from and placed above all other parts of the flower.

TENDRIL   A slender and twining outgrowth used in climbing.

TERNATE   Arranged in three's, or divided into three parts.

THROAT   The opening into the tube of a calyx or corolla having united sepals or petals.

TUBER   A short, thick underground stem.

UMBEL   A flower cluster in which the flower stalks arise from a common point at the tip of a stem.

WHORL   A circle of leaves about a stem.

WING   A thin, flat extension; one of the two side petals of a pea-like or papilionaceous flower.

WOOLLY   Bearing hairs which are curled or more or less matted.

HOW TO USE THIS BOOK

The following key is provided to the flower families which are covered in this book, and keys to the genera of some of the larger or more difficult families will be found following the discussions of the family characteristics elsewhere in the book.

A key is a guide or aid in helping one to identify a flower without thumbing through the book page by page. Insofar as possible, characteristics which may be seen with the naked eye have been used in the keys, but there were a few cases where this was not feasible. At any rate, a serious student of plants will sooner or later find that a good hand lens or magnifying glass is a very handy piece of equipment.

In using the following key, first decide into which class—monocots or dicots—the plant belongs. Next decide into which group it belongs. Having done this, we proceed to use the sets of numbers beginning with number 1, then 2, 3, etc. until the plant family is found. The numbers are based on two sets of opposing characteristics.

Suppose, for example, we have a plant in which the leaves are distinctly netveined and the flower parts—sepals, petals, and stamens—are in fives. From these characteristics we decide that the plant is a dicot from the description given. As our plant has flowers with both sepals and petals— two sets of floral envelopes—it can't belong in Groups I or II, and as the petals are not united it must belong to Group III. Now we will proceed to number 1 under this group, and take the following steps.

1. This first number 1 reads, *"Ovary of the pistil free from other parts of the flower and aparently situated above them."* As the flowers of our plant obviously have the calyx united with the ovary, we proceed to the second number 1 which reads, *"Ovary of the pistil wholly or partly united with the calyx and apparently situated below the other parts of the flower"*. As this fits our flower, we shall proceed to number 2.

2. The first number 2 reads, *"Pistils 2, etc.",* but as our flower has but a single pistil we will go to the second number 2. Here we find, *"Pistil apparently solitary, completely concealed by and more or less united with the calyx tube."* As this is correct, we shall proceed to number 3.

3. The first number 3 reads, *"Petals and stamens numerous. Plants with fleshy, jointed, flattened, and usually spiny stems."* As none of these characteristics fit our plant, we will proceed to the second number 3. Here we find, *"Petals, sepals, and stamens relatively few."* This seems to fit, so we will go on to number 4.

4. The first number 4 reads, *"Sepals and petals usually in 4's."* As the flower of our plant has 5 petals, we shall go to the second 4. This reads, *"Sepals and petals in 5's. The flowers mostly arranged in umbels."* This is correct and the flowers of our plant are arranged in umbels, so we will go on to number 5.

5. The first number 5 reads, *"Pistil with 2 to 5 styles. Fruit a berry."* Our plant has a pistil with but 2 styles and the fruits do not seem to be berries, so we shall try the second number 5. There we read, *"Pistil with 2 styles, surrounded at their base by a prominent disk. Fruits dry and seed-like."* This description seems to fit our plant perfectly and we find that it is a member of the Parsley Family or *Umbelliferae*.

The serious student of flowers should become acquainted with the characteristics of the various flower families. A short discussion of the outstanding characteristics of the various families treated in this book will be found before the accounts of the species. Familiarity with them will make it much easier to identify an unknown flower.

KEY TO THE FLOWER FAMILIES

MONOCOTS

The flower parts of monocots are usually in 3's (rarely in 4's). The leaves have unbranched veins which usually run parallel to each other from the base of the leaf to the tip (Trilliums and some members of the Arum Family are exceptions in that the leaves have branching veins).

GROUP I. FLOWERS WITHOUT FLORAL ENVELOPES OR SOMETIMES WITH INCONSPICUOUS SEPALS.

1. Flowers (sometimes with small sepals) crowded and seated directly upon a thick and fleshy stalk (*spadix*), which is often subtended or partly surrounded by a leaf-like structure (*spathe*). ARUM FAMILY (*Araceae*) Page 35

1. Flowers not crowded on a thick and fleshy stalk.

  2. Flowers in ball-like heads and arranged along a simple or branching stalk. BUR-REED FAMILY (*Sparganiaceae*) Page 32

  2. Flowers in small, scaly-bracted, more or less cone-shaped end clusters. Grass-like plants with usually 3-sided stems, each leaf with a basal sheath surrounding the stem. SEDGE FAMILY (*Cyperaceae*) Page 32

GROUP II. FLOWERS WITH A DEFINITE PERIANTH, USUALLY WITH 3 SEPALS AND 3 PETALS.

1. Flowers in a tightly packed head at the end of a long and leafless stem.

  2. Heads of flowers cone-shaped to cylindrical. Petals yellow. Flowers nearly covered by hard, dry, overlapping scales. YELLOW-EYED GRASS FAMILY (*Xyridaceae*) Page 36

  2. Heads of flowers button-shaped or roundish. The flowers small, whitish, with a perianth of dry scales. PIPEWORT FAMILY (*Eriocaulaceae*) Page 36

1. Flowers not in tightly packed heads.

  2. Pistils 6 or more and crowded in heads or ring-like clusters. Stamens often numerous and sometimes in separate flowers. Flowers with 3 green sepals and 3 white or pinkish petals. WATER-PLANTAIN FAMILY (*Alismataceae*) Page 32

  2. Pistil solitary, composed of 3 united carpels and often showing 3 distinct styles or stigmas. Stamens 6 or fewer.

    3. Ovary of the pistil free from the perianth parts and seemingly situated above the other parts of the flower.

      4. Sepals and petals different in size or color.

        5. Flowers clustered, arising from folded spathes or with leafy bracts at their base. Anthers not much longer than broad and sometimes only 3 of them fertile. Pistil with a single style. Leaves alternate and with bases sheathing the stem. SPIDERWORT FAMILY (*Commelinaceae*) Page 39

        5. Flowers solitary. Anthers much longer than broad. Pistil with 3 styles. Leaves in a whorl of 3 beneath the flower. TRILLIUMS in LILY FAMILY (*Liliaceae*) Page 59

      4. Sepals and petals very much alike in size and color.

        5. Perianth with a bilateral symmetry and somewhat 2-lipped. Stamens 3 or 6, unequal in length and attached to the perianth

tube. Flowers usually blue, solitary or in a spike-like cluster subtended by a leafy bract. Aquatic plants.
PICKERELWEED FAMILY (*Pontederiaceae*) Page 39

5. Perianth with a radial symmetry. Stamens 6 (rarely 4) and about the same length; free from or joined to the base of the perianth tube. Flowers solitary or variously clustered.
LILY FAMILY (*Liliaceae*) Page 40

3. Ovary of the pistil more or less united with the perianth parts or tube and thus appearing to be below the other parts of the flower.

4. Flowers with 6 stamens; arranged in showy umbels.
AMARYLLIS FAMILY (*Amaryllidaceae*) Page 63

4. Flowers with fewer than 6 stamens.

5. Flowers with a radial symmetry or nearly so. Stamens 3.

6. Stamens attached to the base of the 3 larger and inner perianth parts (petals). Flowers woolly on the outside. Plant with a bright red juice.
BLOODWORT FAMILY (*Haemodoraceae*) Page 63

6. Stamens attached to the base of the 3 outer perianth parts (sepals), their filaments sometimes forming a tube about the pistil. Styles united except at the tips, or deeply parted and petal-like. Leaves grass-like or sword-shaped and placed edge to edge.
IRIS FAMILY (*Iridaceae*) Page 64

5. Flowers very irregular and with a bilateral symmetry. Central petal usually markedly different from the other 2 and forming a "lip". Stamens 1 or 2, united with the style to form a central structure or "column".
ORCHID FAMILY (*Orchidaceae*) Page 68

DICOTS

The flower parts of dicots are usually in 4's or 5's (rarely in 3's), in multiples of these numbers, or indefinite in number. The leaves usually have a network of branching veins (net-veined leaves).

GROUP I. FLOWERS WITHOUT FLORAL ENVELOPES, NEITHER SEPALS NOR PETALS PRESENT.

1. Flowers grouped in a calyx-like cup with prominent glands or petal-like lobes on its rim. Flowers consist of single-stalked stamens or a stalked and 3-lobed pistil with 3 spreading styles. The plants have a milky juice.
SPURGE FAMILY (*Euphorbiaceae*) Page 165

1. Flowers arranged in a long and narrow, recurved cluster. Each flower consisting of 6 to 8 stamens and a 3- or 4-parted pistil.
LIZARD'S-TAIL FAMILY (*Sauraceae*) Page 82

GROUP II. FLOWERS WITH BUT ONE SET OF FLORAL ENVELOPES, THE SEPALS. THESE OFTEN COLORED AND PETAL-LIKE.

1. Stamens numerous and indefinite in number. Flower parts all separate and distinct. The pistils usually several or numerous (rarely 1).
BUTTERCUP FAMILY (*Ranunculaceae*) Page 192

1. Stamens 12 or fewer.

2. Sepals 3, these united to form a flask-shaped or urn-shaped cup with 3 lobes on the rim. Plants with aromatic rootstocks and more or less heart-shaped leaves.
BIRTHWORT FAMILY (*Aristolochiaceae*) Page 85

2. Sepals 5 or 6 in number.

3. Sepals 5, these united below into a cup with 5 teeth on its rim. Stamens 5. SANDALWOOD FAMILY (*Santalaceae*) Page 82

3. Sepals 5 or 6 in number, all separate and distinct.

    4. Stamens 10, surrounding the large and somewhat 10-lobed pistil which develops into a purplish-black berry. POKEWEED FAMILY (*Phytolaccaceae*) Page 89

    4. Stamens 6. Sepals often rosy-pink. Stems usually jointed and surrounded by a tube-like sheath above each leaf. BUCKWHEAT FAMILY (*Polygonaceae*) Page 82

GROUP III. FLOWERS WITH TWO SETS OF FLORAL ENVELOPES, BOTH SEPALS AND PETALS. THE PETALS FREE FROM EACH OTHER AND DISTINCT.

1. Ovary of the pistil free from other parts of the flower and apparently situated above them.

  2. Stamens numerous, their number indefinite.

    3. Petals numerous and showing a gradual transition into stamens. Plants aquatic. WATERLILY FAMILY (*Nymphaeaceae*) Page 90

    3. Petals usually 12 or fewer.

      4. Stamens united by their filaments to form a column about the styles of the pistil. MALLOW FAMILY (*Malvaceae*) Page 166

      4. Stamens all separate and distinct.

        5. Sepals 2, falling as the flower opens. Petals usually 4 but sometimes 8 to 12. Plants with a colored or milky juice. POPPY FAMILY (*Papaveraceae*) Page 111

        5. Sepals 4 or 5 and usually persisting.

          6. Flowers with several to many pistils. Leaves usually toothed, cleft, or divided into leaflets.

            7. Stamens attached to the receptacle below the group of pistils. Leaves without stipules. BUTTERCUP FAMILY (*Ranunculaceae*) Page 92

            7. Stamens attached to a disk on the calyx. Leaves usually with prominent stipules. ROSE FAMILY (*Rosaceae*) Page 131

          6. Flowers with but 1 pistil. Leaves with entire margins.

            7. Pistil with 4 or 5 distinct styles. Leaves opposite, often with minute black or transparent dots. ST. JOHN'S-WORT FAMILY (*Hypericaceae*) Page 169

            7. Pistil with a single style or sometimes none. Leaves alternate. ROCKROSE FAMILY (*Cistaceae*) Page 170

  2. Stamens usually no more than twice the number of petals.

    3. Flowers with a radial symmetry.

      4. Sepals 2. Flowers with 5 petals, 5 stamens, and a solitary pistil with 3 styles. Plants fleshy. PURSLANE FAMILY (*Portulacaceae*) Page 86

      4. Sepals more than 2.

        5. Pistil solitary.

6. Sepals and petals not in 5's.
  7. Sepals and petals 4, the latter forming a cross. Stamens 6, two of them shorter.
        MUSTARD FAMILY (*Cruciferae*) Page 115
  7. Sepals 4 or 6. Petals 6 to 9. Stamens as many or twice as many as the petals.
        BARBERRY FAMILY (*Berberidaceae*) Page 108
6. Sepals and petals usually in 5's (rarely in 4's).
  7. Bog plants with leaves in a basal cluster or rosette.
    8. Leaves hollow, pitcher-like or trumpet-shaped.
        PITCHER-PLANT FAMILY (*Sarraceniaceae*) Page 120
    8. Leaves otherwise.
      9. Leaves covered with hairs bearing sticky globules on their tips.
        SUNDEW FAMILY (*Droseraceae*) Page 119
      9. Leaves with broadly winged stalks above which is a trap-like blade with bristles about the margin.
        VENUS'-FLYTRAP FAMILY (*Dionaeaceae*) Page 119
  7. Leaves not in a basal rosette; if in a basal cluster not bog plants.
    8. Tendril-bearing vines. Flowers with a stalked pistil, 5 pendant anthers, and a fringed crown between the sepals and petals.
        PASSION-FLOWER FAMILY (*Passifloraceae*) Page 181
    8. Plants not tendril-bearing vines. Flowers otherwise.
      9. Leaves deeply cut or divided.
        10. Leaves divided into 3 inversely heart-shaped leaflets.
        WOOD-SORREL FAMILY (*Oxalidaceae*) Page 158
        10. Leaves palmately cut or divided with the divisions variously cut or toothed.
        GERANIUM FAMILY (*Geraniaceae*) Page 158
      9. Leaves entire.
        10. Petals and stamens attached to the calyx tube.
        LOOSESTRIFE FAMILY (*Lythraceae*) Page 181
        10. Petals and stamens otherwise.
          11. Sepals more or less united, at least at the base. Leaves opposite. Stems often swollen at the nodes.
        PINK FAMILY (*Caryophyllaceae*) Page 86
          11. Sepals not united. Leaves alternate or opposite; small, narrow, and numerous.
        FLAX FAMILY (*Linaceae*) Page 161
5. Pistils 2 or more.
  6. Pistils 2, more or less united at the base. Sepals and petals 5. Stamens 5 or 10.
        SAXIFRAGE FAMILY (*Saxifragaceae*) Page 123
  6. Pistils 4 or 5. Sepals and petals 4 or 5. Stamens 8 or 10. Plants fleshy.
        ORPINE FAMILY (*Crassulaceae*) Page 123

3. Flowers with a bilateral symmetry.
    4. Flowers with 1 or more sacs or spurs.
        5. Sepals 5, greenish and distinct from the petals. Petals 5, the lowermost one extended backward as a sac or spur.
            VIOLET FAMILY (*Violaceae*) Page 173
        5. Sepals inconspicuous or colored like the petals.
            6. Sepals 2, very small. Petals 4, 2 of them large and 2 small; one or more of the large petals extended backward as a sac or spur. Plants with leaf blades divided and often finely cut.
                FUMITORY FAMILY (*Fumariaceae*) Page 112
            6. Sepals 3, the lower one extended backward as a spurred sac. Petals 5, all very unequal. Leaves with a 1-piece blade. Plants with very watery stems.
                JEWELWEED FAMILY (*Balsaminaceae*) Page 165
    4. Flowers without sacs or spurs.
        5. Sepals 5, united at the base and distinct from the petals. Stamens usually 10 and often united by their filaments into two groups. Petals 5, sometimes nearly equal but more often the flowers pea-like or papilionaceous. Fruit as legume.
            PEA FAMILY (*Leguminosae*) Page 136
        5. Sepals 5 but the 2 side ones petal-like and forming wings. Petals 3, grouped together to form a tube, the lower one often crested or fringed at the tip.
            MILKWORT FAMILY (*Polygalaceae*) Page 161
1. Ovary of the pistil more or less united with the calyx and apparently situated below the other parts of the flower.
    2. Pistils 2, the ovaries partially covered by a cup-like disk.
        SAXIFRAGE FAMILY (*Saxifragaceae*) Page 123
    2. Pistil apparently solitary, the ovary completely concealed by and more or less united with the calyx tube.
        3. Petals and stamens numerous. Plants with fleshy, jointed, flattened and usually spiny stems.
            CACTUS FAMILY (*Cactaceae*) Page 181
        3. Petals, sepals, and stamens relatively few.
            4. Sepals and petals usually in 4's.
                5. Calyx tube urn- or bell-shaped with a narrow neck and 4-lobed rim; united with ovary only near its base.
                    MEADOW-BEAUTY FAMILY (*Melastomataceae*) Page 182
                5. Calyx tube and ovary completely united.
                    6. Stamens 4. Style unbranched. Flowers small, crowded in a head which is surrounded by 4 large and petal-like bracts.
                        DOGWOOD FAMILY (*Cornaceae*) Page 189
                    6. Stamens 8. Style with 4 branches at the tip.
                        EVENING-PRIMROSE FAMILY (*Onagraceae*) Page 185
            4. Sepals and petals in 5's. The flowers usually in umbels.
                5. Pistil with 2 to 5 styles. Fruit a berry.
                    GINSENG FAMILY (*Araliaceae*) Page 189
                5. Pistil with 2 styles, surrounded at the base by a prominent disk. Fruits dry.
                    PARSLEY FAMILY (*Umbelliferae*) Page 190

GROUP IV. FLOWERS WITH TWO SETS OF FLORAL ENVELOPES, BOTH SEPALS AND PETALS. THE PETALS MORE OR LESS UNITED.

1. Ovary of the pistil free from other parts of the flower and apparently situated above them.
2. Flowers with a radial symmetry or very nearly so.
3. Stamens not attached to the corolla.
4. Petals but slightly united at the base.   WINTERGREEN FAMILY (*Pyrolaceae*) Page 199
4. Petals well united at least toward the base.   HEATH FAMILY (*Ericaceae*) Page 200
3. Stamens attached to the corolla.
4. Anther-bearing stamens 5, these alternating with scale-like sterile ones.   GALAX FAMILY (*Galacaceae*) Page 200
4. Anther-bearing stamens not alternating with scale-like sterile ones.
5. Stamens placed opposite the lobes of the corolla.   PRIMROSE FAMILY (*Primulaceae*) Page 203
5. Stamens alternating with the corolla lobes.
6. Pistils 2, at least the stigmas united and maturing into pairs of pod-like fruits. Seeds with silky tufts of hairs. Plants usually with a milky juice.
7. Styles of the pistils united. Stamens separate.   DOGBANE FAMILY (*Apocynaceae*) Page 212
7. Styles of the pistils not united. Anthers of the stamens united in a tube about the disk-like stigma of the pistil.   MILKWEED FAMILY (*Asclepiadaceae*) Page 212
6. Pistil solitary or apparently so.
7. Ovary without partitions and containing many ovules.
8. Leaves opposite and entire.   GENTIAN FAMILY (*Gentianaceae*) Page 204
8. Leaves alternate or all at the base; either toothed, lobed, or divided.   WATERLEAF FAMILY (*Hydrophyllaceae*) Page 224
7. Ovary of the pistil showing 2 or more partitions in cross-section, or with 4 lobes.
8. Stamens 2 or 4 in number.
9. Fruit a group of 4 hard seed-like structures.   VERBENA FAMILY (*Verbenaceae*) Page 228
9. Fruit a 2-celled and many-seeded capsule.   ACANTHUS FAMILY (*Acanthaceae*) Page 250
8. Stamens 5 in number.
9. Pistil with a deeply 4-lobed ovary which develops into a group of 4 hard seed-like structures.   BORAGE FAMILY (*Boraginaceae*) Page 227
9. Pistil with an ovary which is not 4-lobed.
10. Stigma of the pistil with 3 branches.   PHLOX FAMILY (*Polemoniaceae*) Page 220

29

10. Stigma unbranched or with 2 or 4 branches.
    11. Leaves opposite.   **LOGANIA FAMILY** (*Loganiaceae*) Page 204
    11. Leaves alternate.
        12. Ovary with 2 chambers, each containing a pair of ovules.   **MORNING-GLORY FAMILY** (*Convolvulaceae*) Page 219
        12. Ovary with 2 chambers, each containing a number of ovules.   **NIGHTSHADE FAMILY** (*Solanaceae*) Page 237
2. Flowers with a bilateral symmetry.
    3. Aquatic plants with minute bladders on the usually thread-like leaves; or plants of wet places without obvious leaves, or with a basal rosette of pale green leaves and solitary spurred flowers on naked stems.   **BLADDERWORT FAMILY** (*Lentibulariaceae*) Page 249
    3. Plants otherwise.
        4. Plants (of woodlands) which lack green color and true leaves; they are parasitic on roots of other plants.   **BROOM-RAPE FAMILY** (*Orobanchaceae*) Page 246
        4. Plants with green color and normal leaves.
            5. More or less woody vines.   **BIGNONIA FAMILY** (*Bignoniaceae*) Page 246
            5. Plants other than woody vines.
                6. Ovary of the pistil deeply 4-lobed, developing into a group of 4 hard, dry, seed-like structures.
                    7. Anther-bearing stamens 5. Flower clusters unrolling from the tip and straightening as the flowers expand. Leaves alternate.   **BORAGE FAMILY** (*Boraginaceae*) Page 227
                    7. Anther-bearing stamens either 2 or 4, if 4 one pair shorter than the other. Leaves opposite.   **MINT FAMILY** (*Labiatae*) Page 229
                6. Ovary of the pistil not deeply 4-lobed.
                    7. Ovary 1-celled and 1-seeded, in fruit bending sharply downward.   **LOPSEED FAMILY** (*Phrymaceae*) Page 250
                    7. Ovary otherwise.
                        8. Ovary developing into 4 hard, dry, seed-like structures.   **VERBENA FAMILY** (*Verbenaceae*) Page 228
                        8. Ovary 2-celled, each cell containing a number of small ovules.
                            9. Seeds supported by short hooks or cup-like expansions of the ovary wall, forcibly thrown by the exploding capsules.   **ACANTHUS FAMILY** (*Acanthaceae*) Page 250
                            9. Seeds neither thus supported nor thrown by the exploding capsules.   **FIGWORT FAMILY** (*Scrophulariaceae*) Page 238
1. Ovary of the pistil united with the calyx tube and apparently situated below the other parts of the flower.
2. Flowers in dense heads which are surrounded by an involucre of bracts.

3. Stamens 4, separate from one another. Stout and prickly plants with opposite leaves. TEASEL FAMILY (*Dipsacaceae*) Page 257

3. Stamens 5, their anthers united into a ring about the style of the pistil. Heads may have either tubular flowers, flowers with flat and strap-shaped corollas, or both. COMPOSITE FAMILY (*Compositae*) Page 262

2. Flowers not in dense heads.

3. Stamens and pistils in separate flowers. Plants are tendril-bearing vines. GOURD FAMILY (*Cucurbitaceae*) Page 257

3. Stamens and pistils present in the same flowers.

4. Stamens 3. Calyx lobes minute or not evident. VALERIAN FAMILY (*Valerianaceae*) Page 254

4. Stamens 4 or 5. Calyx lobes usually prominent.

5. Plants with usually opposite leaves.

6. Flowers with a radial symmetry. Corolla lobes and stamens 4. MADDER FAMILY (*Rubiaceae*) Page 253

6. Flowers often with a bilateral symmetry. Corolla lobes and stamens usually 5. HONEYSUCKLE FAMILY (*Caprifoliaceae*) Page 254

5. Plants with alternate leaves.

6. Flowers with a radial symmetry. Stamens all separate. BLUEBELL FAMILY (*Campanulaceae*) Page 259

6. Flowers with a bilateral symmetry. Stamens united into a tube about the style of the pistil. LOBELIA FAMILY (*Lobeliaceae*) Page 261

BUR-REED FAMILY (Sparganiaceae)

Bur-reeds are aquatic or marsh plants with long ribbon-like leaves, the bases of which sheath the stems. The flowers are of two kinds—neither of them having sepals or petals —and are arranged in ball-like heads. The one to a few flower heads near the base of the cluster contain the pistil-bearing flowers. Those in the upper part of the cluster are made up of stamen-bearing flowers. The plants get their name from the bur-like heads of pistil-bearing flowers and fruits.

AMERICAN BUR-REED (Sparganium americanum)

This is the most widely distributed species of bur-reed. It is often common on mucky or peaty shores and in the shallow water of marshes. The plants grow from 1 to about 3 feet tall and have ball-like fruit heads from ¾ to about an inch in diameter. It blooms between May and September. RANGE: Nfd. to Minn. south to Fla. and Mo.

WATER-PLANTAIN FAMILY (Alismataceae)

Members of this family are marsh or aquatic plants having leaves in a basal cluster. Their flowers are often quite showy and arranged in clusters on scape-like leafless stems. They have 3 greenish sepals, 3 white to pinkish petals and usually more than 6 stamens and pistils. The best known members of the family are the plants called "arrowheads", as many of them have more or less arrow-shaped leaves. Flowers of the sagittarias or arrowheads are usually in whorls of threes. Those in the lowermost whorls have pistils or sometimes both pistils and stamens, but those in the upper whorls have only stamens.

BROAD-LEAF ARROWHEAD (Sagittaria latifolia)

This is the commonest, best known, and most widely distributed of all the arrowheads. The leaves are quite variable in width but are usually arrow-shaped. Its 3-petalled white flowers with clusters of golden stamens are quite attractive and may be seen from June to September. They are subtended by thin papery bracts. Also called Wapato or Duck-potato, the tubers of the plant were a food of the Indian.
RANGE: N.S. to B.C. south throughout most of the U.S.

COASTAL WAPATO (Sagittaria falcata)

Although recognizable as an arrowhead by its flowers, this species does not have arrow-shaped leaves. Its leaves are pointed at both ends and usually 6 to 15 inches long. It grows in tidal marshes and along streams and ditches near the coast; blooming from June to October. RANGE: Del. south to Fla. and west to Tex.

LANCE-LEAF WAPATO (Sagittaria lancifolia)

This species is similar to the preceeding but it is somewhat larger, with leaves up to 2 feet long. It may be readily distinguished, however, by the minute nipple-like projections on both its sepals and bracts. RANGE: S.C. south to Fla. and west to Tex. (Not illustrated)

GRASS-LEAF SAGITTARIA (Sagittaria graminea)

The leaves of this species are variable, ranging from lance-shaped to narrow and ribbon-like. It is often common in shallow waters, especially where the botton is sandy.
RANGE: Nfd. to Ont. south to Fla. and Tex.

SEDGE FAMILY (Cyperaceae)

Sedges are grass-like plants which usually grow in moist or wet places. Most of them have 3-sided stems which are sheathed by the bases of the leaves. The flowers are small and quite inconspicuous, being arranged in scaly-bracted and usually cone-shaped clusters. Although there are several genera of sedges, some with numerous species, the following, because of their handsome white bracts, are the only ones likely to be considered as wild flowers.

WHITE-TOPPED SEDGE (Dichromena latifolia)

This is a conspicuous plant in the wetter pinelands and savannahs of the Southeast from May until after mid-summer. What appear to be petals are really the white leaf-like bracts which surround the cluster of true flowers. They are 1½ to 3 inches long, mostly white but with green tips, and usually more than 7 in number.
RANGE: N.C. south to Fla. and west to Texas.
Another but less showy species is *Dichromena colorata*. It usually has less than 7 narrower white bracts, and occurs north to the coast of Virginia.

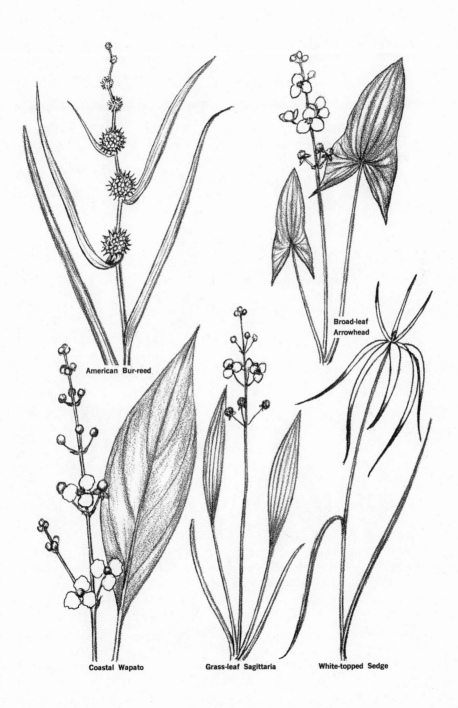

American Bur-reed

Broad-leaf
Arrowhead

Coastal Wapato

Grass-leaf Sagittaria

White-topped Sedge

Jack-in-the-pulpit

Green Dragon

Skunk-cabbage

Sweetflag

Wild Calla

The arums have minute flowers usually consisting of either stamens or a pistil—or sometimes both—which are crowded on a fleshy stem called a *spadix*. Usually this spadix is subtended by a bract—often a very large one—which is called a *spathe*. The plants contain minute crystals of calcium oxylate which cause an intense burning sensation when parts of the plants are eaten. The crystals, however, seem to be destroyed by drying or boiling; thus many of these plants were often used as food by the Indians.

JACK-IN-THE-PULPIT *(Arisaema triphyllum)*

This plant is quite familiar to country boys as the "Indian-turnip". Jack is the club-like spadix which bears tiny flowers toward its base. The spathe forms what looks like an old-fashioned canopied pulpit from which Preacher Jack preaches. The hood portion of the spathe may be green or purple, quite often marked with paler or whitish stripes. Jack-in-the-Pulpits are often quite common in rich, moist woods and thickets. The plants grow from 1 to rarely 3 feet tall, and each of the two leaves are divided into 3 leaflets. Towards fall the spathe withers and discloses a cluster of brilliant red, berry-like fruits. The flowering season is between late March and June.
  RANGE: N.B. to Man. south to n. Fla. and Miss.

GREEN DRAGON *(Arisaema dracontium)*

A unique plant with usually but one leaf which is divided into from 7 to 15 lance-shaped leaflets or leaf segments. The spadix is prolonged into a long, pointed tail-like portion which projects upward through an opening in the spathe. Less common and much less familiar than the Jack-in-the-pulpit, the Green Dragon grows in low wet woodlands or on flats along streams. The plants are from 1 to 3 feet high, and may be found in flower between May and July.
  RANGE: N.H. to Ont. and Minn. south to Fla. and Tex.

SKUNK-CABBAGE *(Symplocarpus foetidus)*

All parts of this plant have a characteristic skunk-like odor when bruised or broken. The large hood-like spathes vary from yellowish-green to reddish-brown and are streaked and spotted with purple. They often appear above the half-thawed ground in late February or March, in wet meadows or swampy woods. These flower spathes are soon followed by big veiny leaves which have heart-shaped bases. They unfurl from tightly wrapped cones as the spathes wither and are very conspicuous throughout the summer.
  RANGE: Que. to Man. south to w. N.C., n. Ga. and Tenn.

SWEETFLAG *(Acorus calamus)*

Rootstocks of the Sweetflag are pleasantly aromatic and in bygone days were often boiled in syrup and eaten as a candy. The spathe in this plant looks very much like the long, narrow, and flattened leaves, being prolonged upward 2 or 3 inches above the outwardly pointing spadix. It grows in wet open places and the flowering season is between May and July.
  RANGE: N.S. to Ore. south to S.C., Tenn., Miss., and Tex.

WILD CALLA *(Calla palustris)*

The Wild Calla or Water-arum grows in cold northern bogs and swamps. It is small plant seldom a foot high; with beautiful dark green, heart-shaped leaves from 2 to 4 inches wide. The nearly flat, snow-white spathe is sometimes 2 inches across and stands behind the spadix on which the real flowers are clustered. It blooms from late April to June or sometimes later. A good plant for bog gardens in regions with cool summers but it must have an acid soil.
  RANGE: Nfd. to Alaska south to n. N.J., n. Pa. and Great Lakes region.

GOLDEN-CLUB *(Orontium aquaticum)*

A plant of swamps, pond margins, bogs, and slow-moving streams. The "club" is a spadix from 4 to 8 inches long, tipped with closely packed yellow flowers. Near its base is a small bract-like spathe. The bluish-green leaves are 6 to 12 inches long and often float on the water. When emersed they show a silvery or coppery iridescence and come out perfectly dry. For this reason the plant is locally known as the Never-wet. The bright yellow clubs are produced between late March and May.

RANGE: Mass. to Ky. south to Fla. and Tex.

ARROW-ARUM *(Peltandra virginica)*

This is a common plant of swamps and shallow waters. The rather large arrow-shaped leaves stand a foot or more above the water. Although they look somewhat like the leaves of the broad-leaf arrowheads, they have an entirely different venation. The narrow greenish spathe is wrapped around the spadix which is covered with small flowers. It blooms during May or June. RANGE: Me. to Ont. south to Fla. and Tex.

WHITE-ARUM *(Peltandra sagittaefolia)*

This is similar to the preceding species but it has spathes which are whitish and spreading. It grows in boggy places in the coastal plain from N.C. south to Fla. and w. to Miss.

YELLOW-EYED-GRASS FAMILY (Xyridaceae)

Yellow-eyed grasses are rush-like plants with narrow leaves and naked flower stalks which terminate in scaly heads of flowers. The flowers have 3 unequal and brownish sepals, 3 yellow petals, 3 anther-bearing stamens alternating with 3 sterile filaments, and a pistil composed of 3 united carpels. Most of the flower parts are hidden by the large overlapping bracts. There are several species in the Southeast, especially in the coastal plain.

SLENDER YELLOW-EYED-GRASS *(Xyris flexuosa)*

This species has a tuft of deeply-rooted chestnut-brown bulbs from which arise the narrow and often twisted leaves and slender, wiry flower stalks. The latter are much longer than the leaves, from 10 to 30 inches tall, 2-edged above and are often slightly twisted. It blooms in June or July. RANGE: N.J. south to Fla. west to Ark. and e. Texas.

PIPEWORT FAMILY (Eriocaulaceae)

Pipeworts are plants of wet places. They have small flowers crowded in a button-like head at the summit of a long stalk, which is naked except for a sheath at the base. They so remind one of the old-fashioned hatpins that hatpins is one of their common names. Their leaves are narrow and grass-like.

TEN-ANGLED PIPEWORT *(Eriocaulon decangulare)*

This common species has a flower stalk 1 to 3 feet tall which is 10- or 12-angled. The blunt-pointed leaves are as long as, or longer than, the sheath at the base of the flower stalk; and the flowers are in a whitish wooly head about ½ inch in diameter. It blooms from June to October. RANGE: N.J. south to Fla. and west to Tex.

FLATTENED PIPEWORT *(Eriocaulon compressum)*

Has basal leaves sharply pointed and shorter than the sheaths of the flower stalks. It grows in shallow waters of the coastal plain from N.J. south to Fla. and west to Tex. (Not illustrated)

SEVEN-ANGLED PIPEWORT *(Eriocaulon septangulare)*

Is smaller and often has flower stalks only 1 to 8 inches long, which are 7-angled. It grows from Nfd. to Ont. south to Va. and the Great Lakes; blooming July to September. (Not illustrated)

SHOE-BUTTONS *(Syngonanthus flavidulus)*

Is often called the Yellow Pipewort. Its straw-colored flower heads are on naked stalks 4 to 12 inches tall and arise from a cluster of short, awl-like leaves which are woolly at the base. It grows in wet pinelands and bogs of the coastal plain from N.C. south to Fla. and Ala.; blooming May to October. (Not illustrated)

36

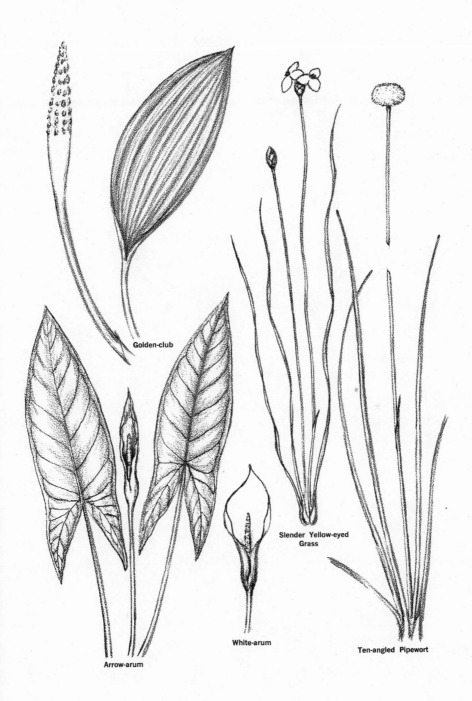

Golden-club

Arrow-arum

White-arum

Slender Yellow-eyed
Grass

Ten-angled Pipewort

Slender Dayflower

Virginia Dayflower

Roseling

Reflexed Spiderwort

Pickerelweed

SPIDERWORT FAMILY (Commelinaceae)

Members of this family have flowers with 3 greenish or bronzy sepals, 3 petals, 6 stamens, and a 3-parted pistil. Only 1 or 2 of the flowers in the cluster open at a time. They open in the morning and by noon the petals become but blobs of liquid.

SLENDER DAYFLOWER *(Commelina erecta)*

Like the flowers of other dayflowers, those of this species appear from folded, spathe-like bracts; and they have 3 perfect stamens and 3 sterile ones with X-shaped anthers. The flowers of this species show but 2 bright blue petals; the lower one being much smaller, white, and inconspicuous. The narrow leaves are from 2 to 6 inches long, and leaf sheaths which surround the stem at the leaf bases have a spreading green flange. The plant itself grows from a few inches to about 2 feet tall. It is found in dry sandy woods and on rock outcrops; blooming between June and October.

RANGE: Pa. to Kan. south to Fla. and Tex.

VIRGINIA DAYFLOWER *(Commelina virginica)*

Flowers of this species have 3 bright blue petals, the lower one being but slightly smaller. It has broader lance-shaped leaves than the preceding species, and the leaf sheaths are fringed at the top with reddish hairs. The Virginia Dayflower becomes 2 to 3 feet tall, and grows in moist woods and thickets. It blooms between July and October.

RANGE: N.J. to Ill. and Kan. south to Fla. and Tex.

COMMON DAYFLOWER *(Commelina communis)*

This is a widely distributed and weedy plant often found in low moist grounds and waste places. It is a sprawling plant which often roots at the joints of the stem. Its flowers have 2 large blue petals and a smaller white one, and the edges of the spathes are not united near the base. The leaves are broadly lance-shaped to egg-shaped. (Not illlustrated)

REFLEXED SPIDERWORT *(Tradescantia ohiensis)*

Spiderworts have flower clusters which are subtended by long, narrow, leaf-like bracts. The flowers of this one have 3 delicate violet or purple petals and the filaments of the 6 stamens are bearded with hairs. The 3 sepals have tufts of hair only at the tips. The plant is 1 to 2 feet tall and both the stem and narrow leaves are smooth and whitened with a bloom. It grows in dry woods and open places, and blooms between April and July.

RANGE: Mass. to Neb. south to Fla. and Tex. Several other species occur in the eastern United States.

ROSELING *(Tradescantia rosea)*

This small spiderwort is distinguished by its slender stems, narrow grass-like leaves, and small flowers which have 3 bright rosy-pink petals. It is usually less than a foot tall and often grows in dense clumps in dry sandy pinelands of the coastal plain and piedmont. It blooms between May and July.

RANGE: Va. south to Florida.

ANEILEMA *(Aneilema keisak)*

This is a low, often creeping plant, that resembles the dayflowers. It has small lilac or bluish-purple, 3-petalled flowers with 2 or 3 fertile stamens which are borne in the axils of the upper leaves, which are narrowly lance-shaped and often folded. It grows along stream banks and in marshes; blooming in September or October.

RANGE: Va. south to Ga. (Not illustrated)

PICKERELWEED FAMILY (Pontederiaceae)

PICKERELWEED *(Pontederia cordata)*

The bright lavender-blue flowers of this plant may be seen from May to September, or even later in Florida. There are 2 yellow spots on the middle upper lobe of the corolla but these can be seen only at close range. The leaves vary from egg-shaped to lance-shaped and they may have heart-shaped or wedge-shaped bases. It grows quite commonly on muddy shores and in shallow waters.

RANGE: N.S. to Ont. south to Fla. and Tex.

This is a large family including many of our most attractive wild and garden flowers. Members of the family typically have flowers with a perianth of 6 similar parts, 6 stamens, and a pistil composed of 3 united carpels. The styles may be separate or united into one style. The ovary of the pistil is separate from any of the other flower parts and it occupies a prominent position in the center of the flower.

There is, however, considerable variation in the structure and appearance of the flowers of the various genera of the family. Some botanists prefer to divide it into the following, and a few other, families.

The *Bunchlily Family* includes members having a flat perianth of 6 similar parts, usually persisting about the bases of the fruits. The pistil has 3 separate styles and often appears to be 3-parted or 3-horned. The underground parts are usually rootstocks but are sometimes bulb-like, and the fruits are capsules.

The *Onion Family* includes members whose flowers have a flat or dish-shaped perianth of 6 similar parts, the flowers being arranged in umbels subtended by 2 or 3 thin and dry bracts. There is a single compound pistil with but 1 style and the fruits are few-seeded capsules. The plants have a bulb at the base.

The *Lily Family* includes members whose flowers are flat to bell-shaped, usually quite large and showy, and have 6 similar perianth parts sometimes united near the base. There is a single compound pistil with but 1 style and the fruits are capsules. The plants usually have a bulb at the base.

The *Lily-of-the-valley Family* includes members with moderate to small-sized, flat to bell-shaped flowers with 6 similar perianth parts sometimes united at the base. There is a single compound pistil with but 1 style and the fruits are berries. The underground parts are rootstocks.

The *Trillium Family* includes members whose 3 petals are more or less distinct from the 3 sepals. The pistil has 3 very prominent stigmas and sometimes a short style and the fruits are berry-like. The plants have their leaves in whorls and the underground parts are rootstocks.

Key to Genera of the Lily Family

1. Plants with only basal leaves.
    2. Flower stalks forking above; the flowers large and tawny-orange.
    $\qquad$ DAY-LILIES *(Hemerocallis)*
    2. Flower stalks not forking above; the flowers medium or small.
        3. Flowers solitary. Leaves mottled. $\quad$ ADDER'S-TONGUES *(Erythronium)*
        3. Flowers in clusters.
            4. Styles 3, the pistil sometimes appearing 3-parted or 3-horned.
                5. Leaves pointed at the tip. $\qquad$ TOFIELDIAS *(Tofieldia)*
                5. Leaves blunt at the tip. $\qquad$ FLY-POISON *(Amianthium)*
            4. Style 1.
                5. Flowers arranged in umbels.
                    6. Flower cluster subtended by 2 or 3 papery bracts.
                        7. Plants with an onion-like odor.
                        $\qquad$ ONIONS, LEEKS, ETC. *(Allium)*
                        7. Plant without an onion-like odor.
                        $\qquad$ FALSE GARLIC *(Nothoscordum)*
                    6. Flower cluster not subtended by bracts. Leaves broad.
                    $\qquad$ CLINTONIAS *(Clintonia)*
                5. Flowers in a long and narrow type of cluster.
                    6. Leaves broad. Flowers bell-shaped, white, and very fragrant.
                    $\qquad$ LILY-OF-THE VALLEY *(Convallaria)*
                    6. Leaves narrow and grass-like.
                        7. Flowers white or yellow, perianth cylindrical bell-shaped.
                        $\qquad$ COLIC-ROOTS *(Aletris)*
                        7. Flowers bluish or lavender, the perianth somewhat bilateral.
                        $\qquad$ CAMAS *(Camassia)*

1. Plants with leafy stems, leaves of the flower stems sometimes reduced in size.
   2. Sepals and petals not alike in size or color.   TRILLIUMS *(Trillium)*
   2. Sepals and petals much alike in size and color.
      3. Flowers large (2 inches or more across); the perianth yellow, orange or red and usually spotted.   LILIES *(Lilium)*
      3. Flowers much smaller.
         4. Leaves in whorls.   INDIAN CUCUMBER-ROOT *(Medeola)*
         4. Leaves alternate.
            5. Styles 3, the pistil sometimes appearing 3-parted or 3-horned.
               6. Flowers in a long and narrow type of cluster.
                  7. Basal leaves broad but those along the flower stalk much smaller and narrow.
                     8. Flowers white; the stamen-bearing and pistil-bearing ones on separate plants.   DEVIL'S-BIT *(Chamaelirium)*
                     8. Flowers pink, anthers bluish.   SWAMP-PINK *(Helonias)*
                  7. Leaves all long and narrow, those of the flower stem smaller.
                     8. Leaves very narrow (almost like pine needles) and wiry. Flowers white.   TURKEY-BEARD *(Xerophyllum)*
                     8. Leaves narrow but flat and grass-like. Flowers greenish-white, each perianth segment with a 2-lobed greenish gland about midway from the base.   POISON-CAMAS *(Zigadenus)*
               6. Flowers in a broad and branching type of cluster.
                  7. Perianth parts with a pair of greenish glands at the base.
                     8. Perianth parts with stalk-like bases, in age turning brown.   BUNCHFLOWERS *(Melanthium)*
                     8. Perianth parts without stalked bases, in age turning pink.   SOUTHERN-CAMAS *(Zigadenus)*
                  7. Perianth parts without glands at the base.
                     8. Flower cluster quite smooth.   BUNCHFLOWERS *(Melanthium)*
                     8. Flower cluster rather downy.
                        9. Leaves narrow and grass-like. Flowers white turning greenish or bronze.   FEATHERBELLS *(Stenanthium)*
                        9. Leaves broad and prominently plaited lengthwise. Flowers yellowish-green   WHITE-HELLEBORE *(Veratrum)*
            5. Style single, the stigmas sometimes 3-parted.
               6. Flowers medium-sized, bell-shaped or cylindrical.
                  7. Flower solitary, or in pairs at the tips of leafy branches.
                     8. Flowers plain yellow.   BELLWORTS *(Uvularia)*
                     8. Flowers greenish-white, or yellow with purple spots.   DISPORUMS *(Disporum)*
                  7. Flowers arising from the axils of the leaves.
                     8. Flowers cylindrical bell-shaped, greenish-white, usually 2 or more grouped together. SOLOMON'S-SEALS *(Polygonatum)*
                     8. Flowers open bell-shaped, greenish-white to rose-purple, usually solitary.   TWISTED-STALKS *(Streptopus)*
               6. Flowers small, neither bell-shaped nor cylindrical, white to creamy-white and borne in end clusters.
                  7. Flower parts in 4's.   FALSE LILY-OF-THE-VALLEY *(Maianthemum)*
                  7. Flower parts in 6's.   FALSE SOLOMON'S-SEALS *(Smilacina)*

TURKEY-BEARD *(Xerophyllum asphodeloides)*

This plant has a dense basal cluster of slender leaves which might easily be mistaken for a tuft of wiry grass or the needles of a young Longleaf Pine. Sometime in May or June it sends up a flower stalk from 2 to 3 feet tall. Along it are a few scattered leaves and at the top there is a densely cylindrical cluster of white flowers. It grows in dry woodlands, southward chiefly in the mountains.

RANGE: Coastal plain N.J. and Del. south to Va.; mountains Va. to Ga.

WOOD-FEATHERLING *(Tofieldia racemosa)*

In June or July the flowers of this plant often whiten the wet pinelands and savannahs of the southeastern coastal plain. The long, narrow, grass-like leaves are all at the base of the plant. Its flower stalk is from 1 to 2 feet tall and bears a long, narrow, more or less interrupted cluster of small white flowers. Both the upper part of the flower stalk and the pedicels of the individual flowers are roughened by minute glandular hairs.

RANGE: N.J. south to Fla. and west to Tex.

VISCID TOFIELDIA *(Tofieldia racemosa* var. *glutinosa)*

This is a northern plant which occurs southward only in the high mountains. It closely resembles the preceding species but it has a sticky-hairy stem 6 to about 20 inches tall which is sprinkled with black dots. A plant of boggy places, flowering in July or August.

RANGE: Nfd. to Man. south to N. Eng, the Great Lakes, and in mts. to n. Ga.

WHITE-FEATHERLING *(Tofieldia glabra)*

September and October are the months to look for the slender white flower clusters of the White-featherling. The plant is quite similar to the prceding species but it has a flower stalk which is entirely smooth. It grows in wet pinelands and savannahs of the coastal plain in the Carolinas. (Not illustrated)

DEVIL'S-BIT *(Chamaelirium luteum)*

Another and much more attractive name for this plant is Fairy-wand. Most of the leaves are in a rosette at the base of its slender 2 to 3 foot flower stalk. Along the stalk are just a few smaller and narrower leaves; and toward the summit there is a long, slender cluster of small white flowers. The flowers on a given plant have either stamens or pistils, but not both. It grows in rich moist woods and thickets; blooming between April and June. A good subject for a woodland wild flower garden.

RANGE: Mass. to Ont. south to Fla., Miss. and Ark.

FLY-POISON *(Amianthum muscaetoxicum)*

Between May and July this plant sends up a practically leafless flower stalk from 1 to 3 feet tall. On it is a dense cylindrical cluster of flowers which are at first white but later become greenish or purplish. Both leaves and flower stalk arise from a very poisonous bulb-like base. Another name for the plant is Crow-poison. Whether or not flies and crows are affected by it we cannot say, but cattle and sheep are often poisoned by eating the leaves. It grows in a variety of places: dry to moist open woods, mountain balds, bogs, and savannahs.

RANGE: N.Y. and Pa. south to Fla., Miss. and Okla.

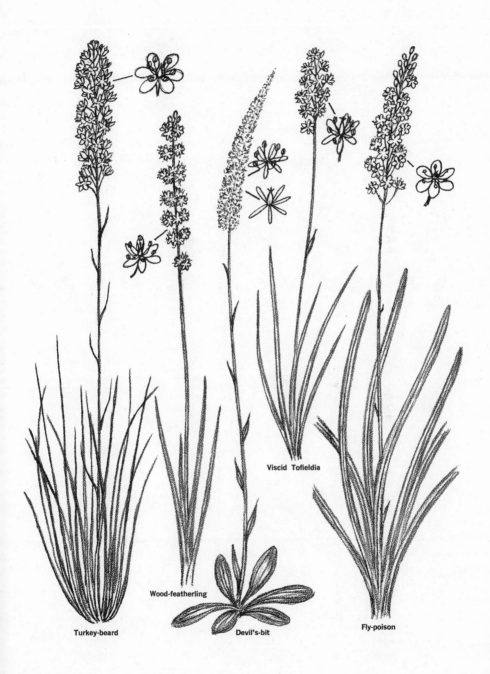

Turkey-beard

Wood-featherling

Viscid Tofieldia

Devil's-bit

Fly-poison

Featherbells

American
White Hellebore

Northern Camas

Virginia Bunchflower

Southern Camas

FEATHERBELLS *(Stenanthium gramineum)*

Often called Feather-fleece, this is an attractive plant with large and more or less drooping clusters of small, starry, white flowers. It grows to a height of 3 to 6 feet and has long, narrow, grass-like leaves which are more numerous and larger toward the base of the plant. This attractive plant grows in moist open woods, meadows, and bogs; and blooms between June and September.

RANGE: Pa. to Ill. and Mo. south to N.C., nw. Fla. and e. Tex.

AMERICAN WHITE HELLEBORE *(Veratrum veride)*

This is often a common and conspicuous plant in swamps and on moist wooded slopes. It has a stout, leafy, more or less downy stem from 2 to 5 feet tall. The large leaves are broadly elliptic, prominently veined and plaited, and have bases which clasp the stem. They are often mistaken for the leaves of some of the lady's-slipper orchids. A large branched cluster of small, downy, yellowish-green flowers is produced between June and August. It is also known as the False Hellebore and Indian-poke.

RANGE: N.B. to Minn. south to Md., n. Ga. and Tenn.

SMALL-FLOWERED HELLEBORE *(Veratrum parviflorum)*

This plant has a slender leafy stem 2 to 5 feet tall, and lower stem leaves which taper at the base into long stalks. Large clusters of small, smooth, greenish flowers are produced between July and September. It grows in dry deciduous woodlands in the mountains from Va. and W.Va. south to Tenn. and n. Ga. (Not illustrated)

NORTHERN CAMAS *(Zigadenus glaucus)*

The narrow and grass-like leaves of this plant are chiefly at the base, with only a few smaller ones along the 1 to 3 foot tall flower stalk. The flowers are rather small, creamy-white tinged with green or purplish on the back, and each of the 6 perianth segments has a 2-lobed greenish gland. It grows in moist rocky places and in bogs, blooming between July and September. Another name for this very poisonous plant is White Camas.

RANGE: N.B. to Minn. south to N.Y., w. N.C., and the Great Lakes region.

SOUTHERN CAMAS *(Zigadenus glaberrimus)*

This is a stout leafy-stemmed plant from 2 to 4 feet tall; with a basal cluster of long, narrow, strongly channelled leaves. The flowers are produced in a large, rather open, pyramid-shaped terminal cluster. They are an inch or more across and white when they first open, but they gradually turn pinkish. There is a pair of prominent greenish glands at the base of each of the six perianth segments. It grows in wet coastal plain pinelands, savannahs and bogs; blooming June to August.

RANGE: Va. south to Fla. and west to La.

ST. AGNES'-FEATHER *(Zigadenus densus)*

This plant has white flowers in a dense cylindrical cluster, and each perianth segment has but one gland. Its 2- to 3-foot tall stem is sparingly leafy, the grass-like leaves being chiefly basal. It grows in bogs and savannahs of the coastal plain from N.C. south to Fla. and west to Miss.; blooming between April and June. (Not illustrated)

VIRGINIA BUNCHFLOWER *(Melanthium virginicum)*

The rather coarse, narrow, grasslike leaves of this plant are chiefly at the base of 3- to 4-foot tall, rough-hairy stem. Its dime-sized flowers are creamy-white at first but later turn greenish or purplish. Each of the six perianth parts are stalked at the base and have a pair of greenish glands. The flowers are produced in rather large showy clusters between June and August. It grows in moist to wet woods, meadows and bogs.

RANGE: N.Y. to Iowa south to Fla. and Tex.

CRISPED BUNCHFLOWER *(Melanthium hybridum)*

This is a similar but more slender plant with broader and thinner leaves. The six perianth parts of its flowers have wrinkled margins and are pointed rather than blunt at their tips. It grows in moist to dry open woods of the uplands from Conn. and s. N.Y. south to n. Fla.; blooming during July and August. (Not illustrated)

SOUTHERN RED LILY *(Lilium catesbaei)*

This beautiful lily grows in the wet pinelands and savannahs of the southeastern coastal plain. It is 1 to 2 feet tall and along the stem are small, scattered, lance-shaped leaves which point upward. Between July and September each stem bears a solitary flower in which the 6 perianth parts have long and slender stalks. Their blades are yellow toward the base but bright scarlet above, thickly spotted with purple, and the long-pointed tips curve gracefully outward. Also called the Pine Lily, Leopard Lily, and Catesby's Lily. It was named for Mark Catesby (1679-1749), one of the earliest southern naturalists.
RANGE: Va. south to Fla. and west to La.

NORTHERN RED LILY *(Lilium philadelphicum)*

Often called the Wood Lily, this species has a stem 1 to about 3 feet tall on which are from 2 to 6 whorls of lance-shaped leaves. At its summit there may be from 1 to 5 flowers which stand upright. Their 6 perianth parts are distinctly stalked, bright orange-red, and purple-spotted. It grows in dry open woods and clearings and southward in mountain meadows and balds, blooming between June and August.
RANGE: Me. to s. Que. and s. Ont. south to Del., n. Ga. and Ky.

TURK'S-CAP LILY *(Lilium superbum)*

The showy Turk's-cap is the tallest of our native lilies, being from 3 to about 5 feet in height. Along its stem are several whorls of leaves and some scattered ones near the summit. They are broadest about the middle and pointed at both ends. Between June and August the plants produce anywhere from a few to as many as 40 handsome flowers. These are orange-red thickly spotted with purple and the 6 perianth parts are curved backward so their tips often touch. It grows in wet meadows and moist woods, southward chiefly in the mountains.
RANGE: Mass. to Ind. south to N. Fla. and Ala.

CAROLINA LILY *(Lilium michauxii)*

This species closely resembles the Turk's-cap but it is usually less than 3 feet tall and generally has but 1 to 3 flowers. The leaves afford the best distinguishing feature. In this species they are thickish in texture and always broadest toward the bluntly-pointed tip; and they may be scattered or arranged in from 1 to 4 whorls along the stem. Although most common in open woods and on dry rocky slopes in the mountains, it often occurs well down into the coastal plain. It blooms during July and August. This lily was named *michauxii* in honor of Andre Michaux, the noted French botanist who discovered it.
RANGE: Va. and W.Va. south to Fla. and Ala.

CANADA LILY *(Lilium canadense)*

On a stem 1 to 4 feet tall this lily usually has several nodding, bell-shaped, red to yellow flowers which are spotted with purplish-brown. The 6 perianth parts of its flowers have spreading or slightly recurved tips. It usually has several whorls of lance-shaped leaves with roughish margins. This northern species is often common in wet woods and meadows and is found southward along the mountains. It blooms in June or July. Another name for it is Wild Yellow Lily.
RANGE: N.S. to Que. south to Va., n. Fla. and Ala.

GRAY'S LILY *(Lilium grayi)*

This attractive but rather rare lily grows in moist meadows and balds in the southern Appalachians. On a stem 2 to 4 feet tall are usually a few whorls of leaves, or the lower ones may be scattered. The few to sometimes numerous bell-shaped flowers are slightly nodding; and their 6 perianth parts are deep orange-red thickly spotted with purple, with the short-pointed tips but slightly spread. This lily was named for Dr. Asa Gray, the famous American botanist; and it is sometimes called the Roan Lily after Roan Mountain where Dr. Gray discovered it. It blooms during June and July.
RANGE: Mts. of Va. south to w. N.C. and e. Tenn.

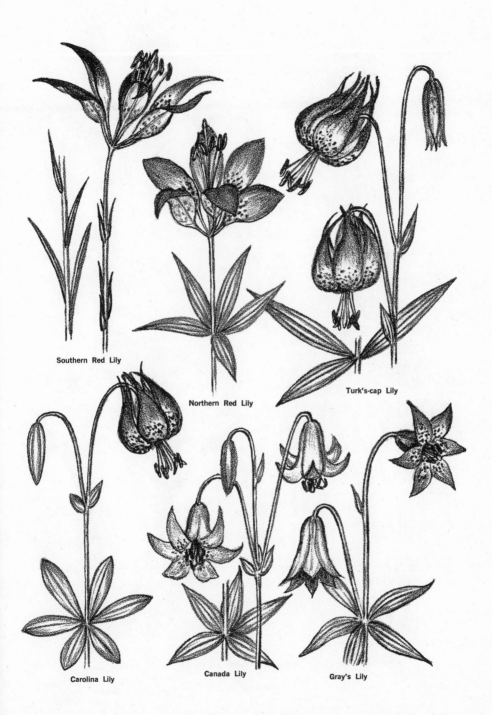

Southern Red Lily

Northern Red Lily

Turk's-cap Lily

Carolina Lily

Canada Lily

Gray's Lily

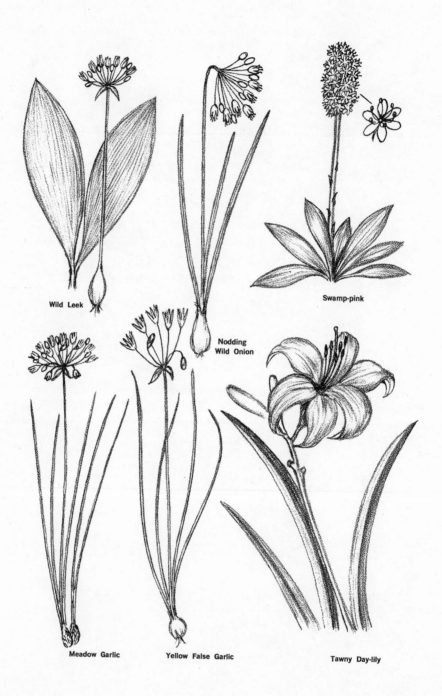

Wild Leek

Nodding
Wild Onion

Swamp-pink

Meadow Garlic

Yellow False Garlic

Tawny Day-lily

WILD LEEK *(Allium tricoccum)*

In the early spring, this plant has broad, flat, elliptical leaves from 6 to 10 inches long but the very definite onion-like odor will aid in identifying it. After the leaves have withered, in June or July, it sends up a naked stalk which bears, at the top, an umbel of greenish-white flowers. The plant grows in rich, moist woodlands. In the southern mountains, where it is often very abundant, the plant is known as the Ramp. The bulbs are eagerly sought by inhabitants of the region, who seem to be very fond of them.
RANGE: N.B. to Que. and Minn.; south to n. Ga., Tenn., and Iowa.

NODDING WILD ONION *(Allium cernuum)*

This species blooms in July or August. It has a flower stalk a foot or more tall which is bent near the top, thus the umbel of lilac-colored or pinkish flowers are in a nodding position. Its flat, soft, long, and grass-like leaves are usually shorter than the stalk which bears the flowers. All of its parts have an onion-like odor. It grows on moist to rather wet, rocky, wooded slopes.
RANGE: N.Y. to B.C. south to Ga., Tex., and N.Mex.

MEADOW GARLIC *(Allium canadense)*

This species has a naked flower stalk from 8 inches to nearly 2 feet tall, topped with an umbel of lilac-pink to whitish flowers. Frequently some or even all of the flowers may be replaced by small bulblets. Its leaves are long and very slender but shorter than the flower stalk. The entire plant has an onion-like odor. It is often abundant in open woods, thickets, and meadows; blooming in May and June.
RANGE: N.B. to Que. and Minn. south to Fla. and Tex.

YELLOW FALSE GARLIC *(Nothoscordum bivalve)*

In its general appearance, the False Garlic resembles the onions and garlics but it has no trace of an onion-like odor. Its flower stalk is 6 to 12 inches tall, leafless, and bears at the summit an umbel of from 6 to 12 starry, greenish-white to yellowish-white flowers. The leaves are narrow and grass-like and do not overtop the flower stalk. It grows in sandy, open woods and open places and blooms in April or May.
RANGE: Va., the Ohio Valley, and Neb. south to Fla. and Tex.

SWAMP-PINK *(Helonias bullata)*

The Swamp-pink, as its name indicates, grows in swamps and bogs. It has a stout, hollow flower stalk from 6 to 15 inches tall with almost scale-like bracts toward the base. Towards the top is a short but dense cluster of pink flowers with lavender-blue stamens. The true leaves are flat, dark green, broadest above the middle, and form a rosette at the base of the flower stalk. It blooms in April and May.
RANGE: Se. N.Y. and N.J. south to Va. and in mts. to n. Ga.

TAWNY DAY-LILY *(Hemerocallis fulva)*

This native of Eurasia long ago escaped from American flower gardens, and it is now so widely naturalized that many think it has always been here. It is often very common along roadsides and in the borders of fields and woods; in fact, it has become a real weed. Unlike the true lilies, the day-lilies have a leafless flower stem which forks repeatedly. Although each flower lasts but a few hours, the plant produces a succession of them from May to about mid-summer. At the base of the plant is a cluster of long, strap-shaped, and channeled leaves. The flowers of this species are quite large and have 6 tawny-orange perianth segments.

49

PERFOLIATE BELLWORT *(Uvularia perfoliata)*

This plant has a slender forking stem 8 to 20 inches tall; and smooth, pale green leaves which are coated with a thin whitish bloom. The bases of the leaves completely surround the stem, which appears to grow through them. It usually has a solitary pale yellow flower about an inch long, which is shaped like a narrow bell. On the inner surface of the 6 perianth parts there are small grain-like hairs. It grows in moist open woods and blooms in April or May.

RANGE: Mass. to Ont. south to Fla. and La.

LARGE-FLOWERED BELLWORT *(Uvularia grandiflora)*

This species looks very much like a larger edition of the preceding one, but it has a stouter stem 1 to 2 feet tall and its leaves are finely downy beneath and brighter green above. Its flowers are about 1½ inches long, deeper lemon-yellow in color, and the 6 perianth parts are smooth within. It also grows in rich woods, southward only in the mountains, and blooms in April and May.

RANGE: Que. to N.D. south to n.Ga., Miss., Ark. and Okla.

SESSILE-LEAF BELLWORT *(Uvularia sessilifolia)*

The leave of this species are stalkless but their bases do not surround the stem. It has a slender, smooth, forking stem 8 to 16 inches tall. The leaves are pale or somewhat whitened on the lower surface. The 6 perianth parts of the inch-long, pale yellow flowers are smooth within. It likewise grows in rich woods and blooms in April or May. It is also known as Wild-oats.

RANGE: N.B. to N.D. south to n. Fla., Ala. and Mo.

MOUNTAIN BELLWORT *(Uvularia pudica)*

Although similar to the preceding species, this plant has leaves which are bright green on both surfaces; and its stem has minute hairy lines. It commonly grows in clumps in deciduous woodlands and is not confined to the mountains. Blooming in April or May.

RANGE: Va. and W.Va. south to Tenn. and Ga.

FLORIDA BELLWORT *(Uvularia floridana)*

This plant grows in deciduous woods and swamps of the coastal plain from S.C. south to Fla. and west to Ala. (Not illustrated)

YELLOW ADDER'S-TONGUE *(Erythronium americanum)*

Other names given to this little lily family member are Fawn-lily, Trout-lily, and Dog's-tooth Violet. The plant has a pair of elliptic leaves 4 to 6 inches long which are pale green and mottled with purplish-brown. Between them rises a flower stalk which bears a nodding, open bell-shaped, yellow flower about 1½ inches across. Its 6 perianth parts are often tinged with purplish on the back, and usually curve gracefully backward. It grows in rich woods and bottomlands and blooms between March and May. It requires several years for the plants to attain the flowering stage. Younger plants have just 'one leaf which arises from a deeply buried corm.

RANGE: Ont. to Minn. south to Ga., Ala., Ark. and Tex.

WHITE ADDER'S-TONGUE *(Erythronium albidum)*

This species is similar to the preceding one but it has white to pale bluish or pale pinkish flowers, and its leaves are less mottled and sometimes plain green. It grows in moist woods or on stream banks from Ont. to Minn. south to Ga., Mo. and Okla. (Not illustrated)

EASTERN CAMAS *(Camassia scilloides)*

This is sometimes called Wild-Hyacinth. The plant has a naked flower stalk from 6 inches to almost 2 feet tall. On it is a long cluster of starry, 6-parted, pale blue flowers. The long, narrow, keeled leaves are in a basal cluster, arising from a bulb which the Indians used as food. The Indian name for the plant was "quamash" and from it both the generic name *Camassia* and the common name "camas" have been derived. It grows in wet open woods and meadows and blooms between April and June.

RANGE: Pa. to Wis. south to Ga., Miss., Mo. and Okla.

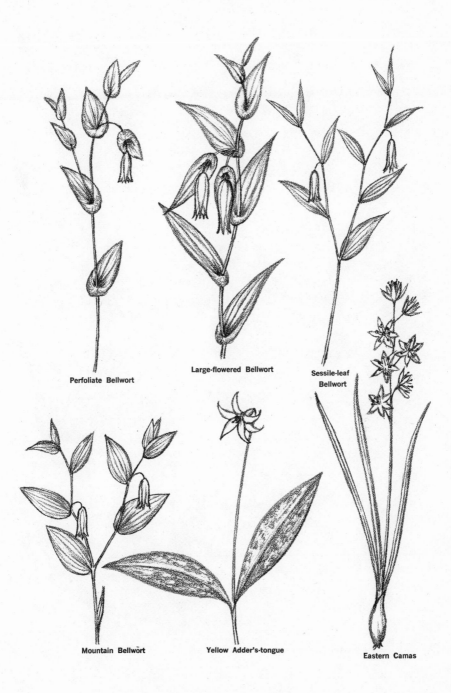

Perfoliate Bellwort

Large-flowered Bellwort

Sessile-leaf Bellwort

Mountain Bellwort

Yellow Adder's-tongue

Eastern Camas

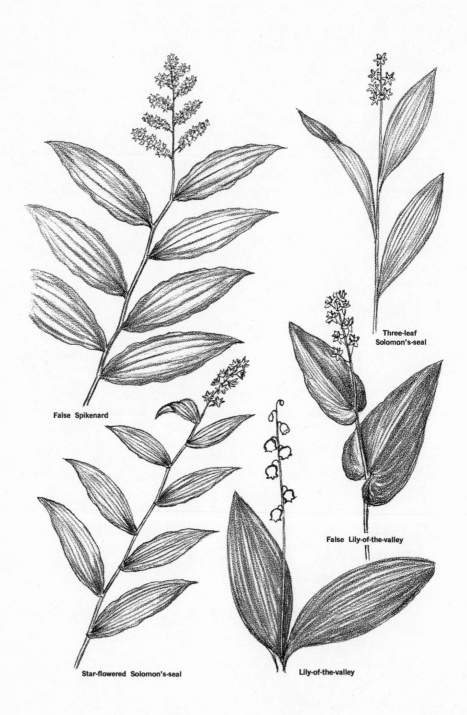

False Spikenard

Three-leaf
Solomon's-seal

Star-flowered Solomon's-seal

Lily-of-the-valley

False Lily-of-the-valley

FALSE SPIKENARD (*Smilacina racemosa*)

The False Spikenard, or False Solomon's-seal, has an arching, slightly zig-zag stem from 2 to 3 feet tall which arises from a rootstock. Scattered along it are a number of conspicuously veined and almost stalkless leaves. It small white or creamy-white flowers are disposed in a plumy-branched end cluster sometime between April and July. They are followed by round berries which at first are yellowish-white and speckled. Later they become translucent and ruby-red. The plant is often common on rocky wooded slopes. It grows well in a woodland flower garden.

RANGE: Que. to B.C. south to Ga. and Ariz.

STAR-FLOWERED SOLOMON'S-SEAL (*Smilacina stellata*)

This species has a leafy stem from 8 to about 20 inches tall. The veiny leaves are stalkless and finely downy beneath. Its flowers, while not very numerous, are larger than those of the preceding species and arranged in a simple, rather than branched, end cluster. It blooms during May or June and grows on moist wooded slopes, shores, bluffs, and meadows. The berries at first are greenish with black stripes, finally becoming a bronzy-black.

RANGE: Nfd. to B.C. south to W. Va., the Great Lakes region, Mo., N.M. and Calif.

THREE-LEAF SOLOMON'S-SEAL (*Smilacina trifolia*)

A small plant usually from 2 to about 8 inches high with from 2 to 4, but usually 3, rather narrow leaves. Its white flowers are in a small, loose, simple end cluster and are produced between late May and August. This is a plant of cold northern bogs and wet woods.

RANGE: Lab. to B.C. south to N. Eng. and the Great Lakes region.

FALSE LILY-OF-THE-VALLEY (*Maianthemum canadense*)

The small white flowers of this plant are unique among members of the Lily Family in that they have a 4-parted perianth and 4 stamens. The plant has an erect stem usually from 3 to 6 inches tall, bearing 2 or 3 smooth leaves which have heart-shaped bases. It has rootstocks which creep extensively and it usually occurs in colonies; in which there are many single, stalked, heart-shaped leaves. The flowers are borne in simple little end clusters above the leaves, sometime between May and July. They are followed by small, round, pale greenish and spotted berries which eventually become a dull red. Other names for the plant are Two-leaf Solomon's-seal and Canada Mayflower. It is often common in damp mossy woods and bogs and not infrequently on the decaying trunks of fallen trees.

RANGE: Lab. to B.C. south to Del., n. Ga., Tenn. and Iowa.

LILY-OF-THE-VALLEY (*Convallaria majalis* var. *montana*)

This native of our southern Appalachian Mountains is considered by most botanists to be a variety of the European Lily-of-the-valley, which is very common in cultivation and sometimes occurs as an escape. Unlike the European plant our native Lily-of-the-valley is not a colony-forming plant. It has nearly the same broad elliptic leaves, and long clusters of fragrant white flowers which resemble little globe-shaped bells. Our native plants grow on rich, rocky wooded slopes and bloom between April and June.

RANGE: Va. and W.Va. south to w. N.C. and e. Tenn.

GREAT SOLOMON'S-SEAL *(Polygonatum canaliculatum)*

Largest of the Solomon's-seals, this species has a stout, arching stem from 2 to nearly 6 feet tall. Along it are a number of broad, more or less corrugated leaves from 3 to 6 inches long; which have clasping bases. From the leaf axils arise drooping clusters of from 2 to 8 greenish-white flowers a half inch or more long, which are shaped like cylindrical bells. Later these flowers develop into ball-shaped, bluish-black berries. The Great Solomon's-seal grows in rich, moist, woods and swampy thickets; and also along the banks of streams. It blooms in May and June. Solomon's-seals get their name from the seal-like scars which the upright leafy branches leave on the underground, creeping rootstocks. RANGE: N.H. to Man. south to S.C., Mo., and Okla.

HAIRY SOLOMON'S-SEAL *(Polygonatum pubescens)*

This is a much smaller plant with an arching stem from about 1 to 3 feet tall, which grows in woods and thickets. On its slender stem are a number of leaves 2 to about 4 inches long, which are pale and somewhat downy beneath. In their axils hang half-inch, narrowly bell-shaped, greenish-white flowers, which are sometimes solitary but usually in pairs. It blooms in May or June, and the flowers are followed by round, bluish-black berries. RANGE: Que. to Man. south to S.C., Ky., and Iowa.

SMOOTH SOLOMON'S-SEAL *(Polygonatum biflorum)*

Like the preceding species, the Smooth Solomon's-seal usually has its flowers in pairs. The most obvious difference between the two species is in their leaves, those of the Smooth Solomon's-seal being smooth on both surfaces. It is often common in dry to moist, often rocky woods and thickets; blooming in May or June.
RANGE: Ont., Mich., and Neb. south to Fla. and Tex. (Not illustrated)

SESSILE-LEAF TWISTED-STALK *(Streptopus roseus)*

Twisted-stalks get their name from the fact that the stalks of their flowers are abruptly bent or twisted near the middle. Instead of arising from the leaf axils, the slender stalks which bear the open bell-shaped flowers arise to the side or more nearly opposite the leaves. In general appearance, the plants resemble the Solomon's-seals but they have somewhat more zig-zag and often forked stems. This species has a stem from 1 to 2 feet tall. The leaves are deeply corrugated and seated directly on the stem but their bases are not clasping. Between April and July it has pink or rose-purple flowers, which are followed by red berries. It grows in cool, moist woods and the borders of swamps. Another name for it is Rose Mandarin. RANGE: Lab. to Man. south to n. Ga., Tenn. and Minn.

CLASPING-LEAF TWISTED-STALK *(Streptopus amplexifolius)*

From the preceding species, this one can be distinguished by its clasping leaf bases. It has a stem from 1½ to 3 feet tall. The flowers are greenish-white (sometimes dark purple) and the fruits are red berries. It grows in cool, moist woods and thickets; blooming between May and July. It is also known as the White Mandarin.
RANGE: Lab. to Alaska south to N.C., the Great Lakes region, and N. Mex.

HAIRY DISPORUM *(Disporum lanuginosum)*

Disporums are plants similar to the twisted stalks but they have 1 or 2 open bell-shaped flowers at the tips of the stems or their branches. This one has a stem 1 to 2 feet tall which is sparingly branched above. Its leaves are stalkless, pointed at the tip, and rounded to slightly heart-shaped at the base. Their lower surfaces, as well as the younger parts of the stems, are minutely woolly-hairy. The 6 perianth parts of the flowers are about ¾ inch long and greenish-white in color. Smooth red berries follow the flowers which bloom in May or June. This plant grows in rather moist, rich woods. It is also known as the Yellow Mandarin. RANGE: N.Y. to Ont. south to Ga., Ala., and Tenn.

SPOTTED DISPORUM *(Disporum maculatum)*

This species has the younger parts of its stems and lower leaf surfaces roughened by small, stiff, spreading hairs. Its flowers are slightly larger and are yellow spotted with dark purple. The red fruits are rather wrinkled and somewhat hairy. It also grows in rich woodlands, blooming in April or May. Another name for it is Nodding Mandarin.
RANGE: Ohio and Mich. south to Ga., Ala., and Tenn. (Not illustrated)

**Sessile-leaf
Twisted-stalk**

Great Solomon's-seal

**Hairy
Solomon's-seal**

Clasping-leaf Twisted-stalk

Hairy Disporum

YELLOW CLINTONIA *(Clintonia borealis)*

This plant usually has 3 oval-shaped, somewhat leathery, lustrous leaves with hairy-fringed margins. They are from 5 to about 10 inches long. The greenish-yellow, bell-shaped flowers are borne in a cluster (umbel) of 3 to 8 at the top of a naked stalk 6 to 8 inches tall. Both leaves and flower stalk arise directly from an underground rootstock. The plants bloom in May or June, the flowers being followed by oval-shaped blue berries. The Yellow Clintonia is a plant of cool, moist woods and thickets.

RANGE: Lab. to Man. south to N. Eng., n. Ga., and the Great Lakes region.

WHITE CLINTONIA *(Clintonia umbellata)*

The White Clintonia has a whorl of 3 or 4 leaves very much like those of the preceding species. It differs in having smaller and more numerous (up to 30) white flowers which are minutely speckled with purple and green. The fruits which follow the flowers are ball-shaped black berries. This species is usually more common in rich woods southward. It blooms between May and early July.

RANGE: N. Y. to Ohio south in the mts. to n. Ga. and Tenn.

INDIAN CUCUMBER-ROOT *(Medeola virginica)*

A distinctive plant with a slender stem usually 1 to 2 feet tall, with a whorl of 5 to 9 leaves near the middle and another whorl of 3 smaller ones near the top. From the axils of the latter leaves arise the slender stalks bearing the nodding, greenish-yellow flowers. Both sepals and petals, as well as the 3 slender stigmas of the pistil, curve backward. The plant blooms in May or June. Later the flowers produce dark purple berries. In the ground, at the base of the stem, is a whitish tuber which has a taste very much like that of a cucumber—hence the common name. It grows in rich, moist woodlands.

RANGE: Que. to Ont. and Minn. south to n. Fla. and La.

WHITE COLIC-ROOT *(Aletris farinosa)*

Close to the ground this plant has a star-like cluster of flat, rather thin, yellowish-green, and grass-like leaves. Sometime between May and July or August, it sends up an almost naked stalk usually 1 to about 3 feet tall. Along the upper part of it are scattered white flowers which are shaped like narrow urns, and have a peculiar mealy surface. The plant grows in moist to dry open woods on sandy or peaty soils. It is abundant in the coastal plain pinelands of the Southeast and is also often common in the mountains. Other names for it are White Star-grass and Mealy Starwort.

RANGE: Me. to Ont. and Wis. south to Fla. and Tex.

Aletris obovata is another white-flowered species found from se. S.C. southward to Florida. It can be distinguished by the fact that the flowers are not constricted below the lobes, and the latter are erect rather than spreading. (Not illustrated)

GOLDEN COLIC-ROOT *(Aletris aurea)*

This plant closely resembles the preceding one but it has a more lax cluster of shorter, broader, bell-shaped, orange-yellow flowers. It grows in the wetter pinelands, bogs and savannahs of the coastal plain; blooming during June and July.

RANGE: Md. south to Fla. and west to Tex.

YELLOW COLIC-ROOT *(Aletris lutea)*

This species resembles both of the preceding species and is best distinguished by its narrowly urn-shaped, somewhat mealy, pale yellow to orange flowers. It blooms in late April and May in wet pinelands of the southeastern coastal plain from Va. south to Fla. and west to La. (Not illustrated)

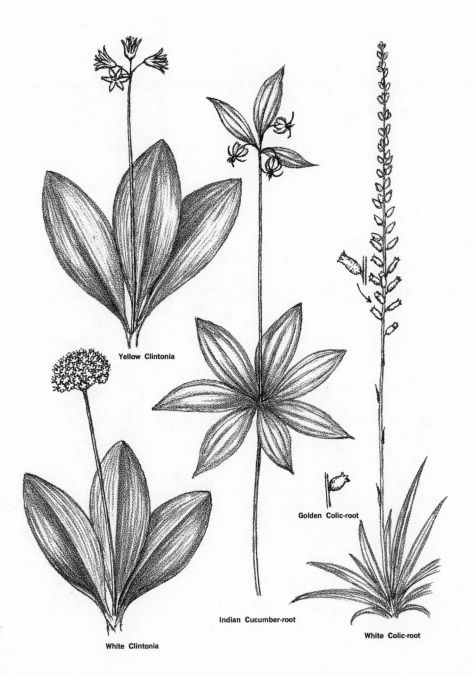

Yellow Clintonia

White Clintonia

Indian Cucumber-root

Golden Colic-root

White Colic-root

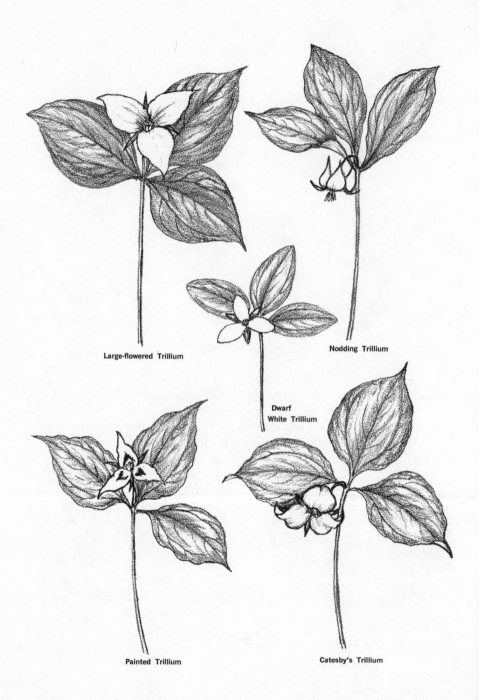

Large-flowered Trillium

Nodding Trillium

Dwarf
White Trillium

Painted Trillium

Catesby's Trillium

Trilliums

Trilliums, or Wake-robins, typically have all of their parts in 3's. At the summit of the stem is a whorl of 3 leaves which are unusual among Lily Family members in that they are net-veined. A solitary flower arises from the center of this whorl of leaves; and they, too, are unusual in that the 3 sepals are narrow and green while the 3 petals are usually much broader and either white or colored. There are 6 stamens and the 3- to 6-angled ovary of the pistil is surmounted by 3 prominent styles.

Some species are highly variable and, especially in the southern Appalachian region, many are difficult to identify. As a group they are among the showiest and best known of our spring wild flowers.

LARGE-FLOWERED TRILLIUM *(Trillium grandiflorum)*

This is one of the most common trilliums, being widespread in rich moist woods and thickets. It has a stout stem 8 to 18 inches tall with 3 large, broadly oval or egg-shaped, nearly stalkless leaves. The flower is 2 to 3½ inches across and stands on an erect or slightly leaning stalk. The 3 broad petals overlap at the base forming a sort of tube. They are white when the flower first opens but turn pink with age. It blooms in April or May.

RANGE: Me. and s. Que. west to Minn. south to n. Ga. and Ark.

NODDING TRILLIUM *(Trillium cernuum)*

Like the flowers of the preceding species, those of this trillium have petals which overlap at the base forming a sort of short tube. A distinctive feature is its purplish anthers and the fact that the flower nods on a slender stalk and hangs below the leaves. The petals are white, creamy-white, or pale pink. It grows in rich moist woods and swamps, blooming between April and June.

RANGE: Nfd. to Que. and Wis. south to n. Ga., Tenn. and Iowa.

DROOPING TRILLIUM *(Trillium flexipes)*

This plant is similar to the Nodding Trillium but is larger and coarser, and the larger flowers have pale anthers. It grows in damp woods and stream bottoms from N.Y. to Minn. south to Md., Tenn. and Mo. (Not illustrated)

DWARF WHITE TRILLIUM *(Trillium nivale)*

Often called the Snow Trillium, this is a small species with a stem 2 to 5 inches tall; with oval, egg-shaped or roundish, stalked leaves from 1 to 2 inches long. The stalked flower, little more than an inch across, has oval-shaped white petals. It grows in rich woods and along streams; blooming between March and early May.

RANGE: w. Pa. to Minn. south to Ky. and Mo.

PAINTED TRILLIUM *(Trillium undulatum)*

This trillium is readily recognized by the V-shaped purplish-pink marks toward the bases of its white, wavy-margined, recurved petals. It is a slender-stemmed plant 5 to about 20 inches tall. The broadly egg-shaped leaves are definitely stalked and are taper-pointed at the tip. It grows in cool wet woods and swamps, blooming between April and June.

RANGE: N.S. to Man. south to N.J., n.Ga., e. Tenn. and Wis.

CATESBY'S TRILLIUM *(Trillium catesbaei)*

This is the pink-flowered trillium so often seen in the piedmont region and lower slopes of the mountains in the Southeast. It has a moderately stout stem 8 to 20 inches tall; and broadly oval leaves with stalked bases and abruptly taper-pointed tips. The flower nods on a slender stalk. A good field mark is the tendency of the sepals to be sickle-shaped; and the stamens have filaments fully as long as the anthers. It grows in rich deciduous woods, blooming in April or May.

RANGE: N.C. and Tenn. south to Ga. and Ala.

LITTLE TRILLIUM *(Trillium pusillum)*

The Little Trillium grows in swamp forests and savannahs of the coastal plain from Va. to S.C. and in s.Mo. and nw. Arkansas. It has a stem 4 to 8 inches tall, with rather narrow oblong-lance-shaped leaves. The white flower turns purplish and is short- to fairly long-stalked. It blooms between March and May. (Not illustrated)

RED TRILLIUM *(Trillium erectum)*

This is one of the commonest and most variable of our trilliums. The flowers are not always red for the petals, varying greatly in width, range from deep purplish red or maroon to pink, greenish-yellow, and even white. The flower stalks may be erect or they may be inclined or even bent downward. The petals, however, do not overlap but spread from the base. Such names as Ill-scented Wake-robin, Stinking-Beth and Stinking-Benjamin attest to the fact that the flowers are ill-scented. Often they are but this is not always true. The plants are commonly 8 to 16 inches tall and have rather broadly oval or somewhat diamond-shaped, stalkless or nearly stalkless leaves. It grows in rich moist woods and thickets, blooming between April and June.

RANGE: N.S. to Ont. south to Del., n. Ga. and n. Ala.

VASEY'S TRILLIUM *(Trillium erectum var. vaseyi)*

By some botanists this is considered to be a distinct species. Its flowers have broad, deep maroon petals and pale anthers; and they are quite sweet-scented. It is sometimes called the Sweet Trillium or Sweet-Beth. A white-flowered form of this is called the Woodland White Trillium *(Trillium simile)* in some manuals. Both grow in rich moist woods from Tenn. and w. N.C. south to nw. S.C. and n. Ga. blooming between April and early June.

SESSILE TRILLIUM *(Trillium sessile)*

Often called the Toadshade Trillium, this species has 3 stalkless, oval or egg-shaped leaves which are strikingly mottled in two or three shades of green. The plant grows from 4 to about 12 inches tall. The stalkless flower has 3 narrow and more or less erect petals from ¾ to 1½ inches long, which vary from maroon or purplish-brown to greenish-yellow. The flowers have a strong odor which is not altogether unpleasant. It grows in rich moist woods and stream bottoms, blooming in April or May.

RANGE: w. N.Y. to Ill. and Mo. south to w. Ga., Miss. and Ark.

HUGER'S TRILLIUM *(Trillium cuneatum)*

Huger's is a striking southeastern trillium which looks like a larger edition of the preceding species. Its flowers have erect maroon-colored petals from 2 to nearly 5 inches long, and they have a fragrance which has been likened to that of crushed strawberries. It grows in rich moist woods from w. N.C. and e. S.C. south to nw. Fla. and Miss. but is most common in the mountains; blooming between late March and May. (Not illustrated.

YELLOW TRILLIUM *(Trillium luteum)*

This striking trillium has a stout stem 8 to 18 inches tall, with broadly oval, stalkless leaves which are beautifully mottled. The stalkless flower has erect lemon-yellow petals from 2 to 3 inches in length, and 3 yellowish-green sepals which spread horizontally. The flowers have a very pleasant odor which suggests that of lemons. It grows in rich moist woods and ravines, blooming in April or May.

RANGE: w. N.C., Ky. and Mo. south to n. Ga., Ala. and Ark.

PRAIRIE TRILLIUM *(Trillium recurvatum)*

A distinguishing feature of this trillium is the slender stalks of its leaves which are ½ to about 1 inch long. The flowers are stalkless but their maroon or reddish-brown to yellowish-green petals are contracted into stalk-like bases. The 3 sepals curve backward between the leaves. This trillium grows in rich woods and blooms during April and May.

RANGE: Ohio and Mich. to Wis. and Neb. south to Ala., Miss. and Ark.

LANCE-LEAF TRILLIUM *(Trillium lanceolatum)*

This species is distinguished by its narrowly oval or lance-shaped, almost stalkless, mottled leaves which top a stem from 4 to 15 inches tall. The stalkless flower has 3 maroon to greenish and erect petals which taper at the base. It grows in deciduous woods and on river bluffs from S.C. and Tenn. south to Fla. and La., blooming in April or May. (Not illustrated)

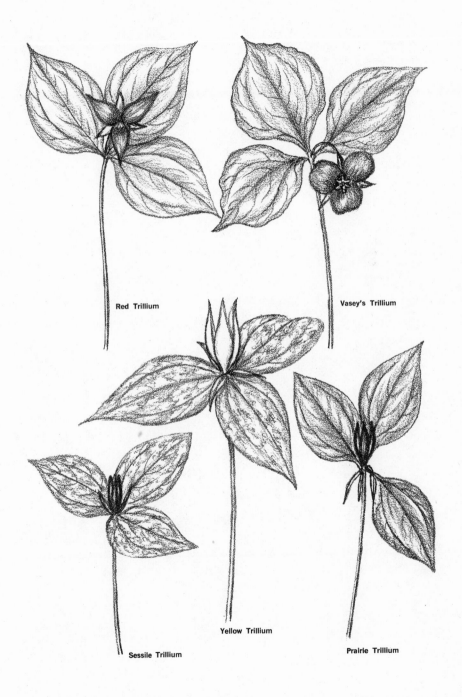

Red Trillium

Vasey's Trillium

Yellow Trillium

Sessile Trillium

Prairie Trillium

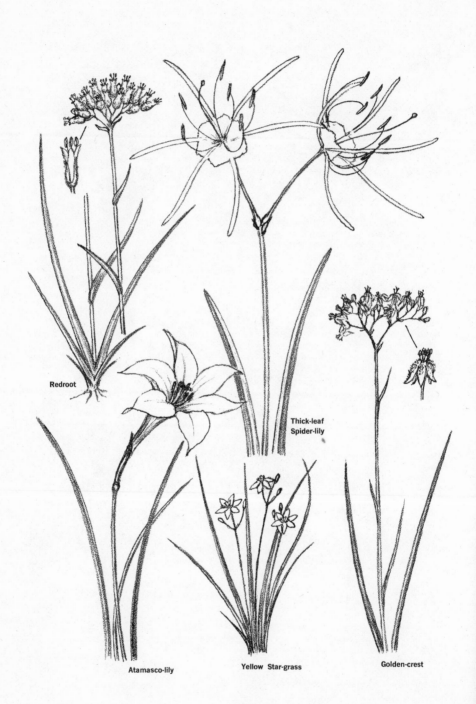

Redroot

Thick-leaf
Spider-lily

Atamasco-lily

Yellow Star-grass

Golden-crest

BLOODWORT FAMILY (Haemodoraceae)

REDROOT *(Lachnanthes caroliniana)*

This is a plant of sandy swamps and peat bogs, which gets its name from its bright red roots. It has a stem 1 to 2½ feet tall which is woolly toward the top; terminating in a dense and nearly flat-topped cluster of narrowly bell-shaped, dull yellow flowers which are about a half inch long. They are densely woolly outside but smooth within, and have 3 stamens which are longer than the corolla tube. The narrow and grass-like leaves are in a basal cluster, with only a few small ones along the stem. It blooms between June and September in the coastal plain.

RANGE: Mass. and Del. south to Fla. and west to Tex.

GOLDEN-CREST *(Lophiola americana)*

In some ways this plant resembles the Redroot. It has a slightly more leafy stem 1 to 2 feet tall which is densely coated with soft,white, matted wool toward the top. At its summit is a flat-topped cluster of small yellow flowers which are hairy within, and their perianth segments bend backward to expose the 6 stamens. It grows in wet pinelands, bogs and savannahs and blooms in June or July,

RANGE: N.J. south to Fla. and west to Miss.

AMARYLLIS FAMILY (Amaryllidaceae)

As in the Lily Family, the flowers of members of this family have 3 sepals and 3 petals which are similar in size and color, 6 stamens, and a solitary pistil composed of 3 united carpels. In this family, however, all of the flower parts are joined at the base. The tube of the perianth is more or less united with the ovary of the pistil, thus the ovary appears to be beneath the other parts of the flower or is *inferior*. The fruits are capsules. These plants have long and narrow or grass-like leaves which, along with the naked flower stalks, arise from a bulb or corm.

ATAMASCO-LILY *(Zephyranthes atamasco)*

Also known as the Zephyr-lily and Wild Easter-lily, this plant has rather large lily-like flowers that are usually borne solitary on a naked stalk 8 to 15 inches tall. The flowers are white when they first open but later turn pink. Both the flower stalks and the long, narrow leaves arise from an onion-like bulb. It grows in rich moist woods, swamps, and meadows; blooming between March and May.

RANGE: Va. south to Fla. and west to Miss.

THICK-LEAF SPIDER-LILY *(Hymenocallis crassifolia)*

At the summit of a naked stalk from 1½ to 2 feet tall, this spider-lily has 2 or 3 large white flowers. The long, green, stalk-like perianth tubes suddenly flare into 6 long and very narrow, petal-like segments. Within them are the 6 stamens, the slender filaments of which are joined toward the base with a cup-shaped white membrane which adds immeasurably to the showiness of the flower. The leaves are all basal, strap-like and up to 20 inches in lenth. This species of spider-lily grows in coastal plain marshes and along the bank of tidewater streams; blooming in May or June.

RANGE: N.C. south to Fla. and west to Ala.

MIDWESTERN SPIDER-LILY *(Hymenocallis occidentalis)*

This species is similar to the preceding species but it usually has from 3 to 6 flowers in a cluster, and blooms between June and September. It grows along the marshy banks of streams from s. Ind., s. Ill and Mo. south to S.C., Fla. and Miss. (Not illustrated)

YELLOW STAR-GRASS *(Hypoxis hirsuta)*

Yellow Star-grasses are small plants with clusters of from 2 to 7 flowers at the summit of a hairy stalk from 2 to 6 inches long. The six-parted perianth is smooth and bright yellow above but usually greenish and hairy beneath, opening to about the size of a dime. Both flower stalks and the narrow grass-like leaves arise from a hard corm. This species grows in dry open woods and meadows, blooming between March and September. Several other species are more commonly found in the southeastern coastal plain.

RANGE: Me. to Man. south to Fla. and Tex.

IRIS FAMILY (Iridaceae)

Flowers of members of this family have 3 petals and 3 sepals, 3 stamens, and a pistil composed of 3 united carpels but with distinct styles. The bases of the flower parts are joined together and form a tube which is completely united with the ovary of the pistil. They are plants which grow from creeping stems or rootstocks, and have narrow or grass-like leaves which are set end to end.

Wild irises resemble the cultivated kinds and are easy to recognize. They have 3 petal-like sepals which generally curve outward and downward, and 3 smaller petals which are erect. The 3 style branches are petal-like and lie over the sepals, while the 3 stamens are hidden beneath the style branches

BLUE-FLAG IRIS *(Iris versicolor)*

Flowers of the Blue-flag are often seen in wet meadows and marshes between May and August. The violet-blue sepals are whitish toward the base and beautifully veined with a darker purple, while the base of each one shows a yellow or greenish-yellow spot. The 3 petals are about half as large and plain blue-violet.

RANGE: Lab. to Man. south to Va., Ohio, Wis. and Minn.

SOUTHERN BLUE-FLAG IRIS *(Iris virginica)*

This species is quite similar to the preceding but the sepals usually have a brighter yellow and usually downy spot at the base. It is the most common of the tall blue-flowered irises in the South and is often abundant in the borders of swamps, marshes, and roadside ditches. It blooms between April and June, and its range extends from Va. northwestward to Minn. and south to Fla. and Tex. (Not illustrated)

THREE-PETALLED IRIS *(Iris tridentata)*

This iris of the southeastern coastal plain seems to have but 3 instead of the usual 6 perianth parts. Actually the 3 petals are so short they are inconspicuous, but the 3 large sepals are deep violet-blue with a bright yellow blotch at the base. The leaves are quite narrow and are usually gracefully curved. It blooms between April and June in wet pinelands and the borders of swamps.

RANGE: N.C. south to Fla.

Iris hexagona has conspicuously zig-zag stems and long leaf-like bracts at the bases of the spathes from which the flowers appear. As its name indicates it has 6-sided seed pods. It is another iris of the coastal plain swamps and is found from S.C. south to Fla. and west to Ala. (Not illustrated)

SLENDER BLUE-FLAG IRIS *(Iris prismatica)*

This iris has slender flower stalks 1 to 2 feet tall and very narrow leaves. Its pale lavender-blue flowers are about 3 inches across, and the 3 sepals have a yellowish spot at the base. The sharply 3-angled capsules are helpful in distinguishing it. It grows in wet meadows, marshes and on shores; blooming between April and June.

RANGE: Along coast from Me. south to S.C.; in mountains from Va. and Ky. south to n. Ga. and Tenn.

CRESTED DWARF IRIS *(Iris cristata)*

This is a little iris with flower stalks 3 to 6 inches tall. The flowers range from pale to a deep lavender-blue and each of the 3 sepals has a white patch and a 3-ridged, fringed, orange and white crest. The leaves tend to be curved and are ½ to about ¾ of an inch wide. It grows on rich rocky wooded slopes or bluffs, and in ravines; blooming in April or May.

RANGE: Md. to Ind. and Mo. south to n. Ga and Miss.

DWARF IRIS *(Iris verna)*

This is another dwarf species with flower stalks from 1 to 3 inches tall. Its flowers range from a deep to a rather pale violet-blue. The 3 sepals are but little larger than the 3 petals and have a smooth orange-yellow spot at the base. Its leaves are rather stiff, straight-sided, and about ¼ of an inch wide; greatly elongating after the flower fades. It grows in sandy or rocky woods, blooming between March and May. Sometimes it is called the Violet Iris.

RANGE: Md. to s. Pa. south to Fla. and Ala.

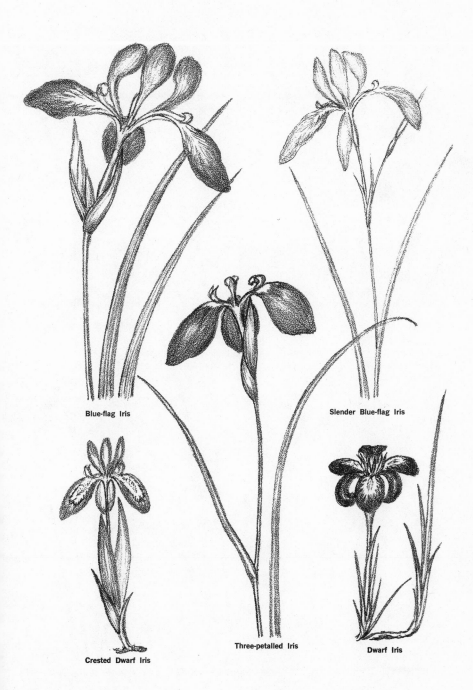

Blue-flag Iris

Slender Blue-flag Iris

Three-petalled Iris

Crested Dwarf Iris

Dwarf Iris

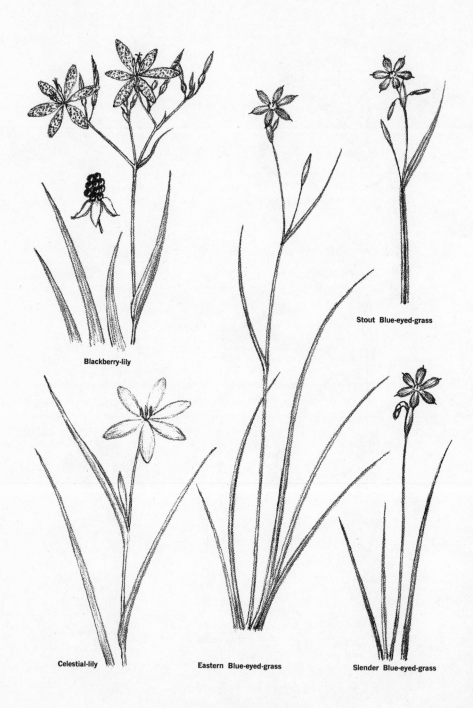

Stout Blue-eyed-grass

Blackberry-lily

Celestial-lily

Eastern Blue-eyed-grass

Slender Blue-eyed-grass

BLACKBERRY LILY *(Belamcanda chinensis)*

The Blackberry-lily has a rather stout, leafless flower stalk from 1½ to about 3 feet tall. It branches above, producing a loose cluster of flowers in which the 6 perianth parts are all alike, orange-yellow, and spotted with crimson or purple. The flower stalks arise from the basal fan-like clusters of leaves which very closely resemble those of the irises. The flowers open between June and August: and are followed by pear-shaped capsules which open to expose a cluster of black, fleshy-coated seeds. The latter are very suggestive of blackberries, hence the common name of Blackberry-lily. This plant, which is a native of Asia, escaped from oldtime flower gardens. It now grows in wayside thickets, open woods, and in waste places throughout much of eastern North America.

CELESTIAL-LILY *(Nemastylis geminiflora)*

Celestial-lilies have stems from 1 to 2 feet tall which bear 3 or 4 long, narrow, folded leaves. This one has very delicate, violet-blue flowers from 1½ to 2½ inches across, which open between late morning and mid-afternoon. Two such flowers appear from each spathe, hence the generic name *geminiflora* which means "twin-flowered". The plant grows on prairies and in open woods or glades; blooming between April and June.
    RANGE: W. Tenn. to Kan. south to La. and Tex.
    A similar species which grows in the marshes, swamps, and flatwoods of northeastern Florida is *Nemastylis floridana*. It blooms in the fall and its flowers open between mid-afternoon and sundown.

BARTRAM'S IXIA *(Ixia coelestina)*

This plant is similar to the Celestial-lily but its nodding flowers are violet with a white "eye", or more rarely entirely white. The flowers open early in the morning but they soon wither. It grows in the flatwoods of southern Georgia and northern Florida where it blooms in the spring. This interesting plant was first discovered by the famous Quaker naturalist William Bartram, probably in the spring of 1766, and was described in his "Travels". It was not rediscovered until about 156 years later. (Not illustrated)

BLUE-EYED-GRASSES

About a dozen species of blue-eyed grasses occur in the eastern part of North America. All of them have tufts of narrow or grass-like leaves which stand stiffly erect. The flowering stems are two-edged and the flowers are in small clusters, more or less enclosed by the spathe-like bracts. The 6 perianth parts of the flower are all similar and are usually tipped with a small bristle-like point.

EASTERN BLUE-EYED-GRASS *(Sisyrinchium atlanticum)*

This species is common in moist meadows, marshes, and low woods. It is a pale green or somewhat whitened plant with tufted stems 8 inches to about 2 feet tall. The stems are slender, wiry, and just barely 2-winged. Its flowers are slightly more than a half inch across and are bright blue-violet with a yellow "eye"; blooming March to July.
    RANGE: N.S. to Mich. south to Fla. and Miss.

SLENDER BLUE-EYED-GRASS *(Sisyrinchium montanum)*

This species has slender wiry stems 6 to 24 inches tall which have a solitary straw-colored spathe without leafy bracts below it. The violet-blue flowers are about a half inch across and have a yellow "eye". It grows in meadows, fields and open woods; blooming between April and June.
    RANGE: Nfd. to B.C. south to Pa., n. Ga., the Great Lakes region, and Colo.

STOUT BLUE-EYED-GRASS *(Sisyrinchium angustifolium)*

The broadly 2-winged stem which usually forks above, and is but slightly longer than the leaves, is helpful in recognizing this species. The violet-blue flowers with a yellow "eye" are a bit more than ½ inch across. It grows in moist meadows and open woods; blooming May to July.
    RANGE: Nfd. to Ont. south to Fla. and Tex.

67

ORCHID FAMILY (Orchidaceae)

The members of this family have highly specialized flowers, many of them apparently being dependent upon a single species of insect to effect their pollination. Seemingly for this reason the flowers are unusually long-lived, but as soon as pollination has taken place the flowers wither.

Orchid flowers have 3, or sometimes only 2, sepals. There are 3 petals. The two side or lateral ones usually form the *wings* while the lower one, which is usually much different from the other two, forms the *lip*. The 1 or 2 stamens are united with the style of the pistil to form the *column*. The pollen grains are very sticky and adhere to one another, forming the 2 pollen masses or *pollinia*. The bases of all of the flower parts are united with the ovary of the pistil, thus this organ appears to be at the very base of the flower (ovary inferior). The fruits of the orchids are capsules which contain a very large number, sometimes even millions, of dust-like seeds.

Many tropical orchids (and those grown in our greenhouses) are epiphytes which grow on the trunks and branches of trees. Only one such species, the Greenfly Orchid, occurs within our range. Aside from this, all of our native orchids are terrestrial plants. Some of them, such as the lady's-slippers, have large and showy flowers, but indiscriminate picking and gathering of the plants is making them increasingly rare. They are very much in need of protection. Others have such small and inconspicuous flowers that only those versed in the subject of botany recognize them as being orchids.

Key to Genera of the Orchid Family

1. Plants with little or no green color; either without leaves or the leaves not present at the time of flowering.
   2. Flower stalks with at least a few scales; the plants entirely leafless. Lip of the flower usually with purple spots and a lobe on either side near the base. CORAL-ROOTS (Corallorhiza)
   2. Flower stalks entirely naked; the leaves not usually present at flowering time.
      3. Lip extended backward as a long and slender spur. CRANEFLY ORCHID *(Tipularia)*
      3. Lip not extended backward as a spur. PUTTYROOT *(Aplectrum)*
1. Plants with a green color; the leaves usually present at flowering time.
   2. Lip large and pouch-like. LADY'S-SLIPPERS *(Cypripedium)*
   2. Lip otherwise.
      3. Lip erect or at the top, at least in the mature flowers.
         4. Flowers fairly large, pink or magenta (rarely white), usually 3 to 12 on a stem. Leaves narrow, grass-like. GRASS-PINKS *(Calopogon)*
         4. Flowers small, greenish or white, and rather numerous.
            5. Plant with a single oval-shaped leaf. ADDER'S-MOUTH *(Malaxis)*
            5. Plant with 2 or more long and narrow leaves. REIN ORCHID *(Habenaria)*
      3. Lip at the bottom of the flower.
         4. Flower solitary, or only 2 or 3 on a stem.
            5. Leaves in a whorl of 5. WHORLED-POGONIAS *(Isotria)*
            5. Leaves otherwise.
               6. Plant with usually 3 nodding flowers from axils of small, oval-shaped, clasping bracts. NODDING-POGONIA *(Triphora)*
               6. Plant with usually 1 (rarely 2) flower and a single leaf.
                  7. Leaf broad and oval-shaped. Lip of the flower slipper-shaped. CALYPSO *(Calypso)*
                  7. Leaf narrow and grass-like. Lip of the flower otherwise.
                     8. Flower not subtended by a large leafy bract; the basal leaf appearing after the flower matures. ARETHUSA *(Arethusa)*
                     8. Flower subtended by a large leafy bract; the lower leaf well developed before the flower opens.

9. Side petals lying over the trough-shaped lip. Sepals narrow and spreading.   SPREADING-POGONIA *(Cleistes)*

9. Side petals spreading and not covering the spoon-shaped lip. Sepals pink.   ROSE POGONIA *(Pogonia)*

4. Flowers several to numerous.

5. Plant with a pair of leaves near the middle of the stem.
 TWAYBLADES *(Listera)*

5. Plant with scattered or only basal leaves.

6. Leaves conspicuously mottled with white.
 RATTLESNAKE-PLANTAINS *(Goodyera)*

6. Leaves otherwise.

7. Lip with a spur at its base.

8. Sepals and petals forming a purple hood above the broad white lip.   SHOWY ORCHIS *(Orchis)*

8. Sepals and petals colored alike, the lip sometimes toothed or fringed.   FRINGED ORCHIDS, ETC. *(Habenaria)*

7. Lip without a spur at the base.

8. Plant with 2 oval-shaped basal leaves.
 TWAYBLADES *(Liparis)*

8. Plant with 2 or more rather narrow or grass-like basal leaves.

9. Plant terrestrial. Flowers stalkless and arranged in 1 or more spiral rows in a slender cluster.
 LADY'S-TRESSES *(Spiranthes)*

9. Plant epiphytic. Flowers stalked and arranged in an open cluster.   GREEN-FLY ORCHID *(Epidendrum)*

GREEN-FLY ORCHID *(Epidendrum conopseum)*

This is the only epiphytic orchid to be found north of Florida. It grows on the trunks or branches of live oaks and other trees, along with the Spanish-moss and the resurrection fern. The plant has a bulb-like base and thick roots which serve as holdfasts; and a basal cluster of thickish, leathery, narrow leaves up to 3 inches in length. The flowers are about ¾ inch across, greenish or tinged with purple, and have a delicate fragrance. Several are borne in a cluster on a stalk from 2 to 8 inches long, between July and September.

RANGE: se. N.C. south to Fla. west to La., near the coast.

YELLOW LADY'S-SLIPPER *(Cypripedium calceolus* var. *pubescens)*

From 1 to 3 flowers are borne on a leafy stem from 8 inches to about 2 feet tall. Often there are several stems in a clump. The prominently veined leaves are hairy and from 3 to 6 inches in length. The flowers have a bright yellow pouch-like lip from ¾ to 2 inches long; and 3 sepals and 2 spirally twisted side petals which are yellowish-green to purplish-brown and often streaked with purple. They are more or less fragrant. Hairs of the plant may cause a dermatitis in sensitive persons. It grows in dry to wet woods and swamps, blooming between April and June.

RANGE: Nfd. and N.S. to B.C. south to N.C., n.Ga., n.La., Tex., Ariz. and Wash.

SMALL WHITE LADY'S-SLIPPER *(Cypripedium candidum)*

This species has a leafy stem 6 to about 15 inches tall which bears 1 or 2 flowers. The lance-shaped, prominently veined leaves are more or less overlapping along the stem. The flowers have a pouch-like lip about ¾ inch long which is white with purple stripes within. The sepals and 2 side petals are greenish-yellow and often streaked with purple. It grows in wet meadows, glades and swamps but is rather local; blooming in May or June.

RANGE: N.Y. west to N.D. south to N.J., Ky. and Mo.

SHOWY LADY'S-SLIPPER *(Cypripedium reginae)*

Often called the Queen Lady's-slipper, this species has a stout, leafy stem from 1 to 2½ feet tall. The large corrugated leaves range up to 7 inches in length and resemble those of the White Hellebore. The flowers are usually solitary and have a pouch-like lip 1½ to 2 inches long which is white but strongly suffused with rose or magenta. The 2 other petals and 2 sepals are white. Hairs of the plant may produce a dermatitis in sensitive persons. It grows in swamps, bogs, and moist wooded slopes; blooming between April and July.

RANGE: Nfd. to Man. south to Pa., w. N.C., e. Tenn., Mo. and N.D.

RAM'S-HEAD LADY'S-SLIPPER *(Cypripedium arietinum)*

The Ram's-head gets its name from its odd flower, the cone-shaped pouch of which is greenish or yellowish at the tip and marked with purple veins. The sepals and 2 side petals are greenish streaked with purple. It has a stem 6 to 12 inches tall on which are from 3 to 5 rather narrow, smooth leaves up to 4 inches in length. The plant grows in wet woods and bogs but it is rather rare, blooming in May or June.

RANGE: Que. to Man. south to N.Y. and Mich.

STEMLESS LADY'S-SLIPPER *(Cypripedium acaule)*

This species is also called the Pink Lady's-slipper and Moccasin-flower and, like other lady's-slippers, it is also known as the Whip-poor-will's-shoe. It is distinctive as the flower stands on a naked stalk 6 to 15 inches tall, at the base of which is a pair of large elliptic leaves. The pouch-like lip is about 2 inches long and pink with deeper colored veins (rarely white). The sepals and 2 side petals are greenish yellow and tinged with purplish. It grows in dry to moist woods and in bogs, blooming between April and July.

RANGE: Nfd. to Alb. south to Ga., Ala., Tenn. and Mo.

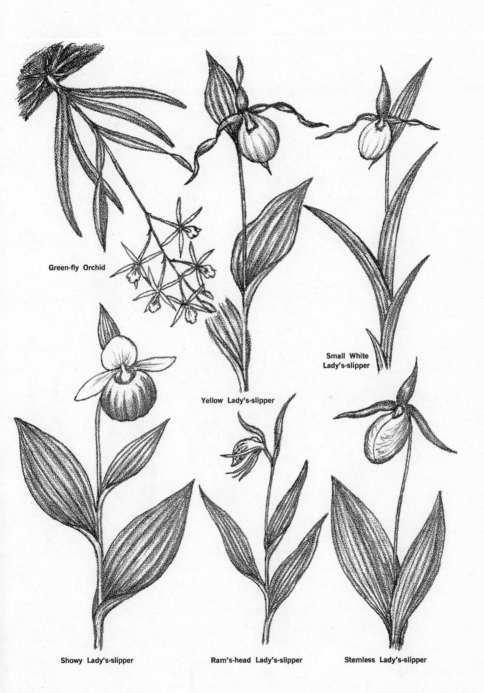

Green-fly Orchid

Small White
Lady's-slipper

Yellow Lady's-slipper

Showy Lady's-slipper

Ram's-head Lady's-slipper

Stemless Lady's-slipper

Showy Orchis

Green Fringed Orchid

Small Purple
Fringed Orchid

Yellow Fringed Orchid

White Fringed Orchid

SHOWY ORCHIS *(Orchis spectabilis)*

On a stem from 5 to 9 inches tall, the Showy Orchis displays several, leafy-bracted, attractive flowers. Each one is about an inch long, and from the base of the flat white lip hangs a spur. The other petals and the sepals are joined together to form a lilac or magenta, erect hood. There are 2 smooth, lustrous leaves, from 4 to 8 inches long, at the base of the upright flower stalk. It is found in rich, moist and usually rocky woodlands and it blooms between April and June.

RANGE: N.B. to Ont. south to N.Eng., n. Ga., Tenn., Mo. and Kan.

GREEN FRINGED ORCHID *(Habenaria lacera)*

Another name for this species is Ragged Orchid; and, indeed, its greenish-yellow or greenish-white flowers really look ragged. The flowers are less than an inch long and their fanshaped lip is cut into 3 wedge-shaped lobes which have long-fringed tips. At its base there is a downward pointing spur. The flowers are arranged in a rather loose but long cluster toward the summit of the 1 to 2½ foot stem along which there are some small, pointed leaves. The basal leaves are much larger, some of them often 8 inches in length. This interesting orchid grows in dry to wet meadows, fields, and thickets. It blooms between June and September.

RANGE: Nfd. to Ont. and Minn. south to Fla. and Tex.

SMALL PURPLE FRINGED ORCHID *(Habenaria psycodes)*

On a leafy stem from 1 to 3 feet tall, this orchid has a narrow but quite dense cluster of lilac-pink to rose-purple flowers. Each flower is less than an inch long and its fan-shaped lip is cut into 3 wedge-shaped and fringed lobes. The lip is also projected backward into a downward pointing spur about ¾ of an inch in length. Leaves at the base may be anywhere from 2 to 10 inches long. It grows in moist meadows, thickets, and woods; and blooms between late June and August.

RANGE: Nfd. to Ont. south to N.J., n. Ga., Tenn., and Iowa.

LARGE PURPLE FRINGED ORCHID *(Habenaria fimbriata)*

This orchid is very similar to the preceding species but larger in every respect. Its flowers are an inch or more long, and the spur of the lip is about 1½ inches in length. It grows in cool, moist, rich woods and in meadows; blooming about 2 weeks earlier than the Small Purple Fringed Orchid.

RANGE: Nfd. to Ont. south to N.J., w. N.C., and e. Tenn.

YELLOW FRINGED ORCHID *(Habenaria ciliaris)*

The bright orange-yellow plumes of this common orchid make it one of our most conspicuous wild flowers, and have earned it the name of Orange-plume. It blooms between July and September. The plant has a leafy stem from 1 to 2½ feet tall, the larger leaves toward the base being 4 to 8 inches in length. The flowers have an oblong-shaped lip which is deeply fringed about the margin; and a slender spur as long as, or longer than, the colored and stalk-like ovary. It grows in moist open places, on slopes, and in thickets from the coast to the mountains.

RANGE: Vt. to Ont. and Wis. south to Fla. and Tex.

CRESTED YELLOW ORCHID *(Habenaria cristata)*

This species is similar to, but smaller than, the preceding species. Perhaps the best distinction lies in the length of the spurs. Those of the Crested Yellow Orchid are only about half as long as the stalk-like ovaries. It grows in bogs and in moist to dry meadows and thickets; blooming between July and September.

RANGE: N.J. to Tenn. and Ark. south to Fla. and Tex. (Not illustrated)

WHITE FRINGED ORCHID *(Habenaria blephariglottis)*

The plume-like clusters of snow-white flowers near the summit of a leafy 1 to 3 foot stem will distinguish this orchid. As in the Yellow Fringed Orchid, the slender spur is longer than the stalk-like ovary; but in this species the lip is quite short-fringed, or not fringed at all in the variety *integriloba*. It is very partial to wet boggy places and blooms between June and September.

RANGE: Nfd. to Ont. and Mich. south to Fla. and Miss.

WHITE REIN ORCHID *(Habenaria nivea)*

This orchid is often abundant in the wet pinelands and bogs of the Southeast, where it is frequently called the Bog-torch or Snowy Orchid. The plant has a slender stem 10 to 30 inches tall, with a few small leaves and a slender cluster of small white flowers. At the base are a few rather firm, keeled or even longitudinally folded, lance-shaped leaves 4 to 8 inches in length. The lip of the flower is smooth-margined and stands at the top of the flower. It is projected backward as a long, slender spur. The plant blooms in August or September.

RANGE: N.J. south to Fla., west to Tex., and north to Ark.

SMALL SOUTHERN YELLOW ORCHID *(Habenaria integra)*

The small yellow or orange-yellow flowers of this orchid have a lip which is slightly toothed but not fringed. The plant has a stiffly erect stem 1 to 2 feet tall along which are scattered, small leaves. The 1 or 2 lowest ones are larger, lance-shaped, and long-pointed at the tip. Toward the summit of the stem there is a long and narrow flower cluster. It grows in wet pinelands and bogs, blooming in August or September.

RANGE: N.J. to e. Tenn. south to Fla. and Tex.

SMALL GREEN WOOD ORCHID *(Habenaria clavellata)*

One could not call this little orchid very conspicuous. It has a slender stem 8 to 16 inches tall, on which are a few small and bract-like leaves. There is a single large leaf at the base which is 2 to 6 inches long and broadest well above the middle. The small greenish-white flowers have a club-like spur about ½ inch in length, and they are in a narrow cluster. It grows in wet or moist woods and boggy places and blooms during July and August.

RANGE: Mass. to Wis. south to Fla. and Tex.

ROUND-LEAF ORCHID *(Habenaria orbiculata)*

This woodland orchid has a pair of large, round, shiny, pad-like leaves which are 4 to 8 inches wide and usually lie flat on the ground. The flower stalk is 8 to 20 inches tall and usually has several small, bract-like leaves below the narrow flower cluster. Its greenish-white flowers are about an inch long and they have slender dangling spurs. It blooms between June and August.

RANGE: Nfd. to Ont. south to n. Ga., Tenn. and Ill.

HOOKER'S ORCHID *(Habenaria hookeri)*

This plant like the preceding species has big, round, pad-like leaves. The somewhat fleshy, leafless flower stalk is 8 to 15 inches tall; and the flowers are greenish-yellow. The lip tapers to an upturned point in the front and is projected backward as a slender spur. This species grows in rather dry woods, blooming between May and August.

RANGE: Que. and Ont. to Minn. south to W.Va., Ill. and Iowa. (Not illustrated)

FRINGELESS PURPLE ORCHID *(Habenaria peramoena)*

Toward the summit of a stout leafy stem 1 to 3 feet tall, this orchid displays a dense, cylindrical cluster of bright rose-purple or violet-purple flowers. Each one has a lip with 3 wedge-shaped lobes which are but slightly toothed at the tip, and projected backward as a slender spur about an inch in length. Leaves toward the base of the stem are 4 to 8 inches long but they become progressively smaller up the stem. It grows in moist woods, meadows, and along streams; blooming between June and October.

RANGE: N.J. to Ill. and Mo. south to nw. S.C., Ga. and Miss.

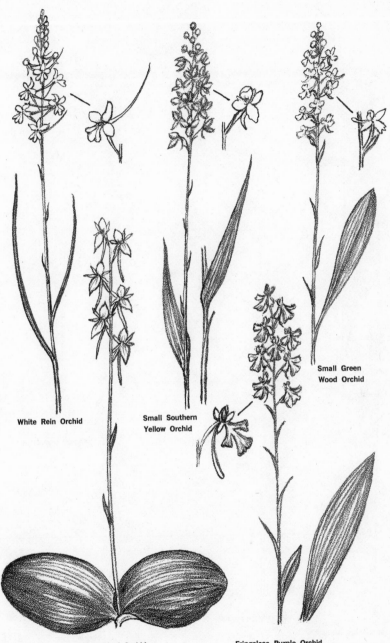

White Rein Orchid

Small Southern
Yellow Orchid

Small Green
Wood Orchid

Round-leaf Orchid

Fringeless Purple Orchid

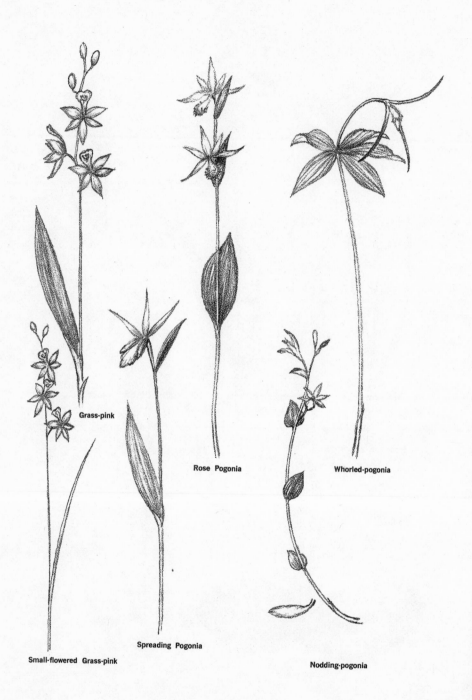

Grass-pink

Rose Pogonia

Whorled-pogonia

Small-flowered Grass-pink

Spreading Pogonia

Nodding-pogonia

GRASS-PINK *(Calopogon pulchellus)*

Several rose-pink to magenta flowers are produced along the 8 to 24 inch tall stem of this plant. As in all grass-pinks the spoon-shaped lip is uppermost and has a tuft of yellow, crimson-tipped, club-shaped hairs. The flowers are an inch or more across and open successively up the stem. There is but one broad grass-like leaf, from 6 to 12 inches long, toward the base. This attractive orchid is quite common in wet meadows, bogs, and southward in the wet pinelands. It blooms between April and August.

RANGE: Nfd. to Que. and Minn. south to Fla. and Tex.

SMALL-FLOWERED GRASS-PINK *(Calopogon barbatus)*

This species of the southern coastal plains has an almost thread-like slender stem 6 to 15 inches tall, with a very narrow grass-like leaf 4 to 10 inches long at the base of the stem. The rose-colored flowers are smaller than those of the preceding species and all open at about the same time. It grows in wet pinelands and savannahs; blooming in April or May.

RANGE: N.C. south to Fla. and west to La.

PALE GRASS-PINK *(Calopogon pallidus)*

This plant closely resembles the preceding species but has pale lilac to whitish flowers. It grows in wet pinelands and bogs of the coastal plain from Va. south to Fla. and west to La., blooming from May to July. (Not illustrated)

SPREADING POGONIA *(Cleistes divaricata)*

At the summit of a 1 to 2 foot stem, this orchid has a solitary, leafy-bracted pink flower an inch to 2 inches long. The trough-shaped lip is veined with purple, lobed at the tip, and crested but not bearded. The other 2 petals lie forward over the lip, while the 3 narrow brownish sepals widely spread. About midway on the stem is a lance-shaped leaf from 2 to 5 inches long. It grows in moist woods, wet meadows and swamps; blooming May to July. Also called Rose Orchid, Rosebud Orchid, and Lady's-ettercap.

RANGE: N.J. south to Fla.; Ky. south to Ga., Tenn. and La.

ROSE POGONIA *(Pogonia ophioglossoides)*

The Rose Pogonia, or Snake-mouth, usually has 1, but sometimes 2, leafy-bracted pink flowers at the top of a slender stem from 10 to 20 inches tall. The flower is an inch to 1½ inches broad, and it has a spoon-shaped lip which is beautifully bearded with yellow-tipped hairs. A solitary and usually broadly lance-shaped leaf 2 to 4 inches long is located about midway on the stem. This orchid grows in wet to moist meadows, thickets, pinelands, and bogs; blooming between May and August.

RANGE: Nfd. to Ont. south to Fla. and Tex.

WHORLED-POGONIA *(Isotria verticillata)*

This orchid of moist woodlands has a stem from 8 to 12 inches tall, on which is a whorl of 5 leaves. The solitary flower at the summit has a greenish-yellow lip which is lobed at the tip, and a ridge-like crest in the center. The 3 wide-spreading sepals are greenish tinged with purple. It blooms in May or June.

RANGE: Me. to Mich. and Mo. south to Fla. and Tex.

SMALL WHORLED-POGONIA *(Isotria medeoloides)*

Like the preceding species, this smaller plant has a whorl of 5 leaves on its 6- to 8-inch stem. At the summit are 1 or 2, inch-long flowers in which the yellow lip is lobed at the tip and bears a broad crest. The other petals and sepals are short and greenish-yellow with a purplish tinge. This orchid grows in dry woodlands but it is quite rare and local. It blooms between May and early July.

RANGE: N.H. and Vt. south to N.C. and Mo. (Not illustrated)

NODDING-POGONIA *(Triphora trianthophora)*

This is a dainty little plant with a fragile stem 3 to 8 inches tall; along which are scattered, small, roundish, clasping leaves. It is often called Three-birds because there are usually 3 flowers nodding from the axils of its upper leaves. They vary from whitish to pink and their lip has 3 greenish lines. It grows in rich hardwood forests, blooming in August or September. Although locally common, it may disappear for a period of several years.

RANGE: Sw. Me. to s. Mich. and Iowa south to Fla. and e. Tex.

ARETHUSA *(Arethusa bulbosa)*

Arethusa has a solitary flower at the summit of a 5 to 10 inch stem; along which are a few, loose, sheathing bracts. Not until the flower matures does the single grass-like leaf protrude from one such sheath, later growing to a length of about 6 inches. The broad tongue-like lip is whitish with conspicuous purple spots, and on it is a crest consisting of 3 rows of fleshy, yellow- and purple-tipped hairs. The other petals and the sepals are magenta-pink. In most places Arethusa is a bog orchid, but nowhere does it grow so abundantly as in the salt marshes along the northern New England coast. It blooms in May or June. It is also known as the Dragon's-mouth and Bog-pink.

RANGE: Nfd. to Ont. and Minn. south to Md., nw. S.C., and the Great Lakes region.

CALYPSO *(Calypso bulbosa)*

The solitary and oddly beautiful flower of Calypso is borne atop a sparsely bracted 3- to 6-inch stem; at the base of which is a broad but pointed, plaited leaf which withers soon after the plant flowers. The lance-shaped sepals and 2 side petals are purplish and spread or ascend over the slipper-shaped, inflated lip. The latter bends downward; its white surface is streaked and spotted with cinnamon-brown and purple within, and in front there are 3 double rows of golden yellow hairs. By many it is considered to have the most beautiful flower of any of our native orchids, and it is often called the Fairy-slipper. It grows in cool, damp, mossy woods and blooms in May or June.

RANGE: Nfd. to Alaska south to N.Y., Mich., Wis., and in mts. to Ariz. and Calif.

DOWNY RATTLESNAKE-PLANTAIN *(Goodyera pubescens)*

This orchid is often called to our attention by its oval-shaped dark green leaves, which have a network of whitish veins. Its small white flowers are arranged in a long, narrow but dense cluster on a downy stalk 6 to 18 inches tall. The leaves are 1 to 2½ inches long. Often common in both moist or dry woods, it blooms during July and August.

RANGE: Me. to Ont. south to Fla., Ala., and Mo.

LESSER RATTLESNAKE-PLANTAIN *(Goodyera repens* var. *ophioides)*

This species has smaller leaves, ½ to 1 inch long with a few broadly bordered white veins. Its small white flowers are in a more loose, 1-sided flower cluster on a 4 to 10 inch stalk. It grows in cool, moist woods and blooms during July and August.

RANGE: Lab. to Alaska south to N.J., w. N.C., e. Tenn., and S.D. (Not illustrated)

SLENDER LADY'S-TRESSES *(Spiranthes gracilis)*

About a dozen species of lady's-tresses occur in eastern North America. All of them have rather small white, greenish-white, or yellowish flowers arranged in a more or less spirally twisted spike. This one has small white flowers which have a green spot on the lip. They are arranged in a single and strongly spiraled row on a leafless stalk 8 to 24 inches tall. The leaves are egg-shaped, stalked, and about 1 to 2½ inches long but they may not be present at flowering time. It grows in dry to moist open woods and fields, blooming from late July to October.

RANGE: N.H. to Wis. and Okla. south to Fla. and Tex.

NODDING LADY'S-TRESSES *(Spiranthes cernua)*

This is a widespread and common little orchid; growing in moist to dry fields, thickets, and open woods. It has white flowers about ⅓ of an inch long, which are arranged in 3 or 4 somewhat twisted rows on stalks 6 to 18 inches tall. The grass-like leaves are basal, several inches long, and narrower downward. It blooms from August to October, and the flowers are sweet-scented.

RANGE: N.S. to Que. and Wis. south to Fla. and Tex.

MARSH LADY'S-TRESSES *(Spiranthes odorata)*

Some botanists consider this plant to be a variety of the preceding species. It is a similar but much larger plant growing from 1½ to about 3 feet tall. The flowers are creamy-white and very fragrant. It grows in fresh water marshes and blooms in September or October.

RANGE: Md. and Tenn. south to Fla. and Tex. (Not illustrated)

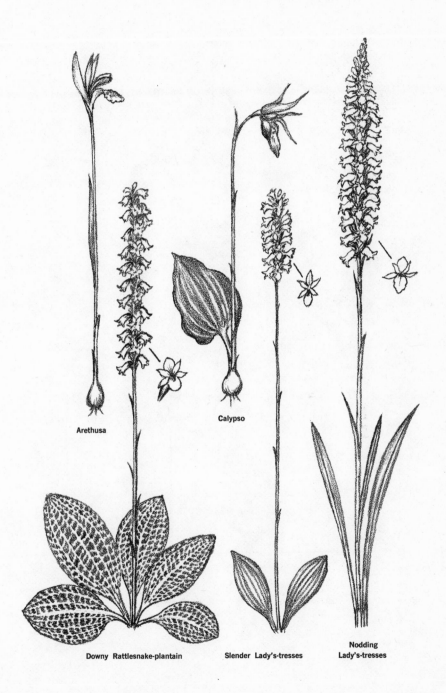

Arethusa

Calypso

Downy Rattlesnake-plantain

Slender Lady's-tresses

Nodding
Lady's-tresses

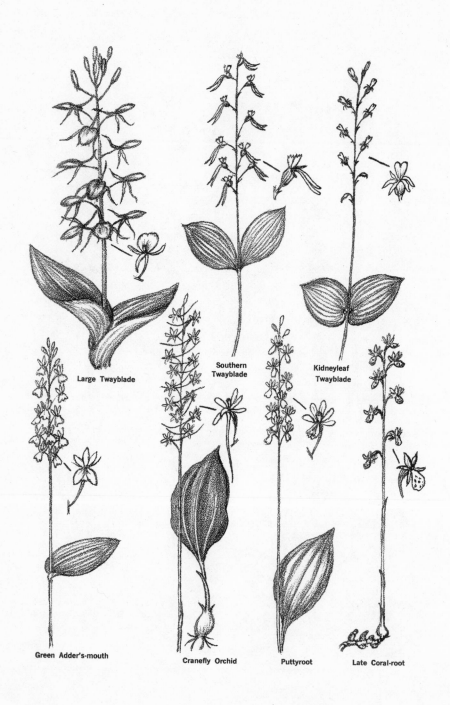

Large Twayblade

Southern Twayblade

Kidneyleaf Twayblade

Green Adder's-mouth

Cranefly Orchid

Puttyroot

Late Coral-root

LARGE TWAYBLADE *(Liparis lilifolia)*

Twayblades get their common name from the fact that they have 2 leaves. Those of *Liparis* are oval-shaped, smooth and lustrous, and all at the base of the plant. A number of half-inch greenish-brown flowers are borne on an angled stalk 4 to 10 inches tall. It grows in rich moist woods and blooms between May and early July.

RANGE: N.H. to Minn. south to n. Ga. and Mo.

SOUTHERN TWAYBLADE *(Listera australis)*

On a slender stem 4 to 10 inches tall this plant has a pair of quite firm, narrowly egg-shaped, stalkless leaves ½ to 1½ inches long. The reddish- to greenish-purple flowers are usually less than ½ inch long, with a lip that is split nearly to the base into 2 parallel lobes. It grows in wet woods and bogs, blooming from April to July.

RANGE: Que. and Ont. south to Fla. and La.

HEARTLEAF TWAYBLADE *(Listera cordata)*

This species is similar to the preceding but has thinner heart-shaped leaves ½ to about 1 inch long. The bronzy- or purplish-green flowers have a lip with 2 spreading lobes. It grows in mossy woods or bogs from Nfd. to Alaska south to N.J., w. N.C., Mich., Minn., N.Mex. and Calif.; blooming between late May and August. (Not illustrated)

KIDNEYLEAF TWAYBLADE *(Listera smallii)*

This species has a stem 4 to 12 inches tall which is densely glandular-hairy above. On it is a pair of roundish kidney-shaped leaves ½ to slightly over 1 inch long. The lip of the small greenish flowers is broadly wedge-shaped and deeply notched. It grows in moist mountain woods and thickets, blooming during July and August.

RANGE: Pa. south to n. Ga.

GREEN ADDER'S-MOUTH *(Malaxis unifolia)*

This orchid has a smooth, slender stem 4 to 10 inches tall with a solitary oval-shaped leaf about midway. Its small greenish flowers stand on slender stalks in a cylindrical cluster. At first the lip is lowermost; but, by a twisting of its stalk, the flower becomes inverted so that the lip is at the top. It grows in dry to moist open woods and thickets, blooming between May and August.

RANGE: Nfd. to Sask. south to Fla. and Tex.

CRANEFLY ORCHID *(Tipularia discolor)*

During the fall this orchid produces a single broadly egg-shaped leaf 2 to 3 inches long, which is purple beneath. By flowering time, in July or August, this leaf withers and disappears. The bronzy or tawny flowers have a long slender spur, and they stand on slender stalks which gives the impression of a long-legged insect. A number of the flowers are arranged in a long cluster on a leafless, smooth, tawny stalk 1 to 2 feet tall. It grows in rich woodlands.

RANGE: Mass. to Ind. and Mo. south to Fla. and Tex.

PUTTYROOT *(Aplectrum hyemale)*

This orchid produces a single dark green leaf with paler stripes, from 4 to 6 inches long. It persists until the flower stalk develops in May or June, then it disappears. The purplish-green to yellowish flowers have a white lip spotted with purple, and are arranged in a narrow cluster on a leafless stalk 10 to 20 inches tall. The name of Puttyroot alludes to the putty-like, sticky contents of the whitish corms which are usually in pairs; hence another name for it is Adam and Eve. It grows in rich woods.

RANGE: Que. to Sask. south to Ga., Tenn. and Ark.

LATE CORAL-ROOT *(Corallorhiza ondontorhiza)*

Coral-roots lack chlorophyll and are yellowish to purplish in color. Their leaves are merely small scales and the underground parts are branching and coral-like. This species has a stalk 4 to 10 inches tall bearing small greenish-purple flowers which have a white, purple-spotted lip. It grows in woodlands, blooming between August and October.

RANGE: Me. to Minn. south to Ga., Miss. and Mo.

LIZARD'S-TAIL FAMILY (Sauraceae)

Flowers of the members of this family have neither sepals nor petals, the 6 to 8 white stamens being the showy part of the flower. They have 3 or 4 pistils which are more or less united at the base. Only the following representative of the family is found in our region.

LIZARD'S-TAIL *(Saururus cernuus)*

The Lizard's-tail is a plant of swamps and shallow waters. It has heart-shaped leaves 3 to 6 inches long which are scattered along the more or less zig-zag 1½ to 3 foot tall stem. The small, fragrant, white flowers are in a long, slender, tapering, and gracefully drooping cluster; blooming between May and September. The extensively creeping rootstocks are aromatic. RANGE: Que. and Ont. south to Fla. and Tex.

SANDALWOOD FAMILY (Santalaceae)

Plants of this family are more or less parasitic on the roots of other plants. The flowers have no petals and the 5 sepals are united to form a cup with a 5-toothed rim. They have 5 stamens and a solitary pistil.

BASTARD-TOADFLAX *(Commandra umbellata)*

This plant has a slender, very leafy, and often a branched stem 6 to 18 inches tall. The thin leaves are stalkless, pale beneath, and from ½ to 1¼ inches long. Its small greenish-white flowers are in clusters at the tip of the stem or its branches. It grows in dry open woods, thickets and fields; blooming between April and June.

RANGE: Me. to Mich. south to Fla. and Ala.

BUCKWHEAT FAMILY (Polygonaceae)

Members of this family may be recognized by the thin tubular sheath about the stem just above each leaf. Their small flowers have 4 to 6 sepals which are often colored and petal-like, no petals, 4 to 6 stamens, and a solitary pistil with 2 or 3 styles. The small, dry, 1-seeded fruits may be flattened or 3-sided.

ARROW-LEAF TEARTHUMB *(Polygonum sagittatum)*

Tearthumbs are well-named as the hooked prickles which line the 4 angles of their stems are capable of scratching the skin. The arrow-shaped leaves of this species are on short stalks and range up to 3 inches in length. Its small greenish to pink flowers are produced between May and late fall. It is often abundant in wet places.

RANGE: Nfd. to Sask. south to Fla. and Tex.

HALBERD-LEAF TEARTHUMB *(Polygonum arifolium)*

This species is similar to the preceding and is best distinguished by its leaves which have the pair of basal lobes pointing outward. It is also common in wet places from N.B. to Ont. and Minn. south to Ga. (Not illustrated)

WATER SMARTWEED *(Polygonum amphibium)*

This is a plant of shallow waters and muddy shores. The sheaths above the leaves have a spreading flange at the top which is rimmed with bristly hairs. Dense clusters of rosy-pink flowers are produced between June and September.

RANGE: Lab. to Alaska south to Pa., Mo., Colo., and Calif.

PENNSYLVANIA SMARTWEED *(Polygonum pensylvanicum)*

A number of smartweeds similar to this one are found in eastern North America, but this is one of the most common and widespread species. It grows to a height of 1 to 3 feet, usually branches freely, and has lance-shaped leaves from 2 to 10 inches long. Showy clusters of pink flowers are produced from July until late fall. The gland-tipped hairs on the stalks of the flower cluster help to distinguish it from similar smartweeds.

RANGE: N.S. to N.D. south to Fla. and Tex.

VIRGINIA KNOTWEED *(Tovara virginiana)*

Often called Jumpseed as the mature fruits seem to spring from the stalk when touched. This is a woodland plant 2 to 4 feet tall; with egg-shaped pointed leaves 2 to 6 inches long, and small greenish-white flowers widely spaced on a long and slender end stalk. It blooms between July and October. RANGE: Que. to Minn. south to Fla. and Tex.

Lizard's-tail

Bastard-toadflax

**Arrow-leaf
Tearthumb**

Water Smartweed

Pennsylvania Smartweed

Virginia Knotweed

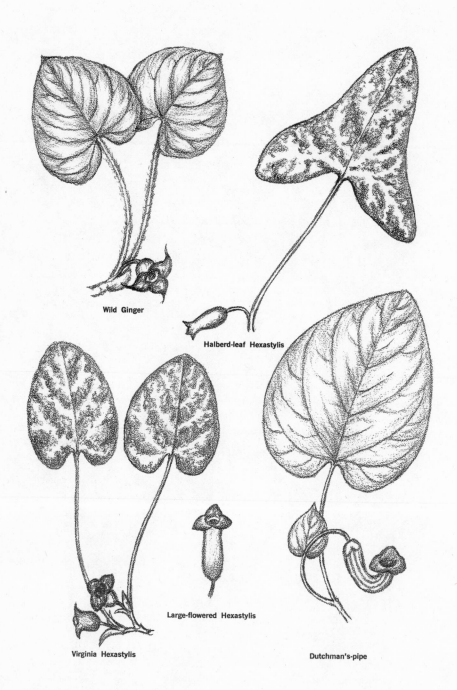

Wild Ginger

Halberd-leaf Hexastylis

Virginia Hexastylis

Large-flowered Hexastylis

Dutchman's-pipe

BIRTHWORT FAMILY (Aristolochiaceae)

Members of this family may be mistaken for monocots as their flower parts are in 3s or multiples of this number. They have 3 sepals which are joined together to form a cup-like structure with 3 lobes on its rim, 6 or 12 stamens, and a pistil which is made up of 6 united carpels, its ovary being more or less united with the calyx tube. The plants have more or less heart-shaped leaves with entire margins, and aromatic rootstocks which often have a ginger-like odor.

WILD GINGER *(Asarum canadense)*

The Wild Ginger is a low hairy plant, with a pair of very veiny leaves at the tip of its creeping underground stem. A solitary flower is produced between the bases of the leaf-stalks and is often hidden among the fallen leaves. It is shaped like a little bell and there are 3 spreading or recurved, pointed, brownish-purple lobes at the summit. In the variety *acuminatum* the lobes have tail-like tips up to 1½ inches long. Often common on rich and usually rocky wooded slopes, it blooms in April or May. The rootstocks have a ginger-like odor.

RANGE: Que. to Man. south to nw. S.C., Mo. and Kan.

HALBERD-LEAF HEXASTYLIS *(Hexastylis arifolia)*

Like the preceding, these plants have rootstocks with a ginger-like odor; but they have evergreen leaves which are more or less leathery in texture. This species has 1 or 2 such leaves on each branch of its underground stem. They vary from triangular to roundish or arrow-shaped and they are 2 to 5 inches long. Usually they are mottled on the upper surface. The flowers are vase-shaped, contracted at the top, and have 3 slightly spreading lobes at the summit. They are about an inch long. Growing in rich woods, it blooms between April and June.

RANGE: Va., W. Va. and Tenn. south to Fla. and La.

VIRGINIA HEXASTYLIS *(Hexastylis virginica)*

This plant is also known as the Heartleaf and Southern Wild Ginger. It differs from the preceding species in having more roundish or heart-shaped leaves 1½ to 3½ inches long and almost as broad. Its flowers are bell-shaped, about ¾ inch long, and they have 3 broadly-pointed, spreading lobes which are purplish-brown and often mottled. It grows in both sandy and rocky soils and blooms between March and May.

RANGE: E. Va. and W. Va. south to Ga. and Tenn.

LARGE-FLOWERED HEXASTYLIS *(Hexastylis shuttleworthii)*

The flowers of this species are narrow and flask-shaped, and from 1 to 2 inches long. Its leaves are similar in shape to those of the preceding species but they are usually thinner and larger. It grows in rocky woods and ravines in the southern Appalachians, blooming in May or June.

RANGE: Mts. of w. Va. and W. Va. south to n. Ga. and n. Ala.

DUTCHMAN'S-PIPE *(Aristolochia durior)*

The Dutchman's-pipe, or Pipe-vine, is a high-twining vine with heart-shaped leaves 6 to 15 inches across. The flowers are on leafy-bracted stalks in the axils of the leaves. The calyx tube is curved like a Dutch pipe, with a flat and somewhat 3-lobed rim. Its color varies from yellowish-green to brownish-purple. It grows on rich, often rocky wooded slopes and along the banks of streams; blooming in May or June. Often cultivated and sometimes found as an escape outside of its range.

RANGE: Sw. Pa. south in the mts. to n. Ga. and n. Ala.

WOOLLY PIPE-VINE *(Aristolochia tomentosa)*

This species is similar to the preceding but it is readily distinguished by its white-downy young branchlets, lower leaf surfaces, and flowers. The leaves are much smaller, being only 3 to about 6 inches broad. It grows in rich woods and stream bottoms and blooms between May and August.

RANGE: Ill. to Mo. and Kan., south to Fla. and Tex. (Not illustrated)

VIRGINIA SNAKEROOT *(Aristolochia serpentaria)*

The Virginia Snakeroot has an erect, slender, wavy stem from 6 to 18 inches tall which is sparingly branched at the base. Its thin leaves have a heart-shaped base, a pointed tip, and are from 2 to 5 inches long. The dull brown to purplish flowers stand on slender, scaly stalks near the base of the plant and appear between May and July. Beneath the ground, the plant has a knotty rootstock which has an agreeable camphor-like odor and is used medicinally. It grows in rich woodlands.
RANGE: Conn. to Ill. and Kan. south to Fla. and Tex.

PURSLANE FAMILY (Portulacaceae)

The members of the Purslane Family are mostly small, fleshy plants. Their flowers have 2 sepals, usually 5 petals, 5 or more stamens, and a pistil made up of 3 united carpels.

VIRGINIA SPRING-BEAUTY *(Claytonia virginica)*

Spring-beauties have 2 to several flower stems which arise from a deeply buried tuber. In this one the stems are usually 4 to 8 inches tall. Near the middle they have a pair of narrow and rather fleshy leaves from 2 to 4 inches in length. Along the upper part of the stem is a narrow cluster of 5-petalled white or pale pink flowers which have deeper pink veins. They are about a half inch across. The lowermost one opens first, the others open progressively up the stem. This plant is often very common in rich, moist woods and thickets; blooming between March and May. It grows well in a woodland flower garden. RANGE: Que. to Ont. and Minn. south to Ga. and Tex.

CAROLINA SPRING-BEAUTY *(Claytonia caroliniana)*

This species closely resembles the preceding one but it has narrowly egg-shaped or elliptic leaves from 1½ to 3 inches long, and ¼ to 1 inch broad. It grows in rich, moist, open woods and thickets; it blooms between March and May, or later northward. It is also called the Broad-leaved Spring-beauty.
RANGE: Nfd. to Sask. south to w. N.C., e. Tenn., Ill., and Minn.

PINK FAMILY (Caryophyllaceae)

Members of the Pink Family usually have opposite and entire leaves. Their flowers usually have 5 petals and 5 sepals (sometimes only 4), 5 or 10 stamens, and a solitary pistil with from 2 to 5 styles. The fruit is a capsule containing many small seeds.

STAR CHICKWEED *(Stellaria pubera)*

The half-inch, bright white, starry flowers of this plant are often seen on rocky, wooded slopes in the early spring. They have 5 petals which are so deeply notched that there appears to be 10, and there are 10 stamens. The weak stems are 4 to 12 inches tall and have 2 finely hairy lines. On them are pairs of elliptic or oblong leaves from ½ to 2 inches long which are pointed at both ends. Blooming between March and May. It is also known as the Great Chickweed.
RANGE: N.J. to Ill. south to n. Fla. and Ala.

FIRE-PINK *(Silene virginica)*

This is one of our most conspicuous wild flowers. The flowers are an inch or more across and have 5 spreading petals of the most brilliant red, each one being 2-pronged at the tip. The sepals are greenish but tinged with red and united into a sticky tube with a 5-toothed rim. The plant has an ascending, sticky-hairy stem becoming a foot to 2 feet tall and branching above. Along it are widely spaced pairs of narrow leaves, the lower ones being 3 to 5 inches long. The Fire-pink is common in open woods and on rocky slopes. In the South it begins to bloom in late March and it may continue to bloom until June or later. RANGE: N.Y. to Ont. and Minn. south to Ga., Ala., and Ark.

CAROLINA WILD-PINK *(Silene caroliniana)*

This species is a low, tufted plant with sticky-hairy stems from 4 to about 10 inches tall. Its flowers are about an inch across and have 5 spreading petals which are bright pink, and slightly if at all notched at the tip. The paired leaves, and the ones at the base, are 2 to 4 inches long and broadest toward the tip. It grows in dry sandy or rocky woods, blooming between April and June. RANGE: N.H. to Ohio south to S.C. and Tenn.

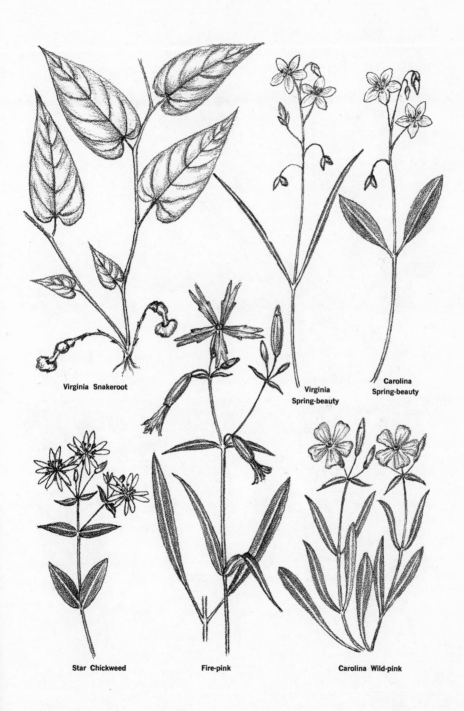

Virginia Snakeroot

Virginia
Spring-beauty

Carolina
Spring-beauty

Star Chickweed

Fire-pink

Carolina Wild-pink

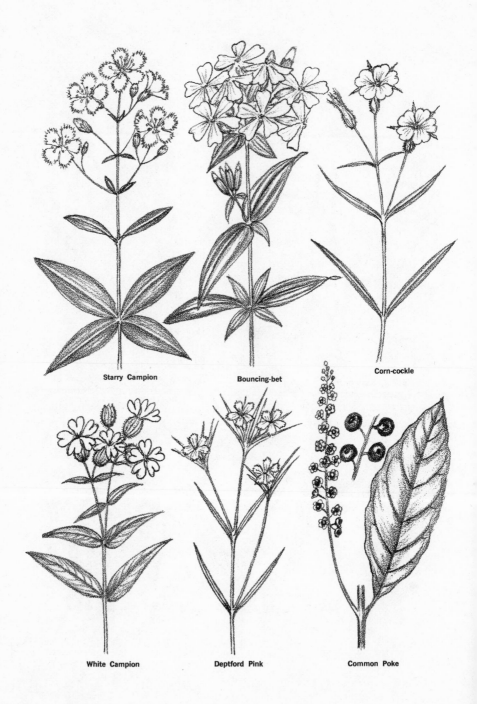

Starry Campion

Bouncing-bet

Corn-cockle

White Campion

Deptford Pink

Common Poke

STARRY CAMPION *(Silene stellata)*

Atop a stem from 2 to 3 feet tall, the Starry Campion has a loose cluster of white flowers. Along the stem below them are whorls of 4 lance-shaped leaves 2 to 4 inches long and minutely downy beneath. The flowers are about ¾ inch across and have an inflated, bell-shaped, usually downy calyx. The 5 petals are delicately fringed at the end. Often common in open woods, clearings, and thickets; it blooms between July and September.

RANGE: Mass. to Minn. south to Ga., Ala., Ark., Okla., and Tex.

BOUNCING-BET *(Saponaria officinalis)*

The Bouncing-bet is a native of Europe but it is now widely naturalized in America. A weed, but a very pretty one, it is often abundant along roadsides, on railroad beds, and in waste places generally. It is a rather coarse but smooth plant from 1 to 2 feet tall; with pairs of broadly lance-shaped, strongly 3- to 5-ribbed leaves which are 2 to 3 inches long. The pale pink or whitish flowers are grouped in quite dense end clusters, and are produced between July and September. Another name for the plant is Soapwort for its juice makes a lather in water.

CORN-COCKLE *(Agrostemma githago)*

This plant is another immigrant from the Old World which has become widely naturalized here. It is a quite slender and silky-hairy plant a foot to nearly 3 feet tall, with pairs of narrowly lance-shaped leaves from 2 to 4 inches long. The showy purplish-pink flowers are 1½ to 2½ inches across. It is frequently found along roadsides, in waste places, and in grain fields; blooming between June and September. The small black seeds often become mixed with grain but must be removed before it is ground into flour as they are poisonous.

WHITE CAMPION *(Lychnis alba)*

This is another European plant which is widely naturalized in America. It is a loosely branching, sticky-hairy plant from 1 to 2 feet tall. Along the stem are pairs of narrowly egg-shaped or lance-shaped leaves from 1 to 3 inches long. The white or pinkish, fragrant flowers open at dusk and close the following morning, being pollinated by night-flying moths. Their 5 petals are deeply notched at the tip and the pistil has 5 slender styles. Often common by roadsides and in waste places, it blooms between May and September.

DEPTFORD PINK *(Dianthus armeria)*

The Deptford Pink is a stiffly erect, slenderly-branched, finely-hairy plant from 6 to 18 inches tall; with pairs of narrow leaves 1 to 3 inches long. Its small flowers are borne in few-flowered clusters, among long and pointed bracts, at the tips of the stems. Each one is about ½ inch across and the 5 petals are pink or rose with whitish dots. It is an Old World plant which is now widely naturalized; frequently being seen in fields, waste places, and along roadsides. It blooms between May and July.

POKEWEED FAMILY (Phytolaccaceae)

Members of this family have small flowers with 5 sepals, no petals, 10 stamens, and a pistil composed of 10 united carpels. The only representative in our region is the following plant.

COMMON POKE *(Phytolacca americana)*

The Common Poke, or Pokeweed, is a smooth, strong-smelling, branching, reddish-tinged plant from 4 to about 10 feet tall. It has broadly lance-shaped leaves from 5 to 10 inches long which are scattered along the stem and its branches. The small flowers have 5 petal-like white sepals and they are arranged in long and narrow clusters on stalks opposite some of the leaves. As the plant continues to bloom from about mid-summer until late fall, it has flowers and fruits in all stages of development. The mature berries are purplish-black; and as they were once used for making ink, the plant is often called Inkberry. The roots, and perhaps the berries, contain a poisonous substance but the young shoots make wholesome greens. This plant is very common in open woods, thickets, old fields, etc.

RANGE: N.Y. to Que. and Ont. south to Fla. and Tex.

WATERLILY FAMILY (Nymphaeaceae)

Members of this family are aquatic plants with rootstocks creeping in the mud, and long-stalked leaves which commonly float on the surface. The flowers have few sepals, usually numerous petals and stamens showing a gradual transition, and numerous pistils.

AMERICAN LOTUS *(Nelumbo lutea)*

The lotus raises its flowers, and usually its leaves, above the surface of the waters of ponds and slowly moving streams. Its pale yellow flowers are 4 to 8 inches across. The numerous pistils are in pits on the disk-like and elevated receptacle. Later their ovaries become acorn-like fruits which are imbedded on the surface of the disk. The leaves are circular, 1 to 2 feet in diameter, and attached to the leaf stalk in the center. It blooms between July and September. Also called Yellow Lotus and Water-chinquapin.

RANGE: N.Y. and Ont. to Minn. and Iowa south to Fla. and Tex.

SWEET-SCENTED WHITE WATERLILY *(Nymphaea odorata)*

Both the leaves and the flowers of the white waterlily float on the surface of the water. Its flowers are white or pinkish, fragrant, and from 3 to 5 inches across. Their petals are broadest at or near the middle. The leaves are roundish with a V-shaped notch at the base, usually purplish beneath, and from 4 to 10 inches in diameter. It is quite common in ponds and slowly moving streams, blooming between June and September.

RANGE: Nfd. to Man. south to Fla. and Tex.

TUBEROUS WHITE WATERLILY *(Nymphaea tuberosa)*

This species resembles the preceding one but it has larger flowers from 4 to 8 inches across which are odorless, with petals that are broadest near the tips. The leaves are also slightly larger than those of the Sweet-scented species and usually green on both surfaces. It grows in ponds and slowly moving streams, blooming between June and September. RANGE: Que. to Ont., Minn. and Neb. south to Md., Ill., and Ark.

DWARF WATERLILY *(Nymphaea tetragona)*

Also known as the Small White Waterlily, this species has leaves only 2 to 3 inches across. The white flowers are 1¼ to 3 inches across, with purple lines on the petals. It grows from Me. west to Wash. and northward, blooming between June and September. (Not illustrated)

YELLOW WATERLILY *(Nymphaea mexicana)*

This waterlily has pale yellow flowers 2½ or 3 inches across. The leaves, up to 8 inches broad, are purple or crimson beneath. It is found in the coastal plain from S.C. south to Fla. and west to Tex. (Not illustrated)

YELLOW PONDLILY *(Nuphar advena)*

This plant of pond margins, swamps, and slow-moving streams is often called Spatter-dock. The flowers and leaves float on the water surface or are raised slightly above it. The leaves are egg-shaped or oval with a deep V-shaped notch at the base, and are 5 to 12 inches long. The bright yellow, globe-shaped flowers are 2 to 3 inches across and produced between April and October. RANGE: Mass. to Wis. and Neb. s. to Fla. and Tex.

ARROW-LEAF PONDLILY *(Nuphar sagittifolium)*

This species with arrow-shaped leaves less than half as wide as long is found in the coastal region from Va. south to S.C.

WATER-SHIELD FAMILY (Cabombaceae)

WATER-SHIELD *(Brasenia schreberi)*

The oval-shaped leaves of this plant are attached to stalks near the center and float on the water. They are 1½ to 4 inches long, and both the lower surface and leaf stalk are coated with a sticky jelly. The flowers are dull purple, about ½ inch across, with 3 or 4 sepals and petals and from 12 to 18 stamens. It grows in swamps, ponds, and slow streams and blooms between June and September.

RANGE: N.S. to B.C. south to Fla., Tex. and Ore.

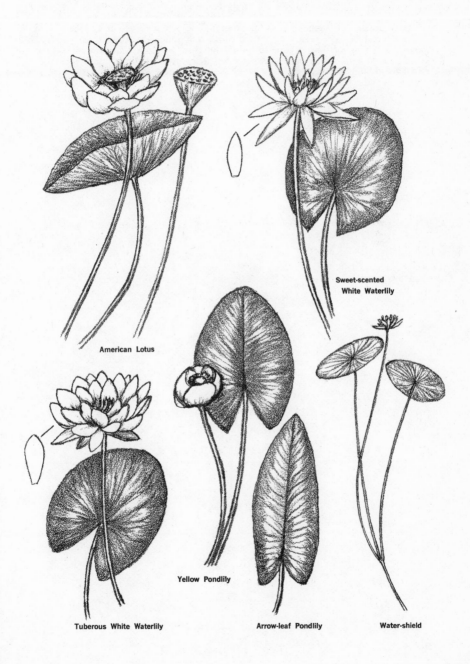

American Lotus

Sweet-scented
White Waterlily

Yellow Pondlily

Tuberous White Waterlily

Arrow-leaf Pondlily

Water-shield

BUTTERCUP FAMILY (Ranunculaceae)

This is quite a large plant family which includes, besides buttercups, many of our most familiar wild flowers. Their flowers have parts which are separate and distinct and they are all attached to a common receptacle. The stamens are usually numerous and indefinite in number. The pistils range from rarely 1 to a great many; in the latter case, being grouped on the knob-like to column-like receptacle in the center of the flower. The petals are usually few (commonly 5) or sometimes none, their place being taken by colorful and petal-like sepals. In some genera which lack petals, the sepals often fall as the flower opens; thus the flowers seem to be without floral envelopes. Most members of the family have flowers with a radial symmetry but those of the larkspurs and monkshoods are bilaterally symmetric.

KEY TO GENERA OF THE BUTTERCUP FAMILY

1. Flowers with a bilateral symmetry.
    2. Upper sepal extended backward as a hollow spur.   LARKSPURS *(Delphinium)*
    2. Upper sepal forming a sort of hood or helmet.   MONKSHOODS *(Aconitum)*
1. Flowers with a radial symmetry.
    2. Flowers with 2 series of floral envelopes—both sepals and petals.
        3. Petals extended backward as hollow spurs.   COLUMBINES *(Aquilegia)*
        3. Petals ordinary, not spurred.
            4. Flowers with green sepals and yellow or white petals; borne solitary or in loose clusters.   BUTTERCUPS *(Ranunculus)*
            4. Flowers with very small white petals, the sepals falling as the flower opens; borne in a long and narrow cluster.   BANEBERRIES *(Actaea)*
    2. Flowers with but 1 series of floral envelopes—the sepals—which may be showy and petal-like.
        3. Flowers seemingly devoid of floral envelopes, the sepals falling as the flower opens.
            4. Flower solitary.   GOLDENSEAL *(Hydrastis)*
            4. Flowers numerous.
                5. Flowers in long, slender, candle-like clusters.
                    BLACK COHOSH *(Cimicifuga)*
                5. Flowers in open and branching clusters.
                    6. Plants with slender stems and long-stalked leaves which are divided into many small leaflets.   MEADOW-RUES *(Thalictrum)*
                    6. Plants with stout stems and large palmately lobed and toothed leaves.   FALSE BUGBANE *(Trautvetteria)*
        3. Flowers with persistent sepals which are colored and petal-like.
            4. Sepals 4. Plants usually vines.   CLEMATIS *(Clematis)*
            4. Sepals usually 5 or more.
                5. Flowers with yellow sepals.
                    6. Sepals 5 to 7, greenish-yellow. Leaves deeply cut or divided.
                        GLOBE-FLOWERS *(Trollis)*
                    6. Sepals usually 5 and bright yellow. Leaves roundish heart-shaped with toothed margins.   MARSH-MARIGOLDS *(Caltha)*
                5. Flowers with white, pinkish, blue or lavender sepals.
                    6. Leaves 3-lobed. Flower with 3 sepal-like bracts beneath the true sepals.   HEPATICAS *(Hepatica)*
                    6. Leaves deeply cut or divided into 3 or more parts. Flowers not with sepal-like bracts beneath the true sepals.
                        7. Flowers on short leafless stalks. Basal leaves divided into 3 leaflets.   GOLDTHREAD *(Coptis)*
                        7. Flower stalks with some leaves or leaf-like bracts.
                            8. Leaves and bracts deeply cut or divided into 3 or more sharply toothed parts. Flower on a stalk rising well above the leaves or bracts.   ANEMONES *(Anemone)*
                            8. Leaves divided into small roundish leaflets which are somewhat lobed. The bracts of the flower stalk similar.
                                9. Plant with several slender-stalked flowers in an end cluster, arising from a whorl of slender-stalked and leaf-like bracts.   RUE-ANEMONE *(Anemonella)*
                                9. Plant with scattered leaves each of which is divided into 3 or 9 leaflets; the flowers arising from their axils.
                                    FALSE RUE-ANEMONE *(Isopyrum)*

EARLY BUTTERCUP *(Ranunculus fascicularis)*

Usually the first buttercup to bloom in the spring, the Early Buttercup may flower between late March and May. It grows on wooded hillsides, usually where the soil is quite thin. The plant may be only a few inches tall when the first flowers appear but it later becomes from 6 to 10 inches in height. It is covered with close-pressed, fine, and silky hairs. The bright yellow flowers are almost an inch across, and the leaves have from 3 to 5 cut or lobed divisions. The specific name, *fascicularis,* refers to the cluster (fascicle) of thick, fibrous roots.

RANGE: N.H. to Ont. and Minn. south to Ga. and Tex.

SWAMP BUTTERCUP *(Ranunculus septentrionalis)*

As its name indicates, the Swamp Buttercup grows in wet or swampy places; and there it may be found in bloom between late April and July. It is a branching plant with smooth to somewhat hairy stems ranging from 1 to about 3 feet tall. The flowers are about an inch across and they have 5 bright yellow petals. Its leaves are long-stalked and divided into 3 lobed and sharply toothed divisions.

RANGE: Que. to Man. south to Md., Ky. and Mo.

SMALL-FLOWERED BUTTERCUP *(Ranunculus abortivus)*

This is not a very showy buttercup for its flowers are barely ¼ inch across. They have tiny yellow petals and somewhat larger sepals which droop. It is a rather smooth plant from 6 to about 24 inches tall. The basal leaves are long-stalked and somewhat heart-shaped or kidney-shaped, but they do not persist very long. Those along the upper part of the stem are quite variable but commonly they have 3 narrow and stalkless segments. It is usually common in low moist woods and thickets where it blooms between late March and June. Another name for it is Kidney-leaf Buttercup.

RANGE: Lab. to Alaska south to Fla. and Tex.

MOUNTAIN BUTTERCUP *(Ranunculus allegheniensis)*

The Mountain Buttercup is quite similar to the preceding species. It can be distinguished from it by the whitish bloom of the plant and also by its achenes which have a strongly recurved or hooked beak. It grows in rich woodlands and blooms between April and June.

RANGE: Mass. and Vt. to Ohio south to nw. S.C. and e. Tenn. (Not illustrated)

ROCK BUTTERCUP *(Ranunculus micranthus)*

This is another small-flowered buttercup similar to both of the preceding species. Usually a smaller plant, it can be distinguished by the fact that it is decidedly hairy. It grows on rocks and in rich, rocky woods, blooming between March and May.

RANGE: Mass. to Ill. and Ark. south to Ga. and Ala. (Not illustrated)

TALL BUTTERCUP *(Ranunculus acris)*

The Tall Buttercup, which is also known as the Common or Meadow Buttercup, is a native of Europe which is now widely naturalized in America. It is the common and weedy buttercup so often seen in fields and meadows or along roadsides, especially in the northeastern United States and Canada. A branching and usually hairy plant from 2 to 3 feet tall, it has deeply 3- to 5-parted leaves in which the divisions are again cut into narrow and toothed lobes. The basal leaves are long-stalked. It has numerous flowers with 5 bright yellow petals, and it blooms between May and August.

CREEPING BUTTERCUP *(Ranunculus repens)*

Like the preceding species, this native of Europe has become a common weed over a large part of North America; and it is commonly found in yards, fields, and in waste places. Its smooth or somewhat hairy trailing stems take root at the nodes, and the plant often grows in rather large patches. Upright stems a few inches high produce bright yellow, 5-petalled flowers about an inch across. The leaves are divided into 3 leaflets which are cleft, lobed, and often mottled. It blooms between May and September.

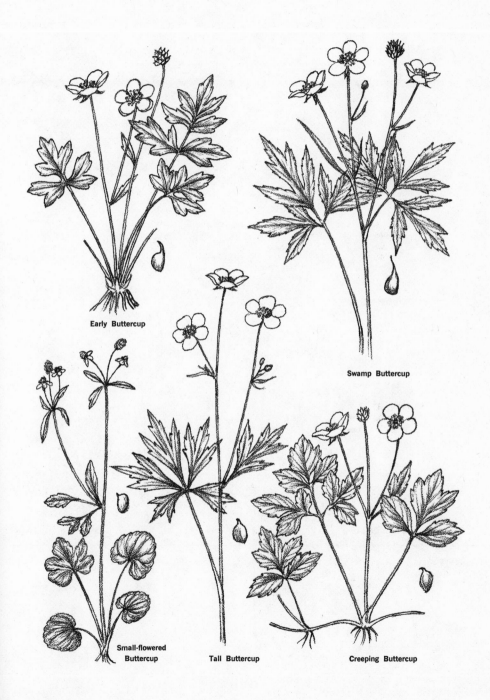

Early Buttercup

Swamp Buttercup

Small-flowered Buttercup

Tall Buttercup

Creeping Buttercup

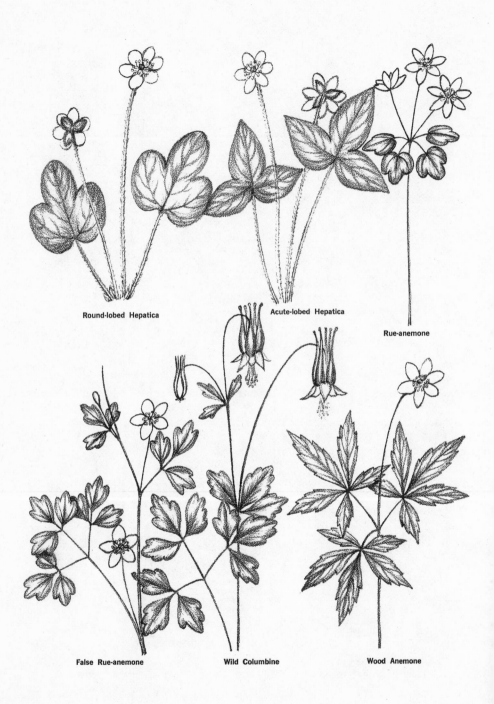

Round-lobed Hepatica

Acute-lobed Hepatica

Rue-anemone

False Rue-anemone

Wild Columbine

Wood Anemone

ROUND-LOBED HEPATICA *(Hepatica americana)*

Hepaticas are among the very first wild flowers to bloom in the spring, their blooming season being between March and May. Each flower stands on a silky-hairy stalk a few inches tall. It has no petals but its 5 to 9 sepals are delicate and petal-like; being white, pink, lilac, or even a deep lavender-blue in color. The numerous stamens have whitish or pale anthers; and in the center of the flower there is a little cluster of pistils. Just beneath the petal-like sepals are 3 green bracts which, in this species, have roundish tips. At flowering time the new leaves of the plant have not yet appeared, or are just beginning to put in their appearance. Usually there are some of the leaves of the previous year still present. Although now mostly brown, they are somewhat thick and leathery and they have 3 roundish lobes. The hepatica grows in woodlands, and it makes a good subject for the shady wild flower garden.

RANGE: N.S. to Man. south to Fla., Ala., and Mo.

ACUTE-LOBED HEPATICA *(Hepatica acutiloba)*

This hepatica is very similar to the preceding species; differing from it chiefly in having the 3 bracts below the flowers, and the lobes of its leaves, pointed instead of being roundish. It is also a woodland plant, blooming between March and May.

RANGE: Me. to Minn. south to Ga., Ala., and Mo.

RUE-ANEMONE *(Anemonella thalictroides)*

The Rue-anemone is a delicate little plant with a very slender stem 4 to 8 inches high. At the summit it bears a whorl of thin, pale green, 3-lobed, leaf-like bracts together with several slender-stalked flowers. The flowers are about ¾ of an inch across and have from 5 to 10 white or pale-pink, petal-like sepals. A bit later the basal leaves develop. They are ternately compound and the leaflets very much resemble the bracts of the flower stalk, but they are not present when the plant blooms in April or May. It grows in rich and rather open woodlands.

RANGE: Me. to Minn. south to Fla., Miss., Ark., and Okla.

FALSE RUE-ANEMONE *(Isopyrum biternatum)*

This plant resembles the Rue-Anemone but it has alternate leaves which are divided into either 3 or 9 leaflets. The leaflets are 3-lobed or divided. Its flowers are about ¾ inch across and are borne at the tip of the stem or on stalks arising from the axils of the leaves. They have 5 white, petal-like sepals. Growing in moist woods and thickets, it blooms during April and May.

RANGE: Ont. to Minn. south to Fla. and Tex.

WILD COLUMBINE *(Aquilegia canadensis)*

The Wild Columbine grows in rocky woodlands and on shaded rocks and cliffs, blooming between April and June. It is a smooth plant from 1 to about 2 feet tall. The flowers, like red and yellow bells, nod from the tips of the long and slender stem or. its branches. Each one is about 1½ inches long, with 5 petal-like sepals and 5 true petals which are prolonged backward as hollow spurs. Nectar is secreted in the ball-like tips of these spurs. The numerous stamens protrude beyond the mouth of the flower. The ovaries of its 5 pistils mature into slender, dry, pod-like fruits which contain many shiny, black seeds. Its leaves are compound, divided into 3s, and the leaflets are more or less 3-lobed and bluntly toothed. It blooms between April and July, and it is quite easy to grow in the wild flower garden.

RANGE: Que. and Ont. to Wis. south to Fla. and Tex.

WOOD ANEMONE *(Anemone quinquefolia)*

The Wood Anemone, or Windflower, has a stem from 4 to 9 inches tall. At its summit is a whorl of 3 leaves, each of which is divided into from 3 to 5 narrow and sharply toothed segments, and a solitary flower. The basal leaves are similar to the ones on the flower stem but they are either not present or just starting to grow at flowering time. The flower is about an inch across and it has from 5 to 7 white, petal-like sepals. It grows in open woods, thickets, and clearings; blooming between April and June.

RANGE: Que. to Man. south to S.C., Tenn., and Iowa.

MOUNTAIN ANEMONE *(Anemone lancifolia)*

The Mountain Anemone bears quite a resemblance to the Wood Anemone but it is a somewhat stouter and taller plant. It has a stem from 6 to 14 inches tall which has a whorl of 3 leaves and a solitary flower at the summit. Each of the 3 leaves is divided into 3 narrowly egg-shaped leaflets which have rather shallowly toothed margins. The flower is an inch or a little more across and it has from 4 to 7 white petal-like sepals. It grows in damp woods and thickets in the mountains, blooming between April and June.
RANGE: S. Pa. south to Ky. and n. Ga.

CAROLINA ANEMONE *(Anemone caroliniana)*

The solitary flower of the Carolina Anemone is from an inch to 1½ inches broad and it has from 10 to 20 white, pink, or violet-colored, petal-like sepals; so many, in fact, that it has the appearance of a daisy. The plant has a stem from 4 to about 10 inches tall, on which are 3 stalkless and deeply cut leaves. The stalked basal leaves are divided into 3 parts which are, in turn, deeply cut and variously toothed. It grows in open woods, fields, and on prairies; blooming in April or May.
RANGE: N.C. to Ind. and Wis. south to Fla. and Tex.

TALL ANEMONE *(Anemone virginiana)*

This is one of several species of *Anemone* popularly called Thimbleweeds because their achenes are crowded on a long and thimble-shaped receptacle. The Tall Anemone has a stout and hairy stem from 2 to 3 feet tall. On it is a whorl of usually 3 stalked and 3-parted leaves, which are variously cleft and sharply toothed. From this whorl of leaves arise the long stalks which end in a solitary flower. The flower is a little more than an inch across and has 5 greenish-white, petal-like sepals. The basal leaves are long-stalked but similar to those of the flower stem. In this species the achenes are crowded in a woolly, cylindrical head an inch or more long. The Tall Anemone grows in usually dry and rocky open woods and thickets; blooming between June and August.
RANGE: Me. to Minn. south to Ga., Tenn., and Kan.

LONG-FRUITED ANEMONE *(Anemone cylindrica)*

In general this species resembles the preceding one. It has a stem from 1 to 2 feet tall which is quite densely hairy, on which is a whorl of from usually 5 to 9 stalked leaves. The achenes are crowded in a narrowly cylindrical head from an inch to 1½ inches long. It grows in dry open woods and on prairies, blooming between May and July.
RANGE: Me. to Alb. south to N.J., the Great Lakes region, Mo., N.Mex., and Ariz.

ROUNDLEAF ANEMONE *(Anemone canadensis)*

This species has a somewhat hairy stem from 1 to 2 feet tall on which are stalkless, broad, and sharply toothed or cut leaves. The basal ones are similar but long-stalked. The flowers are an inch to 1½ inches across and have 5 white, petal-like sepals. The achenes are crowded in ball-like heads. It grows in damp open woods and thickets, blooming between May and July.
RANGE: Lab. to B.C. south to N.J., W.Va., Mo., and N.Mex.

PASQUE-FLOWER *(Anemone patens)*

The beautiful Pasque-flower has a silky-hairy stem from 4 to about 16 inches tall, but at flowering time it is considerably shorter. Its leaves are basal, cut into numerous narrow divisions, and also covered with silvery-silky hairs. The flower is about 2 inches across and has from 5 to 7 large petal-like sepals varying from white to lavender-blue or purple in color. It grows on prairies and on dry, exposed slopes; blooming between April and June. May be grown in a sunny or lightly shaded spot in the flower garden.
RANGE: Mich. to B.C. south to Ill., Mo., Tex., N.Mex., Utah, and Wash.

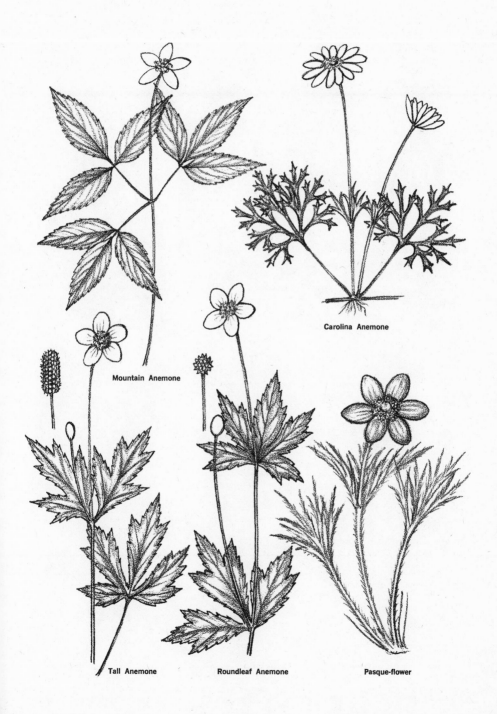

Carolina Anemone

Mountain Anemone

Tall Anemone

Roundleaf Anemone

Pasque-flower

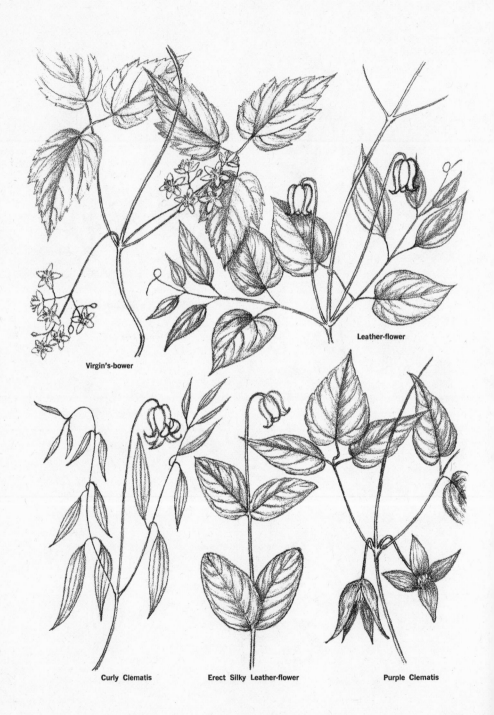

Virgin's-bower

Leather-flower

Curly Clematis

Erect Silky Leather-flower

Purple Clematis

VIRGIN'S-BOWER *(Clematis virginiana)*

The Virgin's-bower is a vine that commonly climbs over other vegetation on the borders of swamps, along streams, and in moist wayside thickets. Between July and September, it produces numerous, showy clusters of white flowers. Each one is a half to ¾ of an inch broad, with 4 or 5 petal-like sepals and tassel-like stamens. In the autumn the clusters of achenes with their long and plume-like tails are just as attractive as the flowers which preceded them. The opposite leaves are divided into 3 egg-shaped leaflets which have a few sharp teeth on their margins. Like other species of *Clematis,* it climbs by means of its leafstalks which act like tendrils. It can be grown in the garden on a fence or trellis.
RANGE: N.S. to Man. south to Ga., La., and Kan.

LEATHER-FLOWER *(Clematis viorna)*

Leather-flowers have bell-shaped flowers which nod from the ends of long stalks arising from the axils of the leaves. They have 4 thick, somewhat leathery, dull purplish sepals in which the tips are recurved. The opposite leaves of this climber are divided into from 3 to 7 egg-shaped to lance-shaped, bright green leaflets. It grows in rich woods and thickets, blooming between May and August. As in other species of *Clematis,* the flowers are followed by clusters of achenes with long, plume-like tails.
RANGE: Pa. to Ill. and Iowa south to Ga. and Tex.

CURLY CLEMATIS *(Clematis crispa)*

The Curly Clematis is also known as the Marsh Leather-flower and the Blue-jasmine. It has attractive bluish-purple flowers an inch or more long, shaped like bells but with the wavy-edged sepals spreading from about the middle. Each one nods from a slender stalk at the tip of a branch. The leaves are divided into from 5 to 9 rather thin, lance-shaped or narrowly egg-shaped leaflets. This species grows in wet woods and about the borders of swamps, blooming between April and August.
RANGE: Se. Va., s. Ill., and Mo. south ot Fla. and Tex.

ERECT SILKY LEATHER-FLOWER *(Clematis ochroleuca)*

Instead of being a vine, this leather-flower is an erect branching plant from 1 to 2 feet tall. It has pairs of simple, egg-shaped, stalkless leaves ranging from 1½ to 2 inches in length. New growth and the lower surfaces of the leaves are silky-hairy but they eventually become smooth. The flowers are bell-shaped, dull yellowish or purplish, silky on the outside, and about an inch long. Each one nods at the end of a slender stalk. It grows in woods, thickets, and on rocky slopes, blooming during April or May. Another name for it is Curly-heads.
RANGE: Se. N.Y. and se. Pa. south to Ga.

PURPLE CLEMATIS *(Clematis verticillaris)*

The showy flowers of the Purple Clematis, or Purple Virgin's-bower, are from 2 to 3 inches broad. They have 4 large, veiny, bluish-purple, petal-like sepals. Some of the outer stamens have the appearance of being small petals. Each flower is on a stalk arising from a leaf axil. The leaves of this trailing or climbing plant are opposite and divided into 3 egg-shaped or heart-shaped leaflets, sometimes with a few teeth on their margins. It grows in open woods and on rocky slopes, blooming during May or June.
RANGE: Que. to Man. south to Md., w. N.C., Ohio, and Iowa.

MARSH-MARIGOLD *(Caltha palustris)*

The Marsh-marigold, or Cowslip, is a smooth plant with a stout, hollow, forking stem from 1 to 2 feet tall. It has flowers an inch to 1½ inches broad, which have 5 or 6 petal-like sepals of the brightest yellow. The roundish, heart-shaped leaves are 2 to 6 inches across and have low teeth on their margins. The young leaves are very popular as spring greens, and in the Northeast they are often sold in the markets. As its name implies, the plant grows in swamps and in wet open woods and meadows. The flowering season is between April and June, or even later in the Far North.

RANGE: Lab. to Alaska south to N.C., Tenn., Iowa, and Neb.

AMERICAN GLOBE-FLOWER *(Trollius laxus)*

Like the preceding species, the Globe-flower grows in swamps and wet meadows or thickets, but it is rather rare and local in occurrence. It has a slender, smooth stem 1 to 2 feet tall. The leaves are divided into from 5 to 7 radiating and cut-toothed segments. They are from 2 to 4 inches wide and all but the uppermost ones are stalked. The flowers are usually solitary, 1 to 1½ inches across, and have from 5 to 7 pale greenish-yellow petal-like sepals. It blooms in April or May.

RANGE: Conn. to Pa. and Mich.

DWARF LARKSPUR *(Delphinium tricorne)*

At the time of flowering, in April or May, the stems of this plant are usually 6 to 12 inches high, but later they become much taller. The larkspurs are unusual among the members of this family in that their flowers have a bilateral symmetry. Those of this species are 1 to 1½ inches long, usually a deep blue-violet or variegated with white, and arranged in a rather loose, cylindrical cluster. As in other larkspurs there are 5 small, irregular, petal-like sepals and the uppermost one is prolonged into a hollow spur. There are also 4 petals but they are quite small, the upper pair having spurs which are enclosed within the spur of the sepal. The leaves are cut into 5 radiating divisions which are themselves cleft and sharply toothed. The Dwarf Larkspur grows in rich woods and on rocky slopes, blooming in April or May.

RANGE: Pa. to Minn. and Neb. south to Ga., Ala., Ark., and Okla.

TALL LARKSPUR *(Delphinium exaltatum)*

This species of larkspur has a slender, leafy stem from 2 to 5 feet tall; bearing toward the summit a long, narrow, but rather dense cluster of lavender-blue to whitish flowers. Each one is about ¾ of an inch long and the upper sepal has a spur which is almost straight. The leaves are deeply cleft into from 3 to 5 narrow divisions which are 3-cleft at the summit. The Tall Larkspur grows in rich woods or thickets and on rocky slopes. Its flowering season extends from July to September.

RANGE: Pa. and Ohio south to N.C. and Miss.

CAROLINA LARKSPUR *(Delphinium carolinianum)*

The Carolina Larkspur usually has a simple, slender stem from 1 to 2 feet tall which is glandular-hairy on the upper portion. Its leaves are deeply 3- to 5-parted and the divisions are cut into very narrow lobes. The flowers are about an inch long, deep blue or violet in color, and have rather long and upcurved spurs. It grows in dry open woods, fields, sandhills, and prairies and blooms during May or June.

RANGE: Va. to Ky., Mo., and Okla. south to Ga. and Tex.

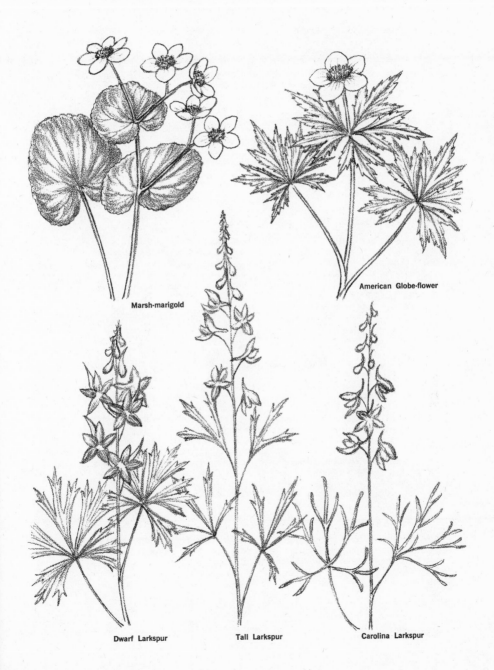

Marsh-marigold

American Globe-flower

Dwarf Larkspur   Tall Larkspur   Carolina Larkspur

BLACK COHOSH *(Cimicifuga racemosa)*

The Black Cohosh, or Black Snakeroot, is one of the most conspicuous plants in our wooded areas during the summer months; for it is then that it displays its long, slender, candle-like clusters of small white flowers. On close inspection, one will find that each flower consists largely of a tassel-like group of white stamens with a pistil in the center. Some of the outermost stamens resemble small petals but there are no true petals, and the sepals drop off as the flowers open. The pistil develops into a small dry pod. The Black Cohosh has a somewhat slender stem from 3 to 6 feet tall, on which are 2 or 3 large compound leaves. The leaflets are mostly egg-shaped, rounded or somewhat pointed at the base, and are cleft or sharply toothed on the margin. It blooms between June and September. The rootstocks are used medicinally.

RANGE: Mass. to Ont. south to Ga., Tenn., and Mo.

HEARTLEAF COHOSH *(Cimicifuga racemosa* var. *cordifolia)*

This plant of the damp southern Appalachian woodlands is almost identical with the Black Cohosh, except for its leaves. They are divided into usually fewer and larger leaflets, and at least the end ones are deeply heart-shaped at the base. It is generally regarded to be merely a variety of the Black Cohosh, although some botanists have considered it to be a distinct species.

RANGE: Mts. of Va., N.C., and Tenn.

AMERICAN BUGBANE *(Cimicifuga americana)*

This plant also closely resembles the Black Cohosh and to identify it one must examine either the flowers or the pod-like fruits which follow them. The flowers of this species usually contain 3 or more pistils (the Black Cohosh usually has only 1); and the resulting pods are stalked and in groups of 3 or more. Also known as the Summer Cohosh and Mountain Bugbane, it grows only in rich woods in the mountain region; blooming during August or September.

RANGE: Pa. south to Ga. and Tenn.

WHITE BANEBERRY *(Actaea pachypoda)*

The White Baneberry is far more likely to attract one's attention when in fruit than in flower. The plant, in general, closely resembles the Black Cohosh but it grows only a foot or two high. Its large leaves are ternately compound with a number of stalked, sharply toothed leaflets. The flowers very much resemble those of the Black Cohosh but they are in shorter, cylindrical clusters. Those of the baneberries actually have petals but they are so small one has to look very carefully to see them. The sepals fall away as the flowers open. In the center of the flower is one pistil with a stalkless stigma seated at the top. It develops into a somewhat egg-shaped and snow-white berry, about ¼ of an inch in diameter, with a purple spot at the end. Each berry stands on a thick and bright red stalk, a number of them being displayed in a cylindrical cluster. The White Baneberry grows in rich woods and thickets. The flowering season is in May and June; the berries are showy between July and October. It is also called the White Cohosh and Doll's-eyes.

RANGE: N.S. to Man. south to Ga., La., and Okla

RED BANEBERRY *(Actaea rubra)*

This species very closely resembles the preceding but it has bright red berries, or sometimes ivory-white ones, on slender rather than stout stalks. It grows in woods and thickets, blooming between May and July. The berries are present between August and October. Another name for it is Snakeberry.

RANGE: Lab. to B.C. south to N.J., W.Va., S.D., Colo., Utah, and Oregon.

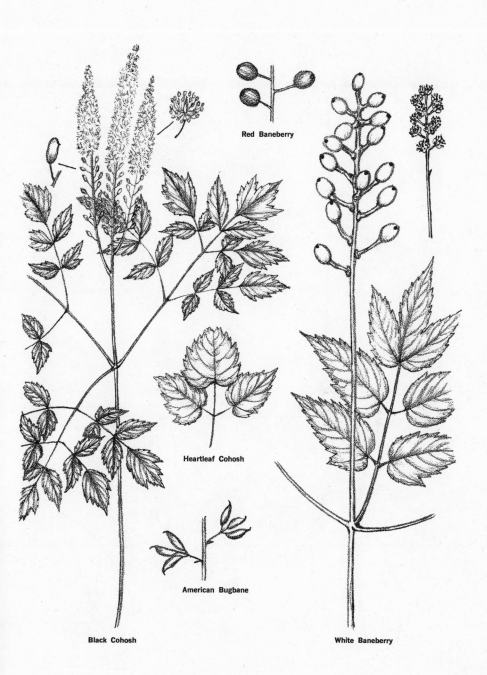

Red Baneberry

Heartleaf Cohosh

American Bugbane

Black Cohosh

White Baneberry

Goldthread

Wild Monkshood

False Bugbane

Goldenseal

WILD MONKSHOOD *(Aconitum uncinatum)*

The Wild Monkshood has a slender, leafy, rather weak, branching stem from 2 to about 3 feet tall; with violet-blue flowers clustered at the ends of the branches. The flowers are about 1 inch across and have a bilateral symmetry. They have 5 very irregular, petal-like sepals, the upper one being much larger and shaped like a hood or helmet. The petals are small and inconspicuous, 2 of them being covered by the hooded sepal. The leaves are deeply divided into from 3 to 5 cut-toothed lobes and they, like the rest of the plant, are smooth or nearly so. The Wild Monkshood is also known as the Wild Wolfsbane. It grows in moist woods, thickets, and on rocky slopes; blooming between August and October.

RANGE: Pa. to Ind. south to Ga. and Ala.

NEW YORK MONKSHOOD *(Aconitum noveboracense)*

This species is similar to the preceding but the stem, at least in the flower clusters, is quite hairy. It grows in rich woods, shady ravines, and on damp slopes; blooming in June and July.

RANGE: Se. N.Y. to Wis. and Iowa. (Not illustrated)

TRAILING WOLFSBANE *(Aconitum reclinatum)*

The Trailing Wolfsbane has a trailing stem from 2 to 8 feet long. It has white to yellowish flowers which are almost an inch long, the hooded sepal being cone-shaped and lying nearly or quite horizontal. The leaves are 3- to 7-cleft and the wedge-shaped divisions are toothed and often deeply cut toward the tips. The lower leaves are roundish and 6 to 8 inches broad; and all but the upper ones are stalked. It grows in mountain woods, blooming between June and September. Also called Trailing Monkshood. (Not illustrated)

RANGE: Va. and W.Va. south to Ga.

GOLDTHREAD *(Coptis trifolia)*

The Goldthread gets its name from its threadlike and bright yellow rootstocks. It is a small plant 3 to 6 inches high, with evergreen leaves which are divided into 3 more or less rounded and toothed lobes. The white flowers are on slender stalks and they have 5 to 6 petal-like sepals. Petals are also present but they are very small and club-shaped. It grows in cold, damp woods and bogs; blooming between May and July.

RANGE: Lab. to Man. south to N.J., e. Tenn., the Great Lakes region, and Iowa.

FALSE BUGBANE *(Trautvetteria carolinensis)*

This plant has a branching stem from 2 to 3 feet tall along which are alternate, deeply-lobed, and sharply toothed leaves. The basal ones are 6 to 8 inches across, 5- to 11-lobed, and long-stalked. The white flowers are borne in clusters at the ends of the branches. They have 3 to 5 sepals which drop off as the flowers open, thus each flower consists of a tassel of white stamens and a head of several pistils. The False Bugbane is also known as Tassel-rue. It grows along the banks of streams and in ravines, flowering between June and August.

RANGE: Sw. Pa. to Mo. south to nw. Fla.

GOLDENSEAL *(Hydrastis canadensis)*

Orangeroot and Yellow Puccoon are other names often given to the Goldenseal; but all three names refer to its thick, knotted, and bright yellow rootstock. In the spring it sends up a simple hairy stem about a foot high; and on it is a pair of large, 5- to 7-lobed, sharply toothed leaves, and there is a similar roundish leaf at the base which is long-stalked. In summer it becomes from 5 to 8 inches broad. From the center of the pair of stem leaves arises a stalk on which is the solitary greenish-white flower. It has a few sepals which promptly drop off, leaving a cluster of stamens and pistils. The latter develop into a little cluster of red berries. The Goldenseal grows in rich woods and blooms in April or May. The rootstock is used medicinally and in many places it has been exterminated by collectors.

RANGE: Vt. to Minn. and Neb. south to Ga., Ala., and Ark.

EARLY MEADOW-RUE (*Thalictrum dioicum*)

The Early Meadow-rue is a smooth, slender-stemmed plant from 1 to 2 feet tall. Its drooping flowers are yellowish-green, or often tinged with purplish, and are borne in a loose terminal cluster. The stamens and the pistils are not only in different flowers but on different plants. The leaves are divided into a number of thin, delicate, roundish leaflets which have from 5 to 9 rounded teeth on their margins. The upper ones are not usually fully expanded at flowering time in April or May. It is quite common in rich, rocky woods and shady ravines.

RANGE: Me. and Que. to Ont., Minn., and S.D. south to Ga., Ala., and Mo.

MOUNTAIN MEADOW-RUE (*Thalictrum clavatum*)

This little meadow-rue differs from all of our other species in that its flowers always contain both stamens and pistils. The flowers are white, long-stalked, and in a relatively few-flowered end cluster. Their stamens have club-shaped, petal-like filaments and the pistils stand on little stalks. The Mountain Meadow-rue is a smooth and very slender-stemmed plant from 6 inches to about 2 feet tall. Its leaves are biternately divided into 9 thin, oval- or egg-shaped leaflets which are pale beneath and usually 3-lobed, but they also have a few additional rounded teeth. It is found in wooded ravines and along streams in the mountains. Another name for it is Lady-rue. It blooms in May or June.

RANGE: Va., W.Va. and Ky. south to n. Ga. and nw. Ala.

TALL MEADOW-RUE (*Thalictrum polygamum*)

The Tall Meadow-rue has a stout, smooth or somewhat hairy stem 3 to 8 feet tall, with white flowers in rather large clusters at the top. Some of the flowers have only stamens, while others have both pistils and a few stamens. The stamens have club-shaped filaments. Its leaves are large and ternately divided into a number of leaflets which usually have 3 lobes. It is the common tall meadow-rue of moist meadows, thickets, and sunny swamps; flowering between June and August.

RANGE: Nfd. to Ont. south to Ga. and Tenn.

WAXY-LEAF MEADOW-RUE (*Thalictrum revolutum*)

From the other species of tall meadow-rues, this one can be distinguished by the tiny waxy particles on the lower surfaces of its leaflets. Its stem and flowers are often purplish, and their stamens have slender and thread-like filaments. The plant has a strong odor which has suggested another common name, that of Skunk Meadow-rue. It grows in open woods, thickets, meadows, and prairies; blooming between May and July.

RANGE: Mass. to Ont. south to Fla., Ala., and Mo. (Not illustrated)

PURPLE MEADOW-RUE (*Thalictrum dasycarpum*)

This is another tall meadow-rue which grows in wet meadows or thickets and swamps. The 4- to 7-foot stem is often purplish, the leaflets commonly downy beneath, and the stamens of its flowers have slender filaments. It blooms between late May and July.

RANGE: Ont. to B.C. south to Ohio, La., N.Mex., and Ariz. (Not illustrated)

BARBERRY FAMILY (Berberidaceae)

Flowers of the members of this family have 4 to 6 sepals, 6 to 9 petals, the stamens as many, or twice as many, as the petals, and a solitary pistil.

BLUE COHOSH (*Caulophyllum thalictroides*)

The leaves of the Blue Cohosh resemble those of the meadow-rues, being divided into a number of leaflets with from 3 to 5 lobes. It is a smooth and more or less whitened plant from 1 to 3 feet tall. About midway on the stem there is a leaf divided into 3 stalked divisions, each of which bears about 9 leaflets. Above this is the stalked cluster of purplish-green flowers. Each flower is about ½ inch across and it has 6 sepals, 6 small gland-like petals, 6 stamens and a single pistil. The 2 ovules within the ovary of the pistil burst the ovary wall as they grow; and they mature as a pair of large, stalked, blue, and berry-like seeds which look like small blue grapes. Another name for the plant is Papoose-root. It grows in rich, moist woods; blooming in April or May.

RANGE: N.B. to Man. south to S.C., Tenn., and Mo.

Early Meadow-rue

Tall Meadow-rue

Mountain Meadow-rue

Blue Cohosh

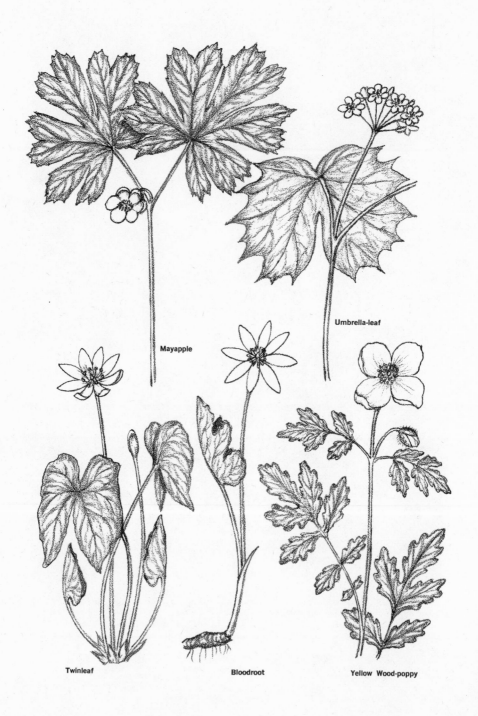

Mayapple

Umbrella-leaf

Twinleaf

Bloodroot

Yellow Wood-poppy

MAYAPPLE *(Podophyllum peltatum)*

The Mayapple is readily recognizable by the pair of large, stalked, umbrella-like leaves on its foot-high stem. They are attached to their stalks near the middle; and deeply divided into from 5 to 7 lobes, each of which is 2-cleft at the end and coarsely toothed. In the fork of the two leafstalks hangs a solitary flower an inch or more across. The 6 sepals are shed as the flower opens but the 6 to 9 large, waxy-white petals remain; and there are from 12 to 18 stamens with bright yellow anthers, and a solitary pistil. The latter develops into a large berry, about the size and color of a small lemon, which is edible and enjoyed by some. Non-flowering plants have but a single umbrella-like leaf at the top of their stem. Mayapples commonly grow in colonies in rich open woods, thickets, and clearings; blooming between April and June. Their rootstocks contain a poisonous substance but they are used medicinally. Another name often given it is Mandrake, but this name properly belongs to an Old World plant of no relationship to the Mayapple. RANGE: Que., Ont., and Minn. south to Fla. and Tex.

UMBRELLA-LEAF *(Diphylleia cymosa)*

This plant gets its name from the single, large, umbrella-like leaf of the non-flowering plants. It is attached to the stem near the center of the leaf. Flowering plants have a pair of similar but smaller leaves which are deeply cleft into two divisions, coarsely toothed, and attached to their stalks near the leaf margin. The white flowers are about ¾ inch across and borne in clusters. They have 6 sepals which are soon shed, 6 oval-shaped petals, 6 stamens, and a pistil. The latter develops into a roundish or oval-shaped, blue berry about ½ inch long. It grows in rich woods, often along streams, in the southern mountains; blooming in April or May. RANGE: Western Va. south to n. Ga.

TWINLEAF *(Jeffersonia diphylla)*

So-called because its leaves are so deeply divided that they seem to have 2 blades, the Twinleaf is very easy to recognize. At flowering time, in April or May, the leaves are only partly developed and 2 halves may be folded together. When fully mature, the leaves are 3 to 6 inches long and from 2 to 4 inches wide. Each flower is on a smooth stalk 6 to 8 inches in length. About an inch across, they have 4 sepals which soon fall, 8 white petals, and 8 stamens. The pistil becomes a many-seeded pod. The Twinleaf grows in rich, moist woods but it is not very common. Its generic name *Jeffersonia* honors our illustrious scientist-president, Thomas Jefferson.

RANGE: N.Y. and Ont. to Wis. south to Va. and Ala.

POPPY FAMILY (Papaveraceae)

Members of the Poppy Family usually have a milky juice which may be whitish, yellowish, or reddish. Their flowers are usually quite large and showy and have a pair of sepals which are quickly shed, 4 petals or petals in multiples of 4, numerous stamens, and a solitary pistil maturing as a many-seeded capsule.

BLOODROOT *(Sanguinaria canadensis)*

In early spring—between March and early May—the bright white flowers of the Bloodroot appear above the fallen leaves in our woodlands. As they open, their 2 sepals fall away; but the 8 to 12 petals spread into a blossom 1½ to 2 inches across. Each flower is accompanied by an enveloping leaf, which has not yet unfolded. Later this 5- to 9-lobed and bluntly toothed leaf may become 6 or more inches in width, persisting until about mid-summer. The Bloodroot gets its name, and another name of Red Puccoon, from the bright orange-red juice of its thick rootstock. It is easily grown in the woodland flower garden. RANGE: Que. to Man. south to Fla. and Tex.

YELLOW WOOD-POPPY *(Stylophorum diphyllum)*

Sometimes called the Celandine-poppy, this plant has a stem 12 to 18 inches tall, with a pair of deeply cut leaves and 2 to 4 flowers at the top. Leaves with similar side-lobes but with long stalks occur at the base. The flowers have 2 hairy sepals which soon drop, and 4 bright yellow petals. The plant grows in rich, moist woodlands and blooms between March and May. It has a yellow juice.

RANGE: Pa. to Wis. south to Va., Tenn., and Mo.

FUMITORY FAMILY (Fumariaceae)

Members of this family have flowers with a bilateral symmetry. They have 2 small sepals; 4 petals, one or both of the outer ones being spurred at the base; 6 stamens in two groups of 3 each; and a solitary pistil composed of 2 united carpels. The plants have a watery juice and compound dissected leaves.

MOUNTAIN-FRINGE *(Adlumia fungosa)*

Also known as the Allegheny-vine, this plant with long and slender stems climbs by means of its coiling leaf stalks. The leaves are divided into many thin, delicate, usually lobed leaflets which are pale beneath. It has pinkish or purplish flowers shaped like narrow hearts, and borne in drooping clusters on stalks arising in the axils of the leaves. The Mountain-fringe grows on damp, rocky, wooded slopes and is sometimes common on recently burned areas. It blooms between June and October.

RANGE: Que. to Ont. and Minn. south to N.Eng. and in mts. to N.C. and Tenn.

WILD BLEEDING-HEART *(Dicentra exima)*

The native Wild Bleeding-heart is sometimes called Turkey-corn and Staggerweed, and in cultivation it is known as the Plumy Bleeding-heart. It is a somewhat whitened, smooth plant from 10 inches to about 2 feet high. The pink to flesh-colored flowers are about ¾ inch long and they are produced between April and September. The leaves are all basal, ternately divided, and cut into numerous oblong segments. It grows in rocky woods and on rock cliffs in the mountains. RANGE: N.Y. and W.Va. south to n. Ga. and e. Tenn.

DUTCHMAN'S-BREECHES *(Dicentra cucullaria)*

This well-known wild flower gets its name from the resemblance of its flowers to a Dutchman's baggy breeches, hanging upside down along the nodding stalks which are 5 to 10 inches long. They are about ¾ inch long, white or faintly pinkish, and their 2 broad spurs are spread like the letter V. The leaves are all at the base and are ternately divided and cut into numerous narrow segments which are pale beneath. Both the flower stalks and the leaves arise from a knobby-scaled bulb. The Dutchman's-breeches grows in rich woods and on rocky slopes; blooming during April or May.

RANGE: N.S. to S.D. south to Ga., Ala., and Kan.

SQUIRREL-CORN *(Dicentra canadensis)*

Leaves of the Squirrel-corn are just like those of the Dutchman's-breeches, but the flowers afford a fine point of distinction. Those of the Squirrel-corn have 2 short and rounded spurs which point upward. They are a little more than ½ inch long, white or pale pinkish, rather heart-shaped, and arranged along an arching stalk 6 to 8 inches high. The plant gets its name from the yellow tubers which occur on its rootstocks. It grows in rich woods and on rocky slopes, blooming in April or May.

RANGE: Que. to Minn. south to Va., N.C., n. Ga., and Mo.

PINK CORYDALIS *(Corydalis sempervirens)*

This is a more or less erect, smooth, and whitened plant 5 to 20 inches tall, with slender and branching stems. Its flowers, like those of other species of Corydalis, are slender and have only 1 petal spurred. They are about ½ inch long, pink or purplish with a yellow tip, and arranged in clusters at the tips of the branches. The leaves are much divided and bluntly lobed, the upper ones being stalkless. It grows on rocky slopes and in recent clearings, blooming between May and September. Another name for it is Pale Corydalis.

RANGE: Nfd. to Alaska south to Ga., Tenn., Minn., and Mont.

YELLOW CORYDALIS *(Corydalis flavula)*

This species is similar to the preceding but it has yellow flowers which have a short, rounded spur. It grows in rocky woods, blooming in April or May.

RANGE: Conn. to Ont. and Minn. south to Va., Tenn., La., and Kan. (Not illustrated)

GOLDEN CORYDALIS *(Corydalis aurea)*

The bright yellow flowers of this species are almost ½ inch long and have a slightly curved spur nearly half the length of the flower. It grows in open woods, on rocky slopes, and on shores; blooming between May and July.

RANGE: Que. to Alaska south to N.Y., W.Va., Mo., Ariz., and Calif. (Not illustrated)

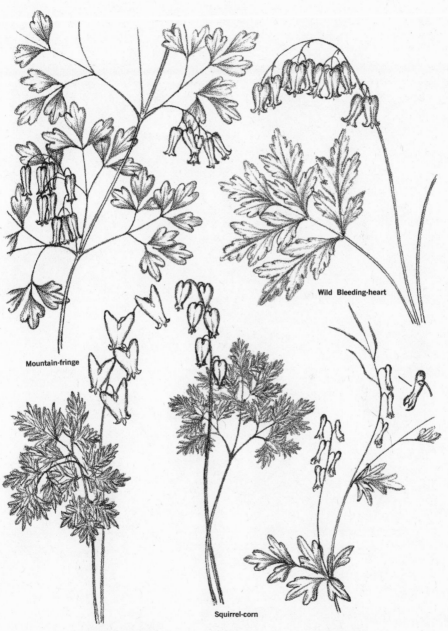

Mountain-fringe

Wild Bleeding-heart

Dutchman's-breeches

Squirrel-corn

Pink Corydalis

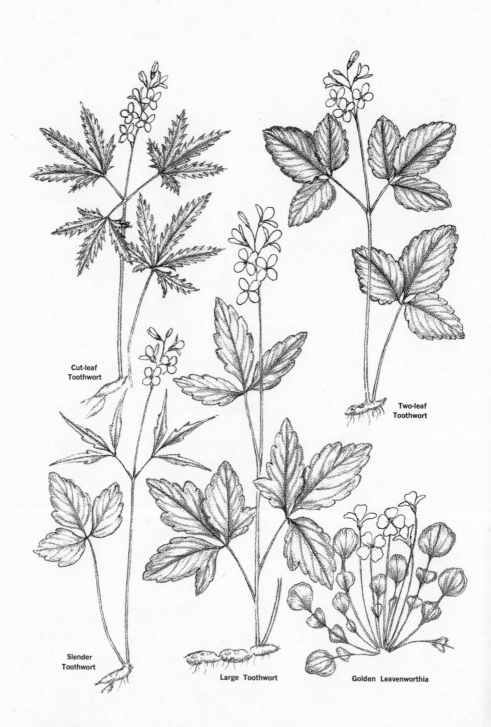

Cut-leaf
Toothwort

Two-leaf
Toothwort

Slender
Toothwort

Large Toothwort

Golden Leavenworthia

MUSTARD FAMILY (Cruciferae)

Flowers of the members of this family have 4 sepals; 4 petals which spead out flat to form a symmetrical cross; 6 stamens, 2 of them shorter than the other 4; and a single pistil composed of 2 united carpels. The latter develops into a flattened or narrow pod containing several seeds.

CUT-LEAF TOOTHWORT *(Dentaria laciniata)*

On a smooth or somewhat hairy stem 8 to 15 inches tall, this toothwort has a whorl of 3 leaves; each of them being divided into 3 narrow and sharply toothed or lobed segments. The basal leaves are similar but they are seldom present at flowering time, between March and May. The flowers are about ½ inch across and have 4 white or lavender tinged petals. Several of them occur along a stalk which stands above the leaves. Beneath the ground the plant has a jointed rootstock which readily separates into inch-long tubers shaped like sweet-potatoes. Being slightly peppery, they afford a quite pleasant nibble. It is often common in rich, moist woods and on rocky slopes. Another name for it is Pepperroot.

RANGE: Vt. and Que. to Minn. and Neb. south to Fla. La., and Kan.

TWO-LEAF TOOTHWORT *(Dentaria diphylla)*

Another name for this plant is Crinkleroot; a name suggested by its long, continuous, crinkled rootstock. It has a smooth stem from 6 to 12 inches tall on which is a pair of leaves, both of them divided into 3 broadly egg-shaped and bluntly toothed leaflets. The basal leaves are similar but they are long-stalked. Along the stem, and above the 2 leaves, is a loose cluster of white flowers with 4 white petals. This toothwort is usually quite common in rich, moist, rocky woods and thickets; blooming between April and June.

RANGE: N.S. and Ont. south to S.C., Ky., and Mich.

SLENDER TOOTHWORT *(Dentaria heterophylla)*

This toothwort has a slender, smooth or somewhat downy stem 6 to 14 inches tall. On it is a pair of leaves which are divided into 3 very narrow and sparingly toothed or untoothed segments. The basal leaves are divided into 3 more or less egg-shaped leaflets which are bluntly toothed or slightly lobed. Along the stem above its 2 leaves is a loose cluster of flowers, each of them about ¾ inch across and with 4 pinkish or pale purplish petals. The rootstock separates into tubers like those of the Cut-leaf Toothwort. It grows in rich, moist and usually rocky woods; blooming in April or May.

RANGE: N.J. to Ohio south to n. Ga., and Tenn.

LARGE TOOTHWORT *(Dentaria maxima)*

One might mistake this toothwort for the Two-leaf Toothwort for the leaves of the two are quite similar. This one, however, usually has 3 leaves which are widely spaced along the stem. Its flowers are about ¾ inch across and they have 4 white or pale purplish petals. The rootstock is jointed but does not separate easily into tubers. It grows on wooded slopes and streambanks but it is rather local, blooming in March or April.

RANGE: Me. to Wis. south to W. Va. and Tenn.

GOLDEN LEAVENWORTHIA *(Leavenworthia aurea)*

Leavenworthias are small plants with basal tufts of leaves which have side lobes. In this species they are divided into a relatively few, large, and blunt lobes. The flowers are not quite ½ inch across and usually solitary on leafless stalks 1½ to about 4 inches in length. They have 4 white or purplish petals which are yellow at the base. The Golden Leavenworthia grows in rocky places; blooming in March or April.

RANGE: Tenn. to Ark. south to Ala. and Tex.

MICHAUX'S LEAVENWORTHIA *(Leavenworthia uniflora)*

This species differs from the preceding in that the leaves are divided into a number of angled and somewhat toothed lobes or segments. It generally has several but slightly smaller flowers on leafless stalks 2 to 6 inches tall. The plant grows in dry rocky woods or sometimes on wet rocks; blooming in March or April.

RANGE: Ohio and Ind. to Mo. south to Ala. and Ark. (Not illustrated)

SMOOTH ROCK-CRESS *(Arabis laevigata)*

A number of rock-cresses occur in eastern North America, but this species is one of the more conspicuous ones. It has a smooth, whitened, leafy stem from 1 to 3 feet tall. The pale, narrow leaves clasp the stem by their eared bases and their margins may have a few teeth. The basal leaves taper to a stalked base and are toothed and sometimes deeply cut. The small whitish flowers are followed by slender pods 3 to 4 inches long, which arch outward and downward. The plant is quite common in rich, rocky woods and slopes; blooming between March and June.

RANGE: Que. to Minn. south to Ga., Ala., Ark., and Okla.

SICKLE-POD *(Arabis canadensis)*

This rock-cress is similar to the preceding but it is somewhat hairy, the stem leaves do not have clasping bases, and their margins are toothed. The slender sickle-shaped pods bend abruptly downward. It grows in rich, rocky woods and on banks; blooming between April and June.

RANGE: Me. to Ont., Minn., and Neb. south to Ga. and Tex. (Not illustrated)

BULBOUS CRESS *(Cardamine bulbosa)*

This smooth, leafy-stemmed plant has a knobby tuber at the base of its 6- to 18-inch stem, hence the name Bulbous Cress. It is also known as the Spring Cress. Between March and June it produces quite showy clusters of white flowers which are about a half-inch across. The leaves along the stem vary from lance-shaped to roundish and they may or may not have wavy-toothed margins. The basal ones are roundish to heart-shaped, often angled, and long-stalked. It is quite common in wet woods and meadows.

RANGE: N.H. to Ont. and Wis. south to Fla. and Tex.

PURPLE CRESS *(Cardamine douglasii)*

The Purple Cress is quite similar to the preceding species. It differs principally in having a somewhat hairy stem and flowers tinged with lavender or rose. It grows quite generally in wet woods, swamps, and about springs; usually blooming about 2 weeks earlier than the Bulbous Cress.

RANGE: Conn. to Ont. and Wis. south to Va., Tenn., and Mo. (Not illustrated)

PURPLE ROCKET *(Iodanthus pinnatifidus)*

This plant has a slender, smooth, leafy stem from 1 to 3 feet tall which branches above. The lower leaves are divided into a large egg-shaped end segment below which there are 2 to 6 pairs of side lobes, all of them with more or less sharply toothed margins. The leaves along the upper part of the stem are much smaller and have bases which clasp the stem. Numerous flowers about ⅓ inch across, with 4 light violet petals, are arrayed in frequently branched end clusters. The Purple Rocket commonly grows on the flood plains of streams and on adjoining slopes; blooming in May or June.

RANGE: Pa. to Minn. south to Ala. and Tex.

COMMON WINTER-CRESS *(Barbarea vulgaris)*

The Winter-cress, or Yellow Rocket, is a common weed which is often abundant in fields, meadows, and wet woods. It is a smooth, branching plant with leafy stems from 1 to 2 feet tall. The lower leaves are stalked and have a terminal segment much larger than the 1 to 4 pairs of side ones. Those along the upper portion of the stem are stalk-less and often have clasping bases. The bright yellow, 4-petalled flowers are about ⅓ inch across; and are borne in rather dense, cylindrical clusters at the end of the stem and its branches; blooming from April to June or later. It is a native of Europe.

EARLY WINTER-CRESS *(Barbarea verna)*

This species quite closely resembles the preceding one, and like it is a native of Europe. It is now widespread in eastern North America as far south as Florida. All of its leaves are deeply lobed, the larger basal ones having from 4 to 8 pairs of side lobes below the larger terminal one. Perhaps the best field mark, however, is its sharply 4-sided pods. It has bright yellow flowers between late March and May. Another name for it is Belle Isle Cress. (Not illustrated)

116

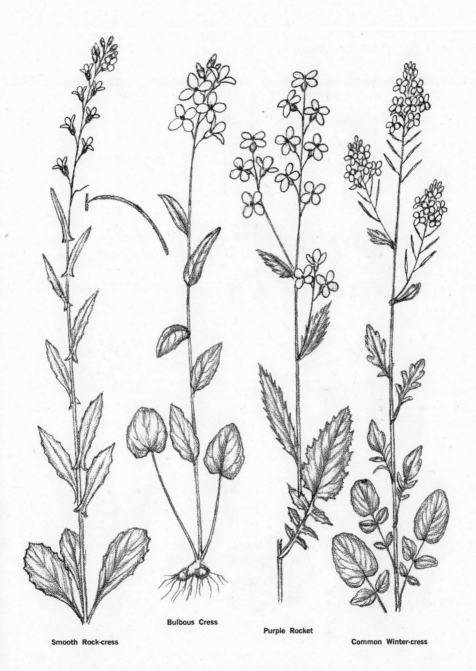

Smooth Rock-cress

Bulbous Cress

Purple Rocket

Common Winter-cress

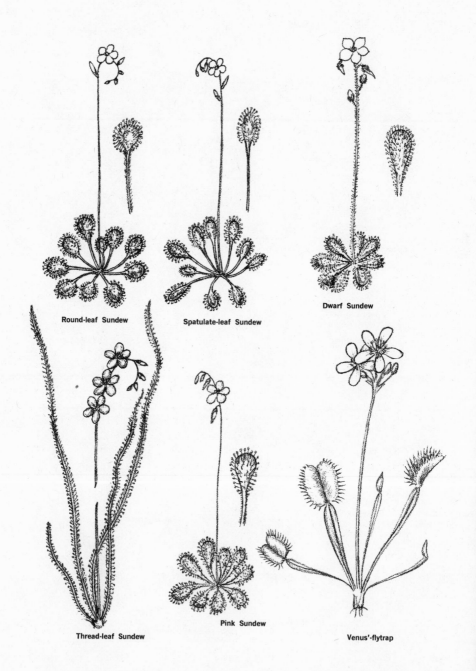

Round-leaf Sundew

Spatulate-leaf Sundew

Dwarf Sundew

Thread-leaf Sundew

Pink Sundew

Venus'-flytrap

SUNDEW FAMILY (Droseraceae)

Sundews are small insectivorous plants found in bogs and other wet places. Their leaves have gland-tipped red hairs which exude little droplets of a sticky fluid. In the sunlight, these little droplets sparkle like dewdrops, hence the name given to the plants. Small insects trapped on this natural "flypaper" are gradually digested by the plant. The flowers have 5 sepals, 5 petals, 5 stamens, and a pistil with usually 3 styles. The leaves are in a basal rosette.

ROUND-LEAF SUNDEW *(Drosera rotundifolia)*

This is the most common and widespread species of sundew. The leaves have disk-shaped blades on slender, minutely hairy stalks from ½ to 2 inches long. Several white flowers about ¼ inch across are borne on a slender, smooth stalk from 3 to 10 inches high. In bogs and on wet sands; blooming between June and August.
RANGE: Lab. to Alaska south to Fla., Ala., Minn., Mont., and Calif.

SPATULATE-LEAF SUNDEW *(Drosera intermedia)*

The leaves of this species have oval-shaped blades up to ¾ inch long on slender, smooth stalks from ½ to 1½ inches long. The several white flowers are about ¼ inch across and are borne on a slender, smooth stalk from 2 to 8 inches high. It grows in bogs and on wet sands, blooming between June and August.
RANGE: Nfd. to Ont. south to Fla. and Tex.

DWARF SUNDEW *(Drosera brevifolia)*

The Dwarf Sundew has top-shaped leaves ¼ to about ⅝ inch long which have very short and glandular-hairy stalks. Its 1 to 3 white flowers are almost ½ inch across and are borne on a slender, glandular-hairy stalk from 2 to 3½ inches high. It grows in wet, sandy, coastal plain pinelands in the Southeast; blooming in May and June.
RANGE: Va., Tenn., and Ark. south to Fla. and Tex.

THREAD-LEAF SUNDEW *(Drosera filiformis)*

This sundew is unmistakable as it has very narrow leaves from 6 to 15 inches in length, which are covered with gland-tipped hairs. Its lavender flowers are ⅜ to ¾ of an inch across and are borne on a slender, smooth stalk from 8 to 20 inches tall. It grows on wet sands in the coastal plain, blooming between June and September. Another name for it is Dew-thread.
RANGE: Mass. to N.J. and S.C. south to Fla. and west to La.

PINK SUNDEW *(Drosera capillaris)*

The Pink Sundew has top-shaped leaves from ½ to 1¼ inches long which taper into short, broad, glandular-hairy stalks. Its pink flowers are about ¼ inch across; several of them being borne on a very slender, smooth stalk from 2½ to 6 inches tall. It grows in peaty bogs and on wet sands, blooming between May and July.
RANGE: Coastal plain se. Va. south to Fla. and west to Tex.; also on the Cumberland Plateau in Tenn.

VENUS'-FLYTRAP FAMILY (Dionaeaceae)

VENUS'-FLYTRAP *(Dionaea muscipula)*

This unique insectivorous plant is the only representative of its family. Its leaves, which are in a basal rosette, are 2 to 5 inches long. The leaf stalk has a pair of wings which taper gradually to the base; and at its summit there is a roundish, 2-lobed blade with a marginal fringe of bristly hairs. The upper surface of the blade is red or reddish and on each of the 2 lobes there are 3 sensitive hairs which serve to trigger the trap. An insect touching these hairs causes the two halves of the blade to snap shut. and the marginal bristles then fit together like the fingers of one's folded hands. Glands on the leaf surface then begin to secrete a fluid which digests the softer parts of the trapped insect. The white flowers are almost ¾ of an inch across and are clustered at the summit of a smooth stalk from 4 to 12 inches tall. They have 5 sepals, 5 petals, 10 to 20 stamens, and a pistil composed of 5 united carpels. The Venus'-flytrap is restricted to bogs in southeastern North Carolina and eastern South Carolina. It blooms during May or June.

PITCHER-PLANT FAMILY (Sarraceniaceae)

Pitcher-plants have hollow leaves with a wing down one side and a lid-like hood at the summit. These leaves contain a watery fluid in which insects drown and are digested. Their flowers are solitary and nod from the summit of a long, naked stalk. They have 5 persistent sepals with 3 bracts at their base; 5 fiddle-shaped petals; a number of stamens; and a solitary pistil which has a conspicuous umbrella-like end, bearing the 5 hooked stigmas on its underside. All grow in wet or boggy places.

PURPLE PITCHER-PLANT *(Sarracenia purpurea)*

This pitcher-plant really has pitcher-shaped leaves which are 4 to 10 inches long, with a rather broad wing and an erect hood which is covered with backward-pointing bristles. The reclining or ascending pitchers are often beautifully veined with purple. Its flower is more or less globe-shaped, about 2 inches across, usually a deep purplish-red, and stands on a stalk 10 to 20 inches tall. It is the only species of pitcher-plant found north of the southern part of Virginia. It blooms between April and August. Sometimes it is called the Huntsmans-cap or Sidesaddle-flower.

RANGE: Nfd. to Sask. south to Fla. and La.

PARROT PITCHER-PLANT *(Sarracenia psittacina)*

The pitcher-shaped leaves of this pitcher-plant are only 2 to 6 inches long. They have a broad wing and a domed hood which resembles the head and bill of a parrot; the opening being on the under side. Its pitchers are beautifully marked with white spots and purple veins. The dark purplish flowers are 1¼ to 2 inches across and each one stands on a stalk 8 to 16 inches tall. It grows in wet coastal plain pinelands and bogs, blooming in April or May.

RANGE: S. Ga. and Fla. west to La.

HOODED PITCHER-PLANT *(Sarracenia minor)*

This species has erect, trumpet-shaped leaves 8 to 16 inches tall, with an arching dome-like hood which covers the open top of the trumpet-like leaf. Toward the summit they have numerous translucent, window-like spots; and they are often veined with purple. The yellow flowers are about 2½ inches across and stand on stalks 6 to 12 inches tall. It grows in wet coastal plain pinelands and bogs, blooming between April and June.

RANGE: N.C. south to Fla.

SWEET PITCHER-PLANT *(Sarracenia rubra)*

The leaves of this species are very slender, trumpet-shaped, erect, and 6 to 16 inches tall. They have a narrow wing down the side and an erect or leaning pointed hood ½ to 1¼ inches wide which is usually veined with purple. Its reddish-purple or maroon flowers are 1½ to 2 inches across and stand on stalks 10 to 18 inches tall; and they have a delightful fragrance. It grows in wet pinelands and bogs of the coastal plain, and also along streams in the mountains; blooming in April or May.

RANGE: N.C. south to Fla. and west to Miss.

TRUMPETS *(Sarracenia flava)*

This distinctive species has trumpet-shaped leaves 1½ to 4 feet tall, which have a narrow wing and an erect hood 3 to 4½ inches broad. The latter is often yellow or strikingly veined with red or purple. Its yellow flowers are 3 to 4½ inches across and stand on stalks from 1½ to 3 feet tall. It grows in bogs and savannahs, chiefly in the coastal plain; blooming in March or April. Also known as the Trumpet-leaf or Huntsman's-horn.

RANGE: Se. Va. south to Fla. and west to Ala.

PURPLE TRUMPET *(Sarracenia leucophylla)*

This species resembles the preceding in having tall trumpet-like leaves. Those of this species, however, are white above and beautifully veined with purple. Its large flowers are purplish-red. It grows is sandy bogs in the coastal plain from sw. Ga. and nw. Fla. west to Miss. (Not illustrated)

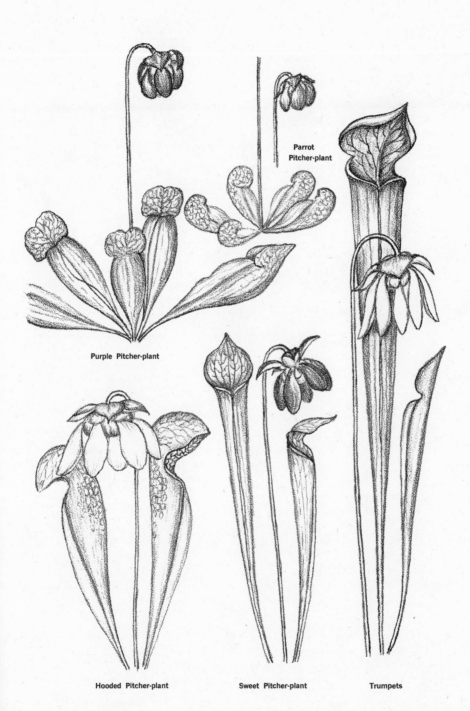

Parrot Pitcher-plant

Purple Pitcher-plant

Hooded Pitcher-plant   **Sweet Pitcher-plant**   **Trumpets**

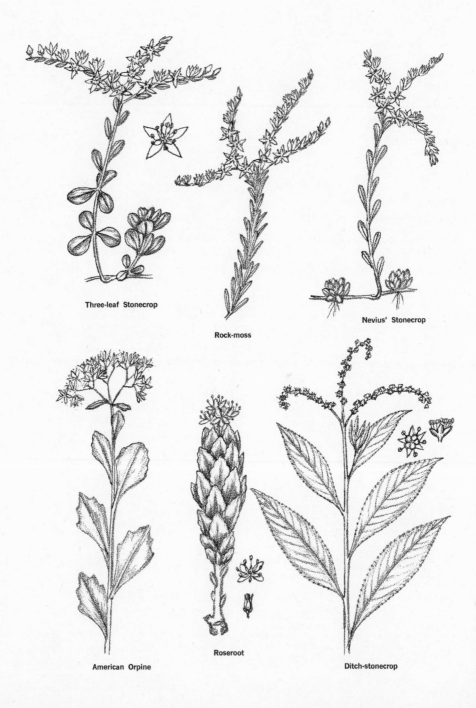

Three-leaf Stonecrop

Rock-moss

Nevius' Stonecrop

American Orpine

Roseroot

Ditch-stonecrop

ORPINE FAMILY (Crassulaceae)

The members of the Orpine Family are mostly small and fleshy plants. Their flowers have 4 or 5 sepals which are united at the base, 4 or 5 petals, 8 or 10 stamens, and a group of 4 or 5 separate pistils.

THREE-LEAF STONECROP *(Sedum ternatum)*

The Three-leaf Stonecrop is a small, succulent plant with a creeping stem and ascending flowering branches from 3 to 6 inches high. Its lower leaves are top-shaped and arranged in whorls of 3's, but those on the upper portion of the stem are scattered singly. Its flowers are almost ½ inch across, starry in appearance, with 5 narrow white petals and twice as many stamens which have dark-colored anthers. They suggest another common name of Pepper-and-salt. This plant is usually common on moist cliffs and rocky, wooded slopes; blooming between April and June. RANGE: N.Y. to Mich. south to Ga. and Tenn.

ROCK-MOSS *(Sedum pulchellum)*

This is a small, succulent plant with a creeping or ascending stem from 4 to 12 inches long. It has numerous, densely crowded leaves ¼ to 1 inch long with slightly clasping bases. The flower cluster has from 4 to 7 spreading or recurved branches which are crowded with starry, 5-petaled, white to rose-pink flowers about ½ inch across. Also known as the Mountain-moss and Widow's-cross, it grows on dry to moist rocks and on rocky soils; blooming in May or June.
RANGE: W.Va. to Ill. and Kan. south to Ga., Ala., Ark., and Tex.

NEVIUS' STONECROP *(Sedum nevii)*

This is another small succulent with a creeping stem and ascending flowering branches from 3 to 5 inches high. Its leaves are narrowly top-shaped, spirally arranged, and somewhat spreading. Those of the sterile shoots are very densely crowded. The flower cluster has 3 branches crowded with starry, 5-petaled, white flowers about ½ inch across. It grows on moist rocks in the mountains, blooming in May and June.
RANGE: Western Va. and W.Va. south to N.C. and Ala.

AMERICAN ORPINE *(Sedum telephioides)*

The American Orpine is an erect plant seldom over 10 inches tall; with thick and fleshy, oval or top-shaded, somewhat toothed leaves from 1 to 2 inches long. It has a flat-topped or slightly dome-shaped end cluster of pale pink flowers from 2 to 4 inches broad. The 5-petaled flowers are about ⅜ inch across, blooming during August or September. The entire plant is smooth, purplish, and is whitened with a bloom. It grows on dry rock outcrops and cliffs. Another name for it is Wild Live-forever.
RANGE: W. N.Y. to Ill. south in the mts. to Ga.

ROSEROOT *(Sedum rosea)*

The Roseroot is a peculiar little fleshy plant with a thick root which is fragrant when bruised. It has ascending or erect, leafy stems from 4 to about 12 inches high. The leaves are pale, oval-shaped, sometimes toothed on the margin, from ½ to 1½ inches long, and are closely crowded on the stems. Some plants have yellowish flowers with usually 8 stamens; others have purplish ones with usually 4 pistils. It grows in rocky places, blooming between May and August.
RANGE: Arctic regions south to Me., N.Y., ne. Pa., and Roan Mt., N.C.

SAXIFRAGE FAMILY (Saxifragaceae)

Members of this family usually have flowers with 5 sepals which are more or less united at the base; 5 petals; 5 or 10 stamens; and either a solitary pistil or a pair of pistils with the ovaries at least partly joined together.

DITCH-STONECROP *(Penthorum sedoides)*

This is a smooth plant with an erect, usually branched, somewhat angled stem from 1 to 2 feet tall. It has scattered, elliptic to lance-shaped leaves 2 to 4 inches long, which are finely saw-toothed on the margin. Its flowers are small and yellowish-green; with 5 sepals, no petals, and 10 stamens. It grows in low wet places, swamps, and along stream banks and ditches; blooming between July and October. It is also known as the Virginia-stonecrop. RANGE: N.B. to Ont., Wis., and Neb. south to Fla. and Tex.

EARLY SAXIFRAGE *(Saxifraga virginiensis)*

When the Early Saxifrage begins to bloom in late March or early April, it has a sticky-hairy flower stalk only 4 to 6 inches high. It continues to bloom for several weeks, often into June, becoming branched and up to a foot high. At the base of the flower stalk it has a rosette of rather fleshy, oval or egg-shaped leaves from 1 to 3 inches long which are often purplish-beneath. Their margins may have low and blunt teeth or be coarsely toothed or scalloped. Similar but smaller leaves subtend the branches of the flower stalk. The flowers are about ¼ inch across and have 5 oblong or top-shaped white petals and 10 stamens with bright yellow anthers. This is our most common and widespread species of saxifrage, growing on wet to dry rock ledges and rocky slopes.

RANGE: N.B. to Ont. and Minn. south to Ga., Tenn., and Mo.

CAROLINA SAXIFRAGE *(Saxifraga caroliniana)*

This is a sticky-hairy plant with a cluster of basal leaves, and a flower stalk from 6 to 18 inches tall which branches above. Its leaves are 1 to 2½ inches long, with an oval or roundish blade contracted to a long, hairy leaf stalk; and from 6 to 10 coarse teeth on each side of the margin. Its flowers are almost ½ inch across and have 5 white petals with 2 yellow spots near the base. Also known as Gray's Saxifrage, it grows on moist, rocky slopes or cliffs in the southern mountains; blooming between May and July.

RANGE: Western Va., w. N.C., and e. Tenn.

LETTUCE SAXIFRAGE *(Saxifraga micranthidifolia)*

The Lettuce Saxifrage has a more or less sticky-hairy flower stalk from 1 to about 3 feet tall, with a cluster of big leaves at the base. The latter are narrowly top-shaped, rather thin, coarsely and sharply toothed on the margin, and from 6 to about 12 inches in length. The flowers are small and have 5 white petals. It grows on wet rocks and along the banks of streams in the mountains, blooming during May and June. Also known as Mountain-lettuce, as the leaves are used as a green by many mountain people.

RANGE: Pa. and W.Va. south to Ga. and Tenn.

SWAMP SAXIFRAGE *(Saxifraga pensylvanica)*

As its name indicates, the Swamp Saxifrage grows in swamps, bogs, and wet meadows. It has a stout and somewhat sticky-hairy flower stalk from 1 to 3½ feet tall, with a rosette-like cluster of leaves at its base. The leaves are oval to narrowly top-shaped, thick and somewhat leathery in texture, and from 4 to about 12 inches long. Its small flowers vary from greenish-white to yellowish or purplish and have 5 narrow petals. The flowering season is between April and June.

RANGE: Me. to Minn. south to Va., w. N.C., Ill., and Mo.

MICHAUX'S SAXIFRAGE *(Saxifraga michauxii)*

Michaux's Saxifrage grows in crevices on the face of rocky cliffs and on sunny, wet rocks in the southern Appalachians. In typical saxifrage fashion, it has a sticky-hairy flower stalk from 6 to about 20 inches tall with a rosette-like cluster of leaves at the base. Its leaves are narrowly top-shaped, from 3 to 7 inches long, and have coarse, sharp teeth on their margins. Among saxifrages, the flowers of this one are unusual in that the white petals are not all alike. There are 3 large ones which are heart-shaped at the base and have a pair of yellow spots, and 2 smaller ones which have tapering bases and no spots. It blooms between June and August.

RANGE: Western Va. and W.Va. south to n. Ga. and e. Tenn.

Early Saxifrage

Michaux's Saxifrage

Carolina Saxifrage

Lettuce Saxifrage

Swamp Saxifrage

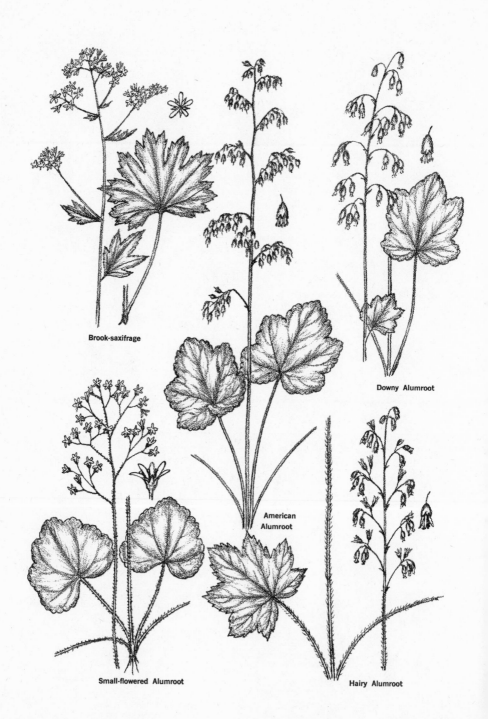

Brook-saxifrage

Downy Alumroot

American
Alumroot

Small-flowered Alumroot

Hairy Alumroot

BROOK-SAXIFRAGE *(Boykinia aconitifolia)*

The Brook-saxifrage is a rather stout-stemmed, erect plant from 1 to 2 feet tall. Most of its leaves are basal and they, as well as the ones on the lower part of the stem, are 5- to 7-lobed, cut-toothed, and long-stalked. Both the stem and the leaf stalks are glandular-hairy. The small flowers clustered at the upper part of the stem have 5 white petals and 5 stamens. It grows in rich woods, on wet rocks, and along the banks of streams, chiefly in the mountains. The flowering season is during June and July. Another name often given it is Aconite-saxifrage, due to the resemblance of its leaves to those of the monks-hoods.
RANGE: Va., W.Va., and Ky. south to Ga. and Ala.

AMERICAN ALUMROOT *(Heuchera americana)*

This is our most common and widespread species of alumroot, being found quite generally in dry woods and on rocky slopes. It has a smooth or sparingly hairy, rather stout stem from 1 to 3 feet tall. The leaves are chiefly basal. They are roundish heart-shaped with from 7 to 9 rounded and bluntly toothed lobes, smooth or nearly so, 3 to 4 inches wide; and have long, slender stalks. The small purplish or reddish-tinged flowers have a cup-like calyx. 5 minute petals, and 5 stamens which extend well beyond the calyx cup. They are very numerous and arranged in a long, loose, several-branched cluster which overtops the leaves. The flowering season extends from April to June. It is often called the Rock-geranium.
RANGE: Conn. to Ont. and Mich. south to Ga., Ala., and Okla.

DOWNY ALUMROOT *(Heuchera pubescens)*

The Downy Alumroot has a rather stout stem 1 to 3 feet tall which usually has a few leaves and is glandular-hairy at least near the summit. Most of the leaves are basal. They are 2 to 4 inches wide, roundish heart-shaped, and the 5 to 7 lobes have abruptly pointed teeth on their margins. The flowers are greenish or purplish-tinged and have a bell-shaped calyx about ¼ inch long which is glandular-downy. The purplish petals are a trifle longer than the calyx cup. This species grows in rich woods and in crevices among rocks in our mountains, blooming between May and July.
RANGE: Pa. and Md. south to Ky. and w. N.C.

SMALL-FLOWERED ALUMROOT *(Heuchera parviflora)*

Both this and the following species have small flowers in which the 5 petals are 2 or 3 times as long as the bell-shaped calyx cup. In this one the petals are usually white. It usually produces 2 or more slender, hairy flowering stems from 6 to 18 inches tall. The leaves are quite thin, kidney-shaped, broader than long, 2 to 5 inches wide, and have very low rounded lobes. They are commonly whitish-downy beneath and also have stalks which are quite hairy. It grows on moist rocks and shaded cliffs, blooming between July and September.
RANGE: W.Va. to Ill. south to N.C., Ala., and Mo.

HAIRY ALUMROOT *(Heuchera villosa)*

The Hairy Alumroot has rusty-hairy flowering stems 1 to 2½ feet tall, and often rusty-hairy leaf stalks. The small flowers have white or pink petals which are 2 to 3 times as long as the bell-shaped calyx. Its leaves are chiefly basal, long-stalked, 2 to 4½ inches wide more or less hairy, and have 7 to 9 triangular and sharply toothed lobes. It grows on damp rocks and rich, rocky wooded slopes; blooming between June and August.
RANGE: W.Va. and s. Ohio south to Ga., Ala., and Mo.

FOAMFLOWER *(Tiarella cordifolia)*

The Foamflower, or False Miterwort, is a low plant which spreads by means of slender runners and forms little colonies. It usually has a leafless flower stalk 6 to 12 inches tall, with a narrow cluster of small white flowers along the upper portion. Occasionally the flower stalks do have a pair of small leaves, in which case one will have to look closer at the flowers to distinguish it from the true miterwort. The flowers have 5 small petals which taper into stalked bases, and 10 very conspicuous long stamens. The leaves are roundish to egg-shaped, heart-shaped at the base, and have from 3 to 7 rather shallow but sharply toothed lobes. They are 2 to 4 inches broad and have long stalks. The entire plant is more or less hairy. It grows in cool, moist, rich and often rocky woodlands; blooming between April and June.

RANGE: N.B. to Ont. and Mich. south to N.Eng., w. N.C. and e. Tenn.

WHERRY'S FOAMFLOWER *(Tiarella cordifolia* var. *collina)*

This variety is quite similar to the preceding one but the plants are not stoloniferous. It also has more narrow flower clusters and leaf blades which are mostly longer than broad. Of more southern distribution than the preceding, it grows in similar situations from Va. and Tenn. south to Ga. and Miss.; blooming in April or May. (Not illustrated)

TWO-LEAF MITERWORT *(Mitella diphylla)*

The Two-leaf Miterwort has a flower stalk 10 to 18 inches tall with a pair of quite stalkless, heart-shaped, 3-lobed, and toothed leaves about the middle. Above them is a slender cluster of small, short-stalked, starry flowers in which the 5 white petals are delicately fringed. The 10 stamens are short and in the mouth of the cup-like calyx. The basal leaves are broadly egg-shaped, heart-shaped at the base, 3- to 5-lobed, and sharply toothed. The entire plant is minutely hairy. It grows in rich and often rocky woodlands, blooming in April or May. Another name is Bishop's-cap.

RANGE: N.H., Que., and Minn. south to w. S.C., Tenn., Miss., and Mo.

NAKED MITERWORT *(Mitella nuda)*

This is a little plant of cold northern woods and bogs, spreading by means of runners. The slender flower stalks are 3 to 7 inches tall, either leafless or with a single small leaf. The basal leaves are roundish kidney-shaped, deeply and doubly blunt-toothed but not lobed, and 1 to 1½ inches wide. It has greenish-yellow flowers; blooming between May and August.

RANGE: Lab. to Mackenz., south to New Eng., Pa., N.D., and Mont. (Not illustrated)

EASTERN GRASS-OF-PARNASSUS *(Parnassia glauca)*

This is a smooth plant with a basal cluster of roundish leaves which are often slightly heart-shaped at the base, 1 to 2½ inches long, and long-stalked. Like other species of *Parnassia* the solitary flower is on a long stalk on which there is a stalkless leaf between the middle and the base. The flower is 1 to 1½ inches across and has 5 sepals, and 5 broadly oval white petals with greenish veins. There are 5 anther-bearing stamens which alternate with the petals; and 5 sterile stamens (staminodia) with 3 prongs usually shorter than the stamens, and placed at the bases of the petals. It grows in wet meadows and thickets, blooming between July and October.

RANGE: Nfd. to Man. south to Pa., the Great Lakes region, Iowa, and S.D.

LARGE-LEAF GRASS-OF-PARNASSUS *(Parnassia grandifolia)*

This is similar to the preceding species but coarser, with leaves 2 to 4 inches long. The flowers are 1 to 2 inches across; the staminodia having 3 to 5 prongs which are very slender and much longer than the stamens. It grows on moist soil or on wet rocks; blooming between August and October.

RANGE: Va., W. Va., Tenn. and Mo. south to Fla. and Tex.

KIDNEY-LEAF GRASS-OF-PARNASSUS *(Parnassia asarifolia)*

The petals of the flowers in this species are abruptly contracted at the base into a distinct stalk or claw; and the staminodia are 3-pronged and shorter than the stamens. The inch-broad flower is at the summit of a stalk 10 to 20 inches tall; and the stem leaf is nearly round, almost surrounding the stalk. The basal leaves are kidney-shaped, 2 to 4 inches broad and long-stalked. It grows in wet woods, bogs, and on rocky banks in the mountains; blooming between August and October.

RANGE: Western Va. and W.Va. south to n. Ga. and n. Ala.

Foamflower

Two-leaf Miterwort

Large-leaf Grass-of-Parnassus

Eastern Grass-of-Parnassus

Kidney-leaf Grass-of-Parnassus

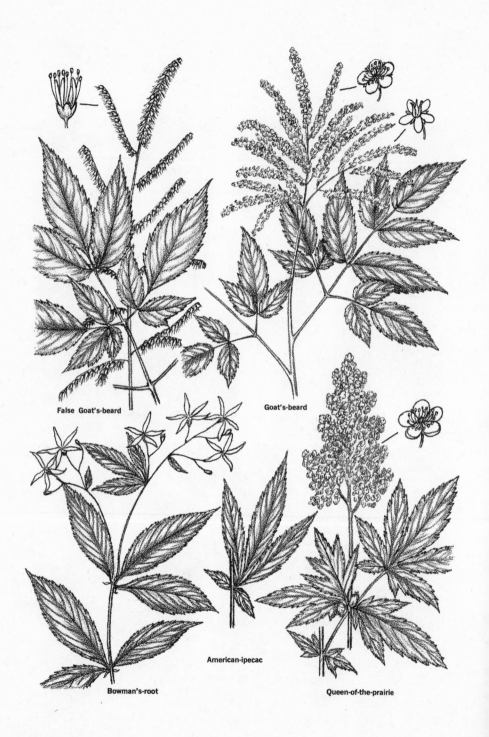

False Goat's-beard

Goat's-beard

Bowman's-root

American-ipecac

Queen-of-the-prairie

FALSE GOAT'S-BEARD *(Astilbe biternata)*

This is a large, somewhat hairy plant from 3 to 6 feet tall; with large leaves, sometimes 2 feet across, which are divided ternately 2 or 3 times into a large number of leaflets. These leaflets are 2 to 5 inches long, more or less egg-shaped or often heart-shaped, with sharply toothed and sometimes lobed margins. The small flowers are yellowish-white, with 4 or 5 narrow petals, from 8 to 10 stamens which have long filaments, and 2 pistils. Although the individual flowers are small, they are crowded together on the numerous branches of the inflorescence; forming a showy, pyramid-like cluster often a foot in length. It grows in mountain woodlands, blooming between May and July.
RANGE: Western Va. and W.Va. south to Tenn. and n. Ga.

ROSE FAMILY (ROSACEAE)

This family to which the roses, the blackberries and raspberries, and most of our common fruit trees belong is a large and varied one. In general, its members have flowers with a radial symmetry with 5 sepals united at the base and borne on a disk-like expansion of the receptacle, usually 5 free petals, numerous stamens, and 1 or more pistils. The leaves are usually alternate, often compound, and nearly always have a pair of prominent stipules.

GOAT'S-BEARD *(Aruncus dioicus)*

This plant quite closely resembles the preceding species in size and in leaf characteristics. Its flowers are likewise arranged in similar large, showy, plume-like clusters. Each flower is less than ¼ inch across and has 5 oval-shaped petals. Those of some plants have about 15 stamens with long, slender filaments. On other plants they have a group of 3 pistils but only tiny rudiments of stamens. When in bloom between May and July, this plant is very conspicuous in rich woods, and ravines.
RANGE: Pa. to Iowa south to Ga., Ala., and Okla.

BOWMAN'S-ROOT *(Gillenia trifoliata)*

The Bowman's-root, or Indian-physic, is often conspicuous in rich, open woods and thickets when it is in flower between May and July. It grows from 2 to 3 feet high and its slender and often somewhat twisted branches terminate in loose clusters of showy flowers. They are about an inch across, with a reddish calyx cup and 5 strap-shaped white or pale pinkish petals. The leaves are stalkless and divided into 3 sharply toothed leaflets 2 to 3 inches in length. There is a pair of small stipules at the base of each leaf.
RANGE: N.Y. to Ont. and Mich. south to Ga. and Ala.

AMERICAN-IPECAC *(Gillenia stipulata)*

This plant closely resembles the Bowman's-root but its leaves are short-stalked, its leaflets somewhat more deeply cut or toothed, and there is a pair of large leaf-like stipules at the base of each leaf. The latter are so large that the leaves appear to have 5 rather than just 3 leaflets. It grows in woods, thickets, and on rocky slopes; blooming between May and July.
RANGE: N.Y. to Ill., Mo. and Kan. south to Ga. and Tex.

QUEEN-OF-THE-PRAIRIE *(Filipendula rubra)*

Moist thickets, meadows, and prairies to the west of the Appalachians seem to have been the original home of this plant; but it has escaped from gardens eastward. It is a smooth plant 2 to 6 feet tall with an angled or grooved, leafy stem. Its small but numerous flowers are grouped in a dense, showy, end cluster and bloom between June and August. Each flower is about ¼ inch across and has 5 pink petals and a large cluster of stamens. The leaves are deeply cut or divided and sharply toothed. Those along the upper portion of the stem have but 3 divisions. The larger ones toward the base have from 5 to 7 divisions or leaflets; the end one being much the larger, 4 to 8 inches broad, and cleft into 7 to 9 radiating lobes.
RANGE: Pa. to Mich. and Iowa south to Ga. and Ky. Escaped from cultivation eastward into N.Y., N. Eng., and N.S.

WILD STRAWBERRY *(Fragaria virginiana)*

Like our cultivated strawberries, the Wild Strawberry is a low plant with a very short stem. From it grow the leaves, the flower clusters, and the slender runners on which new plants are produced. The long-stalked leaves are divided into 3, elliptic or oval shaped, sharply toothed leaflets which are usually 2 to 4 inches long. The flowers are about ¾ inch across and have 5 oval-shaped white petals, a large number of stamens with yellow anthers, and numerous pistils on a cone-shaped receptacle in the center of the flower. This receptacle develops into an egg-shaped red "berry" with the small fruits (achenes) imbedded in pits on its surface. This native species grows in open woods, fields, and on grassy slopes; blooming between April and June.

RANGE: Nfd. to Alb. south to Ga., La., and Okla.

AMERICAN WOOD STRAWBERRY *(Fragaria vesca* var. *americana)*

This is a more slender, paler green, and less hairy plant than the preceding species. It has thinner leaflets and more narrowly egg-shaped or cone-shaped "berries", with the achenes or "seeds" on its surface rather than in pits. This wild strawberry is usually found on rocky, wooded slopes; blooming in May or June. It is sometimes called the Sow-teat Strawberry.

RANGE: Nfd. to Alb. south to N.Eng., w. Va., w. N.C., Ill., Mo., Neb., and N.Mex.

BARREN-STRAWBERRY *(Waldsteinia fragarioides)*

The Barren- or Dry-strawberry is a low, smooth or slightly hairy plant which also has creeping rootstocks. It resembles a strawberry plant and is often mistaken for one. The long-stalked leaves are divided into 3 broadly wedge-shaped and cut-toothed leaflets from 1 to 2 inches long. The flowers are about ½ inch across and have 5 bright yellow petals, a number of stamens, and 2 to 6 pistils which are within a cup-shaped calyx with 5 lobes on its rim. In the variety *parviflora*, the petals are shorter or barely as long as the calyx lobes. It grows in woods, thickets, and clearings; blooming between April and June.

RANGE: N.B. to Ont. and Minn. south to n.Ga., Tenn., Ind., and Mo.

BARREN-STRAWBERRY *(Waldsteinia lobata)*

This plant resembles the short-petalled variety of the preceding species, but its leaves are merely 3-lobed instead of being divided into 3-leaflets. It grows on river banks from the coast inland from Ga. north to N.C. (Not illustrated)

THREE-TOOTHED CINQUEFOIL *(Potentilla tridentata)*

The Three-toothed Cinquefoil is a low, tufted, woody-based, evergreen plant which has extensively creeping rootstocks. Its leaves are divided into 3 wedge-shaped leaflets, ½ to about 2 inches long, which are 3-toothed at the broad summit; hence its name. The flowers are about ⅓ inch across and have 5 white petals and numerous stamens. They are in few-flowered clusters atop leafy or leafy-bracted stems a few inches high. It grows in dry, open, rocky places; in the south at high elevations in the mountains. The flowering season is between June and September.

RANGE: Lab. to Machenz. south to N.Eng., Ont., N.D. and in mts. to n. Ga.

COMMON CINQUEFOIL *(Potentilla canadensis)*

A large number of cinquefoils occur in eastern North America. Many are native plants and a few have been introduced from Europe. Some are erect plants with leafy stems and they have leaves which are variously divided. None are more common or better known than this creeping plant of dry open places. Its leaves are divided into 5 radiating and wedge-shaped leaflets which are sharply toothed on the margin, at least above the middle. The flowers are about ⅓ inch across and have 5 broadly top-shaped, bright yellow petals and a number of stamens. They are borne singly on slender stalks which arise from the axils of the leaves. Another name for the plant is Five-finger. It blooms between March and June.

RANGE: N.S. to Ont. south to Ga., Tenn., and Mo.

132

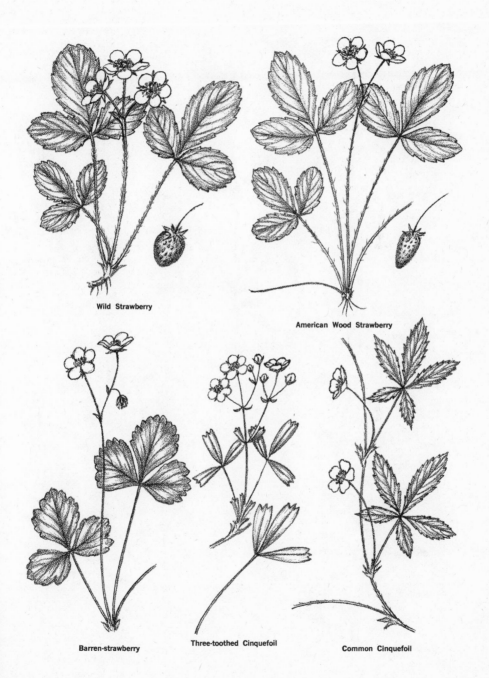

Wild Strawberry

American Wood Strawberry

Barren-strawberry

Three-toothed Cinquefoil

Common Cinquefoil

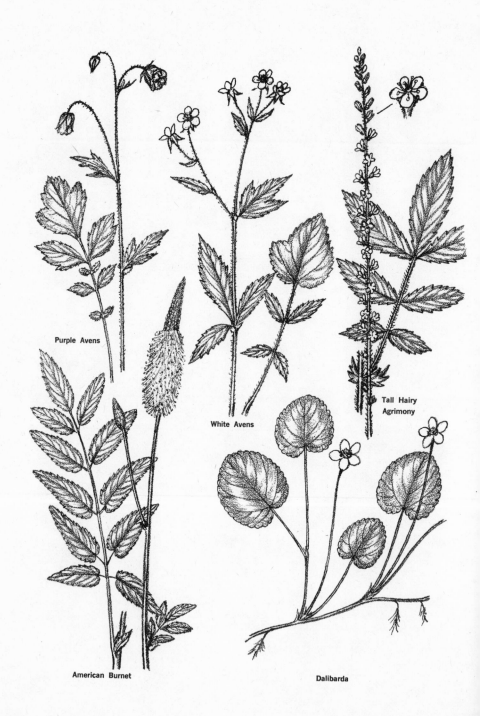

Purple Avens

White Avens

Tall Hairy
Agrimony

American Burnet

Dalibarda

PURPLE AVENS *(Geum rivale)*

The Purple or Water Avens is at home in wet meadows, swamps, and bogs; and there it blooms between May and August. The plant has an erect, downy, and nearly simple stem from 1 to 3 feet tall; along which there are a few 3-parted and toothed leaves. The leaves at the base are much larger, with a large segment at the end and several smaller ones along the sides. Its flowers are about an inch wide and nod at the tips of slender stems. They have a bell-shaped calyx, 5 erect petals, and are usually purple or purplish in color.

RANGE: Lab. to B.C. south to N.J., W.Va., Minn. and N.Mex.

WHITE AVENS *(Geum canadense)*

The White Avens is usually common in open woods and thickets; blooming between June and August. It has an erect, downy or smoothish, branching stem from 1½ to 2½ feet tall; with mostly 3-parted, sharply toothed leaves. The basal leaves have a large terminal leaflet with usually 2 pairs of smaller ones below it, all of which are sharply toothed and sometimes lobed. The flowers are about ½ inch broad and have 5 rather small white petals.

RANGE: N.B. to Minn. south to Ga. and Tex.

ROUGH AVENS *(Geum virginianum)*

This plant closely resembles the preceding species but its stem and leaf stalks are bristly-haired. Its flowers are also somewhat smaller and the petals are creamy-white to greenish-yellow. It grows in dry woods and thickets and on rocky banks from Mass. to Ind. south to S.C. and Tenn; blooming between June and August. (Not illustrated)

TALL HAIRY AGRIMONY *(Agrimonia gryposepala)*

The agrimonies, of which there are a number of species in eastern North America, have a top-shaped hypanthium or calyx-tube with many hooked bristles at the summit. They also have leaves which are pinnately divided, often with small segments between the larger one. This species has a leafy stem usually 2 to 4 feet tall which is minutely glandular and has scattered spreading hairs. The small flowers have 5 yellow petals and between 5 and 15 stamens. They are arranged in a long and very slender cluster and are produced between June and August. Its leaves usually have 7 of the larger leaflets which are coarsely and sharply toothed. It grows in the borders of woods and thickets.

RANGE: N.S. to Que. and N.D. south to S.C., Tenn., and Kan.

AMERICAN BURNET *(Sanguisorba canadensis)*

This is a decidedly attractive plant with a smooth, erect, simple or branching stem from 1 to 5 feet tall. The small white flowers are arranged in dense, showy, terminal clusters from 2 to about 6 inches long, blooming from the base upward. Each flower has 4 whitish sepals and 4 stamens which have very long white filaments. The leaves are divided into from 7 to 15 oval or egg-shaped leaflets with sharply toothed margins. It grows in marshes and in wet meadows or thickets, blooming between May and September. Another name for it is Great Burnet.

RANGE: Lab. to Mich. south to N.J., w. N.C., and Ill.

DALIBARDA *(Dalibarda repens)*

The Dalibarda is a dainty little plant which grows in moist woods and bogs. It has creeping and densely tufted stems or rootstocks from which arise slender stalks bearing a solitary flower. This flower is about ½ inch across and has 5 white petals and numerous stamens, but it usually produces no fruit or seeds. There are other flowers which look like mere buds on short, curved stalks and they produce the little, dry, seed-like fruits. The leaves are roundish heart-shaped, bluntly toothed on the margin, and are somewhat downy on both surfaces. From 1 to 2 inches wide and long-stalked, they might easily be mistaken for the leaves of a violet. Some other names for it are False-violet, Dewdrop, and Robin-run-away. It blooms between June and August.

RANGE: N.S. and Que. to Ont. south to Conn. w. N.C., and the Great Lakes region.

This is a very large plant family which includes a great many important food, forage, and ornamental plants. They are popularly referred to as "legumes", a legume technically being the peculiar bilaterally symmetric pod which is characteristic of the members of the family. This pod is developed from a simple pistil, and at maturity it usually splits into two parts sometimes with considerable force. The flowers vary from a regular or nearly regular form to the decidedly bilateral or papilionaceous (meaning butterfly-like) flowers seen in the typical peas. Botanists sometimes divide the family into 3 separate families, or into the following subfamilies.

Mimosoideae. Members of this subfamily have small flowers with a radial symmetry which are arranged in dense and often ball-like heads. The petals are often united into a 4- or 5-lobed cup with the stamens protruding far beyond it. This subfamily is sometimes called the Mimosa Family.

Caesalpinioideae. Members of this subfamily have flowers with an almost radial symmetry or ones which are somewhat bilateral. They have 5 sepals united at the base, 5 petals, and usually 10 separate stamens. This subfamily is sometimes called the Cassia Family.

Papilionoideae. Members of this subfamily have papilionaceous flowers in which the upper petal forms a broad banner or *standard;* the 2 side ones are more or less parallel and form the *wings;* and the 2 lower ones are united into a *keel,* which encloses the stamens and the pistil. The 5 sepals are more or less united and the 10 stamens are united by their filaments into 1 or 2 groups. This subfamily includes most of the family members.

KEY TO GENERA OF THE PEA FAMILY

1. Plants with undivided (simple) leaves.
  2. Flowers blue or lilac-purple. Leaves mostly over 2 inches long. LUPINES *(Lupinus)*
  2. Flowers yellow. Leaves usually smaller.
    3. Leaves stalkless or nearly so. RATTLEBOXES *(Crotalaria)*
    3. Leaves long-stalked. DOLLARWEED *(Rhynchosia)*
1. Plants with divided (compound) leaves.
  2. Leaflets 3.
    3. Plants with twining and climbing stems.
      4. Keel of the flowers spirally twisted or strongly incurved.
        5. Keel spirally twisted. WILD BEAN *(Phaseolus)*
        5. Keel merely strongly incurved. SAND-BEANS *(Strophostyles)*
      4. Keel of the flowers otherwise.
        5. Flowers large, the standard often an inch or more broad.
          6. Standard with a spur on back near the base. SPURRED BUTTERFLY-PEA *(Centrosema)*
          6. Standard very large, notched at the tip but not spurred. BUTTERFLY-PEA *(Clitoria)*
        5. Flowers smaller, the standard ½ inch or less broad.
          6. Plant brownish-hairy. HOG-PEANUT *(Amphicarpa)*
          6. Plant at most minutely hairy. MILK-PEAS *(Galactia)*
    3. Plants with erect or reclining stems.
      4. Margins of the leaflets with minute teeth.
        5. End leaflet stalked. Flowers in long and narrow clusters. Plant very fragrant when crushed. SWEET-CLOVERS *(Melilotus)*
        5. End leaflet not stalked. Flowers in ball-shaped, egg-shaped, or cylindrical heads. CLOVERS *(Trifolium)*
      4. Margins of the leaflets untoothed.
        5. Filaments of the stamens all separate and distinct.

6. Pods inflated or plump. FALSE INDIGOS *(Baptisia)*

6. Pods flattened. THERMOPSIS *(Thermopsis)*

5. Stamens united by their filaments into 1 or 2 groups.

    6. Flowers 1½ to 2 inches long, the corolla slender and bright red.
CORAL-BEAN *(Erythrina)*

    6. Flowers otherwise; mostly quite pea-like.

        7. Leaflets with small stipules on their stalks.

            8. Pods jointed and separating into flat 1-seeded segments which adhere to clothing, etc. TICK-TREFOILS *(Desmodium)*

            8. Pods merely flattened and pea-like. MILK-PEAS *(Galactia)*

        7. Leaflets without small stipules.

            8. Flowers yellow, solitary or in few-flowered clusters; their calyx tube stalk-like. PENCIL-FLOWERS *(Stylosanthes)*

            8. Flowers whitish to purplish, in many-flowered clusters.

                9. Leaves and pods with small dark or translucent dots.
SCURF-PEAS *(Psoralea)*

                9. Leaves and pods not dotted. BUSH-CLOVERS *(Lespedeza)*

2. Leaflets more numerous than 3.

    3. Leaves palmately divided, with radiating leaflets.

        4. Leaflets 4. Flowers yellow. BRACTED ZORNIA *(Zornia)*

        4. Leaflets 7 to 11. Flowers blue. LUPINES *(Lupinus)*

    3. Leaves pinnately divided into numerous leaflets.

        4. Leaves ending in a tendril.

            5. Wing petals adhering to the keel. Style bearded near the summit. Leaves with rather small stipules. VETCHES *(Vicia)*

            5. Wing petals not adhering to the keel. Style bearded along its inner side. Leaves with large stipules. VETCHLINGS *(Lathyrus)*

        4. Leaves not ending in a tendril.

            5. Flowers not at all pea-like or papilionaceous.

                6. Flowers pinkish and in dense ball-shaped heads. Plants prostrate and prickly. SENSITIVE-BRIERS *(Schrankia)*

                6. Flowers yellow, the corolla often with a nearly radial symmetry.
WILD SENNAS *(Cassia)*

            5. Flowers pea-like or papilionaceous.

                6. Plants twining and climbing.

                    7. Leaflets 5. Flowers brownish-purple, the keel coiled.
GROUND-NUT *(Apios)*

                    7. Leaflets 9 to 15. Flowers lilac-colored. Plant woody.
WISTERIAS *(Wisteria)*

                6. Plants erect or prostrate.

                    7. Plant prostrate. Flowers white, turning red.
GOAT'S-RUE *(Tephrosia)*

                    7. Plants erect.

                        8. Flowers creamy-white and purple. GOAT'S-RUE *(Tephrosia)*

                        8. Flowers yellow. Plants quite tall.

                              9. Standard petal red on the back. Pods very slender and 5 or more inches long. SESBAN *(Sesbania)*

                              9. Standard petal yellow on both sides. Pods plump and bladder-like, 2 to 3 inches long. BAGPOD *(Glottidium)*

CAT-CLAW SENSITIVE-BRIER *(Schrankia nuttallii)*

Sensitive-briers have long, slender, trailing or sprawling stems often 2 to 4 feet in length. They, as well as the leaf stalks and those of the flower clusters—and even the fruit pods —are well-armed with small and hooked prickles. The small pink to rose-purple flowers are in puffy ball-shaped heads which are borne on long stalks arising from the leaf axils. The sensitive leaves are doubly compound, each of the primary leaf divisions being divided again into from 8 to 16 small leaflets. In this species the leaflets show conspicuous veins on the lower surface. It has a densely prickly and narrow pod 2 to 3½ inches long which is short-pointed at the tip. Quite common in dry fields, open woods, and pinelands; it blooms between June and September.

RANGE: Ill., Neb. south to Ala. and Tex.

SMALL-LEAF SENSITIVE-BRIER *(Schrankia microphylla)*

This eastern species is very similar to the preceding one but it has somewhat smaller and narrower leaflets without obvious veins on the lower surface. The slender and prickly pods are 3 to 6 inches long and have long-pointed tips. It grows in dry sandy open woods, thickets, or fields; flowering between June and September.

RANGE: Va. and Ky. south to Fla. and Tex.

WILD SENNA *(Cassia marilandica)*

The wild, or American, Senna has an erect, simple or sparingly branched stem 3 to 5 feet tall; with clusters of numerous flowers arising from the axils of the upper leaves. Its flowers are about ¾ inch across and have 5 yellow petals, 7 anther-bearing stamens, and 3 sterile ones. The leaves are pinnately divided into from 6 to 10 pairs of lance-shaped to narrowly egg-shaped leaflets from 1 to 2 inches long. There is a conspicuous cone-shaped gland near the base of the leaf stalk. It grows in dry thickets and along roadsides, blooming during July and August.

RANGE: Pa. to Iowa and Kan. south to Fla. and Tex.

MEDSGER'S WILD SENNA *(Cassia hebecarpa)*

This wild senna is similar to the preceding species but the gland on its leaf stalks is stalked and club-shaped. The segments of its pods are about as long as broad, while those of the preceding species are much shorter than they are broad. It grows in moist open woods or in stream bottoms from N.Eng. to Wis. and south to w. N.C. and Tenn.; blooming during July and August. (Not illustrated)

LOW SENNA *(Cassia obtusifolia)*

This species is also called Sicklepod on account of its slender, 4-sided, and curved pods which are 4 to 6 inches long. It is a smooth plant 1½ to 2 feet high; its leaves having from 2 to 3 pairs of top-shaped leaflets. There is a long gland on the stalk between or just above the lowest pair of leaflets. It grows in rich soil, often along streams, from Pa. to Mich. and Kan. south to Fla. and Tex.; blooming between July and September. (Not illustrated)

PARTRIDGE-PEA *(Cassia fasciculata)*

Also known as the Golden Cassia or Large-flowered Sensitive-plant, this is a branching plant 1 to 2 feet high. Its leaves are pinnately divided into 10 to 15 pairs of small leaflets which fold together when the leaf is touched. The flowers are 1 to 1½ inches across and have 5 bright yellow petals often with reddish-purple spots at the base. Four of the 10 stamens have yellow anthers and 6 have purple ones. It grows in open thickets, meadows, and along roadsides; blooming between July and September.

RANGE: Mass. to Ont. and Wis. south to Fla. and Tex.

WILD SENSITIVE-PLANT *(Cassia nicitans)*

The Wild Sensitive-plant resembles the preceding species but it grows only 6 to 15 inches high; its flowers are short-stalked and less than ½ inch across, and they have but 5 stamens. Its sensitive leaves have from 9 to about 20 pairs of narrow leaflets. This species grows on dry and sandy soils and also blooms from July to September.

RANGE: Mass. to Ill. and Kan. south to Ga. and Tex.

138

**Small-leaf
Sensitive-brier**

**Cat-claw
Sensitive-brier**

Partridge-pea

Wild Senna

Wild Sensitive-plant

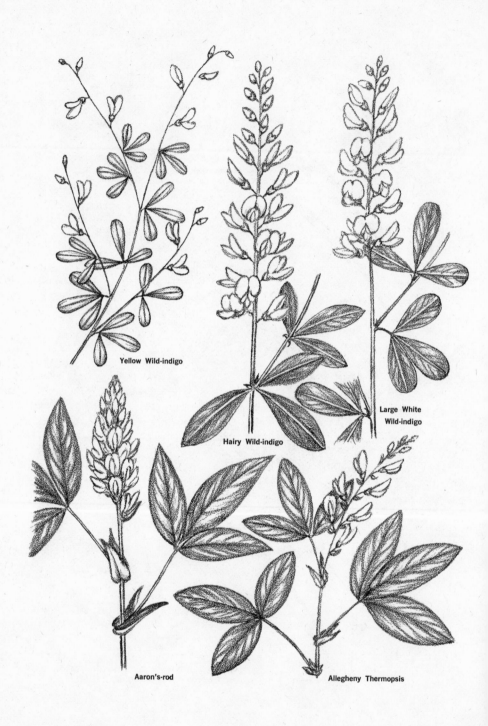

Yellow Wild-indigo

Hairy Wild-indigo

Large White Wild-indigo

Aaron's-rod

Allegheny Thermopsis

YELLOW WILD-INDIGO *(Baptisia tinctoria)*

Some of the wild indigos, including this one, were once used as a substitute for the true indigo in dyeing cloth. This species is a smooth, slender, bushy-branched plant 2 to 3 feet high. Its yellow flowers are ½ inch or less long and in numerous but few-flowered clusters at the ends of the branches; blooming between May and September. The short-stalked leaves are divided into 3 wedge-shaped leaflets from ½ to 1½ inches long. Usually a common plant in dry open woods, clearing, etc. It is used to a limited extent in medicine.

RANGE: Me. to Ont. and Minn. south to Fla. and La.

HAIRY WILD-INDIGO *(Baptisia cinerea)*

This is an erect, branching plant 2 to 3 feet tall which may be softly hairy or merely downy on the younger growth. It has many inch-long yellow flowers arranged in narrow clusters up to 10 inches in length. Its leaves are stalkless or nearly so and divided into 3 lance-shaped to narrowly top-shaped leaflets 2 to 4 inches in length; with a pair of prominent stipules at the base of each leaf. It grows in dry sandy pinelands and on sand-hills in the coastal plain blooming in April or May.

RANGE: se Va. south to S.C.

LARGE WHITE WILD-INDIGO *(Baptisia leucantha)*

The large white flowers which are about an inch long, and the stalked, drooping pods serve to identify this species. It is a smooth plant 2 to 4 feet tall with ascending branches; and stalked leaves which are divided into 3 narrowly top-shaped leaflets 1 to 2¼ inches long. Blooming between May and July, the flowers are arranged in rather loose clusters up to a foot long. It grows in rich woods, and on prairies and river-banks.

RANGE: Ont. to Wis. and Neb. south to Fla. and Tex.

WHITE WILD-INDIGO *(Baptisia alba)*

In this species the white flowers are a little more than ½ inch long, and the pods which follow them stand erect. It is a smooth plant 1 to 3 feet tall with rather spreading slender branches. There are numerous flowers in a narrow and long-stalked cluster; blooming during May or June. The leaves are stalked and have 3 leaflets from 1 to 2 inches in length. It grows in dry woods and pinelands, from the coast to the mountains.

RANGE: Va. and Tenn. south to Fla. (Not illustrated)

BLUE WILD-INDIGO *(Baptisia australis)*

This is our only species of wild indigo with blue flowers. They are about ¾ inch long and violet-blue in color. It is a smooth and branching plant 3 to 4 feet tall, with stalked leaves divided into 3 narrowly top-shaped leaflets 1 to 2½ inches in length. It grows in rich woods and along streams, blooming in May or June; and is frequently cultivated.

RANGE: Pa. to s. Ind. south to Ga. and Tenn. (Not illustrated)

AARON'S-ROD *(Thermopsis villosa)*

Members of the genus *Thermopsis* resemble the wild indigos but they have flattened rather than plump or inflated pods. Aaron's-rod is a somewhat woolly-hairy plant 1 to 3 feet tall with spreading branches. It has yellow flowers nearly an inch long which are in crowded, long, and narrow erect clusters. The leaves are divided into 3 ellpitic or top-shaped leaflets 2 to 4 inches long; and they have large, leafy stipules at the bases of the leafstalks. It grows in dry open woods and along roadsides, blooming between May and July. Often cultivated as Carolina Thermopsis.

RANGE: N.C. and Tenn. south to Ga.

ALLEGHENY THERMOPSIS *(Thermopsis mollis)*

This is an erect, finely downy, branched plant 2 to 3 feet tall. Its yellow flowers are about ⅔ inch long and are in long but rather loose clusters. Its leaves are divided into 3 elliptic to top-shaped leaflets from 1 to 3 inches in length, and there is a pair of prominent stipules at the base of the leafstalk. It grows in dry woods and on rocky ridges in the mountains, blooming in May or June. Another name given it is Bush-pea.

RANGE: Western Va. and Tenn. south to n. Ga. and n. Ala.

WILD LUPINE *(Lupinus perennis)*

This is the only lupine found north and west of the Carolina coastal plain. Usually it has several erect or ascending stems from 1 to 2 feet tall. Between April and June these terminate in elongate clusters of showy flowers which are about ⅔ inch long and usually lavender-blue to purplish-blue in color. Occasional plants have flowers which are pinkish or white. The leaves are divided into from 7 to 11 leaflets which radiate from the summits of the long leaf stalks like the spokes of a wheel. The leaflets are narrowly top-shaped and from 1 to 2 inches in length. This plant grows in dry open woods, thickets, and on sandhills. It is often called the Sundial Lupine.

RANGE: Me. to Ont. and Minn. south to Fla. and La.

LADY LUPINE *(Lupinus villosus)*

This is a striking plant of the dry pinelands and sandhills of the southeastern coastal plain. The stalked leaves are 1-foliate with lance-shaped or elliptic blades from 2 to 6 inches long, and are so densely covered with silky hair that they appear quite a grayish-green. The plant has several radiating stems or branches which are more or less prostrate, but turn up at the ends and terminate in dense clusters of flowers from 4 to 7 inches in length. The flowers are about ¾ inch long and are deep lilac to purple, with a very dark purple or red spot in the center of the standard petal. They are followed by pods so densely covered with silvery-gray hairs that they suggest pussy willows. It blooms in April or May.

RANGE: e. N.C. south to Fla. and west to Miss.

BLUE SANDHILL LUPINE *(Lupinus diffusus)*

While this lupine closely resembles the preceding species, its stems and leaves have shorter and less spreading hairs. Its flowers are a bright deep blue with a white or cream-colored spot on the standard petal, and they often appear a few weeks earlier than those of the Lady Lupine. It also grows in dry woods and on sandhills of the coastal plain.

RANGE: e. N.C. south to Fla. and west to Miss.

RABBIT-BELLS *(Crotalaria angulata)*

The slender trailing stems of this little plant often form mats up to 2½ feet across. Scattered along the stems are short-stalked, oval-shaped leaves from ½ to slightly more than 1 inch long. The 2 to 6 yellow flowers are borne on slender erect stalks from 3 to 6 inches in length, appearing between May and August. They are followed by inflated pods, sometimes an inch long, which look like miniature punching-bags. When mature and dry the many seeds within them become loose and rattle. Sometimes it is called the Prostrate Rattlebox. It grows in dry sandy pinelands, chiefly in the coastal plain.

RANGE: se. Va. south to Fla. and west to La.

RATTLEBOX *(Crotalaria sagittalis)*

This plant has a simple to bushy-branched hairy stem seldom more than a foot tall. Its leaves are oval or lance-shaped, nearly stalkless, and 1 to 2½ inches long. Each leaf usually has a pair of arrow-shaped stipules at its base and these extend down the stems as wings. The 2 to 4 yellow flowers are on slender stalks 1 to 3 inches in length, and are followed by bag-like pods similar to those of the preceding species. It grows in dry open woods and clearings, blooming between June and September.

RANGE: Mass. to Wis. south to Fla. and Tex.

SHOWY CROTALARIA *(Crotalaria spectabilis)*

This species is a tall branching plant with showy yellow flowers and large top-shaped leaves, which has escaped from cultivation and is often seen in fields and along roadsides from Va. and Ky. south to Fla. and La. It blooms between July and September. (Not illustrated)

142

Wild Lupine

Lady Lupine

Blue
Sandhill Lupine

Rabbit-bells

Rattlebox

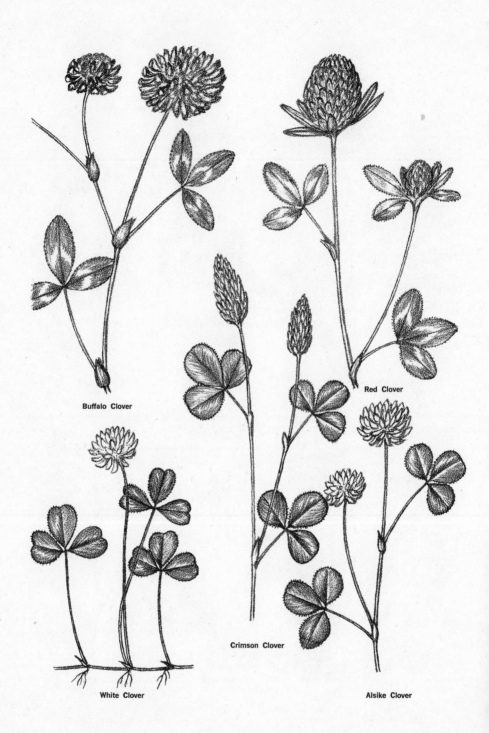

Buffalo Clover

Red Clover

White Clover

Crimson Clover

Alsike Clover

BUFFALO CLOVER *(Trifolium reflexum)*

This native clover is a smooth to somewhat hairy plant 10 to 20 inches tall. Its flowers have a deep pink or rose-colored standard petal but the rest of the flower is white or a very pale pink. Each flower is about ½ inch long and they are crowded in globe-shaped heads 1 to 2 inches across. The 3 leaflets are oval to broadly top-shaped, with a paler green V-shaped spot and minutely toothed margins. Rather large, egg-shaped and pointed stipules are present at the bases of the leaf stalks. This clover grows in open woods, fields, and along roadsides; blooming between April and August.

RANGE: N.Y. and Ont. to Iowa south to Fla. and Tex.

RED CLOVER *(Trifolium pratense)*

Although introduced from Europe as a forage plant, the Red Clover is now widely naturalized in North America. It is a more or less hairy, usually branched plant, from 6 to about 24 inches tall. The purplish-pink flowers are in dense, roundish to somewhat egg-shaped heads about an inch in diameter, with a pair of leaves at the base. Each of the 3 oval or top-shaped leaflets have toothed margins and have a prominent pale V-shaped spot. It is common in fields, waste places and along roadsides; blooming between April and October.

WHITE CLOVER *(Trifolium repens)*

This is another immigrant from Europe which is now common in fields, lawns, and along roadsides throughout most of North America. It is a creeping plant with long, smooth, mat-forming stems. The inversely heart-shaped leaflets are minutely toothed on their margins; and the white or pinkish flowers are in globe-shaped, long-stalked heads about ¾ inch in diameter. It blooms between April and October.

RUNNING BUFFALO CLOVER *(Trifolium stoloniferum)*

This plant is a native creeping species found in open woods and on prairies from W.Va. to S.D. south to Ky., Mo. and e. Kan. Its white flowers are tinged with purple and are in heads an inch or more across, on stems often 4 or more inches tall. The stalks bearing the flowers have a pair of leaves toward the summit. It blooms between May and August. (Not illustrated)

CRIMSON CLOVER *(Trifolium incarnatum)*

This is still another immigrant from Europe which is now naturalized in waste places, fields, and along roadsides. It is an erect, branching, soft-hairy plant 6 to 24 inches tall; with crimson or scarlet flowers in narrowly cone-shaped heads 1 to 2½ inches in length. It is sometimes called the Italian Clover. In bloom from April to July.

ALSIKE CLOVER *(Trifolium hybridum)*

Often called the Alsatian Clover, this European species is now widely naturalized in fields and along roadsides throughout much of North America. A smooth plant, it has erect or ascending, branched stems often 1 to 2 feet tall. Its flowers are white or pink-tinged but turn brown when old, very fragrant; and in long-stalked, globe-shaped heads about ¾ inch across. The broadly oval to top-shaped leaflets have minutely toothed margins. It blooms between April and October.

CAROLINA CLOVER *(Trifolium carolinianum)*

This is a native species with somewhat downy, tufted, ascending or reclining stems 3 to 8 inches in length. Its purplish flowers are in roundish heads about ¼ inch across; and the 3 leaflets are broadly oval or top-shaped, slightly notched at the top, and minutely toothed on the margin. It grows in fields and on rocks from N.C. to Mo. and se. Kan. south to Fla. and Tex. (Not illustrated)

VIRGINIA CLOVER *(Trifolium virginicum)*

This species is a tufted hairy plant with white flowers in heads about an inch across; and long-stalked leaves which have 3 very narrow leaflets. It grows on shady slopes in the mountains from s. Pa. to W.Va., Md. and Va.; blooming in May or June. (Not illustrated)

YELLOW SWEET-CLOVER *(Melilotus officinalis)*

The two sweet-clovers are smooth and branching plants from 3 to 6 feet tall; with numerous, small, flowers arranged in long and narrow clusters arising from the axils of the leaves. They get their name of "sweet-clover" from the sweet-scented, vanilla-like odor the plants give off when they are crushed or dried. Both species are natives of Europe which have become widely naturalized here in America; being found in fields, waste places, and along roadsides. They bloom almost continuously between May and October. This species is distinguished by its yellow flowers. The leaves are divided into 3 narrowly top-shaped leaflets which are toothed on the margin and rounded at the tip.

WHITE SWEET-CLOVER *(Melilotus alba)*

This species is practically identical to the preceding one but it is readily distinguished by its white flowers. The 3 leaflets of its leaves are also notched at the tip. (Not illustrated)

GOAT'S-RUE *(Tephrosia virginiana)*

Among the other names given to this plant are Devil's-shoestring, Cat-gut, Wild Sweet-pea, and Dolly Varden. It is quite an attractive, more or less whitish silky-hairy plant with an erect stem 1 to 2 feet tall. The showy flowers are about ¾ inch long. They have a yellow standard petal which is commonly flushed with pink, and a rose-pink keel. The leaves are pinnately divided into from 14 to 28 narrowly oblong leaflets. It grows in dry open woods, thickets, or fields in usually sandy soils; blooming between May and August.

RANGE: Mass. to Ont., Wis. and Okla. south to Fla. and Tex.

FEW-FLOWERED GOAT'S-RUE *(Tephrosia hispidula)*

Instead of being erect, the stems of this species are reclined upon the ground and range between 1 and 2 feet in length. It is a somewhat hairy or smoothish plant and its leaves are pinnately divided into from 7 to 19 lance-shaped leaflets. The half-inch long flowers are white when they first open but change to red, and are in few-flowered and long-stalked clusters arising from the axils of the leaves. It grows in dry, sandy, coastal plain pinelands; blooming between May and August.

RANGE: Va. south to Fla. and west to La.

AMERICAN VETCH *(Vicia americana)*

One of our few native vetches, this species is found in moist thickets and meadows where it blooms between May and July. It is a rather smooth plant which, like most members of the genus, climbs by means of a tendril at the tip of its leaves. The leaves are pinnately divided into from 8 to 14 leaflets which are egg-shaped or elliptic, blunt but usually tipped with a minute point, and ¾ to 1¼ inches long. Its flowers are about ¾ inch long, bluish-purple, and in rather loose and rather 1-sided clusters. Another name for it is Purple Vetch.

RANGE: Que. to Alaska south to Va., Kan., N.Mex. and Ariz.

CAROLINA VETCH *(Vicia caroliniana)*

The flowers of this native vetch are about ½ inch long, white, with a blue tip on the keel. The long and narrow clusters have from 8 to 20 flowers, and it blooms between April and June. It is a smooth or slightly hairy plant with slender stems 2 to 3 feet long. Its leaves are divided into from 10 to 18 narrowly oblong leaflets which are blunt but with a minute point at the tip, and ½ to ¾ inch long. It grows in rich woods, thickets, and along the banks of streams. Also known as the Pale Vetch.

RANGE: N.Y. and s. Ont. to Minn. south to Ga., La. and Okla.

The following are among the more common and widespread introduced species of vetch naturalized in our region.

COMMON VETCH *(Vicia sativa)* has usually 2 bluish-purple or rose-colored flowers about an inch long in the axils of the leaves. (Not illustrated)

COW VETCH *(Vicia cracca)* has blue to purple flowers in a dense 1-sided cluster. It is also called Canada-pea.

HAIRY VETCH *(Vicia villosa)* is similar to the preceding but more spreading and hairy, with violet to whitish flowers.

Yellow Sweet-clover

Goat's-rue

Few-flowered Goat's-rue

American Vetch

Carolina Vetch

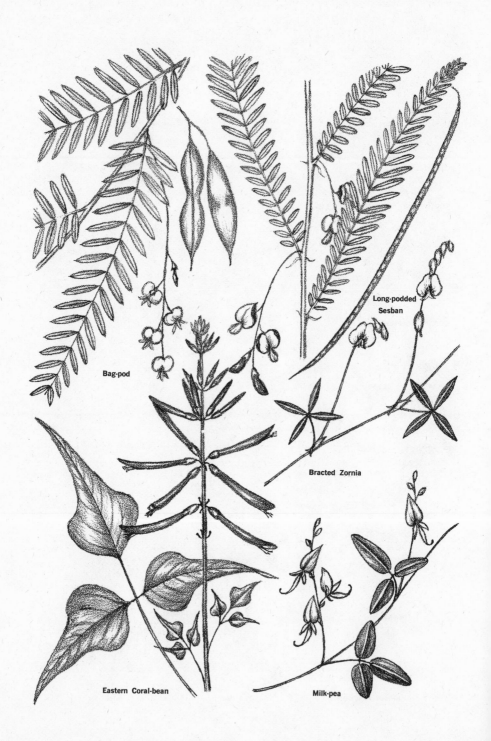

Bag-pod

Long-podded
Sesban

Bracted Zornia

Eastern Coral-bean

Milk-pea

BAG-POD *(Glottidium vesicarium)*

The Bag-pod is a branching plant from 4 to about 12 feet tall, with leaves pinnately divided into 24 to 50 narrowly oblong leaflets. Between July and September it has yellow, or sometimes dark purple flowers about ½ inch long which are borne in open, drooping clusters from the axils of the leaves. It is often conspicuous in thickets, or along roadsides in the coastal plain. The 2-seeded, bladdery pods remain on the dry brown stalks during the winter. Another name for it is Bladder-pod.
RANGE: E. N.C. south to Fla. and west to Tex.

LONG-PODDED SESBAN *(Sesbania exaltata)*

Most of the 15 or so members of this genus grow in tropical lands. This one is a smooth, branching plant from 3 to 10 feet in height. Its leaves are pinnately divided into 24 to 70 narrowly oblong leaflets an inch or less in length. The flowers are yellow, often spotted with red, and the back side of the standard petal is largely red. They are about ¾ inch long and borne in long-stalked, few-flowered clusters which arise from the axils of the leaves. The flowers are followed by very slender bean-like pods from 6 to 12 inches long. It grows in low wet fields, moist thickets, and about the borders of swamps; blooming between June and September.
RANGE: N.C., Mo., and Okla. south to Fla. and Tex; occasionally adventive north to se. Pa. and se. N.Y.

BRACTED ZORNIA *(Zornia bracteata)*

The Bracted Zornia has slender, wiry, much-branched stems up to 3 feet in length which lie flat on the ground. The plant often forms broad carpets in the dry, sandy pinelands or along sandy roadsides in the coastal plain. Its leaves are divided into 4 dark green, lance-shaped leaflets from ½ to 1 inch long which are spread like the letter X. At the base of the leaf stalks there are large stipules which taper to a tail-like base, and the flowers appear from pairs of similarly shaped but broader bracts on long stalks arising from the axils of the leaves. The flowers are bright yellow, the broad standard with usually some red at the base. It blooms between May and September.
RANGE: Se. Va. south to Fla. and west to Tex.

EASTERN CORAL-BEAN *(Erythrina herbacea)*

Between May and July, the brilliant red flowers of this plant are conspicuous in coastal plain pinelands, thickets, and the borders of woods; the long and open clusters being held aloft on leafy stems from 2 to 4 feet tall. Its flowers are slender-looking and about 2 inches long, consisting of a long and narrow standard which turns up only toward the tip. Stamens protrude slightly beyond the end of the standard but the wing and keel petals are quite small. These flowers are followed by bean-like pods which have conspicuous constrictions between the bright red seeds. The leaves are long-stalked and divided into 3 rather triangular leaflets. At the base there is a broad and roundish lobe on each side, above which they taper to a long-pointed tip. Some of the other names given this plant are Cardinal-spear, Cherokee-bean, and Firecracker-plant; the latter because the color and shape of its flowers suggest firecrackers.
RANGE: e. N.C. south to Fla. and west to Tex.

MILK-PEA *(Galactia regularis)*

The Milk-peas, in spite of their name, have nothing milky about them. They are plants with slender, prostrate, or climbing stems. Most species, like this one, have their leaves divided into 3 leaflets; and have violet-purple flowers. The leaves of this species have 3 narrowly egg-shaped or elliptic leaflets from ½ to 1½ inches long, with stalks shorter than the ones bearing the flowers. It grows in open woods, thickets, and roadsides in dry sandy soils; blooming between June and August.
RANGE: N.Y. south to Fla. and west to La.

ELLIOTT'S MILK-PEA *(Galactia elliottii)*

This species is unusual in that its somewhat evergreen leaves have from 7 to 9 leaflets, and its flowers are white. It grows in pinelands from N.C. and Tenn. south to Fla. (Not illustrated)

SPURRED BUTTERFLY-PEA *(Centrosema virginianum)*

This is a trailing or climbing plant with minutely rough-hairy stems from 2 to 4 feet in length. It has clusters of from 1 to 4 flowers on stalks which arise from the axils of the leaves. They are violet colored and have a big, broad standard an inch or more across. On its back, and near the base, is a spur-like projection from which the plant gets its name. The leaves are divided into 3 narrowly egg-shaped to lance-shaped leaflets from 1 to 2 inches long. It grows in dry sandy open woods and fields; blooming between June and August.

RANGE: N.J. to Ky. and Ark. south to Fla. and Tex.

BUTTERFLY-PEA *(Clitoria mariana)*

The showy, 2-inch long, pale lavender-blue or violet flowers of the Butterfly-pea are really impressive. They owe their beauty, however, to the large, rounded standard which is notched at the tip, for the keel and wing petals are quite short and far from conspicuous From 1 to 3 such flowers are borne on stalks arising from the axils of the leaves between June and August. Late in the season, small and bud-like flowers are produced; and, although hardly noticeable they form pods with viable seeds. The Butterfly-pea has trailing but seldom climbing stems from 1 to 3 feet in length; and stalked leaves which are divided into 1-to 2-inch egg-shaped or lance-shaped leaflets. It grows in dry open woods, thickets, and pinelands.

RANGE: se. N.Y. to W. Va. and Iowa south to Fla. and Tex.

SAND-BEAN *(Strophostyles umbellata)*

The Sand-bean has slender, branching, and trailing stems 1 to 5 feet in length which are minutely hairy near the tips. Its flowers are about ½ inch long and are borne in a close cluster at the summit of a stalk from 4 to 8 inches tall. They are pink at first but become yellowish or tawny in fading. The keel is noticably curved. Its leaves are divided into 3 egg-shaped leaflets. The Sand-bean grows in dry sandy woods, thickets, and fields; blooming between June and September. It is also called the Pink Wild-bean.

RANGE: N.Y. to s. Ill. and Mo. south to Fla. and Tex.

TRAILING WILD-BEAN *(Strophostyles helvola)*

This species has trailing or twining and climbing stems from 2 to 8 feet long which are usually somewhat hairy. Its flowers are about ½ inch long and are borne in compact clusters at the summit of a stalk from 2 to 7 inches long. They are pink or purplish and turn greenish with age. The keel is strongly curved. Its leaves are divided into 3 leaflets which are often somewhat 3-lobed. It grows in moist sandy thickets and on shores; blooming between June and September.

RANGE: Mass. to Ont., Wis. and S.D. south to Fla. and Tex.

AMERICAN WISTERIA *(Wisteria frutescens)*

One can readily recognize this woody-stemmed climber as a wisteria, for it closely resembles the cultivated ones. It has rather dense clusters of lilac-purple flowers from 2 to about 5 inches in length, and it blooms in April or May. Its leaves are from 4 to 8 inches long and are pinnately divided into from 9 to 15 narrowly egg-shaped or lance-shaped leaflets, from 1 to 2 inches in length. It grows about the borders of swamps and along the banks of streams.

RANGE: Va. south to Fla. and west to Ala.

KENTUCKY WISTERIA *(Wisteria macrostachya)*

This native wisteria closely resembles the preceding species but it has clusters of flowers from 6 to about 12 inches long. A more sure clue to its identity is found in the minute club-shaped glands which are present on its flower stalks. It grows in rich, moist woods and in swamps; blooming during April or May.

RANGE: Ky., s. Ill. and Mo. south to La. and Tex. (Not illustrated)

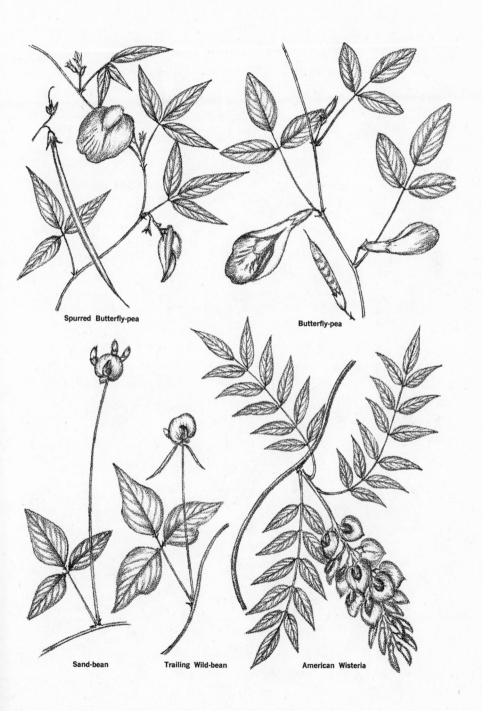

Spurred Butterfly-pea

Butterfly-pea

Sand-bean

Trailing Wild-bean

American Wisteria

Sampson's Snakeroot

Ground-nut

Beach-pea

Hog-peanut

Wild Bean

SAMPSON'S SNAKEROOT *(Psoralea psoralioides)*

Another name for this erect, slender-stemmed, sparingly branched plant is the Congoroot. It grows a foot to 2½ feet tall, producing a dense cluster of bracted, small, lilac-purple flowers toward the end of a long stalk. As the cluster gradually grows longer, the flowers become more spread apart. Its leaves are divided into 3 lance-shaped but rather blunt-tipped leaflets, each from 1½ to 3 inches long. Growing in dry open woods, fields, and clearings; it blooms between May and July.

RANGE: Va. to Ohio, Ill., Mo., and Kan. south to Ga. and Tex.

GROUND-NUT *(Apios americana)*

The Ground-nut is a slender-stemmed, twining plant which often climbs over other vegetation to a height of several feet. It has purplish-brown, fragrant flowers about ½ inch long which are in compact clusters on stalks arising from the axils of the leaves. The keel is strongly upturned. Its leaves are divided into 5 or 7 egg-shaped or broadly lance-shaped leaflets. The "nuts" are tubers which occur in necklace-like strings underground, and were a source of food for the Indians. Also known as the Wild-bean or Potato-bean, the plant is quite common in moist thickets; blooming between June and August.

RANGE: N.B. to Minn. and Colo. south to Fla. and Tex.

BEACH-PEA *(Lathyrus maritimus)*

One might detect a kinship between this and other species of *Lathyrus* and the sweet-peas of our gardens. The Beach-pea is a somewhat fleshy plant with angled, branching, and trailing stems 1 to 2 feet in length. Its leaves are pinnately divided into 6 to 12 broadly egg-shaped or oval leaflets. They have branching tendrils at the leaf tip; and a pair of very large, leaf-like, often more or less arrow-shaped stipules at the base of the leaf stalk. The flowers are purple, violet and purple, or bluish, about ¾ inch long, and are in rather compact clusters on stalks arising from the axils of the leaves. It grows on sandy and gravelly beaches and shores; blooming between June and August.

RANGE: Arctic region south to coast of N.J. and the Great Lakes.

VEINY-PEA *(Lathyrus venosus)*

The Veiny-pea has strongly 4-angled, reclining, ascending, or climbing stems to 3 feet in length. Its leaves are pinnately divided into from 8 to 14 egg-shaped or oval leaflets which are usually very veiny beneath. The stipules are decidedly smaller than the lowest leaflets and shaped like an arrowhead split lengthwise. The flowers are between ½ and ¾ inch long, purple, with 5 to 19 in a stalked cluster. It grows in rich woods, thickets, and along streams; blooming between April and June.

RANGE: Que. to Sask. south to Ga., La., and e. Tex. (Not illustrated)

HOG-PEANUT *(Amphicarpa bracteata)*

Often called the Wild-peanut, this plant has twinging stems more or less clothed with brownish hairs. Purplish or sometimes whitish flowers, about ½ inch long, are produced in nodding clusters on stalks arising from the axils of the upper leaves. They form curved pods containing a few seeds. But like the true peanut, the plant also has small bud-like flowers near the ground; and these mature their 1-seeded pods beneath its surface. The leaves are divided into 3 egg-shaped leaflets and have small stipules at the bases of the leaf stalks. It grows in rich, moist woods and thickets; blooming from July to September.

RANGE: Me. to Que., Man. and Mont. south to Fla. and Tex.

WILD BEAN *(Phaseolus polystachios)*

A close relative of our garden beans, the Wild Bean has lilac or purple flowers about ⅓ inch long in which the keel is spirally coiled. They are produced between July and September in narrow and long-stalked clusters; and are followed by somewhat curved and flattened, bean-like pods 1½ to 2½ inches long. The leaves are quite bean-like in appearance and have 3 broadly egg-shaped leaflets with pointed tips. It grows in dry open woods and thickets.

RANGE: N.J. to W. Va., Ill., Iowa and Neb. south to Fla. and Tex.

The Tick-trefoils, or Tick-clovers, are common plants in woods, thickets, and clearings. They get their name from the fact that the leaves are divided into 3 leaflets; and the fruits, which are called "loments", are made up of several one-seeded joints which separate very easily at maturity, adhering to one's clothing. There are two dozen or more species of these plants in eastern North America.

SMOOTH TICK-TREFOIL *(Desmodium laevigatum)*

This plant has an erect, simple or branched stem from 2 to 4 feet tall, which is smooth or sometimes minutely downy. It has rose-pink or purple flowers about ½ inch long, arranged in a large, branched cluster at the summit. The leaves are divided into 3 egg-shaped leaflets from 1½ to 3½ inches long. It grows in dry sandy woods and clearings, blooming from June to August or September. The fruits usually have 3 or 4 joints.

RANGE: N.Y. to Ind. and Mo. south to Fla. and Tex.

PROSTRATE TICK-TREFOIL *(Desmodium rotundifolium)*

This species has a slender and trailing stem from 2 to 6 feet in length which may be downy or softly white-hairy. It has purple flowers about ⅓ inch long, arranged in rather loosely-branched clusters. The leaves are divided into 3 roundish leaflets from 1 to 2 inches in length, and have prominent stipules at the bases of the leaf stalks. The fruits are 3- to 5-jointed. It grows in dry woods, blooming between June and September. Often called Dollarleaf.

RANGE: Mass. to Ont. and Mich. south to Fla. and Tex.

DILLEN'S TICK-TREFOIL *(Desmodium perplexum)*

This species is an erect plant from 2 to 3 feet tall and somewhat hairy or downy. It has purple flowers about ⅓ inch long which are in a loosely-branched end cluster. The leaves are divided into 3 egg-shaped or oval leaflets 1½ to 4 inches long. The fruits are 2- to 4-jointed. It grows in woods and thickets, blooming between June and September.

RANGE: Me. to Wis. south to Ga. and Tex.

NAKED-FLOWERED TICK-TREFOIL *(Desmodium nudiflorum)*

This tick-trefoil gets its name from the fact that there are no leaves on the flowering stem which usually overtops the one bearing the leaves. The leaves are clustered at the summit of a stem generally less than a foot high. They have 3 leaflets from 1 to 3 inches long; the end one usually somewhat diamond-shaped, the others rather unevenly egg-shaped. Its rose-purple flowers are about ⅓ of an inch long. The fruits are 2- to 4-joined and are not constricted along the top edge. It grows in rather dry but rich woodlands, blooming between June and August.

RANGE: Me. to Que. and Minn. south to Fla. and Tex.

PANICLED TICK-TREFOIL *(Desmodium paniculatum)*

This species has an erect, slender, smooth or minutely downy stem from 2 to 3 feet tall. It has rose-purple flowers about ⅓ inch long which are in a much-branched end cluster. The leaves are divided into 3 lance-shaped leaflets from 1 to 2 inches long, being noticeably narrower than those of most tick-trefolds. The fruits are 4- to 6-jointed. It grows in the borders of dry woods and in clearings, blooming between June and September.

RANGE: N.H. to Ont., Iowa and Neb. south to Fla. and Tex.

SESSILE-LEAF TICK-TREFOIL *(Desmodium sessilifolium)*

The leaves of this species are almost stalkless and have 3 very narrow, blunt-tipped leaflets 1 to 3 inches long. The plant is quite hairy, the stem having small hooked hairs. Its flowers are small and purplish. The fruits being 2- or 3-jointed. It grows in dry sandy soils.

RANGE: Mass. to Mich., Ill., s. Mo. and e. Kan. south to e. S.C., W.Va., La. and e. Tex. (Not illustrated)

HAIRY SMALL-LEAF TICK-TREFOIL *(Desmodium ciliare)*

The name of this species is quite descriptive. It is a hairy plant up to about 5 feet tall. The leaves have 3 egg-shaped or elliptic leaflets usually less than an inch long. Its flowers are very small. The fruits are 2- or 3-jointed. It grows in dry sandy woods and clearings.

RANGE: Mass. to N.Y., Ohio, Mich. and Mo. south to Fla. and Tex. (Not illustrated)

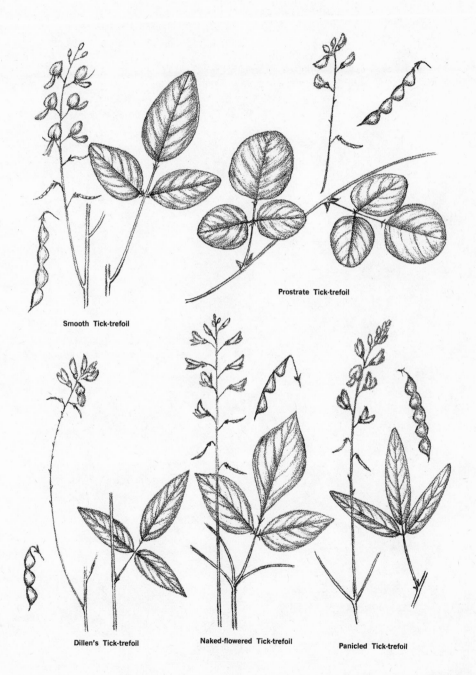

Smooth Tick-trefoil

Prostrate Tick-trefoil

Dillen's Tick-trefoil

Naked-flowered Tick-trefoil

Panicled Tick-trefoil

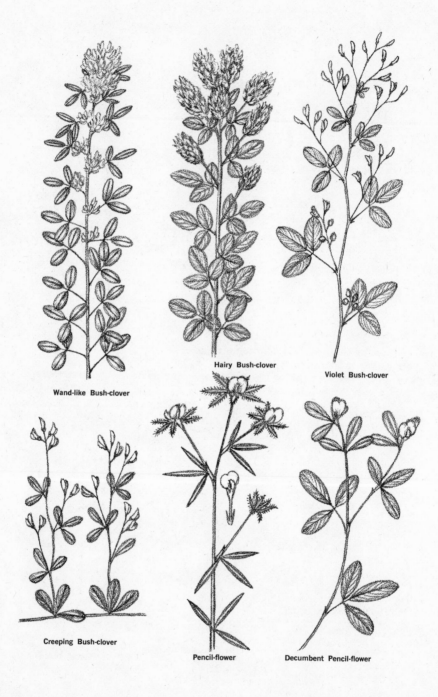

Wand-like Bush-clover

Hairy Bush-clover

Violet Bush-clover

Creeping Bush-clover

Pencil-flower

Decumbent Pencil-flower

WAND-LIKE BUSH-CLOVER *(Lespedeza intermedia)*

This is a stiffly erect, smooth or somewhat hairy plant with a simple or branched stem from 1 to 3 feet tall. It has small violet-purple flowers in short-stalked clusters in the axils of the leaves, and generally crowded toward the top of the stem. Its leaves are divided into 3 elliptic leaflets which are about ¾ inch long and very dark green above. It grows in dry open woods and thickets, blooming between July and September.
RANGE: Me. to Ont. and Wis. south to Fla. and Tex.

HAIRY BUSH-CLOVER *(Lespedeza hirta)*

The Hairy Bush-clover is a densely hairy or silky-hairy plant with an erect, usually branched stem from 2 to 4 feet tall. Its small flowers are whitish or yellowish-white with a purplish base, and are crowded in cylindrical heads on stalks which are longer than the leaves. The latter are divided into 3 oval, top-shaped, or roundish leaflets from ½ to 2 inches in length. It grows in dry open woods, thickets, and on slopes; blooming between July and October. RANGE: Me. to Ont. south to Fla. and Tex.

VIOLET BUSH-CLOVER *(Lespedeza violacea)*

The Violet Bush-clover has rather slender, upright or spreading, bushy-branched stems from 1 to 2½ feet tall. The violet-purple flowers are about ⅓ inch long and are borne in loose and slender-stalked clusters. Its leaves are divided into 3 thin, oval or elliptic leaflets which are ½ to 2 inches in length. It grows in dry woods, thickets, and clearings; blooming between July and September.
RANGE: N.H. to Wis. and Kan. south to Fla. and Tex.

CREEPING BUSH-CLOVER *(Lespedeza repens)*

This species of bush-clover has trailing stems from 6 to 24 inches long which are smooth or minutely hairy. Between May and September it has small violet-purple flowers, which are in loose clusters on slender stalks longer than the leaves. The latter are divided into 3 oval or top-shaped leaflets from ¼ to ¾ of an inch long. It is found in dry open woods, thickets, and fields. RANGE: Conn. to Wis., Iowa, and Kan. south to Fla. and Tex.

TRAILING BUSH-CLOVER *(Lespedeza procumbens)*

The stems of this little bush-clover are also low and trailing, but it is a somewhat stouter and softly hairy plant. Its leaves and flowers ar quite similar to those of the preceding species. It grows in dry sandy or rocky woods and clearings, blooming between August and October. RANGE: Mass. to Wis., Iowa, and Kan. s. to Fla. and Tex. (Not illustrated)

PENCIL-FLOWER *(Stylosanthes biflora)*

Pencil-flowers get their name from the peculiar stalk-like calyx tubes of their flowers. This species has a wiry stem from 6 to 20 inches tall, which is either simple or with a few stiffly ascending branches. It has a few orange-yellow flowers about ⅓ of an inch long; which are grouped at the tips of the stiff stem or its branches, and surrounded by bristly-margined leaflets. The leaves lower on the stem are divided into 3 lance-shaped leaflets ¾ to 1½ inches long and with smooth margins. It grows in dry woods, thickets, and fields; blooming between June and September.
RANGE: se. N.Y. to s. Ill. and Kan. south to Fla. and Tex.

DECUMBENT PENCIL-FLOWER *(Stylosanthes riparia)*

This species has slender reclining or ascending stems from 3 inches to about a foot high, usually with a downy line running between the points where the leaves are attached. Its orange, yellow, or cream-colored flowers are about ⅓ of an inch long. The leaves are divided into 3 elliptic to top-shaped leaflets which are ½ to almost an inch long. It grows in dry woods and on barren slopes, blooming between June and September.
RANGE: N.J. to W.Va., Ill., Mo. and Okla. south to Fla. and Tex.

DOLLAR-WEED *(Rhynchosia reniformis)*

This is an erect, hairy little plant from 3 to about 9 inches high. Its slender-stalked leaves have 1-pieced blades; which are roundish or somewhat broader than long, often slightly heart-shaped at the base, and from 1 to 2 inches long. The yellow flowers are usually less than ½ inch long and in fairly dense end clusters. It grows in sandy open woods, pinelands, and fields; blooming all summer.
RANGE: se. Va. south to Fla. and west to La. (Not illustrated)

GERANIUM FAMILY (Geraniaceae)

Members of this family have flowers with 5 sepals, 5 petals, 10 stamens, and a pistil composed of 5 united carpels which matures into a capsule splitting at the base into 5 parts.

WILD GERANIUM *(Geranium maculatum)*

On a hairy stem usually 1 to 2 feet tall, the Wild Geranium has a pair of deeply 5-parted and sharply toothed leaves 3 to 6 inches wide. Other ones at the base are similar but long-stalked. Between April and June it has lavender-purple flowers an inch or more across. This is one of our most common woodland wild flowers and it sometimes is found in open areas. It is also known as the Spotted Cranesbill. The slender capsules have a fancied resemblance to a crane's bill.

RANGE: Me. to Man. south to Ga., Tenn., Mo., and Kan.

HERB-ROBERT *(Geranium robertianum)*

This smaller relative of the Wild Geranium is a strongly scented plant with a weak, branching, and sparsely hairy stem about a foot long. It has purple flowers about ½ inch across, borne in pairs on long axillary stalks. The leaves are divided into 3 or 5 deeply cut divisions. It grows in rocky woods and ravines, blooming between May and October. RANGE: Nfd. to Man. south to Md., W.Va., and Ill.

CAROLINA CRANESBILL *(Geranium carolinianum)*

This species is a bushy-branched, hairy plant 5 to 15 inches high; readily recognizable as a *Geranium* by its deeply cleft and toothed leaves with spreading divisions; and the long, bill-like capsules. Small, pale-purple flowers in 4- to 12-flowered clusters are produced between May and July. It is found in dry woods, thickets, waste places, etc. and in many places it is a common weed.

RANGE: Mass. to Wyo., Idaho, and s. B.C. south to Fla. and Calif. (Not illustrated)

WOOD-SORREL FAMILY (Oxalidaceae)

Members of this family all have long-stalked leaves with blades divided into 3 inversely heart-shaped leaflets. The flowers have 5 sepals, 5 petals, 10 stamens, and a pistil composed of 5 united carpels which matures into a slightly 5-lobed or 5-sided capsule. The 5 styles are distinct.

COMMON WOOD-SORREL *(Oxalis acetosella)*

This low and creeping plant is usually common in cool, moist northern and mountain woodlands. The solitary flowers are about ¾ inch across, borne on 2- to 6-inch stalks which usually overtop the leaves. Their 5 white petals are veined with pink and are usually deeply notched at the tip. Also called the White or True Wood-sorrel and Wood-shamrock, it blooms between May and August.

RANGE: Nfd. to Man. south to N. Eng., w. N.C., e. Tenn. and the Great Lakes region.

VIOLET WOOD-SORREL *(Oxalis violacea)*

Both leaves and flower stalks of this species arise from scaly-coated bulbs. Usually 3 to 12 flowers are clustered on leafless stalks from 4 to 8 inches high. They are about ⅜ inch across and have rose-purple or violet petals. The leaves have shorter stalks than the flowers. It grows in rich or alluvial woods, thickets, meadows, and on slopes; blooming in April and May and August to October.

RANGE: Mass. to Minn. south to Fla. and N. Mex.

UPRIGHT YELLOW WOOD-SORREL *(Oxalis stricta)*

This is a grayish-green and somewhat whitish-hairy plant with leafy, erect or ascending stems 5 or 6 inches tall. The flowers are about ⅔ inch across and the yellow petals are often red at the base. It grows in dry open woods and in fields, blooming between May and October.

RANGE: N.S. to B.C. south to Fla. and Tex.

GREAT YELLOW WOOD-SORREL *(Oxalis grandis)*

The leafy stalk of this species is 1 to 3 feet tall, its yellow flowers about ¾ in across, and its leaflets 1 to 2 inches broad. The latter usually have purplish margins. It grows in woods and on shady slopes; blooming in May and June.

RANGE: Pa. to Ill. south to Ga. and Ala. (Not illustrated)

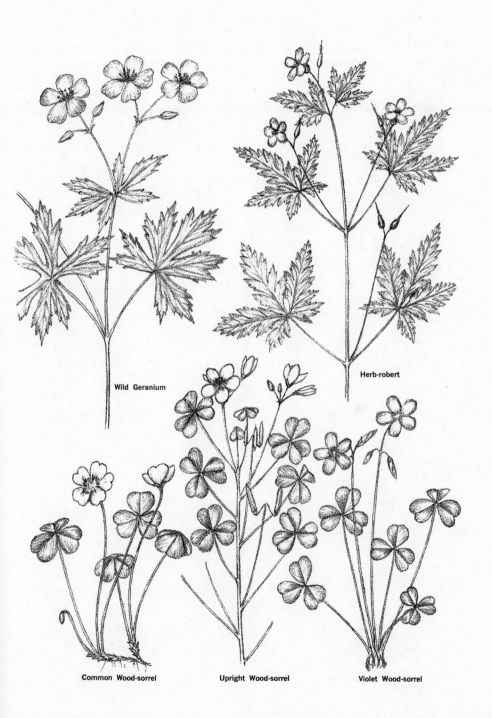

Wild Geranium

Herb-robert

Common Wood-sorrel   Upright Wood-sorrel   Violet Wood-sorrel

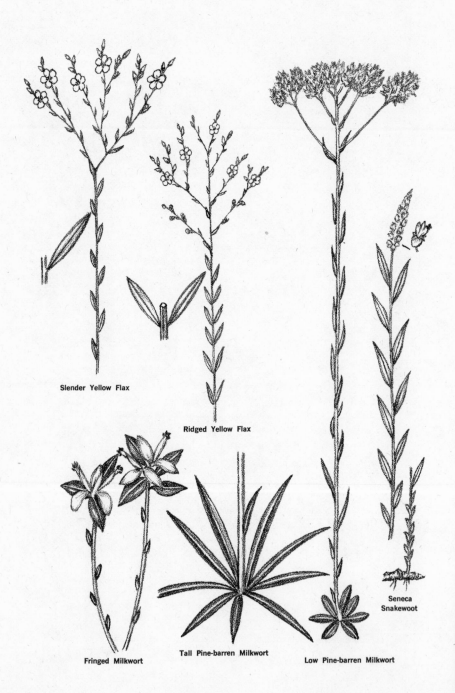

Slender Yellow Flax

Ridged Yellow Flax

Seneca
Snakewoot

Fringed Milkwort

Tall Pine-barren Milkwort

Low Pine-barren Milkwort

FLAX FAMILY (Linaceae)

Members of the Flax Family usually have flowers with 5 sepals, 5 petals, 5 stamens with the filaments united at the base, and a pistil composed of 5 carpels with their ovaries united but the styles separate.

SLENDER YELLOW FLAX *(Linum virginianum)*

Flaxes are very slender-stemmed plants with numerous, small, simple, and narrow leaves. This species is 1 to 2 feet tall, with ascending thread-like branches toward the top. Its flowers are about ⅜ inch across and have 5 yellow petals. The scattered lance-shaped or elliptic leaves are ¼ to ½ inch long. It grows in rich upland or alluvial woods; blooming between June and October. RANGE: Mass. to Ont. south to Ga. and Ala.

RIDGED YELLOW FLAX *(Linum striatum)*

From the preceding species, this one can be distinguished by the sharp angles and ridges which run down its stem from the leaf bases. The leaves on the lower part of the stem are also in pairs. Its flowers are somewhat less than ¼ inch across, blooming between June and October. It grows in moist woods, bogs, and wet sandy places.
RANGE: Mass. to Mich., Mo. and Okla. south to Fla. and Tex.

GROOVED YELLOW FLAX *(Linum sulcatum)*

This species has grooved and wing-angled stems but its leaves are very narrow and all scattered; and the flowers are about ½ inch across. It grows in dry open places, blooming between July and September.
RANGE: Mass. to Man. south to Ga., Ala., Ark., and Tex. (Not illustrated)

MILKWORT FAMILY (Polygalaceae)

Members of this family have flowers with a bilateral symmetry. They have 5 sepals, the 2 lateral ones being petal-like; 3 petals which form a tube, the lower one having a fringed or crested tip; 6 or 8 stamens; and a pistil consisting of 2 united carpels.

FRINGED MILKWORT *(Polygala paucifolia)*

Also known as the Flowering Wintergreen, Gay-wings, and Bird-on-the-wing, this milkwort has very showy, rose-purple flowers about ¾ of an inch long, with a beautifully fringed crest. The plant has slender creeping rootstocks which, in the spring, send up stems 3 to 6 inches high; bearing from 1 to 4 of the pretty flowers and a few small, egg-shaped leaves, with smaller scale-like leaves down along the stem. It grows in rich woods and on rocky slopes, blooming between April and July.
RANGE: N.B. to Man. south to Va., n. Ga., Ill., and Minn.

LOW PINE-BARREN MILKWORT *(Polygala ramosa)*

This plant is very conspicuous in the low, wet, coastal plain pinelands when it blooms between June and September. It has a smooth, erect stem, or stems, from 6 to about 16 inches high, along which are numerous small and narrow leaves. At the top it has a flat-topped cluster of small sulfur-yellow flowers which may be from 3 to 6 inches across. At the base of the plant there is a rosette of broader, top-shaped leaves up to about an inch in length. RANGE: Del. south to Fla. and west to La.

TALL PINE-BARREN MILKWORT *(Polygala cymosa)*

In a general way, this plant is quite similar to the preceding species, but it has a much stouter stem from 2 to about 3 feet tall. The cluster of leaves at the base of the plant are narrowly lance-shaped or grass-like and from 2 to 3 inches in length. Its flowers are no larger than those of the low species and they are in only slightly bigger flat-topped clusters. It also grows in the wet coastal plain pinelands and cypress ponds, blooming between May and August. RANGE: Del. south to Fla. and west to La.

SENECA SNAKEROOT *(Polygala senega)*

The Seneca Snakeroot is a smooth plant with several stems 6 to 15 inches tall, which arise from a thick crown and hard, woody rootstock. Each stem bears a number of narrowly lance-shaped leaves from ½ to 2½ inches long; and small white or whitish flowers in a dense, cone-shaped, 1- to 2-inch end cluster. It grows in dry rocky woodlands and blooms between April and July. Its rootstock is used medicinally.
RANGE: Que. to Alb. south to Me., n. Ga., Tenn., Ark. and S.D.

YELLOW MILKWORT *(Polygala lutea)*

The bright orange-yellow flower heads of this milkwort are conspicuous in coastal plain bogs and wet pinelands between April and October. It is the only milkwort having flowers of this color, which makes its identification easy. It is a smooth plant with several erect or ascending stems from 6 to about 12 inches high. Along them are numerous narrow leaves from ¾ to 1½ inches long. Other names for it are Orange Milkwort and Yellow Bachelor's-button.

RANGE: se. N.Y. south to Fla. and west to La.

CROSS-LEAF MILKWORT *(Polygala cruciata)*

This species has a simple or branched, 4-sided, smooth stem from 4 to 16 inches tall. The leaves are in whorls of 4's, thus forming crosses. They are narrow and ½ to 1½ inches long. The small flowers may be purplish or greenish-white and grouped in dense, cylindrical or barrel-shaped end clusters; blooming between June and October. It grows in bogs and in wet meadows and pinelands.

RANGE: Me. to Minn. south to Fla. and Tex.

FIELD MILKWORT *(Polygala sanguinea)*

The Field or Purple Milkwort is common in fairly moist fields, meadows, and open woods. It is a smooth little plant with a simple or branched stem 6 to about 15 inches high; along which are numerous, scattered, narrow leaves from ¾ to 1½ inches long. Its small flowers vary from a bright rose-purple to greenish and white; and are borne in dense, round to oval-shaped heads from ¼ to ½ inch in diameter. The flowering season is between June and August.

RANGE: N.S. to Ont. and Minn. south to S.C., Tenn., La., and Okla.

WHORLED MILKWORT *(Polygala verticillata)*

This little milkwort has a very slender stem from 6 to 16 inches high which is often branched. It has very narrow leaves which are arranged in whorls of from 3 to 7. The small purplish, greenish, or whitish flowers are in dense cone-shaped clusters at the ends of slender stalks. It grows in moist to dry fields and open woods on more or less sterile soils, blooming between June and September.

RANGE: Me. to Ont. and Minn. south to Fla. and Tex.

RACEMED MILKWORT *(Polygala polygama)*

The numerous simple, erect stems of this milkwort are 4 to 18 inches high; and on them are numerous, rather crowded, and usually narrowly top-shaped leaves from ⅓ to 1½ inches in length. The rose-pink to purple flowers are almost ¼ inch long and arranged in loose but narrow end-clusters from 1 to 4 inches long. It grows in open woods, fields, and meadows but practically always in dry and sandy soils. The flowering season is during June and July.

RANGE: N.S. to Man. south to Fla. and Tex.

PINK MILKWORT *(Polygala incarnata)*

This milkwort has a very slender, stiff, somewhat whitened stem between 5 and 16 inches tall. Its leaves are relatively few, widely scattered, very narrow, and from ⅛ to ½ inch long. The pinkish or flesh-colored flowers have a slender tube formed by the bases of the true petals, about ¼ inch long and far surpassing the wing-like sepals. They are arranged in a dense terminal cluster and the fruits often persist below the tuft of flowers. Another name often given it is Procession-flower. The plant grows in dry fields and meadows, blooming between June and October.

RANGE: N.Y. and Ont. to Wis., Iowa and Neb. south to Fla. and Tex.

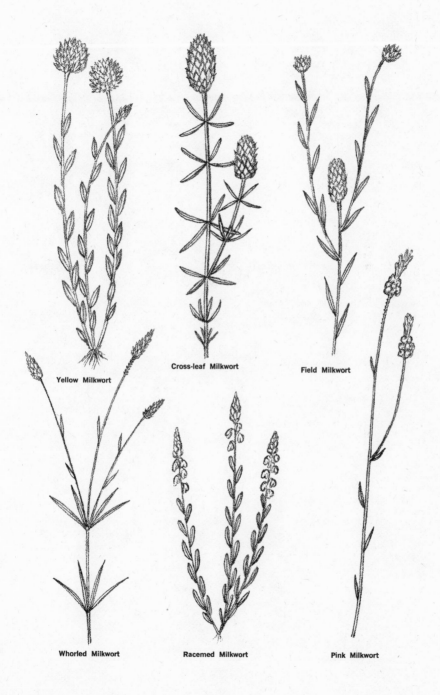

Yellow Milkwort

Cross-leaf Milkwort

Field Milkwort

Whorled Milkwort

Racemed Milkwort

Pink Milkwort

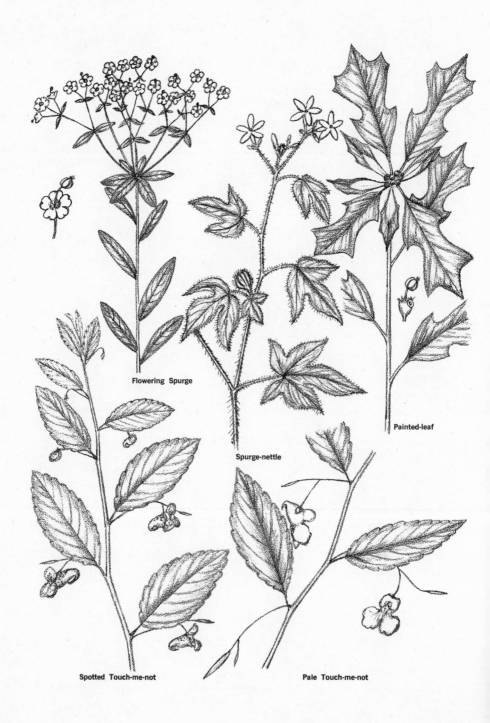

Flowering Spurge

Spurge-nettle

Painted-leaf

Spotted Touch-me-not

Pale Touch-me-not

SPURGE FAMILY (Euphorbiaceae)

This is a large and varied family of plants, most of them occurring in the warmer regions of the world. Many of them have a milky juice. Some have a calyx which may be petal-like. In the true spurges *(Euphorbia)* the flowers consist of only a stalked stamen, or a stalked pistil consisting of 3 united carpels. These flowers are borne within a cup-like involucre which may have prominent glands or corolla-like lobes on its rim. The stamen-bearing and pistil-bearing flowers are always in separate involucres.

FLOWERING SPURGE *(Euphorbia corollata)*

This is a smooth plant with leafy stems from 1 to 3 feet tall, with a branching flower cluster at the summit. What appear to be 5-petalled white flowers are not flowers at all, but really cup-shaped structures which contain the real flowers. The white "petals" are lobes on the rim of the cup, and each one has a yellowish-green gland at the base which might be mistaken for a stamen. The numerous leaves are stalkless and from 1 to 2 inches long. Like other true spurges, the plant has a milky juice. It grows in dry open woods, thickets, fields, and by roadsides. The flowering season is between May and September. RANGE: N.Y. and Ont. to Minn. and Neb. south to Fla. and Tex.

SPURGE-NETTLE *(Cnidoscolus stimulosus)*

This bristly plant of dry sandy pinelands, fields, and sandhills has such other descriptive names as Bull-nettle, Tread-softly, and Finger-rot. It is a branching plant from 6 inches to about 2 feet high, covered with bristle-like and stinging hairs. The stamen-bearing flowers have a corolla-like calyx with 5 spreading, petal-like lobes. The ones which bear the pistils are greenish and not so showy. The leaves are roundish heart-shaped, deeply 3- to 5-lobed, toothed on the margin, from 2½ to 10 inches broad, and are long-stalked. The flowering season is between March and August.

RANGE: Va. south to Fla. and west to Tex.

PAINTED-LEAF *(Euphorbia heterophylla)*

It is easy to see that this plant is a close relative of the familiar Christmas Poinsettia. Its leaves are variable, commonly oval- to fiddle-shaped and coarsely toothed, and from 2 to 5 inches long. Those surrounding the cup-shaped structures containing the flowers have bright red blotches at the base. As in the Poinsettia, there are prominent glands on the flower cups. It grows in open woods, thickets, and waste places usually with a moist sandy soil; flowering between June and September. Other names are Fiddler's Spurge and Annual Poinsettia. It is frequently cultivated under the latter name.

RANGE: Va., Ind., Minn. and S.D. south to Fla. and Tex.

JEWELWEED FAMILY (Balsaminaceae)

Members of this family have flowers with a bilateral symmetry. They have 3 sepals, the lower one extended backward as a spur; 5 petals, all very unequal; 5 stamens; and a pistil composed of 5 united carpels. The fruit is a capsule which splits explosively into 5 spirally twisted parts at maturity, hurling the seeds in all derections.

SPOTTED TOUCH-ME-NOT *(Impatiens capensis)*

This is the smooth, branching, watery-stemmed plant so often met with in moist woods, swamps, and in springy places. It grows from 2 to 5 feet tall and has alternate, thin, elliptic to egg-shaped leaves with coarsely toothed margins. They are from 1½ to about 3½ inches long and are noticeably stalked. The orange flowers are more or less spotted with red, about ¾ inch long, and have a tail-like spur. Usually they are in pairs on slender stalks arising from the leaf axils and are produced continuously between June and September. Other names for it are Jewelweed and Snapweed.

RANGE: Nfd. to Alaska south to Fla., Ala., Ark., and Okla.

PALE TOUCH-ME-NOT *(Impatiens pallida)*

This species is quite similar to the preceding one but somewhat larger and stouter; the canary-yellow to creamy-white flowers being about an inch long, and either unspotted or sparingly spotted with reddish-brown. It is often common in wet or springy woods and in moist, shaded ravines; blooming between July and September. Pale Snapweed or Pale Jewelweed are other names sometimes given to it.

RANGE: Nfd. to Sask. south to Ga., Tenn., Mo., and Kan.

Members of the Mallow Family have flowers with 5 sepals which are united at the base, 5 petals and numerous stamens united by their filaments to form a hollow column about the style, or styles, of the compound pistil.

SWAMP ROSE-MALLOW *(Hibiscus moscheutos)*

Between June and September, this plant of marshes and wet spots produces a succession of showy flowers along its 4- to 7-foot tall stem. They are 4- to 6-inches across and their white or creamy white petals have purplish or dark crimson bases. The flower stalks are united for part of their length with the leaf stalks, thus appearing to grow out of the latter. Its leaves are 3 to 8 inches long, narrowly egg-shaped or lance-shaped, and toothed on the margin. It is also known as the Mallow-rose and Wild-cotton.

RANGE: Md. and W.Va. to Ohio and Ind. south to Fla. and Ala.

PINK SWAMP ROSE-MALLOW *(Hibiscus palustris)*

This rose-mallow is a plant similar to the preceding one, growing in either salt or fresh-water marshes. It differs from it in having pink flowers, and broadly egg-shaped leaves which are often 3-lobed as well as toothed. The flower stalks are distinct from those of the leaves or joined with the leaf stalks very close to their bases. It blooms between June and September. Some other names for it are Mallow-rose and Sea-hollyhock.

RANGE: Mass. south to e. N.C., w. N.Y. and Ont. west about the Great Lakes.

VELVETY ROSE-MALLOW *(Hibiscus incanus)*

As its name indicates, this rose-mallow is a pale or grayish velvety-hairy plant. It has whitish, pale yellow, or pinkish flowers with a crimson center. The leaves are egg-shaped to lance-shaped, long-stalked, and pale velvety beneath. It grows in coastal plain swamps from N.C. south to Fla. and west to Ala. (Not illustrated)

HALBERD-LEAF ROSE-MALLOW *(Hibiscus militaris)*

Leaves of this rose-mallow are arrow-shaped with the basal lobes pointing outward, and from 4 to 5 inches long. It is a smooth plant 3 to 5 feet tall; its 3- to 5-inch flowers being pink or flesh-colored with a reddish-purple center. Growing in wooded swamps and on wet stream banks, it blooms between June and August.

RANGE: Pa. to Minn. and Neb. south to Fla. and Tex.

ROUGH ROSE-MALLOW *(Hibiscus aculeatus)*

This is a very rough-hairy plant 3 to 6 feet tall with leaves deeply 3- to 5-lobed or parted. Its flowers are yellow or cream-colored with a reddish-purple base. It grows in woods and pinelands in the coastal plain from S.C. south to Fla. and west to La. (Not illustrated)

RED HIBISCUS *(Hibiscus coccineus)*

This is a smooth plant up to 10 feet tall with leaves divided into from 5 to 7 narrow and toothed lobes. The crimson or deep red flowers are often 6 inches across. It grows in swamps near the coast from Ga. and Fla. west to Tex. (Not illustrated)

COASTAL-MALLOW *(Kosteletzkya virginica)*

The Coastal-mallow is an erect, branching, more or less downy or sometimes roughish-hairy plant 1½ to 4 feet tall; growing in salt or brackish marshes and on shores. The leaves are egg-shaped to somewhat arrow-shaped, often 3-lobed, always coarsely toothed, and 2 to 5 inches long. It has pink flowers 1½ to 2½ inches across which bloom between July and October. Other names for it are Saltmarsh-mallow and Seashore-mallow.

RANGE: se. N.Y. and Del. south to Fla. and west to Tex.

SOUTHEASTERN POPPY-MALLOW *(Callirhoe papaver)*

There are several species of poppy-mallows and most of them are plants of the mid-west. This one has smoothish or somewhat hairy, reclining stems 8 to 24 inches long. Its leaves are 3- to 5-parted or lobed, with narrow but untoothed segments. It has solitary reddish-purple flowers from 1 to 2½ inches broad which bloom between June and August. The plant grows in sandy or rocky woods, glades, and on prairies.

RANGE: Ga. to Mo. south to Fla. and Tex.

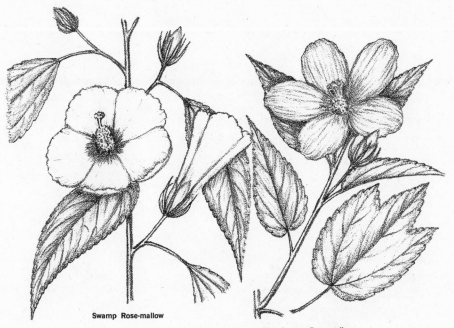

Swamp Rose-mallow

Pink Swamp Rose-mallow

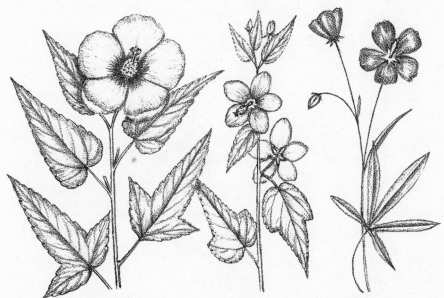

Halberd-leaf Rose-mallow   **Coastal-mallow**   **Southeastern Poppy-mallow**

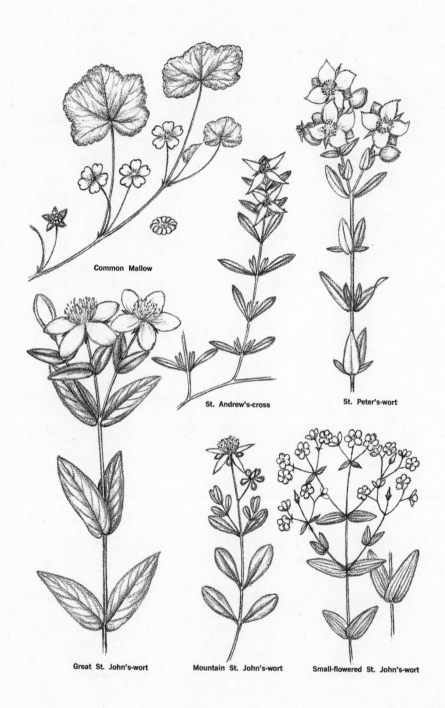

Common Mallow

St. Andrew's-cross

St. Peter's-wort

Great St. John's-wort

Mountain St. John's-wort

Small-flowered St. John's-wort

COMMON MALLOW *(Malva neglecta)*

Another common name for this little trailing plant is Cheeses, as its rings of small fruits suggest a tiny cheese and have a mildly pungent taste. Its flowers are pale lilac or whitish, about ½ inch across, and are clustered in the axils of the leaves; blooming over a long period between April and October. The leaves are roundish heart-shaped, shallowly lobed, bluntly toothed, from 1 to 3 inches wide, and have long stalks. A native of Europe, it has become widely naturalized here in America; growing in yards, barnyards, and waste places.

ST. JOHN'S-WORT FAMILY (Hypericaceae)

Members of this family have opposite, entire leaves with tiny translucent or black dots. Their flowers have 4 or 5 sepals and a like number of petals, usually numerous stamens, and a pistil composed of from 2 to 5 united carpels which are indicated by the number of styles.

ST. ANDREW'S-CROSS *(Hypericum hypericoides)*

This is a woody-based little plant with ascending, flattened and 2-edged, often branching stems from 5 to 10 inches high. Its flowers are about ¾ across and have 2 broadly egg-shaped sepals and 2 very much smaller and narrow ones. The 4 yellow petals form an oblique cross. The pistil is composed of 2 carpels and there are 2 distinct styles. It develops into a pod enclosed by the pair of large sepals. The leaves are oblong or top-shaped and ½ to 1½ inches long. This plant grows in dry sandy or rocky woods and thickets; blooming between May and August.
RANGE: Mass. to Ill. and Kan. south to Fla. and Tex.

ST. PETER'S-WORT *(Hypericum stans)*

The St. Peter's-wort is a woody-based plant with a simple or sparingly branched, 2-edged stem from 1 to 2 feet high. Its flowers are ¾ to an inch across and have 4 broad, bright yellow petals; a pair of large sepals and a pair of smaller ones; and a pistil with 3 or 4 styles. The leaves are oval or oblong, whitened beneath, from ¾ to 1½ inches long, and have heart-shaped bases which clasp the stem. It grows in moist to dry, sandy, open woods and in fields; blooming between June and October.
RANGE: se. N.Y. and N.J. to Ky. south to Fla. and Tex.

GREAT ST. JOHN'S-WORT *(Hypericum pyramidatum)*

This plant has a stout, erect, branching stem from 2 to 5 feet tall; its branches being 2- to 4-angled. The flowers are 1 to 2 inches across and have 5 bright yellow petals, and a pistol with 5 styles. Its leaves are narrowly egg-shaped, from 2 to 5 inches long, and have somewhat clasping bases. It grows on rich, rocky, wooded slopes and along the banks of streams; blooming between July and September.
RANGE: Me. to Man. south to N.J., Md., Ill., Mo. and Kan.

MOUNTAIN ST. JOHN'S-WORT *(Hypericum buckleyi)*

On rocky mountain summits and cliffs in the Southern Appalachians, the Mountain St. John's-wort blooms between June and August. It is a trailing or straggling little plant from 4 to 12 inches high, with pairs of top-shaped or elliptic leaves from ¼ to ¾ of an inch long. Its flowers, between ¾ and an inch across, have 5 yellow petals about twice as long as the spoon-shaped sepals, and a pistil with 3 styles.
RANGE: w. N.C. south to n. Ga.

SMALL-FLOWERED ST. JOHN'S-WORT *(Hypericum mutilum)*

This is one of several species of St. John's-worts having small flowers less than ¼ inch across. This one has branching, slender, weak stems 6 inches to 2½ feet tall; and oblong or egg-shaped leaves ½ to an inch long, usually with a clasping base and 5 main veins. The numerous flowers are about 3/16 inch across, with 5 yellow petals and about 10 stamens. They are arranged in rather large, loose, leafy-bracted end clusters; blooming between June and October. It grows in low, moist, open woods and meadows.
RANGE: N.S. to Ont. and Wis. south to Fla. and Tex.

DOTTED ST. JOHN'S-WORT *(Hypericum punctatum)*

This is a smooth and sparingly-branched plant from 1½ to 3 feet tall, with a crowded flower cluster at the summit. The flowers are about ½ inch across and the 5 yellow petals have several rows of small black dots. The pistil has 5 styles. Its leaves are 1 to 3 inches long, oblong in shape, rounded at the tip, and more or less clasping at the base. They are liberally sprinkled with both translucent and black dots. This is a common plant in open woods, thickets, and fields; blooming between June and September.

RANGE: Que. to Ont. and Minn. south to Fla. and Tex.

COMMON ST. JOHN'S-WORT *(Hypericum perforatum)*

A native of Europe, this St. John's-wort is now widely naturalized here in America and generally abundant in fields, waste places, and along roadsides. It somewhat resembles the preceding species but it is usually less tall, much more branched, and the yellow petals of the flowers are black-dotted only on their margins. The pistil has but 3 styles. It blooms between June and September. (Not illustrated)

CANADA ST. JOHN'S-WORT *(Hypericum canadense)*

This is a slender-stemmed, branching plant from 6 to 20 inches high. It has very narrow leaves with 1 to 3 main veins, and they are ½ to 2 inches long. The small flowers are ¼ inch or less across and have 5 yellow petals and 5 to 10 stamens. It grows in swampy places, on wet rocks, or on moist banks; blooming between July and September.

RANGE: Nfd. to Man. south to Ga., Ala., Ill. and Iowa.

MARSH ST. JOHN'S-WORT *(Hypericum virginicum)*

The Marsh St. John's-wort has a smooth, simple or branched stem 1 to 2½ feet tall. Its leaves are 1 to 3 inches long, egg-shaped or oblong, rounded at the tip, clasping at the base, black-dotted, and often whitish beneath. The flowers are about ⅔ inch across, pink to greenish-purple, and have 9 stamens. The latter are united by the bases of their filaments into 3 groups which alternate with 3 large orange-colored glands. It grows in swamps, bogs, and wet sandy places; blooming between July and September.

RANGE: Nfd. to Man. south to Fla. and Tex.

LARGER MARSH ST. JOHN'S-WORT *(Hypericum tubulosum)*

This is usually a larger and more branched plant than the preceding. It can be distinguished by its leaves which are short-stalked or almost stalkless but not clasping.

RANGE: Md. and W.Va. to Ind. and Mo. south to Fla. and Tex. (Not illustrated)

ROCKROSE FAMILY (Cistaceae)

Members of this family have flowers with 5 sepals, 2 of which are small or sometimes lacking; 3 or 5 petals; numerous stamens; and a solitary pistil with 1 style, or the style sometimes absent. The plants usually have alternate leaves.

FROSTWEED *(Helianthemum canadense)*

The Frostweed branches near the base into several grayish-downy stems from 8 to 16 inches high. Usually each one has a solitary flower between May and July, with 5 bright yellow petals and an inch to 2 inches across. Later there are smaller bud-like flowers which are rather inconspicuous but produce most of the seeds. The leaves are lance-shaped or inversely lance-shaped and broadest near the tip, stalkless or nearly so, and from ½ to 1½ inches long. In late autumn ice crystals shoot from the bases of the stems, hence the common name. It grows in rocky open woods and on sandy barrens.

RANGE: N.S. to Que. and Wis. south to Ga., Miss. and Mo.

CAROLINA ROCKROSE *(Helianthemum carolinianum)*

The Carolina Rockrose is a plant of the drier coastal plain pinelands. In May or June it usually has 1 or 2 showy flowers 1 to 1½ inches across, with 5 bright yellow petals. As in the preceding species, it also produces small bud-like flowers which are quite inconspicuous. The plant has a hairy stem from 2 to about 10 inches tall on which there are a few scattered leaves, most of its leaves being in a basal cluster. They are elliptical or inversely lance-shaped and from ¾ to 1½ inches long.

RANGE: e. N.C. south to Fla. and west to Tex.

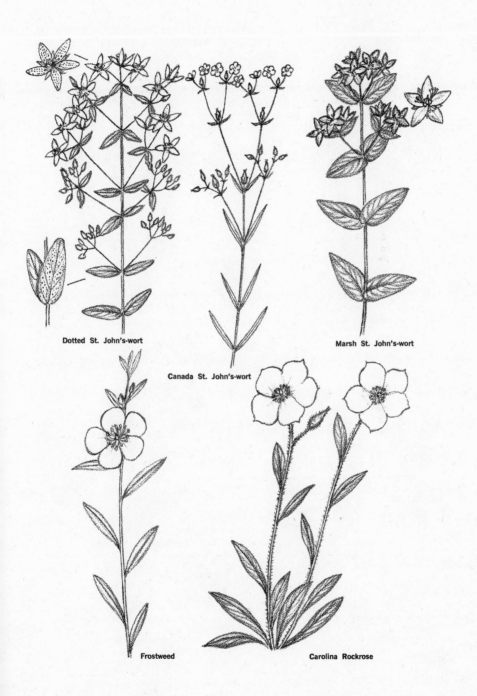

Dotted St. John's-wort

Canada St. John's-wort

Marsh St. John's-wort

Frostweed

Carolina Rockrose

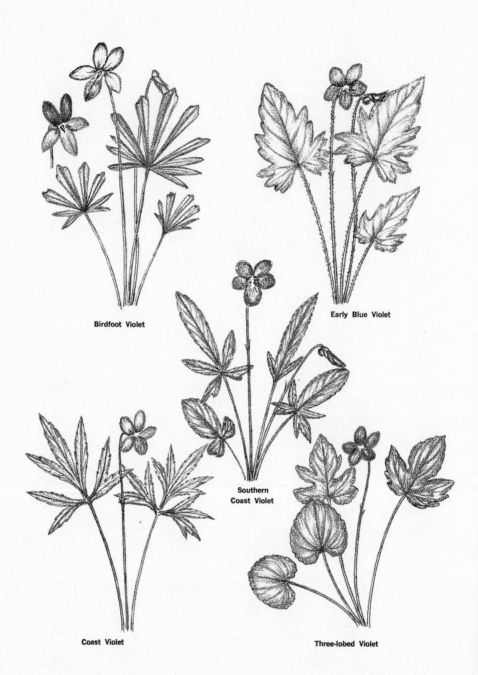

Birdfoot Violet

Early Blue Violet

Southern
Coast Violet

Coast Violet

Three-lobed Violet

VIOLET FAMILY (Violaceae)

Members of this family are among our most common and best known wild flowers. Although they are easy to recognize as being violets, it is often very difficult to identify the numerous species. This is especially true of the so-called "stemless" blue violets, among which there are many confusing hybrids.

The flowers have a bilateral symmetry. There are 5 sepals; 5 petals, the lower one being extended backward as a hollow sac or spur; 5 stamens in which the anthers form a cone-shaped cluster about the base of the pistil; and a solitary pistil with a club-shaped style and stigma. Besides the showy flowers, many violets also have bud-like flowers which produce large quantities of seeds. The fruit is a capsule containing numerous seeds.

BIRDFOOT VIOLET (Viola pedata)

This is certainly one of our most striking species of violet, and one that is very easy to recognize. Its showy flowers are often an inch or more across. Usually all 5 petals are lilac-colored but in one variety the 2 upper petals are dark violet. The stamens are a bright orange-yellow. Its name comes from the leaves which are deeply cut into narrow and radiating segments. Both leaves and flowers arise from a short, erect, fleshy rootstock. It grows on dry, sunny, sandy, rocky, or clayey banks and open woods; blooming between March and June.

RANGE: Mass. to Ont., Minn. and Kan. south to Ga. and Tex.

EARLY BLUE VIOLET (Viola palmata)

From March to May this violet blooms on dry but rich wooded hillsides. It is best distinguished by its leaves which have from 5 to 11 lobes or segments, the middle one being largest and all variously toothed and cleft. The violet-purple flowers are about an inch across. Both they and the leaves arise from a thick, erect, fleshy rootstock and both have stalks which are somewhat hairy.

RANGE: N.H. to Ont. and Minn. south to Fla. and Miss.

COAST VIOLET (Viola brittoniana)

Often the earliest leaves of this violet are merely toothed, but the ones which follow are 3-parted and the segments are cut into 2 to 4 narrow and pointed lobes. The flowers are a rich violet with a conspicuous white throat and are an inch or more across. Both the flowers and leaves arise from a thick, erect, fleshy rootstock and have stalks which are quite smooth. This one grows in moist sandy or peaty soils, blooming between April and June.

RANGE: Coast of s. Me. south to coast and mts. of N.C.

SOUTHERN COAST VIOLET (Viola septemloba)

In spite of its scientific name, the leaves of this violet are not always 7-lobed. They are very variable, ranging from some that are just heart-shaped to others which are variously lobed or divided. The flowers are an inch across and usually well above the leaves. They are a deep blue-violet with a broad white center, and all 3 of the lower petals have tufts of hair at the base. Both flowers and leaves arise from a thick, erect, fleshy rootstock and have stalks which are sparingly hairy. It is the common blue violet of the sandy coastal plain pinelands; blooming from late March to May.

RANGE: Va. south to Fla. and west to La.

THREE-LOBED VIOLET (Viola triloba)

The earliest leaves, as well as some of those developed later in the summer, are heart-shaped with toothed margins. Those produced in between may be 3- to 5-lobed with the middle segment always the largest. The flowers are about an inch across, deep violet, and all 3 of the lower petals have a hairy tuft at the base. Both flowers and leaves arise from a thick, erect, fleshy rootstock and have stalks which are somewhat hairy. It grows in rich but dry woodlands, blooming from late March to May.

RANGE: Pa. to Ill., Mo. and Okla. south to Fla. and Tex.

173

MARSH BLUE VIOLET *(Viola cucullata)*

As its name implies, this violet grows in wet meadows, bogs, and springy places. Its violet-blue flowers are darker toward the center, about an inch broad, and are on long stalks which overtop the leaves. The side petals have hairy tufts containing many club-shaped hairs. The leaves are heart-shaped with rather bluntish teeth on the margin, and they are smooth or very nearly so. The plant is usually tufted with several crowns; and both flowers and leaves arise from a thick, erect, fleshy rootstock. It blooms between April and July.

RANGE: Nfd. to Ont. and Minn. south to Va., n.Ga., Ark. and Neb.

COMMON BLUE VIOLET *(Viola papilionacea)*

This is undoubtedly the commonest of our blue violets; growing in open woods, meadows, door-yards, and along roadsides everywhere. Its rich violet-colored flowers are about an inch across, whitish toward the center, and are on smooth stalks no longer than the leaves. Both of the side petals are "bearded" but none of the hairs are club-shaped. Its smooth leaves are broadly heart-shaped and by midsummer may become 5 inches wide. Both flowers and leaves arise from a thick and fleshy rootstock. It blooms between late February and June. Also called Hooded Blue Violet.

CONFEDERATE VIOLET is a color variety of the Common Blue Violet with white or whitish flowers marked with contrasting purple veins. It seems to be especially common about door-yards in the South.

RANGE: Me. to Que., N.D. and Wyo. south to Ga. and Okla.

WOOLLY BLUE VIOLET *(Viola sororia)*

This species closely resembles the Common Blue Violet but the leafstalks and the lower surfaces of its leaves are somewhat downy or woolly. It grows in low woods, moist meadows, and on damp slopes; blooming between March and June. (Not illustrated)

RANGE: Que. to Minn. and S.D. south to N.C., Ky., Mo. and Okla.

TRIANGLE-LEAF VIOLET *(Viola emarginata)*

The triangular-shaped leaves of this blue violet are on very long, smooth, and slender stalks. Their blades are coarsely toothed toward the base but become obscurely toothed above the middle. Its flowers are violet-blue and the petals are often notched at the ends. They are usually on stalks longer than the leaves, both arising from a stout and matted rootstock. It grows in dry woods and fields, blooming between late March and May.

RANGE: Mass. to Ohio, Mo. and Kan, south to Ga. and Tex.

OVATE-LEAF VIOLET *(Viola fimbriatula)*

This little violet has narrowly egg-shaped (ovate) leaves which have a few prominent teeth or lobes at the base, smaller teeth elsewhere on the margin. They are usually finely hairy, at least on the lower surface. The flowers are violet-purple, about ¾ inch across, and are on hairy stalks about as long as the leaves. Both leaves and flowers arise from a long, stout rootstock. It grows in dry open woods, fields, and on hillsides; blooming in April or May.

RANGE: N.S. to Minn. south to Fla., La. and Okla.

ARROW-LEAF VIOLET *(Viola sagittata)*

The leaves of this violet are shaped like narrow arrow-heads, tapering to a pointed tip; usually with 1 or more pairs of lobes or coarse teeth at the base. At maturity they become from 1½ to 4 inches long. They are usually smooth but sometimes finely hairy, or with a hairy fringe on the margin. The flowers are violet-purple with a white center, about ¾ inch across, and are on stalks about as long as the leaves; both arising from a stout, fleshy rootstock. It grows on moist banks and in fields and upland woods; blooming between late March and June.

RANGE: Mass. to Minn. south to Ga. and Tex.

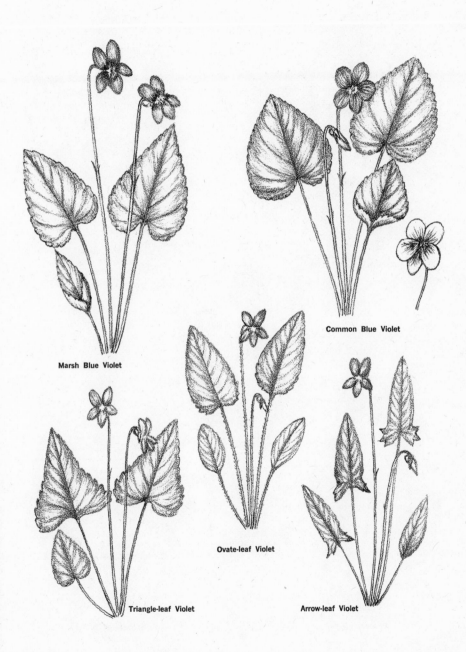

Marsh Blue Violet

Common Blue Violet

Triangle-leaf Violet

Ovate-leaf Violet

Arrow-leaf Violet

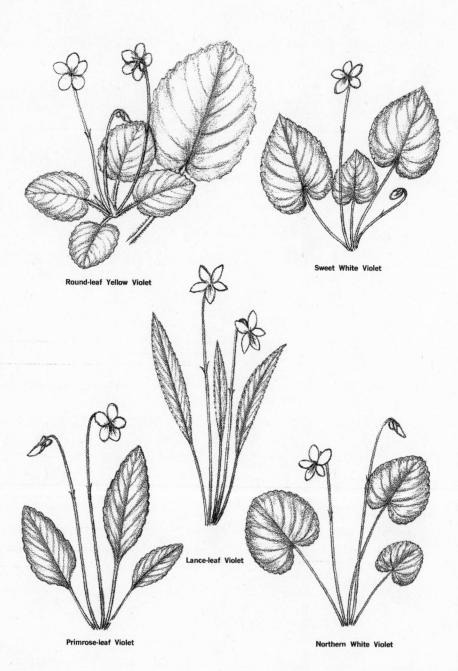

Round-leaf Yellow Violet

Sweet White Violet

Lance-leaf Violet

Primrose-leaf Violet

Northern White Violet

ROUND-LEAF YELLOW VIOLET *(Viola rotundifolia)*

This is our only "stemless" violet with yellow flowers. It has roundish or oval leaves with a wavy-toothed margin. At flowering time, between March and May, they are only about an inch wide and are finely hairy. Later they become 2 to 4 inches broad, thickish, quite smooth, and lie flat on the ground. The flowers are about ½ inch across, bright yellow, the 3 lower petals being veined with brown. Both leaves and flowers arise from a long, stout, jagged rootstock. Look for it in cool, moist, rich woods or on banks; southward in the mountains.

RANGE: Me. to Ont. south to Del., Pa., n. Ga. and e. Tenn.

SWEET WHITE VIOLET *(Viola blanda)*

Expect to find this little white-flowered violet in cool, moist woods and ravines, where it blooms in April or May. Its fragrant flowers are about ½ inch across. The 3 lower petals are veined with purple; the 2 upper ones plain but often twisted or bent backward. The leaves are heart-shaped, 1 to 2 inches wide, the sinus at the base being very narrowly V-shaped. They are smooth except for a few small and widely scattered hairs on the upper surface. Both leaves and flowers usually have reddish-tinged stalks and arise from a slender rootstock.

RANGE: N.H. and Que. to Minn. south to Md., n.Ga., Tenn., Ohio, Ill. and Wis.

NORTHERN WHITE VIOLET *(Viola macloskeyi* var. *pallens)*

The flowers of this species resemble those of the preceding one and are very fragrant. Its leaves are ½ to 2½ inches wide, entirely smooth, heart-shaped, and have a very broadly V-shaped basal sinus. It grows in wet or springy woods, bogs, and along stream banks; blooming between April and July.

RANGE: Lab. to Alaska south to Pa., mts. of Ga. & Tenn. Ill., Iowa, N.D. and Mont.

LARGE-LEAF WHITE VIOLET *(Viola incognita)*

While this species resembles both of the preceding species, it is a coarser plant; its leaves having a wrinkled-veiny appearance and being downy beneath. The 2 side petals of its flowers have hairy tufts at the base, and the flowers are slightly, if at all, fragrant. It grows in wet or moist woods, thickets, and clearings; blooming between April and June.

RANGE: Nfd. to Ont. south to N.Y., e. Tenn., the Great Lakes region, and N.D. (Not illustrated)

LANCE-LEAF VIOLET *(Viola lanceolata)*

This violet can be recognized very easily by its long and narrow, lance-shaped leaves which have low and rounded teeth on the margin. The leaves are commonly from 2 to 6 inches long, but sometimes as much as a foot in length. The white flowers are a half inch or a little more across, the 3 lower petals having conspicuous purple veins. Both leaves and flowers arise from a slender rootstock, and the plants spread by means of runners. Look for this violet in wet meadows, marshy places, and bogs. It blooms between March and July.

RANGE: N.S. to Que., Minn. and Neb. south to Fla. and Tex.

PRIMROSE-LEAF VIOLET *(Viola primulifolia)*

This little white-flowered violet may be recognized by its egg-shaped or elliptic leaves which taper at the base into their stalks. They have rather inconspicuous teeth on the margin and are more or less hairy. The flowers are about ½ inch across and the 3 lower petals are veined with purple. Both flowers and leaves arise from a slender rootstock, and the plants spread freely by means of runners. It grows in moist open woods, clearings, and meadows; blooming between March and June.

RANGE: N.S. to Que., Minn. and Okla. south to Fla. and Tex.

CANADA VIOLET *(Viola canadensis)*

This is a smooth or slightly hairy plant with 1 or more leafy stems usually between 8 and 14 inches tall. The flowers have white petals which are tinged with lilac on the back. They are about ¾ inch across and on slender stalks arising from the axils of the heart-shaped leaves. This violet grows in cool, moist, rich woodlands; blooming between April and July.

RANGE: N.H. and Que. to Mont. south to Md., nw. S.C., n. Ga., Tenn., Iowa, S.D., Colo. and Utah.

HALBERD-LEAF VIOLET *(Viola hastata)*

On a slender stem 4 to 10 inches tall, this violet has from 2 to 4 narrowly triangular, taper-pointed leaves. Its yellow flowers are about ½ inch across and on slender stalks arising from the axils of the leaves. The petals are tinged with violet on the back. It grows in rich, often rocky woods; blooming late March to May.

RANGE: Pa. and Ohio south to Fla. and Ala.

STRIPED VIOLET *(Viola striata)*

The large and conspicuously fringed stipules afford a good field mark in identifying this violet. It usually has several smooth, angled, leafy stems from 6 to 12 inches long; and heart-shaped leaves 1 to 1½ inches broad. The flowers are white or creamy-white, about ¾ inch across, and the 3 lower petals are conspicuously veined with purple. They are on slender stalks arising from the axils of the leaves; and bloom between March and June. It is often common in low, moist woods and meadows, and along streams. Other names given it are Pale Violet or Cream Violet.

RANGE: N.Y. to Ont. and Wis. south to Ga., Tenn. and Ark.

SMOOTH YELLOW VIOLET *(Viola pensylvanica)*

This violet has smooth, leafy stems 6 to 12 inches tall with from 1 to 3 basal leaves. The latter, and the few stem leaves are smooth, heart-shaped, and from 2 to 4 inches wide. The yellow flowers are about ¾ inch across, their 3 lower petals being veined with purple. It grows in moist woods and on cool rocky slopes; blooming in April or May.

RANGE: Conn. to Minn. south to Ga., Ala., Ark. and Okla.

DOWNY YELLOW VIOLET *(Viola pubescens)*

This violet resembles the preceding one but its stems, and the lower surfaces of its leaves, are somewhat soft-hairy. Usually there are no basal leaves, or occasionally only 1. It grows in somewhat drier woodlands; blooming in May or June.

RANGE: Me. to Que., Minn. and S.D. south to Del., w. Va., Tenn., Mo. and Neb. (Not illustrated)

LONG-SPURRED VIOLET *(Viola rostrata)*

The flowers of this violet are lilac-colored and have a slender spur about ½ inch long, or fully as long as the petals. It is a smooth little plant with several leafy stems 4 to 8 inches high. The flowers are on slender stalks which arise from the axils of the heart-shaped leaves. It grows in moist rich woodlands and on rocky slopes, blooming between April and June.

RANGE: Vt. to Que. and Wis. south to n. Ga. and n. Ala.

AMERICAN DOG VIOLET *(Viola conspersa)*

This is a small, smooth plant with branching and leafy stems 3 to 6 inches high at flowering time between late March and June. The flowers are about ½ inch across, pale violet, and have a blunt-tipped spur about half as long as the petals. It grows in moist woods and meadows.

RANGE: Que. to Minn. south to Md., n. Ga., n. Ala. and Tenn. (Not illustrated)

FIELD PANSY *(Viola rafinesquii)*

This little annual has smooth, slender, branching stems 3 to 8 inches high; and mostly top-shaped leaves an inch or less long, with large and deeply cut stipules at their base. Its flowers are about ½ inch across, creamy-white to pale blue or lilac, the 3 lower petals with purple veins. Naturalized from Europe.

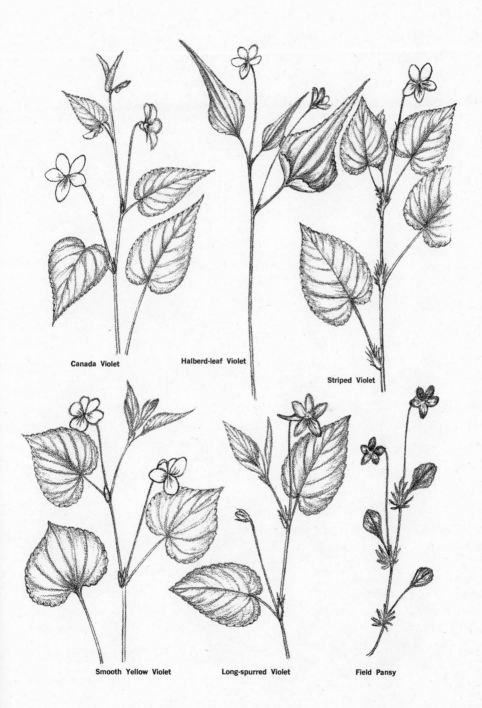

Canada Violet   Halberd-leaf Violet

Striped Violet

Smooth Yellow Violet   Long-spurred Violet   Field Pansy

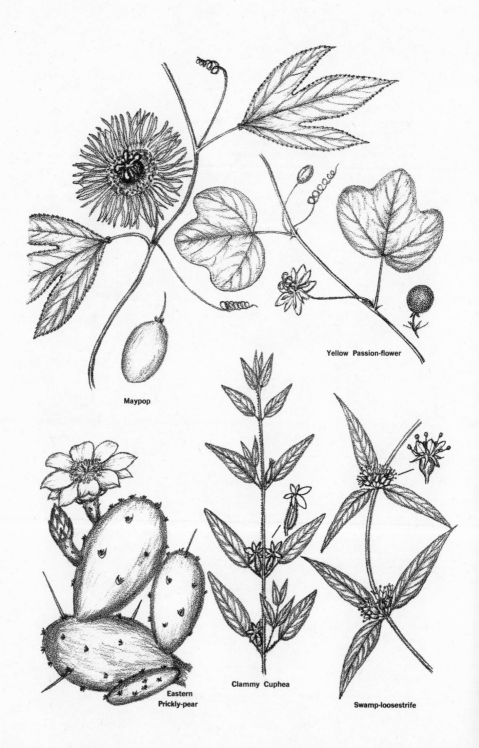

Yellow Passion-flower

Maypop

Eastern
Prickly-pear

Clammy Cuphea

Swamp-loosestrife

PASSION-FLOWER FAMILY (Passifloraceae)

Our members of this family have flowers with 5 sepals united at the base, the throat of the calyx bearing a "crown" of numerous fringe-like segments; 5 petals which are insterted on the calyx; 5 stamens, their filaments united to form a tube about the long stalk of the ovary but the large anthers separate. The fruits are many-seeded berries.

MAYPOP (Passiflora incarnata)

Also known as the Purple Passion-flower, this trailing or climbing vine grows abundantly in open woods, thickets, and dry fields in the South. Its leaves are 3-lobed, toothed on the margin, from 3 to 5 inches wide, and have stalks 1 to 2 inches long with a pair of prominent glands at their summits. The odd-looking lavender flowers are 2 to 3 inches broad and have a very striking fringed "crown". They bloom between May and August and are followed by egg-shaped fruits about 2 inches long. When ripe they are yellowish and edible. Passion-flowers get their name from a fancied resemblance of the flower parts to various implements of the crucifixion.

RANGE: Md. to s. Ohio, Ill., Mo. and Okla. south to Fla. and Tex.

YELLOW PASSION-FLOWER (Passiflora lutea)

This is a slender-stemmed trailing or climbing vine which grows in thickets and the borders of woods. It has leaves which are much broader than long, shallowly 3-lobed, untoothed on the margin, and 2 to 3 inches wide. Their stalks are ½ to 1½ inches long and have no glands at the summit. The greenish-yellow flowers are usually less than an inch across and bloom between June and September. They are followed by roundish, dark purple fruits about ½ inch in diameter.

RANGE: Pa. to Ill., Mo. and Kan. south to Fla. and Tex.

CACTUS FAMILY (Cactaceae)

Members of the Cactus Family have flowers in which the several to many sepals and petals have their bases joined to the ovary; numerous stamens which are inserted on the inside of the cup or tube formed by the union of the sepals and petals; and a pistil with 1 style.

EASTERN PRICKLY-PEAR (Opuntia compressa)

Prickly-pears have fleshy, flat, jointed stems which are green. The leaves are small and scale-like and are soon shed; but in their axils there are clusters of barbed hairs and occasional slender spines. The flowers are 2 to 3 inches across, yellow sometimes with a red star-shaped "eye", and have from 8 to 12 petals. They are followed by pear-shaped, dull purplish-red, fleshy fruits 1 to 1½ inches long. It grows in dry sandy and rocky places, blooming between May and July. Another name for it is Indian-fig, the fruits being edible. RANGE: Mass. to Minn. south to Fla., Ala., Mo. and Okla.

LOOSESTRIFE FAMILY (Lythraceae)

Members of this family have flowers with 4 to 6 sepals united into a tube; 4 to 6 petals and 4 to 12 stamens which are both inserted on the calyx tube; and a solitary pistil which is within but not united with the calyx tube.

CLAMMY CUPHEA (Cuphea viscocissima)

This is an erect, branched, very sticky-hairy little plant 6 to 20 inches tall; often very common in dry fields. It has broadly lance-shaped and slender stalked leaves from 1 to 1½ inches long. The purple flowers borne in the axils of the leaves are not very large and have 6 petals of varying size. It blooms between July and October. Another name for it is Blue Waxweed. RANGE: N.H. to Ill. and Iowa south to Ga. and La.

SWAMP-LOOSESTRIFE (Decodon verticillatus)

This plant with angled and arching stems 2 to 8 feet long is often common in swamps and other shallow waters. The submerged portions of the stems are thickened and spongy, and the tips often bend over and take root. It has lance-shaped leaves 2 to 5 inches long which are usually in whorls of 3. Pinkish-purple flowers about an inch long are clustered in the axils of the upper leaves, blooming from July to September. They have 5 petals, 5 long-stalked stamens and 5 shorter ones. It is sometimes called the Water-willow. RANGE: Me. to Ont. and Minn. south to Fla. and La.

181

MEADOW-BEAUTY FAMILY (Melastomaceae)

This is a large family of chiefly tropical plants. Our members of the family—the Meadow-beauties—are small plants with opposite 3- to 7-ribbed leaves. Their flowers have 4 sepals united to form an urn-shaped or vase-like tube with 4 lobes at the summit; 4 somewhat oblique, showy, and delicate petals; 8 stamens; and a pistil composed of 4 united carpels but with 1 long style and 1 stigma. The petals and sepals are attached near the rim of the calyx tube. The flowers open early in the morning and the petals are usually dropped by mid-day.

VIRGINIA MEADOW-BEAUTY *(Rhexia virginica)*

Deergrass is another name often given this attractive plant of bogs and moist, open, sandy places. It is a more or less hairy plant 1 to 2 feet tall, with a simple or branched stem which is 4-sided and has narrow wings. The leaves are oval or egg-shaped, 1 to 2 inches long, and have small bristly teeth on their margins. Its bright purple flowers are an inch or so across and have a glandular-hairy calyx tube. They bloom between May and September. RANGE: N.S. to Ont. south to Ga., Ala., Tenn. and Mo.

CILIATE MEADOW-BEAUTY *(Rhexia petiolata)*

This meadow-beauty has a smooth square stem from 1 to 2 feet tall which is simple or but slightly branched above. Its leaves are oval or egg-shaped, ½ to 1 inch long, and have a bristly fringed margin. The flowers are violet-purple, 1 to 1½ inches across, and are stalkless or very nearly so. They have a calyx tube which is quite smooth. This species grows in wet pinelands in the Southeast, blooming between June and September.
RANGE: se. Va. south to Fla. and La.

MARYLAND MEADOW-BEAUTY *(Rhexia mariana)*

The Maryland Meadow-beauty has a hairy, roundish or slightly 4-sided stem from 1 to 2 feet tall which is simple or somewhat branched above. Its leaves are lance-shaped or elliptic, 1 to 1½ inches long, bristly toothed on the margin, and are narrowed at the base to very short stalks. The flowers vary from pale purplish to whitish, are about an inch across, and have a glandular-hairy calyx tube shaped like a long-necked vase. It grows in coastal plain pinelands, swamps, and other moist sandy places; blooming between May and September.
RANGE: se. Mass. and e. Pa. south to Fla.; inland from Va. and Ky. south to Ga. and La.

SAVANNAH MEADOW-BEAUTY *(Rhexia alifanus)*

This, the largest and certainly the most beautiful of our meadow-beauties, is often abundant in the wetter coastal plain pinelands and savannahs of the Southeast. There it blooms between May and September. It is a smooth plant, more or less whitened by a waxy bloom, with roundish, slender, simple or sparingly branched stems from 1 to about 3 feet tall. The pairs of 1- to 3-inch lance-shaped leaves point upward. Its flowers are a bright rose-purple, about 2 inches across, and have a calyx tube bristling with reddish glandular hairs. RANGE: e. N.C. south to Fla. and west to La.

YELLOW MEADOW-BEAUTY *(Rhexia lutea)*

Of all our meadow-beauties, this is the only one having yellow flowers. It is a sparsely hairy plant with a 4-sided and branching stem from 6 to 10 inches tall; with pairs of narrow, pale green, and bristly margined leaves an inch or less long. The flowers are an inch or less across, with a calyx tube shaped like a narrow-necked vase and stamens with relatively short anthers. It grows in wet coastal plain pinelands, blooming between April and July. RANGE: e. N.C. south to Fla. and west to La.

AWN-PETALLED MEADOW-BEAUTY *(Rhexia aristosa)*

This meadow-beauty is distinguished by the little tail-like tips on its magenta or rose-purple petals. It has a slender, smooth, 4-sided stem 1 to 2 feet tall which is sometimes branched above. The leaves are ¾ to 1½ inches long, narrow, stalkless, and may have a few inconspicuous teeth. It grows in sandy swamps and wet coastal plain pinelands, blooming between June and September.
RANGE: N.J. and Del. south to Ga. and Ala. (Not illustrated)

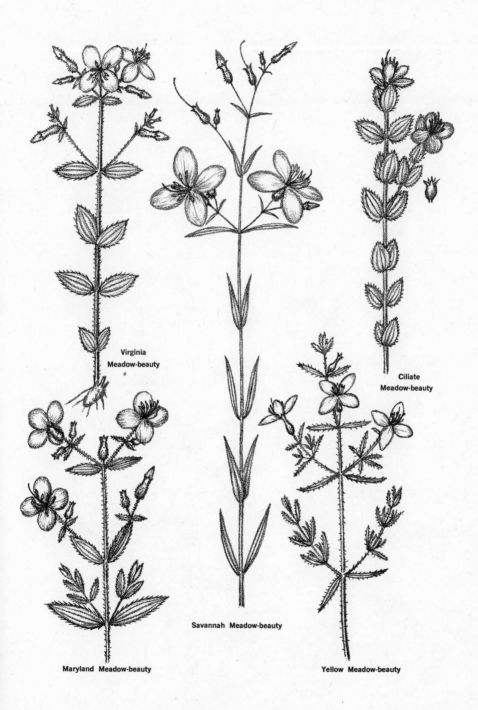

Virginia
Meadow-beauty

Ciliate
Meadow-beauty

Savannah Meadow-beauty

Maryland Meadow-beauty

Yellow Meadow-beauty

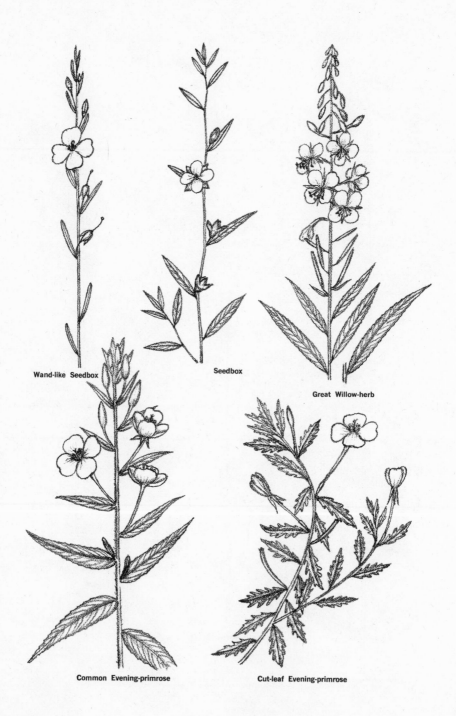

Wand-like Seedbox

Seedbox

Great Willow-herb

Common Evening-primrose

Cut-leaf Evening-primrose

EVENING-PRIMROSE FAMILY (Onagraceae)

Members of the Evening-primrose Family have flowers with usually 4 sepals which are united with the ovary of the pistil, and with each other to sometimes form a long tube; 4 petals, attached to the top of the calyx tube; 4 or 8 stamens, also attached to the calyx tube; and a solitary pistil consisting of 2 or 4 united carpels.

WAND-LIKE SEEDBOX *(Ludwigia virgata)*

Seedboxes have the 4 calyx lobes, and their 4 petals and stamens seated on the summit of the ovary, which later becomes a little box-like capsule full of tiny seeds. This one has an erect, simple or branching, smooth or minutely downy stem from 1 to 2½ feet tall. Its narrow, stalkless leaves are ¾ to about 1½ inches long and point upward. The flowers are about an inch across and the 4 yellow petals are much longer than the calyx lobes, which turn abruptly backward soon after the petals fall. It grows in wet coastal plain pinelands and bogs, blooming between June and September.

RANGE: e. Va. south to Fla.

SEEDBOX *(Ludwigia alternifolia)*

While similar in general appearance to the preceding species, this plant has lance-shaped leaves 1½ to 4 inches long which taper at the base to a short stalk. Its flowers are a little smaller and their 4 yellow petals are about the same length as the calyx lobes. The latter remain erect or spreading after the petals fall. It grows in marshes, wet meadows, and swamps; blooming between May and October.

RANGE: Mass. to Ont., Iowa and Kan. south to Fla. and Tex.

HAIRY SEEDBOX *(Ludwigia hirtella)*

This species is very similar to the preceding except that it is hairy throughout. It grows in wet pinelands and swamps from N.J. and Ky. south to Fla. and Tex. (Not illustrated)

GREAT WILLOW-HERB *(Epilobium angustifolium)*

The Great Willow-herb, or Fireweed, is one of some 20 species found in northeastern North America. It is an erect, smooth, leafy-stemmed plant 2 to 6 feet tall; with inch-wide, 4-petalled, bright purple or magenta flowers in a long terminal cluster. The leaves are almost stalkless, willow-like and 2 to 6 inches long. It grows in open woods, clearings, and in burned-over areas; blooming between July and September. The slender pods which follow the flowers contain numerous seeds with a tuft of silky hairs at one end.

RANGE: Lab. to Alaska south to Md., w. N.C., the Great Lakes region, S.D., Ariz. and Calif.

COMMON EVENING-PRIMROSE *(Oenothera biennis)*

This common plant has an erect, stout, more or less hairy, often red-tinged, leafy stem 2 to 6 feet tall. The flowers, which open in the evening and close the following morning, are 1 to 2 inches across; with 4 pale yellow petals atop the long and slender calyx tube. The lance-shaped leaves are stalkless, elliptic or lance-shaped, wavy-toothed on the margin and 1 to 6 inches in length. It grows in dry open places and along roadsides, blooming between June and September.

RANGE: Lab. to Alaska south to Fla. and Tex.

CUT-LEAF EVENING-PRIMROSE *(Oenothera laciniata)*

The smooth to somewhat hairy, branching stems of this often weedy plant sprawl close to the ground; and the numerous leaves are deeply toothed or lobed and mostly 1 to 2½ inches long. Its flowers are ¾ to 1½ inches across and have 4 pale yellow or yellowish-white petals. They are borne in the axils of the leaves and turn reddish in fading. It is a common plant in fields, waste places and along roadsides; blooming between March and October.

RANGE: N.J. to N.D. south to Fla. and Tex.

SEASIDE EVENING-PRIMROSE *(Oenothera humifusa)*

This species is a similar but hoary plant which grows on coastal sand dunes from N.J. south to Fla. and west to La.; blooming between May and October. (Not illustrated)

SHOWY EVENING-PRIMROSE *(Oenothera speciosa)*

The original home of this attractive little plant was on the prairies of the midwest, but it has escaped from cultivation and now grows wild in fields and along roadsides in the Southeast. It forms colonies by means of creeping underground stems which send up 6- to 12-inch stems bearing leaves and flowers. The nodding flower buds open into pink or white, 4-petalled flowers from 1½ to about 3 inches across; the flowering season being between May and July. Its leaves are lance-shaped, 1 to 3 inches long, and have wavy-toothed margins.

RANGE: Mo. and Kan. south to Tex.; naturalized from Va. and Ill. s. to Fla. and La.

COMMON SUNDROPS *(Oenothera fruticosa)*

This is quite a variable plant and botanists recognize several varieties. As a rule it has erect or ascending and usually branched stems from 1 to 3 feet high which may be hairy or nearly smooth. Its leaves range from narrowly lance-shaped or narrowly egg-shaped to oblong, and the margins may be untoothed or wavy-toothed. They are usually 1 to 4 inches long. The flowers are an inch to 2 inches across and have 4 inversely heart-shaped, bright yellow petals and a slender calyx tube; the ovary being distinctly club-shaped. As the flowers open during the daytime, the name "sundrops" is quite appropriate. It is common in dry to moist open woods, fields, and meadows; blooming between April and August. RANGE: N.H. to Mich. south to Fla., La. and Okla.

SMALL SUNDROPS *(Oenothera perennis)*

The Small Sundrops is a little plant with slender stems a few inches to nearly 2 feet tall, along which are small and narrow leaves. Usually it has a basal rosette of top-shaped leaves from 1 to 2 inches long. Its yellow flowers are in leafy-bracted end clusters. They are about ¾ inch across and open during the daytime. It grows in dry to moist fields and meadows, blooming between May and August; from Nfd. to Man. south to e. Va., n. Ga., nw. S.C., Tenn. and Mo. (Not illustrated)

BIENNIAL GAURA *(Gaura biennis)*

This is an erect, much-branched, leafy plant 2 to 5 feet tall; with a hairy or downy stem and flowers in long, narrow end clusters. The flowers are about ½ inch across, white at first but turning pinkish, with 4 petals turned upward and 8 stamens which are directed downward. The lance-shaped leaves have a few widely spaced teeth on the margin, and are 2 to 4 inches in length. It grows in dry thickets, fields and along roadsides; blooming between June and October. RANGE: Que. to Minn. south to n. Ga., Tenn. and Mo.

NARROW-LEAF GAURA *(Gaura angustifolia)*

This species, found in the coastal plain from N.C. south to Fla. and west to Tex., has very narrow leaves and capsules which are sharply angled. (Not illustrated)

ENCHANTER'S-NIGHTSHADE *(Circaea lutetiana* var. *canadensis)*

The Enchanter's-nightshades are woodland plants with opposite, rather long-stalked, wavy-toothed, egg-shaped leaves. The small white flowers are in long and narrow end clusters. They have but 2 petals which are so deeply notched that they appear to be four, and a pair of stamens. The fruits are oval-shaped pods covered with hooked bristles, and they often hitch a ride on one's clothing. This species has leaves from 2 to 4 inches long, rather firm in texture, dark green, and usually rounded at the base; and the stem is 8 inches to 3 feet tall. It blooms between June and August.

RANGE: N.S. to s. Ont. and N.D. south to Ga., Tenn., Mo. and Okla.

SMALLER ENCHANTER'S-NIGHTSHADE *(Circaea alpina)*

This is a smaller plant with leaves 1 to 2½ inches long which are heart-shaped at the base; and its rootstocks are thickened and tuber-like. It grows in cool moist woods and bogs and blooms between June and September.

RANGE: Lab. to Alaska south to N.Y., n.Ga., e.Tenn., the Great Lakes region, S.D., Colo., Utah and Wash.

CANADA ENCHANTER'S-NIGHTSHADE *(Circaea canadensis)*

This species is a similar plant with heart-shaped leaves 1½ to 4 inches long which are more coarsely toothed. It grows from Lab. to Que. and Minn. south to Me., Conn., and the mts. of Va. and W.Va.

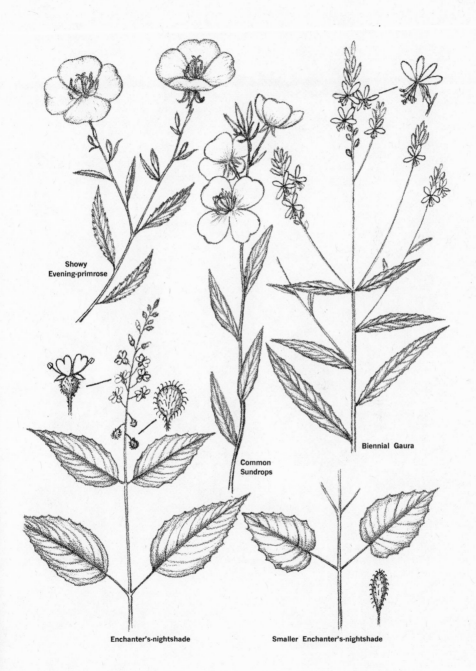

Showy
Evening-primrose

Common
Sundrops

Biennial Gaura

Enchanter's-nightshade

Smaller Enchanter's-nightshade

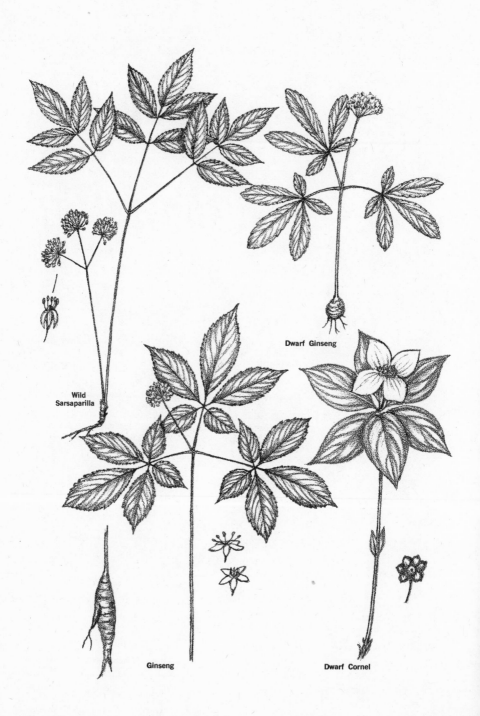

Dwarf Ginseng

Wild
Sarsaparilla

Ginseng

Dwarf Cornel

GINSENG FAMILY (Araliaceae)

Members of this family have small flowers in umbels. Our species have 5 sepals united with the ovary which has a disk at the top, 5 petals, 5 stamens, and a pistil composed of 2 to 5 united carpels with the same number of distinct styles. The fruit is a berry.

WILD SARSAPARILLA *(Aralia nudicaulis)*

This plant has but one long-stalked leaf which is divided into 3 parts; each of which are again divided into usually 5 egg-shaped or oval, sharply toothed leaflets 2 to 5 inches long. The naked flower stalk usually has 3 clusters of small greenish-white flowers; which are followed by round, purplish-black berries. Beneath the ground the plant has a creeping aromatic rootstock. It grows in rich moist woods, blooming from May to July.

RANGE: Nfd. to Man. south to Va., n. Ga., e. Tenn. and Mo.

AMERICAN SPIKENARD *(Aralia racemosa)*

This species is a coarse, herbaceous plant 4 to 10 feet tall. Its leaves are 2 to 3 feet in length and breadth. They are divided into 3 parts which are again pinnately divided into a number of heart-shaped leaflets 2 to 6 inches in length. The numerous umbels of small white flowers are in a large terminal cluster. It is often common in rich moist woods from N.B. to Man. south to n.Ga., Miss., Mo. and Kan.; blooming from June to August. (Not illustrated)

BRISTLY SARSAPARILLA *(Aralia hispida)*

This plant resembles the preceding but it is somewhat woody and bristly toward the base, and the bases of the leaflets are not heart-shaped. It grows in rocky or sandy open woods from Nfd. to Man. south to N.J., W.Va., Ill. and Minn.; blooming June to August. (Not illustrated)

GINSENG *(Panax quinquefolium)*

This is an erect plant 8 to 15 inches tall, bearing 3 leaves and a solitary umbel of 6 to 20 small yellowish-green flowers at the summit. The leaves are divided into 5 radiating leaflets which are 2 to 5 inches long and sharply toothed on the margin. The flowers are followed by bright crimson berries. Ginseng or "Sang" grows in rich, moist deciduous forests, and blooms between May and August. Excessive gathering of its rootstocks has eliminated it in many places.

RANGE: Que. to Man. south to Ga., Tenn. and Okla.

DWARF GINSENG *(Panax trifolium)*

Dwarf Ginseng has a stem 3 to 8 inches tall which bears 3 leaves and a solitary umbel of small white flowers. Each leaf is divided into 3 to 5 stalkless leaflets which are 1 to 1½ inches long and blunt at the tip. The flowers are followed by yellowish berries. The plant grows from a roundish pungent tuber about ½ inch in diameter, which gives it the common name of Groundnut. It grows in rich moist woods and blooms between May and August.

RANGE: N.S. to Minn. south to n. Ga., Tenn., Iowa and Neb.

DOGWOOD FAMILY (Cornaceae)

Most members of this family are trees or shrubs. The small flowers have 4 or 5 sepals united with the ovary, 4 or 5 petals, usually 4 stamens, and a solitary pistil which consists of 2 united carpels. The fruits are fleshy but have a large 2-seeded stone.

DWARF CORNEL *(Cornus canadensis)*

Often called the Bunchberry, this plant has a slender stem which runs underground and sends up erect branches from 2 to 10 inches tall. On them is what appears to be a whorl of usually 6 oval-shaped leaves, from 1 to 3 inches long, and what appears to be a solitary flower. Actually it is a dense little cluster of small greenish-yellow or sometimes purplish flowers, and the flower cluster is surrounded by usually 4 petal-like white bracts. Roundish bright red fruits follow the flowers which bloom between May and July. It grows in cool moist woods and bogs.

RANGE: Lab. to Alaska south to Md., W.Va., the Great Lakes region, S.D., N.Mex. and Calif.

189

All but a very few members of this large family have their flowers arranged in umbels. Usually the umbels are compound; the primary branches or rays of the flower cluster bearing the umbels at their tips. The flowers are small and have the 5 sepals united with the ovary. The 5 petals and 5 stamens are attached to the disk-like summit of the ovary which surrounds the 2 styles of the pistil. The pistil consists of 2 united carpels which mature as a pair of dry 1-seeded fruits, at maturity separating at the bottom but remaining joined at the tip to the stalk which rises between them. They have 5 primary ribs and sometimes 4 additional secondary ones, and through the walls run tubes containing a usually aromatic oil. Many members of the family are plants used for food or flavorings but some members are extremely poisonous.

KEY TO GENERA OF THE PARSLEY FAMILY

1. Flowers in dense heads.   ERYNGOS *(Eryngium)*
1. Flowers in umbels.

  2. Leaves simple, on long stalks arising from a creeping underground stem.

    3. Leaves roundish or kidney-shaped. Umbels with several flowers.
         WATER-PENNYWORTS (Hydrocotyle)

    3. Leaves egg-shaped. Umbels only 2- to 4-flowered.
         MARSH-PENNYWORT *(Centella)*

  2. Leaves compound, the blades divided into leaflets.

    3. Plants with yellow (sometimes purplish) flowers.

      4. Margins of the leaflets untoothed.   YELLOW PIMPERNEL *(Taenidia)*

      4. Margins of the leaflets toothed.

        5. Central flower in each umbel stalkless. Fruits with narrow and rounded ribs.   ALEXANDERS *(Zizia)*

        5. Central flower in each umbel stalked like the others. Fruits with winged ribs.   MEADOW-PARSNIPS *(Thaspium)*

    3. Plants with white or whitish flowers.

      4. Umbels 2- to 4-flowered, each umbel with a ternately divided leaf at its base.   HARBINGER-OF-SPRING *(Erigenia)*

      4. Umbels many-flowered.

        5. Bracts of the primary umbel large and pinnately divided into narrow segments. Fruits bristly.   CARROTS *(Daucus)*

        5. Bracts of the primary umbel rather small or absent.

          6. Fruits very slender, several times as long as broad. Plants with a licorice-like odor.   SWEET-CICELIES *(Osmorhiza)*

          6. Fruits not more than twice as long as broad.

            7. Leaflets often 6 inches or more broad. Plant stout and very woolly-hairy.   COW-PARSNIP *(Heracleum)*

            7. Leaflets much smaller. Entire plant not woolly-hairy and often quite smooth.

              8. Leaves merely pinnately compound, the leaflets narrow and evenly toothed.   WATER-PARSNIPS *(Sium)*

              8. Leaves doubly or even triply compound.

                9. Uppermost leaves reduced to large sheath-like stalks, or with blades much shorter than the sheaths. ANGELICAS *(Angelica)*

                9. Uppermost leaves otherwise.

                  10. Leaflets thin and deeply cut-toothed, cleft, or dissected. Primary umbel with small bracts at its base. Fruits with wavy ribs.   POISON-HEMLOCK *(Conium)*

                  10. Leaflets firm and merely toothed. Primary umbel without bracts at its base. Fruits with broadly rounded ribs.   WATER-HEMLOCK *(Cicuta)*

BUTTON-SNAKEROOT *(Eryngium yuccifolium)*

The Button-snakeroot, Eryngo, or Rattlesnake-master is a rather unique plant with a stout, stiffly erect, and smooth stem from 2 to 6 feet tall. At the base it has a cluster of long, narrow, stiff, and bristly-margined leaves which range from 6 inches to sometimes nearly 3 feet in length. The few and much smaller ones on the stem are similar but have clasping bases. Its flowers are whitish and crowded into globe-shaped heads from ½ to an inch across. This plant grows in dry to moist open woods or thickets and on prairies, blooming between June and August.

RANGE: N.J. to Mich., Minn. and Kan. south to Fla. and Tex.

WILD CARROT *(Daucus carota)*

This weedy ancestor of our cultivated carrots is a native of Europe which is now widely naturalized here in North America. It is frequently abundant in old fields, waste places, or along roadsides; blooming between May and September. The plant has a very bristly-hairy stem from 1 to 3 feet tall, and leaves which are pinnately divided and deeply cut into innumerable narrow segments. Its many umbels of small white flowers are disposed into a lacy-looking and flat-topped cluster usually 3 or 4 inches broad, most often with a solitary and deep purple floret in its center. Before the flower cluster is in full bloom, and again as the fruits form, it is hollow and its shape suggests that of a bird's nest. In fact it is often called the Queen Anne's-lace or Bird's-nest.

AMERICAN CARROT *(Daucus pusillus)*

This native American carrot is apt to be passed by as a poor specimen of the preceding species, for it looks very much like it. It is a smaller plant usually 6 inches to 2 feet high, and it has a minutely bristly stem and even more finely dissected leaves. It grows in dry fields and on barren hillsides from S.C. to Mo., se. Kan. and B.C. south to Fla. and Calif.; blooming in April and May. (Not illustrated)

MANY-FLOWERED WATER-PENNYWORT *(Hydrocotyle umbellata)*

Water-pennyworts get their name from their simple, roundish leaves; and the fact that they grow in wet places. This one has leaves ½ to 2 inches across which are attached to their stalks in the center of the leaf. Both the leaf and the flower stalks arise from creeping stems and are 2 to 6 inches long. The umbels of tiny white flowers appear between June and September. It grows in wet areas, swamps, and on shores.

RANGE: Mass. to Mich. south to Fla. and Tex.

AMERICAN WATER-PENNYWORT *(Hydrocotyle americana)*

This species has its leaves attached to the stalks at a heart-shaped base; and the flowers are in small, short-stalked clusters at the bases of the long-stalked leaves. It grows in wet meadows and woods from Nfd. to Minn. south to Md., w. N.C. and e. Tenn.; blooming between June and September. (Not illustrated)

Hydrocotyle bonariensis is a southern species with shield-shaped leaves and umbels in a branching cluster. It grows among beach dunes and in wet sandy areas in the coastal plain from N.C. south to Fla. and west to Tex.; blooming April to September. (Not illustrated)

OVATE-LEAF WATER-PENNYWORT *(Centella asiatica)*

The stems of this plant creep through the wet sand about the margins of pools, and from them the long-stalked leaves and flower clusters arise. The leaves are egg-shaped, 1 to 2 inches long, with a wavy-toothed margin and heart-shaped base. Flower clusters of 2 to 4 small flowers and a pair of bracts are produced between June and August.

RANGE: Del. south to Fla. and west to Tex.

HARBINGER-OF-SPRING *(Erigenia bulbosa)*

This is a dainty and smooth little plant 3 to 8 inches tall, with 1 or 2 finely dissected leaves and small umbels of white flowers with brown anthers. Both the leaves and the flower stalk arise from a small round tuber. It grows in rich deciduous woods and thickets, blooming between late February and April. Another name for it is Pepper-and-salt.

RANGE: w. N.Y. to Ont. and Wis. south to w. N.C., Ala., Miss. and Mo.

192

Button Snakeroot

Wild Carrot

**Many-flowered
Water-pennywort**

**Ovate-leaf
Water-pennywort**

Harbinger-of-spring

Smooth Sweet-cicely

Golden Alexanders

Heart-leaf Alexanders

Yellow Pimpernel

Meadow-parsnip

SMOOTH SWEET-CICELY *(Osmorhiza longistylis)*

The sweet-cicelies get their name from the pleasant licorice- or anise-like odor of their carrot-like roots. This species has a stem from 1 to about 3 feet tall which is usually smooth except at the points where the leaves are attached. The leaves are divided into 3 segments which are again divided, being quite fern-like in their appearance. Its small white flowers are in few-flowered umbels, blooming April to June. They are followed by slender fruits which taper at both ends and are bristly along the ribs. Those of this species are tipped with a pair of styles about ⅛ inch long. It grows in rich woodlands and on wooded slopes. Sometimes called Sweet-myrrh.

RANGE: N.S. to Alb. south to e. Va., n. Ala., and e. Tex.

HAIRY SWEET-CICELY *(Osmorhiza claytoni)*

This plant very closely resembles the preceding species but it is quite hairy or downy throughout. The slender fruits have very short styles, not more than $\frac{1}{16}$ inch long. It grows in woods and on wooded slopes, blooming between April and June.

RANGE: Que. to Sask. south to w. S.C., n. Ga., Ala., Ark. and Kan. (Not illustrated)

YELLOW PIMPERNEL *(Taenidia integerrima)*

The Yellow Pimpernel is an erect, smooth, slender-stemmed plant 1 to 3 feet tall, which is more or less whitened with a bloom. Its leaves are ternately divided into oval, egg-shaped, or lance-shaped leaflets ½ to an inch long which have untoothed margins. The small yellow flowers are in several long-stalked umbels, blooming April to June. It is a plant of dry rocky or sandy woods and thickets; southward only in the piedmont and mountains. RANGE: Que. to Minn. south to Ga. and Tex.

HEART-LEAF ALEXANDERS *(Zizia aptera)*

This is an erect and usually smooth plant from 1 to 2 feet tall. At the base it has long-stalked leaves which are egg-shaped to roundish, heart-shaped at the base, bluntly toothed on the margin and sometimes lobed, and 2 to 3 inches long. Those upward along the stem are short-stalked and divided into 3 leaflets. The small yellow flowers are in several umbels, the central flower in each umbel being stalkless. It grows in wooded bottomlands and meadows, blooming between April and June. The plant closely resembles the Meadow-parsnip.

RANGE: R.I. to Minn. and B.C. south to n. Fla., Miss., Mo., Col., Utah, and Ore.

GOLDEN ALEXANDERS *(Zizia aurea)*

Golden Alexanders is a smooth, erect plant 1 to 2 feet tall. Its leaves are all ternately divided and sometimes redivided into lance-shaped or egg-shaped, finely-toothed leaflets 1 to 2 inches long. The several umbels of small yellow flowers form a more or less flat-topped cluster. The central flower in each umbel is stalkless. It grows in wet woods and meadows, blooming between April and June. RANGE: Que. to Sask. south to n. Fla. and Tex.

BEBB'S ZIZIA *(Zizia trifoliata)*

This species has somewhat leathery textured and more coarsely toothed leaflets than the preceding, and the umbel has very slender primary rays. It is found from Va. and W. Va. south to n. Fla. and Ala., blooming in April or May. (Not illustrated)

MEADOW-PARSNIP *(Thaspium trifoliatum)*

One variety of this plant has greenish or purplish flowers and is called the Purple Meadow-parsnip or Purple Alexanders. More common and widespread is the variety which has yellow flowers. Both are smooth erect plants 1 to 2½ feet tall. The long-stalked basal leaves may be undivided, or divided into 3 egg-shaped to lance-shaped, toothed leaflets 1 to 2 inches long. All of the flowers in the umbels are stalked. It grows in open woods and thickets, blooming between April and June. It closely resembles the Heart-leaf Alexanders. RANGE: N.Y. to Minn. south to Fla. and La.

HAIRY-JOINTED MEADOW-PARSNIP *(Thaspium barbinode)*

This plant has its basal leaves more dissected and has whitish hairs surrounding the stems at the nodes. It grows in rich woods and along streams from N.Y. to Minn. south to Fla., Miss. and Okla. (Not illustrated)

COW-PARSNIP *(Heracleum maximum)*

This is a conspicuous woolly-hairy plant 4 to 8 feet tall, with a stout grooved stem and very large leaves. Between June and August it displays umbels of white or purple-tinged flowers 6 inches to nearly a foot across. Although it has a rank odor the plant is not poisonous. It grows in moist open places and thickets.

RANGE: Lab. to Alaska south to n. Ga., Tenn., Mo., N. Mex. and Calif.

WATER-HEMLOCK *(Cicuta maculata)*

The roots of water hemlocks resemble small sweet-potatoes, have an odor similar to parsnips, and are deadly poisonous. This species, often called the Spotted Cowbane, Musquash-root and Beaver-poison, has a stout erect stem 3 to 6 feet tall which is usually streaked or spotted with purple. The lower leaves are often a foot long and pinnately divided, or redivided, into a number of lance-shaped, sharply toothed leaflets 1 to 5 inches long. The small white flowers are in umbels 2 to 5 inches across. It grows in swamps, wet meadows and thickets; blooming between May and August.

RANGE: N.B. to Man. south to Fla. and Tex.

BULB-BEARING WATER-HEMLOCK *(Cicuta bulbifera)*

This is a slender plant 1 to 3 feet tall, with very narrow leaflets, and bearing small bulbs in the axils of the upper leaves. It grows in wet places from Nfd. to B.C. south to Va. Ind., Neb., Mont. and Ore. (Not illustrated)

WATER-HEMLOCK *(Cicuta mexicana)*

This species is common southeastward but the amateur will find it difficult to separate it from *Cicuta maculata.* (Not illustrated)

WATER-PARSNIP *(Sium suave)*

The Water Parsnip has an erect, branching stem 2 to 6 feet tall which is longitudinally furrowed. Its leaves are pinnately divided into 5 or more very narrow, lance-shaped, sharply and evenly toothed leaflets 1½ to 5 inches long. The lower ones are long-stalked and submersed leaves are often finely dissected. Its small white flowers are in umbels 2 to 4 inches across. It grows in swamps, wet meadows, and on muddy shores; blooming between June and September.

RANGE: Nfd. to B.C. south to Fla., La. and Calif.

POISON-HEMLOCK *(Conium maculatum)*

This is a European plant, the one used by the ancient Greeks for putting prisoners to death. It is a dangerous plant for all parts of it are poisonous, and it is now widely naturalized here in bottomlands, waste places, etc. It is an erect, much-branched, smooth plant with purple-spotted and hollow stems 2½ to 5 feet tall. Its large leaves are divided and redivided into numerous, thin, egg-shaped leaflets which are sharply toothed and deeply cut. The small white flowers are in umbels from 1 to 3 inches across, blooming between June and August. The fruits are rather roundish, somewhat flattened, and have prominent wavy ribs.

HAIRY ANGELICA *(Angelica venenosa)*

This is a rather slender-stemmed plant from 2 to about 6 feet tall, which is somewhat hairy toward the summit. The lower and basal leaves are often a foot long and divided into rather thickish, oval to lance-shaped leaflets 1 to 2 inches long, with toothed margins. Those on the upper part of the stem are reduced to sheathing leaf stalks, with or without small blades. The small white flowers are in umbels 2 to 4 inches across, blooming between July and September. It grows in dry woods, thickets, and clearings.

RANGE: Conn. to Mich. and Ill. south to Fla., Ala., Miss. and Mo.

PURPLE-STEMMED ANGELICA *(Angelica atropurpurea)*

This is a stouter plant with a purple or purple-blotched, smooth stem 3 to 10 feet tall. The leaf stalks have large, swollen, and veiny sheathing bases; and the umbels are 4 to 10 inches broad. It grows in swamps and wet bottomlands from Lab. to Wis. south to Md., W. Va., Ohio and Ill. Blooming May to September. (Not illustrated)

196

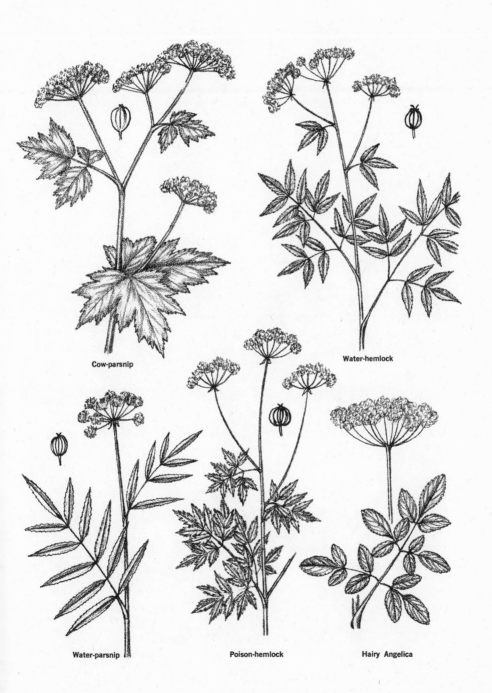

Cow-parsnip

Water-hemlock

Water-parsnip

Poison-hemlock

Hairy Angelica

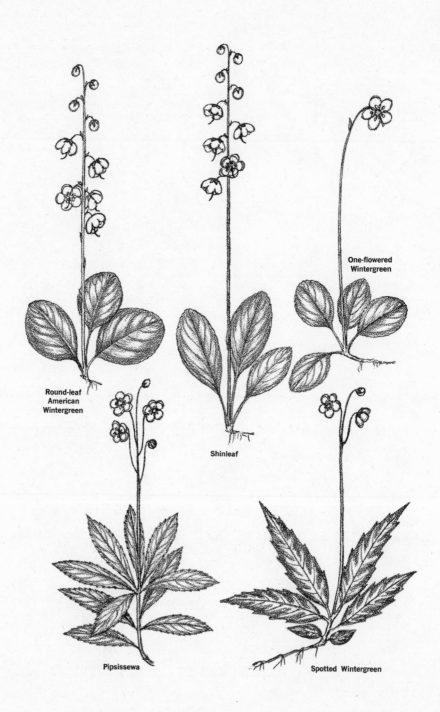

One-flowered
Wintergreen

Round-leaf
American
Wintergreen

Shinleaf

Pipsissewa

Spotted Wintergreen

WINTERGREEN FAMILY (Pyrolaceae)

Members of this family have flowers with a radial or slightly bilateral symmetry. They have 5 sepals, somewhat united at the base; 5 petals, barely united at the base; 10 stamens; and a solitary pistil consisting of 5 united carpels, with 1 style and stigma. The fruits are capsules containing a large number of very small seeds. The name "wintergreen" refers to the evergreen leaves.

ROUND-LEAF AMERICAN WINTERGREEN *(Pyrola rotundifolia var. americana)*

On an erect flower stalk 6 to 20 inches tall, this plant has a few scaly bracts and a narrow cluster of nodding white flowers. Each one is about ⅔ inch across and they are quite fragrant. At the base of the flower stalk are several oval or roundish leaves which are somewhat leathery in texture, lustrous above, obscurely toothed on the margin, and from 1 to 3 inches long. It grows in rather dry woods and clearings, blooming between May and August. RANGE: N.S. to Ont. south to N.C., Ky., Ind., and Wis.

SHINLEAF *(Pyrola elliptica)*

The Shinleaf has an erect, naked flower stalk 5 to 10 inches tall; on which is a narrow cluster of nodding, white, fragrant flowers about ⅔ inch across. At the base of this stalk are several leaves which are oval or elliptic, rather thin in texture, dull green above, obscurely toothed, and from 1 to 3 inches in length. It grows in dry to fairly moist, rich woods; blooming between June and August.
RANGE: Nfd. to B.C. south to W. Va., Ohio, Ill., Iowa, S.D. and N. Mex.

ONE-SIDED WINTERGREEN *(Pyrola secunda)*

This species has whitish or greenish yellow flowers in a dense 1-sided cluster; and elliptic or egg-shaped, somewhat leathery, lustrous leaves which are usually pointed at the tip. It grows in dry or moist woods and thickets and bogs from Nfd. to Alaska south to Va., the Great Lakes region, Iowa, S.D., N. Mex. and Calif. (Not illustrated)

PINK WINTERGREEN *(Pyrola asarifolia)*

The Pink Wintergreen has distinctive pale pink to crimson flowers; and heart-shaped, leathery, lustrous leaves. It grows in rich, wet woods and swamps from Nfd. to Yuk. Ter. south to N.Y., n. Ind., Wis., S.D. and N. Mex. (Not illustrated)

ONE-FLOWERED WINTERGREEN *(Moneses uniflora)*

This plant can be distinguished from the *pyrolas* by its solitary flower at the tip of its erect 2- to 6-inch stem. It is about ¾ inch across, white or pink-tinged, and quite fragrant. Below the flower the stalk bears only 1 or 2 small bracts. The leaves at the base of it are roundish or egg-shaped, rather thin, obscurely toothed, and from ½ to 1¼ inches long. It grows in cool, mossy woods and in bogs, blooming between June and August. RANGE: N.S. to Ont. south to n. Ga., Ohio, Ill. and Minn.

PIPSISSEWA *(Chimaphila umbellata)*

Our Pipsissewa, or Prince's-pine, is a variety of a plant found throughout the northern portion of the Northern Hemisphere. It is a little plant with erect leafy flowering stems 6 to 12 inches high, arising from extensively creeping underground stems. Its leaves are nearly whorled, 1 to 2½ inches long, bright green and shining, sharply toothed, and distinctly broadest toward their tips. The white or pale pinkish flowers are ½ to ⅔ inch across and in an umbel-like end cluster. The Pipsissewa grows in dry woodlands, blooming between May and August. RANGE: N.S. to Ont. south to Ga., Ohio, Ill. and Minn.

SPOTTED WINTERGREEN *(Chimaphila maculata)*

The Spotted Wintergreen, or Spotted Pipsissewa, is similar in habit and stature to the preceding species. Its leaves, however, are broadest toward the base, egg-shaped or lance-shaped, from 1 to 3 inches long and have sharp but rather widely spaced teeth on the margin. Even in winter, the plant is brought to our attention by the white mottling along the veins of its otherwise dark green leaves. Between May and August a few white or pinkish flowers, about ¾ inch across, are borne in an end cluster. It usually grows in rather dry rich woodlands.
RANGE: N.H. to Ont. and Mich. south to Ga., Ala. and Tenn.

INDIAN-PIPE *(Monotropa uniflora)*

This is a strange and ghostly-looking plant which grows in dimly lighted, rich, moist woodlands. Containing no chlorophyll, the entire plant is waxy-white, or sometimes pinkish, and in drying becomes blackish. A solitary flower about ¾ inch long, with 4 or 5 petals and 10 stamens, nods at the end of a scaly stalk from 4 to 10 inches tall. The flower stalks are usually in clusters, arising from a ball-like mass of roots. The plant is a saprophyte, obtaining its nourishment from the decaying vegetable matter in the soil. Also known as the Corpse-plant, it blooms between June and October.
RANGE: Nfd. to Alaska south to Fla., Tex. and Calif.

PINE-SAP *(Monotropa hypopithys)*

The Pine-sap is a somewhat hairy or downy plant with stalks and flowers ranging from lemon-yellow to tawny or red, and darkening in drying. It has several flowers, each about ¾ inch long, toward the top of a scaly stalk 4 to 14 inches in height. Growing in rich woodlands, it blooms between May and October. Another name for it is False Beech-drops. RANGE: Nfd. and Que. to Ont. south to Fla. and La.

HEATH FAMILY (Ericaceae)

Members of this family are chiefly woody plants. Their flowers have 4 or 5 sepals, united toward the base; 4 or 5 petals, which are more or less united; 8 to 10 stamens; and a solitary pistil consisting of 5 to 10 united carpels.

TEABERRY *(Gaultheria procumbens)*

The Teaberry has slender stems which creep on or beneath the surface of the ground, sending up erect branches 2 to 6 inches high which bear the leaves and flowers. Its urn-shaped white flowers are about ⅜ inch long and usually solitary in the leaf axils. They are followed by globular, bright red, berry-like fruits about ⅜ inch in diameter. The leaves are elliptic, oval, or top-shaped, ¾ to 2 inches long, somewhat leathery, and have low bristle-tipped teeth on their margins. The plant has an oil of wintergreen odor and taste. It grows in woods and thickets, blooming between June and August. Other names for it are Mountain-tea, Checkerberry, and Spicy Wintergreen.
RANGE: Nfd. to Man. south to Ga., Ala., Wis. and Minn.

TRAILING ARBUTUS *(Epigaea repens)*

Trailing Arbutus is a prostrate or trailing plant with branches 6 to 15 inches long; and evergreen, veiny, oval to roundish leaves 1 to 3 inches long, which are heart-shaped at the base. Its fragrant whitish or pink flowers are about ⅝ inch long, and are in small axillary or end clusters; blooming between late February and May. Also known as the Mayflower and Ground-laurel, it grows in sandy or rocky woods and banks.
RANGE: Lab to Sask. south to Fla. and Miss.

GALAX FAMILY (Galacaceae)

Members of this family have flowers with 5 sepals, united at the base; 5 petals, united toward the base; 5 stamens alternating with 5 sterile ones or staminodia, either attached to the corolla or joined with one another to form a tube; and a pistil composed of 3 united carpels, with a single style.

GALAX *(Galax aphylla)*

Galax has long-stalked, roundish heart-shaped, thickish, shiny leaves 1 to 3 inches across, with small bristly teeth on their margins. Bright green in summer, they become bronzed or reddish during the winter. The small white flowers are arranged in a narrow cluster on a naked flower stalk 10 to 18 inches tall, blooming May to July. It grows chiefly in mountain and upland woods. Another name for it is Beetleweed.
RANGE: Va. and W. Va. south to n. Ga. and n. Ala.

SHORTIA *(Shortia galacifolia)*

The Shortia, or Oconee-bells, is an interesting little plant which spreads by means of short runners and often forms large colonies. It has a very short stem with long-stalked, shiny, oval or roundish, wavy-toothed leaves ¾ to 2½ inches long. The white or pinkish flowers are about an inch across, with 5 irregularly toothed petals, and are on naked stalks 3 to 6 inches long; blooming during March and April. It grows in wooded ravines and along streams in the foothills and lower slopes of the mountains from sw. Va. south to n. Ga.

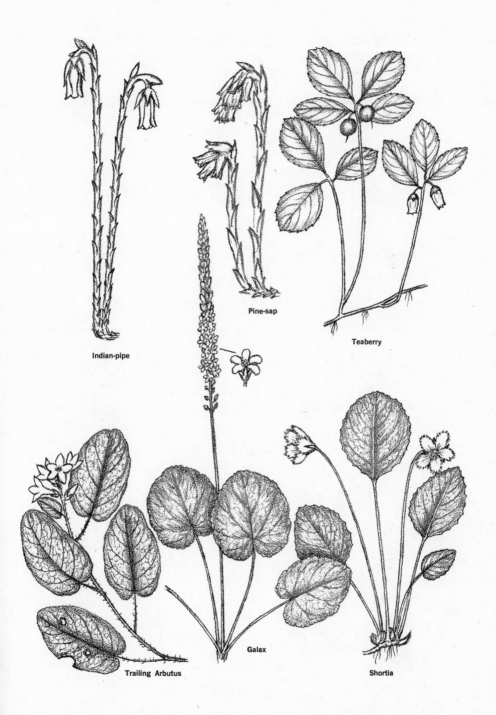

Indian-pipe

Pine-sap

Teaberry

Trailing Arbutus

Galax

Shortia

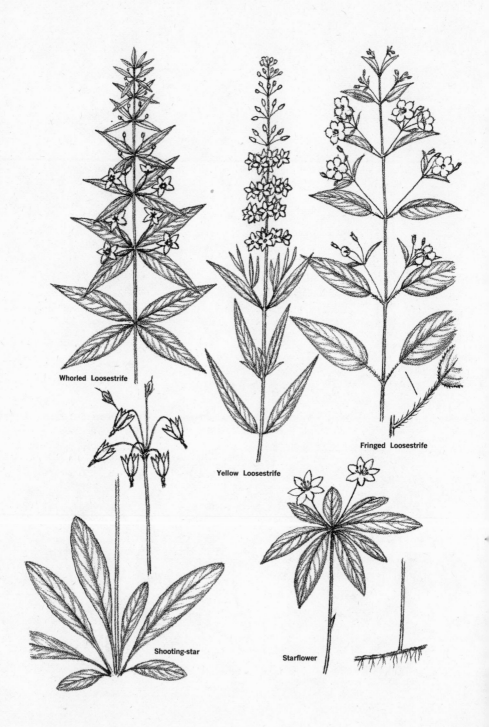

Whorled Loosestrife

Yellow Loosestrife

Fringed Loosestrife

Shooting-star

Starflower

PRIMROSE FAMILY (Primulaceae)

Members of the Primrose Family have flowers with 5 to 8 sepals which are united at the base to form a sort of cup; 5 to 8 petals, somewhat united at the base; 5 to 8 stamens which are attached to the bases of the petals; and a single pistil with a 1-chambered ovary, the seeds being attached to a stalk in its center.

WHORLED LOOSESTRIFE *(Lysimachia quadrifolia)*

This common plant of open woodlands and thickets has a simple, smooth or sparingly hairy stem from 1 to 2 feet tall. Along it are several whorls of usually 4 lance-shaped, stalkless leaves from 1½ to 3½ inches long. The star-like, 5-petalled, yellow flowers are about ½ inch across and have a reddish center. They are on thread-like stalks arising from the axils of the leaves; blooming between May and August. It is also known as the Four-leaf Loosestrife.

RANGE: Me. to Ont. and Wis. south to Ga., Ala., Tenn. and Ill.

YELLOW LOOSESTRIFE *(Lysimachia terrestris)*

Often called Swamp-candles, this loosestrife has a simple or branched stem 8 inches to about 2 feet tall, which ends in a long and narrow cluster of flowers. Each flower is about ⅓ inch across, star-like and 5-petalled, and yellow with purplish streaks or dots. It grows in swamps and low wet woods, blooming between May and August.

RANGE: Nfd. to Ont. and Wis. south to Ga., Ky. and Iowa.

FRINGED LOOSESTRIFE *(Lysimachia ciliata)*

The Fringed Loosestrife has an erect, simple or branched stem from 1 to 4 feet tall. On it are pairs of narrowly egg-shaped leaves from 2 to 6 inches long, which have slender leaf stalks which are fringed with hairs—hence the name of the plant. Its flowers are about ¾ inch across, the 5 yellow petals being ragged-toothed and with a minute point at the summit. They bloom between June and August, nodding on slender stalks at the tip of the stem or its branches.

RANGE: N.S. to B.C. south to Fla. and Tex.

SOUTHERN LOOSESTRIFE *(Lysimachia tonsa)*

This species resembles the preceding species but the leaf stalks are not hairy-fringed. It grows in dry upland woods and rocky slopes from Va., Ky. and Ark. south to Ga. and Ala.; blooming between May and July. (Not illustrated)

LANCE-LEAF LOOSESTRIFE *(Lysimachia lanceolata)*

This plant has lance-shaped leaves which taper at both ends and often have no evident leaf stalks. The flowers are similar to those of the preceding species. It is a slender-stemmed plant which grows in dry to moist open woods from Pa. to s. Mich. and Wis. south to Fla. and La. (Not illustrated)

SHOOTING-STAR *(Dodecatheon meadia)*

The Shooting-star or American Cowslip is a smooth plant with a basal cluster of narrowly elliptic or top-shaped leaves 3 to 10 inches long, their bases often marked with red. The distinctive flowers are about an inch long and have 5 lilac, pink or white petals which point backward; the stamens forming a beak-like cone in the center of the flower. From a few to sometimes a hundred or more of the flowers are arranged in an umbel, and nod from the summit of a naked flower stalk 8 inches to 2 feet tall. It grows in rich moist woods, meadows, prairies and cliffs; blooming between late March and June.

RANGE: D.C. to w. Pa., Wis. and Alb. south to n. Ga., La. and Tex.

STARFLOWER *(Trientalis borealis)*

Also known as the Chickweed-wintergreen, this little plant has a creeping rootstock which sends up erect branches 3 to 9 inches tall. These have a whorl of leaves at the summit; and 1 or 2 white, usually 7-petalled flowers about an inch across, which stand on long and thread-like stalks. The leaves vary considerably in size, from 1½ to about 4 inches in length, and are lance-shaped, pointed at both ends, and are stalkless or nearly so. It grows in moist woods, thickets, and on hummocks in swamps; blooming between May and July

RANGE: Lab. to Sask. south to Va., Ohio, Ill. and Minn.

LOGANIA FAMILY (Loganiaceae)

Members of this family have flowers with 4 or 5 partly united sepals; 4 or 5 petals partly united to form a tube; 4 or 5 stamens, united with the corolla tube; and pistil composed of 2 united carpels, with 1 to 4 style branches or stigmas. They typically have opposite leaves with untoothed margins.

YELLOW-JESSAMINE *(Gelsemium sempervirens)*

The Yellow-jessamine grows most profusely in the woods and thickets in the coastal regions of the South, where it often begins to bloom in late February. Elsewhere it may be as late as April or early May before the showy, trumpet-shaped, and very fragrant yellow flowers appear. They are 1 to 1½ inches long, with 5 rounded lobes, and have a slightly bilateral symmetry. The plant is a climber with slender, smooth, shining stems often 20 feet in length. It has pairs of lance-shaped, short-stalked leaves 1½ to 3 inches long which remain on the vine over winter. Also called the Carolina-jessamine and Evening-trumpet flower, it has found favor in cultivation. Its rootstocks are used medicinally, and children have been poisoned by sucking nectar from its blossoms.
RANGE: Va. and Ark. south to Fla, and Tex.

INDIAN-PINK *(Spigelia marilandica)*

This is a smooth plant with a simple erect stem from 6 to 18 inches tall. It has pairs of stalkless, egg-shaped to broadly lance-shaped, pointed leaves from 2 to 4 inches long; and a terminal cluster of showy flowers which bloom during May or June. They are shaped like slender trumpets 1½ to 2 inches long, with 5 rather small lobes at the summit. On the outside they are bright red or scarlet, but inside they are yellow. Several are borne in a 1-sided cluster. Also known as the Carolina Pinkroot or Wormgrass, its rootstocks have medicinal properties. It grows in rather rich and moist woodlands.
RANGE: Md. to Ohio, Ind., Mo. and Okla. south to Fla. and Tex.

GENTIAN FAMILY (Gentianaceae)

Members of the Gentian Family have flowers with from 4 to 12 partially united sepals; 4 to 12 partially or often well united petals; stamens as many as the petals or corolla lobes and attached to them; and a solitary pistil composed of 2 united carpels, the ovary having a single chamber which contains many ovules. They typically have opposite leaves with untoothed margins.

LARGE MARSH-PINK *(Sabatia dodecandra)*

Also known as the Sea-pink, this plant has attractive flowers 1½ to 2½ inches across, usually pink but sometimes white with a bright yellow "eye", and from 8 to 12 petal-like corolla lobes. They bloom between July and September. The plant has a simple or sparingly branched stem 1 to 2 feet high, on which are pairs of lance-shaped or narrower leaves and the terminal flowers. The basal leaves are larger, 1½ to 3 inches long, and are rather spoon-shaped. It grows on the sandy borders of pools and in brackish or salt marshes, blooming between June and August. RANGE: Conn. south to Fla. and west to La.

MANY-PETALLED MARSH-PINK *(Sabatia gentianoides)*

Very attractive when in flower, this species has a simple or branched stem 1 to 2 feet high; on which are pairs of rather stiff, very narrow, stalkless and pointed leaves from 1½ to 4 inches long. Its flowers are 1½ to 2 inches across, lilac to purplish-pink, with 8 to 12 petal-like corolla lobes but no yellow "eye"—just the yellow stamens in the center. They differ from the flowers of most marsh-pinks in having curved rather than coiled anthers. It grows in bogs and savannahs in the southern coastal plain, blooming during July and August. RANGE: se. N.C. south to Fla. and west to Tex.

SEA-PINK *(Sabatia stellaris)*

The Sea-pink has starry 5-petalled deep pink to white flowers 1 to 1½ inches across, with a central yellow "star" which is bordered with red. They are usually numerous but solitary at the tips of the branches. The plant has a roundish or slightly 4-angled stem from 6 inches to about 20 inches tall; and narrowly lance-shaped or top-shaped leaves from ½ to 2 inches long. It grows in salt and brackish marshes along the coast; blooming between July and October.
RANGE: Mass. south to Fla, and west to La.

204

Yellow-jessamine

Indian-pink

Large Marsh-pink

Many-petalled Marsh-pink

Sea-pink

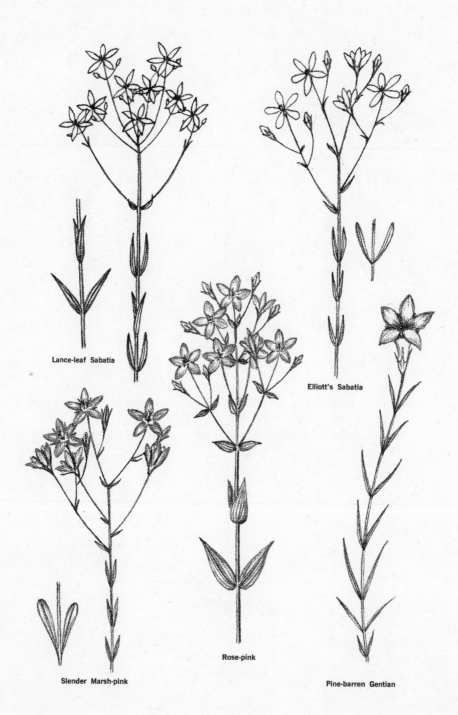

Lance-leaf Sabatia

Elliott's Sabatia

Rose-pink

Slender Marsh-pink

Pine-barren Gentian

LANCE-LEAF SABATIA *(Sabatia difformis)*

This is a smooth plant with a somewhat 4-angled and slender stem from 1 to about 3 feet tall. On it are pairs of narrowly lance-shaped leaves 1 to 2 inches long. Its flowers are white, ¾ to an inch across, and have 5 petal-like corolla lobes. They are quite numerous and arranged in a terminal flower cluster which has opposite, or forking branches. It is often exceedingly abundant in the wet coastal plain pinelands and savannahs, blooming between July and September.

RANGE: N.J. south to Fla.

ELLIOTT'S SABATIA *(Sabatia brevifolia)*

Elliott's Sabatia is a smooth plant with a roundish or slightly ridged stem from 1 to 2 feet high; with pairs of very narrow leaves ½ to nearly an inch long. The flowers are white or cream-colored, about ¾ inch across, and have 5 petal-like corolla lobes. They are quite numerous but arranged in a terminal flower cluster which has alternate branches. It grows in coastal plain pinelands, blooming September and October.

RANGE: se. S.C. south to Fla. and Ala.

SLENDER MARSH-PINK *(Sabatia campanulata)*

The Slender Marsh-pink has pale crimson, pink, or occasionally white flowers about an inch across, with 5 petal-like corolla lobes and a yellow "eye". It is a smooth plant with a very slender stem, or stems, from 1 to 2 feet high; with pairs of often very narrow leaves 1 to 1½ inches long, tapering to the tip from below the middle. The flowers are generally numerous and the flower cluster has alternate branching. It grows in savannahs and wet sandy or boggy places, blooming between June and August.

RANGE: Coast from Mass. south to Fla. and La.; inland from Va. and Ind. south to Ga. and Ala.

ROSE-PINK *(Sabatia angularis)*

This is our most common and best known species of *Sabatia* for it grows in open woodlands, thickets, meadows and marshes over a wide range. Known also as the Bitterbloom, it has a much branched and sharply 4-angled stem from 1 to about 3 feet tall. The paired leaves are egg-shaped, ¾ to 1½ inches long, and have heart-shaped clasping bases. The numerous flowers are rose-pink, rarely white, about an inch across, with 5 petal-like corolla lobes and a greenish-yellow star-shaped "eye". The branching of the flower cluster is opposite. This is one of our more attractive mid-summer wild flowers. It blooms in July and August.

RANGE: N.Y. and Ont. to Wis. and Mo. south to Fla., La. and Okla.

PINE-BARREN GENTIAN *(Gentiana autumnalis)*

This is a distinctive plant which has a solitary flower at the tip of a slender, simple or few-forked stem 6 to 18 inches tall. Along the stem are a number of pairs of rather thick and very narrow leaves from 1 to 2 inches in length. The flower has an almost lily-like, funnel-shaped corolla about 2 inches long, which is bright indigo-blue or rarely lilac or whitish, and is often spotted with greenish or brown within. The corolla lobes are much longer than the small fringed lobes between them. It grows in savannahs and moist, sandy coastal plain pinelands; blooming from September to early December. It is also known as the One-flowered Gentian.

RANGE: N.J. south to S.C.

FRINGED GENTIAN *(Gentiana crinita)*

The Fringed Gentian has violet-blue flowers about 2 inches long, with the 4 petals united below into a bell-shaped tube and with the free ends conspicuously fringed. It has a stem 1 to 3 feet tall, with pairs of lance-shaped leaves 1 to 2 inches long on the stem and spoon-shaped ones at the base. It grows in cool, moist, open woods and meadows; blooming in September and October. RANGE: Me. to Man. south to Ga., Ind. and Iowa.

SMALLER FRINGED GENTIAN *(Gentiana procera)*

This species is similar to the preceding but is only 6 to 18 inches tall, and the very narrow leaves show only a prominent midrib. The flowers are 1 to 2 inches long and the corolla lobes are much shorter fringed. It grows in wet or boggy places from w. N.Y. and s. Ont. to Alaska south to Ohio, Iowa and N.D. (Not illustrated)

CLOSED GENTIAN *(Gentiana andrewsii)*

The club-shaped flowers of this and the next species do not open, nor do they show prominent corolla lobes at the tip. If spread open, the pale appendages between the narrower corolla lobes show a fringed margin in this species. The deep violet-blue (rarely white) flowers are 1 to 2 inches long, and clustered in the axils of the upper leaves. It grows in moist open places and thickets, blooming between August and October. Often called the Blind or Bottle Gentian. RANGE: Mass. and Que. to Man. south to Ga. and Ark.

CLOSED GENTIAN *(Gentiana clausa)*

This species is very similar to the preceding. It has porcelain blue flowers which turn violet-blue. The membranes between the corolla lobes are 2- to 3-cleft but not fringed, and are no wider than the corolla lobes. It grows in rich moist woods and meadows from Me. to Minn. south to w. N.C., Tenn. and Mo. (Not illustrated)

STRIPED GENTIAN *(Gentiana villosa)*

This species has slender, smooth stems 6 inches to 2 feet tall; with pairs of egg-shaped leaves ½ to 2 inches long, which are stalkless and have clasping bases. Its flowers are 1 to 3 inches long, club-shaped, greenish-white to purplish-green with purple stripes, and have 5 corolla lobes which become erect. It grows on wooded slopes and stream banks, blooming from August to November. Also called Samson's Snakeroot.
RANGE: N.J. and Pa. south to Fla. and La.

SOAPWORT GENTIAN *(Gentiana saponaria)*

This plant has a corolla open only slightly at the summit and the pleats or membranes are nearly or quite equal to the corolla lobes. It grows in wet places and moist woods from N.Y. to Ind. and Minn. south to Fla. and Tex., blooming September to November. (Not illustrated)

STIFF GENTIAN *(Gentiana quinquefolia)*

Also called Agueweed and Gall-of-the-earth, this species has stiffly erect, wing-angled stems 6 inches to 2 feet tall. The paired leaves are egg-shaped, ½ to 2 inches long, stalkless, and with clasping bases. Its flowers are about ¾ inch long, funnel-shaped, violet-blue to lilac, and have no pleats between the 5 triangular lobes. They are borne in both end and axillary clusters and bloom between August and October. It grows in dry to moist open woods, and along stream banks and roadsides.
RANGE: Me. to Ont. south to Fla., La. and Mo.

CATESBY'S GENTIAN *(Gentiana catesbaei)*

This gentian of the wet coastal plain pinelands and savannahs is readily identified by its bell-shaped, deep blue or violet-purple flowers which are about 2 inches long. It has a simple or sparingly branched stem 8 inches to 2 feet tall, with pairs of egg-shaped or lance-shaped leaves 1 to 2½ inches in length. It blooms from September to November.
RANGE: Del. south to Fla.

DOWNY GENTIAN *(Gentiana puberula)*

This species has a minutely downy stem 8 to 18 inches tall on which are many pairs of narrowly lance-shaped leaves. Its flowers are 1½ to 2 inches long, violet-blue, and have a funnel-shaped corolla. It grows on prairies and sandy ridges.
RANGE: N.Y. to Ont. and Minn. south to Ga. and Kan.

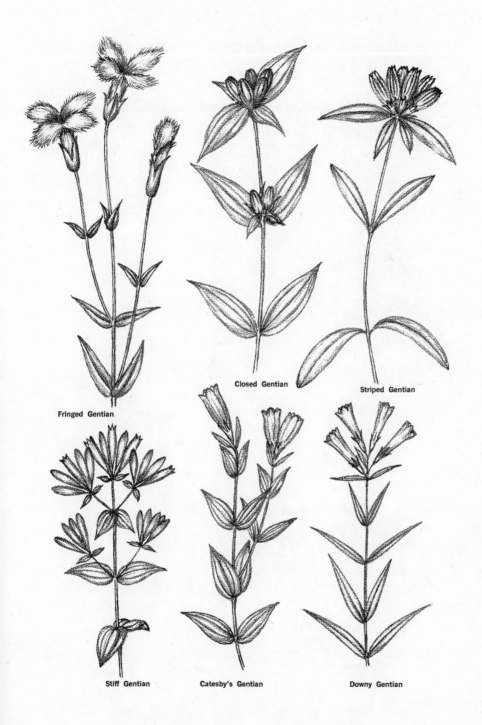

Fringed Gentian

Closed Gentian

Striped Gentian

Stiff Gentian

Catesby's Gentian

Downy Gentian

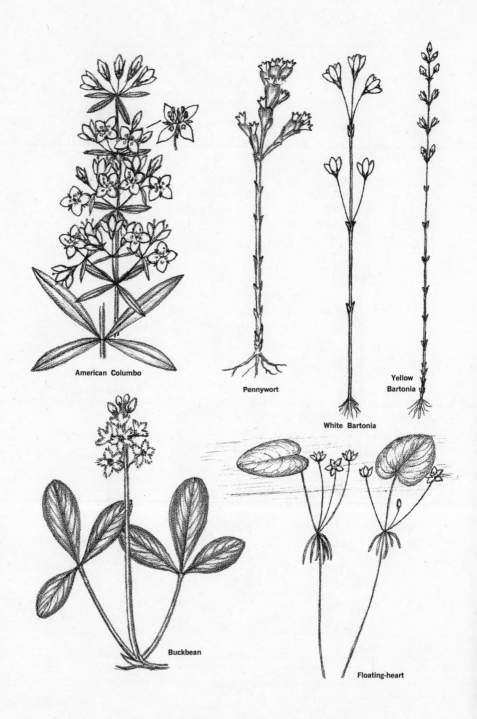

American Columbo

Pennywort

White Bartonia

Yellow Bartonia

Buckbean

Floating-heart

AMERICAN COLUMBO *(Swertia carolinensis)*

Pyramid-plant is another name for this tall member of the Gentian Family. It is a smooth plant with a stout stem 3 to 6 feet high, which is terminated by a branched flower cluster which may be 1 to 2 feet long. Each flower is about an inch across, yellowish-white dotted with brownish-purple; with a large, round, fringed gland on each of the 4 petals. The lance-shaped leaves are 3 to 6 inches long, mostly in whorls of 4, and the ones toward the base of the plant are broader toward the tip. It grows in dry open woods, thickets, and meadows; blooming in May or June.

RANGE: N.Y. and Ont. to Wis. south to Ga. and La.

PENNYWORT *(Obolaria virginica)*

This is a smooth, fleshy, purplish-green plant from 3 to 6 inches high. Near the summit of the stem there are pairs of top-shaped leaves which have 1 to 3 flowers in their axils. Lower on the stem there are 2 to 6 pairs of small bracts in place of leaves. The flowers are about ½ inch long, white to dull purplish, and have 4 lobes at the summit. It grows in rich, moist woods and thickets, getting much of its nourishment from the decaying humus. Flowering season is between March and May.

RANGE: N.J. to Ill. south to Fla. and Tex.

WHITE BARTONIA *(Bartonia verna)*

This plant has a very slender, yellowish-green stem 2 to 15 inches high; with a few widely-spaced, scale-like leaves. Its flowers are white, about ⅓ inch long, 4-petalled, and loosely clustered on the upper part of the stem. It grows in moist pinelands, prairies, and lake shores in the coastal plain; blooming during March and early April.

RANGE: e. N.C. south to Fla. and west to La.

YELLOW BARTONIA *(Bartonia virginica)*

Yellow Bartonia has a fine, wiry, yellowish-green stem 4 to 15 inches high, usually simple but sometimes with a few ascending branches above. Along it are many pairs of small, awl-like scales in place of leaves. Its flowers are small, yellowish, and in the axils of bracts on the upper part of the stem. It grows in moist to fairly dry open woods and on grassy banks; blooming between July and October.

RANGE: N.S. to Que. and Minn. south to Fla. and La.

PANICLED BARTONIA *(Bartonia paniculata)*

This one differs from the preceding Bartonias in having a branched cluster of slender stalked flowers, and scattered rather than paired scale-like leaves. It grows in wet peaty or sandy places from Mass. to Ky. and Ark. south to Fla. and La.; blooming between August and October. (Not illustrated)

BUCKBEAN *(Menyanthes trifoliata* var. *minor)*

The Buckbean has a thick, scaly, creeping stem from which its leaves and flower stalks arise. The former are divided into 3 elliptic or narrowly top-shaped, untoothed leaflets 1½ to 3 inches long; on leaf stalks 2 to 10 inches in length. Its white flowers are about ½ inch across, and the 5 petals have glistening hairs on their upper surface. They are clustered on stalks 3 to 12 inches long and bloom between May and July. Bogbean and Marsh-trefoil are other names often given this plant of shallow waters and boggy places.

RANGE: Lab. to Alaska south to Del., W.Va., the Great Lakes region, Mo., Neb. and Wyo.

FLOATING-HEART *(Nymphoides cordata)*

At first glance, this plant may be mistaken for a miniature water-lily. It grows in ponds and the waters of slowly moving streams with its roots in the bottom mud. Between June and September, it sends up to the surface a long stalk which produces a single 1- to 2-inch long heart-shaped leaf, several small white flowers, and a cluster of tuber-like roots.

RANGE: NFD. to Ont. south to Fla. and La.

LARGE FLOATING-HEART *(Nymphoides aquatica)*

This is a much coarser plant with leaves 2 to 6 inches across, and larger flowers about ¾ inch wide. It grows in ponds and sluggish streams of the coastal plain from N.J. south to Fla.; blooming between May and August. (Not illustrated)

Members of this family have flowers with 5 partly united sepals; 5 petals united to form a corolla tube; 5 stamens with anthers converging around the stigma; and 2 pistils which have their styles and stigmas united and appearing as one, maturing as a pair of long and slender pods. The seeds very often have long, silky hairs. Most species belonging to the family have a milky juice.

BLUE-DOGBANE *(Amsonia tabernaemontana)*

The Blue-dogbane, or Willow Amsonia, is a smooth or slightly downy plant with clustered stems from 1 to 3 feet high. It has scattered lance-shaped or narrowly egg-shaped leaves 2 to 4 inches long. In April or May, it produces rather large but open end clusters of numerous pale blue flowers about ¾ of an inch across. The slender corolla tube abruptly expands into 5 narrow and pointed lobes, giving the flowers a starry appearance. The plant grows in rich, moist woods and along the banks of streams. It is often cultivated and has become naturalized northward and eastward of its normal range.
RANGE: Va. to s. Ill., Mo. and Kan. south to Ga. and Tex.

SPREADING DOGBANE *(Apocynum androsaemifolium)*

The Spreading Dogbane has a stem which forks repeatedly into wide-spreading, mostly smooth, and usually reddish branches. It attains a height of between 1 and 4 feet. Its leaves are paired, egg-shaped or oval, short-stalked, 2 to 4 inches long, and are pale and either smooth or downy beneath. The flowers are about ⅓ inch across, bell-shaped, and rosy-pink. It grows in dry, open woods, thickets, and fields; blooming between June and August. RANGE: Nfd. to Alska south to n. Ga., Ohio, Ill., Ark., Neb. and N.Mex.

INDIAN-HEMP *(Apocynum cannabinum)*

This is a common but less attractive looking plant than the preceding species, usually with a rather erect main stem and ascending, greenish side branches. It has smaller, more urn-shaped, greenish-white flowers which bloom between May and August. The plant apparently got its name from the use of the fibers of its stems by the Indians. It grows in open places and thickets from Que. to Alb. and Wash. south to Fla., Tex. and Calif. (Not illustrated)

MILKWEED FAMILY (Asclepidaceae)

Members of this family have flowers with 5 sepals, barely united at the base; 5 petals, united at the base; 5 stamens which are united at the base and have their anthers adhering to the stigma; and a double pistil, the 2 ovaries having a common stigma and maturing as a pair of pod-like fruits containing seeds usually with silky hairs. Most members of the family have opposite leaves and a milky juice.

In the milkweeds proper, the flowers have 5 reflexed corolla lobes and a central crown of 5 trowel-shaped hoods which are attached to the filaments of the stamens. Within each hood there is usually a slender horn that curves up and over the stigma. The flowers have a remarkable adaptation to insect pollination.

BUTTERFLYWEED *(Asclepias tuberosa)*

This is the beautiful orange-flowered milkweed so often seen in dry fields, on rocky open slopes, and along the roadside. It is a roughish-hairy plant with reclining, ascending, or even somewhat erect stems 1 to 2 feet high, which usually branch toward the summit. The numerous leaves are lance-shaped or narrowly egg-shaped, stalkless or very short-stalked, 1 to 4 inches long, and usually scattered singly along the stems. The flowers are orange-yellow to orange-red but vary considerably in their brilliance. Although it is a milkweed, the plant does not have a milky juice. It blooms between May and September. Other names for it are Yellow Milkweed and Pleurisy-root.
RANGE: Vt. and Ont. to Minn., Neb. and Colo. south to Fla., Tex. and Ariz.

LANCE-LEAF MILKWEED *(Asclepias lanceolata)*

Also known as the Few-flowered Milkweed, this is a smooth plant with usually a simple stem 2 to 4 feet tall. Along it are very widely spaced pairs of narrow or lance-shaped leaves from 4 to 10 inches in length. There are from 1 to 3 umbels at the summit of the stem, each having from 5 to 12 flowers with bright orange-yellow hoods and a deep red corolla. It grows on the borders of swamps and in wet pinelands from Del. south to Fla. and west to Tex.

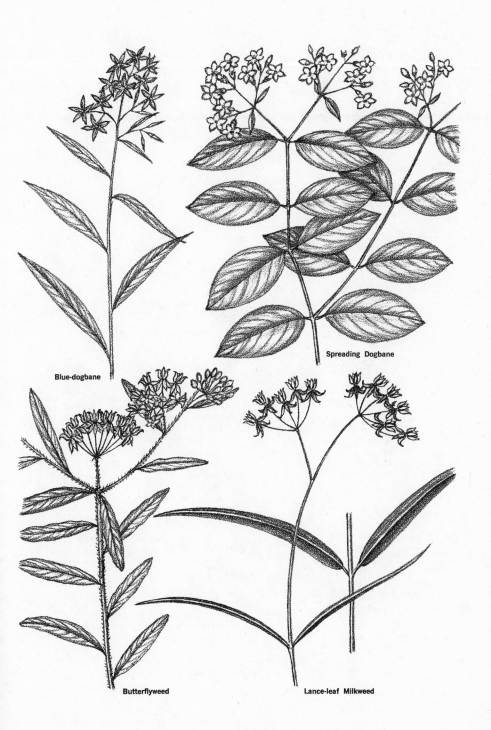

Blue-dogbane

Spreading Dogbane

Butterflyweed

Lance-leaf Milkweed

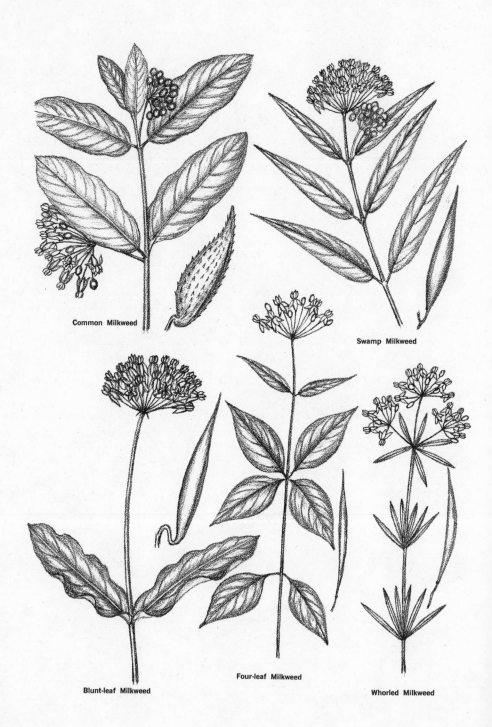

Common Milkweed

Swamp Milkweed

Blunt-leaf Milkweed

Four-leaf Milkweed

Whorled Milkweed

COMMON MILKWEED *(Asclepias syriaca)*

The Common Milkweed has a stout, usually simple stem from 3 to 5 feet in height. Its paired leaves are oblong or oval, more or less rounded at both ends or abruptly pointed at the tip, softly downy beneath, and from 3 to 8 inches long. The dull lavender to greenish-white flowers are about ⅓ inch long and in rather densely crowded umbels a few inches across. This is our commonest species of milkweed, growing in dry fields, thickets, and along roadsides everywhere. It blooms between June and August.
RANGE: N.B. to Sask. south to Ga., Tenn., Mo. and Kan.

SWAMP MILKWEED *(Asclepias incarnata)*

This is another common milkweed and, as its name indicates, it grows in swamps and other wet places. It has a slender and often branched stem from 2 to 4 feet in height; and numerous pairs of leaves which are lance-shaped, taper-pointed, from 3 to 6 inches long and either smooth or downy beneath. They are very short-stalked or practically stalkless. Its flowers are about ¼ inch long, pink or rose-colored, and in many-flowered umbels. The flowering season extends from July to September.
RANGE: N.S. to Man. and Wyo. south to Ga., Tex. and N.Mex.

RED MILKWEED *(Asclepias rubra)*

This is a smooth plant usually with a simple stem 1 to 4 feet tall; and pairs of broadly lance-shaped to egg-shaped leaves 2 to 7 inches long which taper from the rounded or heart-shaped base to a long and slender tip. It has from 1 to 4 many-flowered umbels of purplish-red flowers, blooming in June and July. The plant grows in wet pinelands and bogs in the coastal plain from se. N.Y., N.J. and e. Pa. south to Fla. and west to Tex. (Not illustrated)

BLUNT-LEAF MILKWEED *(Asclepias amplexicaulis)*

The Blunt-leaf Milkweed is a rather smooth, pale green and somewhat whitened plant 2 to 3 feet tall. It has stalkless elliptic or oblong leaves 3 to 5 inches long which have broad and clasping bases, rounded and abruptly short-pointed tips, and conspicuously wavy margins. The dull purple or greenish-purple flowers are about ½ inch long, in a usually solitary and densely-flowered umbel which terminates a long stalk. It grows in dry and usually sandy fields, blooming between May and July.
RANGE: Mass. to Minn. and Neb. south to Fla. and Tex.

FOUR-LEAF MILKWEED *(Asclepias quadrifolia)*

This dainty little milkweed grows in dry open woods, blooming between May and July. On a usually unbranched, slender stem 1 to 2 feet tall, it has 1 or 2 whorls of leaves near the middle and a pair of leaves both above and below the whorled ones. All are quite thin, egg-shaped to lance-shaped, definitely stalked and from 2 to 6 inches long. The flowers have pale pink corolla lobes and white hoods. They are in from 1 to 4 rather small terminal umbels.
RANGE: N.H. to Ont. and Minn. south to n. Ga., Ala., Ark., and Kan.

WHORLED MILKWEED *(Asclepias verticillata)*

The Whorled Milkweed gets its name from its very narrow leaves which are arranged along the stem in several whorls of from 3 to 7. They are stalkless, ¾ to 2¼ inches long, and have the margins rolled. The plant has a slender, simple or sparingly branched stem from 1 to 2½ feet tall. Its flowers are about ¼ inch long and have greenish-white corolla lobes and white hoods. They are in several small umbels, blooming between June and September. It grows in dry woods and fields.
RANGE: Mass. to Ont. and Sask. south to Fla. and Tex.

THIN-LEAF MILKWEED *(Asclepias perennis)*

This is another of our smaller milkweeds, one which grows in the wet woods and along stream banks. It has a slender, ascending or somewhat erect stem 1 to 3 feet high; often rooting near the base and somewhat downy above. Its leaves are paired, rather lance-shaped to narrowly egg-shaped, thin in texture, 2 to 6 inches long, and have slender leaf stalks. The flowers are small, white, and have hoods much shorter than the needle-shaped horns. They are in rather small umbels, blooming between June and August. RANGE: S.C. to s. Ind., s. Ill. and se. Mo. south to Fla. and Tex. (Not illustrated)

215

PURPLE MILKWEED (Asclepias purpurascens)

The Purple Milkweed has a moderately stout, smooth or minutely downy, and usually simple stem 2 to 3 feet tall. It has pairs of elliptic or egg-shaped, short-stalked leaves 3 to 8 inches long which are minutely downy beneath. The flowers are about ⅓ inch long, deep purple, and in several many-flowered umbels; blooming between May and July. It grows in dry to moist open woods, thickets, and fields.

RANGE: N.H. and Ont. to Minn. and S.D. south to N.C., Tenn., Miss. and Okla.

POKE MILKWEED (Asclepias exaltata)

The Poke or Tall Milkweed is a smooth plant, usually with a simple stem 3 to 6 feet tall; and pairs of rather thin, egg-shaped to broadly lance-shaped leaves 4 to 9 inches long, which taper at both ends and are long-stalked. Its flowers are about ⅔ inch long, with greenish or greenish-purple corolla lobes and white hoods. They are in rather large but loosely-flowered and usually nodding umbels; blooming between June and August. It grows in rich open woods and thickets.

RANGE: Me. to Minn. south to Ga., Ky., Ill. and Iowa.

WHITE MILKWEED (Asclepias variegata)

The White Milkweed has a moderately stout, usually simple stem 1 to 3 feet tall, which is somewhat downy on the upper portion. It has pairs of egg-shaped or broadly lance-shaped leaves 3 to 6 inches long, which are definitely stalked and rounded to broadly pointed at both ends. The flowers are about ⅓ inch long, white with a purplish center, and their roundish hoods have a half-moon-shaped horn with a horizontal point. They are arranged in 1 to 4 many-flowered umbels, blooming between May and July. It grows in open woods and thickets.

RANGE: Conn. and se. N.Y. to Ill., Mo. and Okla. south to Fla. and Tex.

SANDHILL MILKWEED (Asclepias humistrata)

This unusual milkweed grows in the driest of sandy places: chiefly in coastal plain pine and oak woods, and on sandhills. It is a pale green and smooth plant which is whitened by a bloom. The often purplish stem is prostrate, 1 to 3 feet long, and the paired leaves stand almost vertically. They are egg-shaped, pointed at the tip, stalkless, and from 2 to 5 inches long. Both surfaces of the leaves are alike—pale green and strikingly veined and bordered with white or coral-pink. The flowers are about ⅓ inch long and have grayish or greenish-purple corolla lobes and white hoods. They are arranged in rather loosely-flowered umbels and bloom in May or June. It cannot possibly be mistaken for any other species of milkweed. RANGE: e. N.C. south to Fla. and west to Miss.

GREEN MILKWEED (Asclepias viridiflora)

The flowers of this milkweed are greenish ½ inch or less long, and the hoods have no horns. They are arranged in quite dense and practically stalkless umbels in the axils of the leaves; blooming between June and August. The plant has reclining or erect stems 1 to 2½ feet long, along which are many pairs of oval to lance-shaped or very narrow leaves which may be smooth or slightly downy. It grows in dry woods, openings, and on prairies from Mass. to Ont. and Man. south to Fla., Tex. and N.Mex. (Not illustrated)

LARGE-FLOWERED ANGLEPOD (Matelea obliqua)

The anglepods are vining plants with opposite heart-shaped leaves. Six species besides this one occur in the eastern United States. The heart-shaped leaves of this species are 2 to 8 inches long, downy beneath, and have rather long downy leaf stalks. Its flowers are ½ to ⅔ inch across and have 5 narrow corolla lobes which are greenish and downy on the back and reddish-purple above. They are arranged in somewhat flat-topped and branching clusters, blooming between May and July. It grows in rather dry but rich thickets, woods borders, and on rocky slopes. The pods have small fleshy protuberances.

RANGE: Pa. to Ill. south to Ga., Tenn. and Mo.

SANDVINE (Ampelamus albidus)

This is also a vine but it has pairs of egg-shaped leaves which are heart-shaped at the base and pointed at the tip. It has small whitish flowers which are bell-shaped with 5 nearly erect corolla lobes, and are in stalked axillary clusters; blooming from July to September. It grows along stream banks from e. Pa. to Ill. and Neb. south to w. Ala. and Tex. (Not illustrated)

216

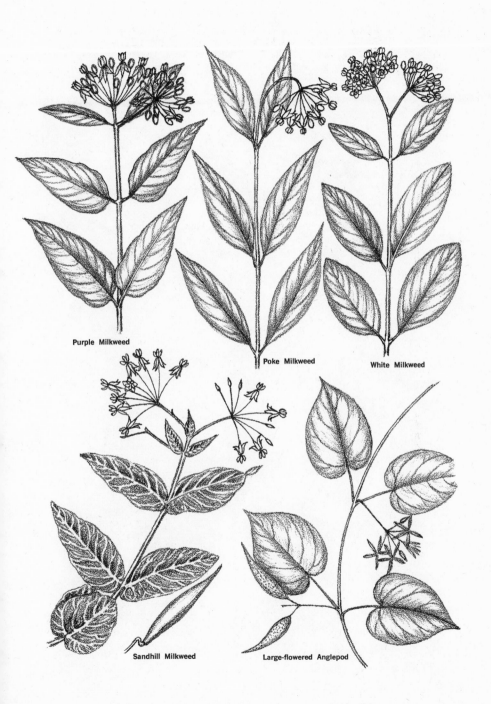

Purple Milkweed

Poke Milkweed

White Milkweed

Sandhill Milkweed

Large-flowered Anglepod

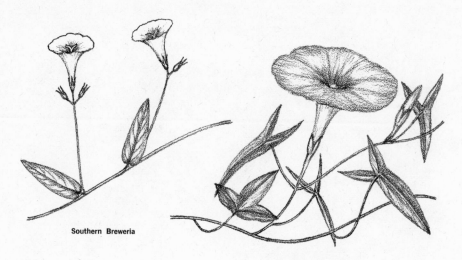

Southern Breweria

Arrow-leaf Morning-glory

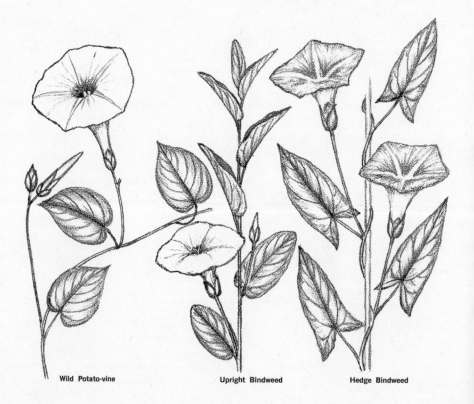

Wild Potato-vine

Upright Bindweed

Hedge Bindweed

MORNING-GLORY FAMILY (Convolvulaceae)

This is chiefly a family of twining and climbing or trailing plants. The flowers usually have 5 (sometimes 4) sepals, united at the base; a like number of petals united to form a funnel-shaped or sometimes bell-shaped corolla; 5 (sometimes 4) stamens which are attached to the corolla tube; and a pistil consisting of 2 united carpels, with from 1 to 4 styles or style-branches. The fruits are capsules with 1 or 2 seeds in each of the chambers.

SOUTHERN BREWERIA *(Bonamia humistrata)*

This is a little plant which grows in dry, sandy coastal plain pinelands. It has a slender, trailing, often branched stem 1 to 2 feet long; and scattered erect or ascending, short-stalked, oblong or elliptic leaves 1 to 2 inches long. Stalks bearing from 1 to 7 white, trumpet-shaped, ¾-inch flowers arise from the leaf axils and overtop the leaves. They have a style with 2 branches. It blooms in June to August.
RANGE: e. Va. south to Fla. and west to Tex.

WATER BREWERIA *(Bonamia aquatica)*

Similar to the preceding, this species is a hairy plant with pink or purple flowers. It grows in wet pinelands and about pond margins from se. Va. south to Fla. and west to Tex. (Not illustrated)

ARROW-LEAF MORNING-GLORY *(Ipomea sagittata)*

This native morning-glory has attractive rosy-pink flowers about 3 inches across. Its leaves are quite variable but most often arrow-shaped with the 2 basal lobes pointing outward, and usually 1½ to 3 inches long. It creeps over the ground or climbs in bushes on the borders of coastal sand dunes, swamps, and marshes; blooming between July and September. RANGE: e. N.C. south to Fla. and west to Tex.

WILD POTATO-VINE *(Ipomea pandurata)*

The slender, smooth or minutely downy trailing or slightly twining stems of this plant arise from an enormous root often weighing as much as 15 to 30 pounds. Its leaves are heart-shaped, 2 to 6 inches long; and often have a purplish midrib, stalks, and margin. The flowers are white with a purple blotch in the center and are about 3 inches across. It grows quite commonly in dry fields, thickets, and along roadsides; blooming between June and September. Another name frequently given it is Man-of-the-earth.
RANGE: Conn. to Ont. and Mich. south to Fla. and Tex.

UPRIGHT BINDWEED *(Convolvulus spithamaeus)*

The flowers of bindweeds resemble those of the morning-glories but they have 2 stigmas, and usually have large bracts surrounding the calyx. This one is a smooth or downy plant with an erect or ascending stem 6 to 12 inches high, sometimes feebly twining toward the tip. Its oval-shaped leaves are short-stalked or nearly stalkless and 1 to 2 inches long. From 1 to 4 flowers are produced in the axils of the lowermost leaves. They are white and between 1½ and 2 inches long. It grows in dry sandy or rocky open woods and fields, blooming between May and August. It is also known as the Low Bindweed. RANGE: Me. and Que. to Ont. and Minn. south to Va., n. Ga., n. Ala. and Iowa.

HEDGE BINDWEED *(Conolvulus sepium)*

The Hedge Bindweed has smooth or somewhat hairy, trailing or twining stems up to 10 feet long; and triangular or arrow-shaped leaves from 2 to 5 inches long, the 2 basal lobes being rather short and blunt. The white or pink trumpet-shaped flowers are 2 to 3 inches across, and on long stalks arising from the leaf axils. At the base they have a pair of large, heart-shaped bracts. It is often abundant in fields, thickets, waste places, and along roadsides; blooming between May and September. It is often called the Wild Morning-glory. RANGE: Nfd. to B.C. south to Fla., Tex. and N.Mex.

FIELD BINDWEED *(Convolvulus arvensis)*

This immigrant from Europe is now widely naturalized here in America, and is often a troublesome weed in cultivated fields. It has a slender, usually trailing stem 1 to 2½ feet long; arrow-shaped leaves from 1 to 2 inches long; and pink or white flowers an inch or less across, which lack bracts at the base. It is also known as the Small Bindweed. (Not illustrated)

COMMON DODDER *(Cuscuta gronovii)*

Dodders are parasitic plants with thread-like, twining and climbing, yellow to bright orange stems on which the leaves are reduced to scales. The small, waxy-white, 4- or 5-parted flowers have globe- or bell-shaped corollas, and are usually in dense clusters. This is one of the more common and widespread of about a dozen species found in our range, but they are not easily identified. The Common Dodder has its flower parts in 5's. It usually occurs in low grounds and is parasitic on a wide variety of plants. It blooms between August and October or later.

RANGE: Que. to Man. south to Fla., Tex. and Ariz.

PHLOX FAMILY (Polemoniaceae)

Members of this family have flowers with 5 united sepals, 5 petals united to form a tube with 5 spreading lobes above; 5 stamens attached to the corolla tube; and a pistil composed of 3 united carpels, with a 3-chambered ovary and a 3-branched style. The fruits are capsules.

GREEK-VALERIAN *(Polemonium reptans)*

This is a native plant with branching, smooth or sparsely hairy stems 6 to 15 inches long. Its leaves are divided into from 3 to 15 lance-shaped or elliptic leaflets. The flowers are about ½ inch across, light blue-violet; with their stamens included within the somewhat bell-shaped, deeply 5-lobed corolla. It grows in rich woods and bottomlands, blooming between April and June.

RANGE: N.Y. to Minn. south to Ga., Miss., Mo. and Okla.

AMERICAN JACOB'S-LADDER *(Polemonium van-bruntiae)*

This is a taller plant with bluish-purple flowers almost an inch across, with the stamens extending well beyond the bell-shaped corolla. The basal leaves are 6 to 12 inches long and have 11 to 17 narrow leaflets. Those on the upper part of the stem are much smaller and have 3 to 7 leaflets. It grows in bogs, marshy meadows, and along streams; blooming between May and July.

RANGE: Vt. and N.Y. south to Md. and W.Va.

WILD BLUE PHLOX *(Phlox divaricata)*

This phlox has slender, upright, more or less hairy stems 6 inches to 1 foot tall; with widely-spaced pairs of lance-shaped or narrowly egg-shaped leaves 1 to 2 inches long. The pale bluish to lilac flowers have a slender corolla tube with 5 spreading lobes which are often notched at the tip; and the stamens are completely within the tube. Often called the Wild Sweet-William, it is often common in open woods and on rocky slopes; blooming from April to June. Often cultivated as a border plant.

RANGE: Vt. and Que. to Minn. and Neb. south to Fla. and Tex.

HAIRY PHLOX *(Phlox amoena)*

The Hairy Phlox has tufted, simple, slender and more or less hairy stems 6 to 18 inches tall; with pairs of lance-shaped or narrowly egg-shaped leaves from ½ to 2 inches long, which tend to stand erect and are rather bluntly pointed. The purplish or pink flowers have 5 narrowly top-shaped lobes which are rarely notched; and the stamens are included within the corolla tube. It grows in dry woods and on rocky slopes and banks; blooming between April and June.

RANGE: N.C. and Ky. south to Fla. and Miss.

SWORD-LEAF PHLOX *(Phlox buckleyi)*

This rather rare phlox has a sticky-hairy stem 4 to 10 inches tall, with pairs of mostly lance-shaped leaves. At the base it has a tuft of evergreen, sword-shaped leaves up to 6 inches in length. The bright purple flowers have corolla tubes and flower stalks densely glandular, and the anthers of the stamens reach the summit of the corolla tube. It grows in open woods and on shaly slopes in western Va. and W.Va., blooming between May and July. (Not illustrated)

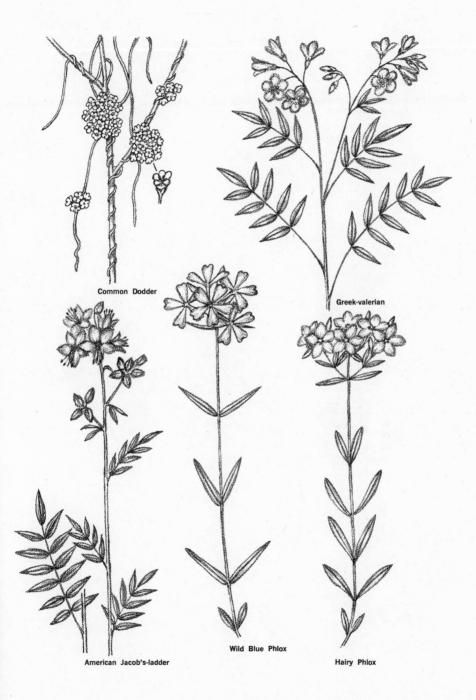

Common Dodder

Greek-valerian

American Jacob's-ladder

Wild Blue Phlox

Hairy Phlox

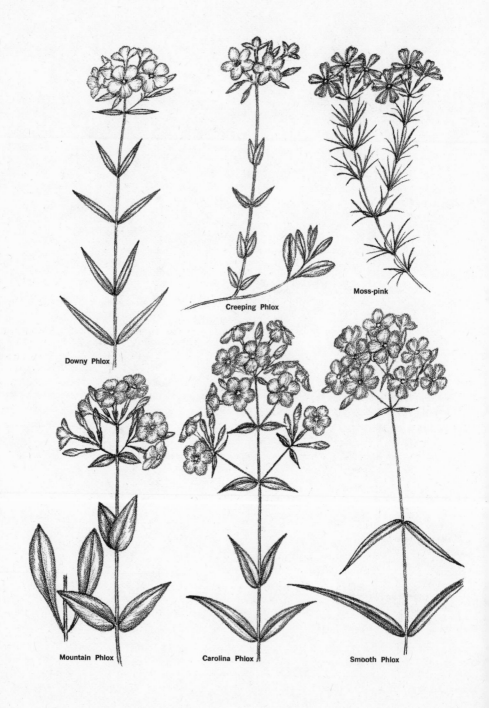

Creeping Phlox

Moss-pink

Downy Phlox

Mountain Phlox

Carolina Phlox

Smooth Phlox

DOWNY PHLOX *(Phlox pilosa)*

This phlox is quite similar to the Hairy Phlox, and most apt to be confused with it. It is a slightly higher plant which is softly hairy or downy. The leaves are more spreading, 1 to 4 inches long, and taper to sharp-pointed tips. Another difference is found in the usually glandular and sticky-hairy calyx of this species. It grows in dry open woods, thickets, sandhills and prairies; blooming between April and June. It is also called Prairie Phlox. RANGE: Ont. to Sask. south to Fla. and Tex.

CREEPING PHLOX *(Phlox stolonifera)*

The Creeping Phlox produces creeping leafy stems which often form sizeable colonies of the plant. It has upright flowering stems 4 to 10 inches high with a few pairs of lance-shaped or narrowly oblong leaves up to ¾ inch long. Those of the sterile shoots are often 1 to 3 inches long, top-shaped, and taper into stalks. The flowers are bright pink or violet-purple, about ¾ inch across, and have rounded corolla lobes. A few of the orange-yellow anthers usually protrude from the summit of the corolla tube. It grows in moist woods and on flats along streams, chiefly in the mountain region; blooming between April and June. RANGE: Pa. and Ohio south to n. Ga. and Tenn.

MOSS-PINK *(Phlox subulata)*

This is a low and mat-forming plant with trailing or creeping stems; and numerous pairs of very narrow, almost needle-like leaves ½ to 1 inch long. Its flowers are about ½ inch across and usually rose-pink or purplish (rarely white), the spreading corolla lobes commonly being deeply notched at the tip. It grows in dry, rocky or sandy, open woods and rocky slopes; blooming between April and June. The plant is widely cultivated, in the South generally under the name of Thrift.
RANGE: N.Y. and Ont. to Mich. south to N.J., w. N.C. and e. Tenn.

TRAILING PHLOX *(Phlox nivalis)*

This plant resembles the preceding one in habit and general appearance. It differs in that the corolla lobes of its flowers are slightly if at all notched at the tip, but they often have some small ragged looking teeth. The stamens in this species are well included within the corolla tube, while those of the preceding one protrude slightly from its opening. This is chiefly a plant of dry woods and pinelands of the coastal plain and piedmont, from s. Va. south to Fla. It blooms between March and May. (Not illustrated).

MOUNTAIN PHLOX *(Phlox ovata)*

The flowering stalks of this phlox arise from reclining leafy stems. They are usually slender, quite smooth, 1 to 2 feet tall; and have from 3 to 7 pairs of leaves which are 1 to 2 inches long, rounded at the base, and pointed at the tip. The lower ones are somewhat larger and narrowed to a stalked base. The flowers are about ¾ inch across, pink to reddish-purple, and have rounded corolla lobes. It grows in moist to rather dry open woods, thickets, and meadows; blooming during May and June.
RANGE: Pa. to Ind. south to S.C. and Tenn.

CAROLINA PHLOX *(Phlox carolina)*

This phlox has tufted, minutely downy to hairy stems from 1 to 3 feet tall; with from 5 to 12 pairs of lance-shaped to narrowly egg-shaped leaves 1½ to 4 inches long. The flowers are almost an inch across, deep to pale reddish-purple, and have 5 rounded corolla lobes. It grows in moist or dry open woods, chiefly in the mountains; blooming in May to July. RANGE: Md. to Ky. and s. Ind. south to Fla. and Miss.

SMOOTH PHLOX *(Phlox glaberrima)*

The Smooth Phlox resembles the preceding species but it is smooth or very nearly so. It has slender stems 1 to 4 feet tall and usually from 10 to 20 pairs of lance-shaped or even narrower leaves from 1½ to 6 inches long. Its flowers are similar but the corolla lobes tend more to be notched at the tip. It grows in moist open woods and meadows, blooming between April and June.
RANGE: Va. to Ky., south to N.C. and Ala.

WILD SWEET-WILLIAM *(Phlox maculata)*

This phlox has fairly smooth and usually purple-spotted stems 1 to 3 feet tall; with 7 or more pairs of lance-shaped or narrowly egg-shaped leaves, rounded at the base, and 2 to 5 inches long. Its flowers are about ⅔ inch across, pinkish-purple or rarely white, and are in narrowly cylindrical end clusters. It grows in moist meadows, bottomlands, and along the banks of streams; blooming between June and September.
RANGE: Conn. and N.Y. to Que. and Minn. south to Md., w. S.C., Tenn. and Mo.

FALL PHLOX *(Phlox paniculata)*

The Fall Phlox has smooth or somewhat downy stems 2 to 4 feet tall; with 14 or more pairs of short-stalked or stalkless, oblong to broadly lance-shaped, and conspicuously veined leaves from 2 to 6 inches long. Its flowers are about ¾ inch across, pinkish-purple to white, and have lobes shorter than the somewhat downy corolla tube. They are arranged in a large, dense, pyramidal end cluster; blooming between July and October. It grows in rich open woods, thickets, and on stream banks. Often cultivated as the Garden or Perennial Phlox, it has escaped beyond its original range.
RANGE: N.Y. to Iowa south to S.C., n. Ga., n. Miss. and Ark.

BROADLEAF PHLOX *(Phlox amplifolia)*

This phlox resembles the preceding species in having pyramidal flower clusters and veiny leaves. It has 7 to 15 pairs of broader leaves which are roughish above; stems which are glandular-hairy above; and flowers with smooth rather than downy corolla tubes. It grows on rocky wooded slopes and the banks of streams, often high in the mountains from sw. Va. to Ind. and Mo. south to w. N.C., Tenn. and Ala. Flowering during July and August. (Not illustrated)

WATERLEAF FAMILY (Hydrophyllaceae)

Members of the Waterleaf Family have flowers with 5 barely united sepals; 5 petals, united to form a tubular or bell-shaped corolla; 5 stamens with filaments more or less united with the corolla tube; and a solitary pistil consisting of 2 united carpels, the style having 2 branches.

VIRGINIA WATERLEAF *(Hydrophyllum virginianum)*

Often a very common plant in rich, moist woodlands, the Virginia Waterleaf is made conspicuous by its usually mottled leaves which are pinnately divided into 5 or 7 cut-toothed segments. It is a smoothish or sparingly hairy plant 1 to 2 feet high with a few leaves on the slender flowering stems, the lower ones being 6 to 10 inches long and long-stalked. Its bell-shaped flowers are white to lavender or purple, about ⅓ inch long; with narrow, bristly, spreading sepals; and stamens with hairy filaments longer than the corolla tube. They are in fairly dense end clusters and bloom between May and August.
RANGE: Que. to Man. south to Va., Tenn. and Kan.

LARGE-LEAF WATERLEAF *(Hydrophyllum macrophyllum)*

This plant is similar to the Virginia Waterleaf but it is quite bristly-hairy. Its leaves are pinnately divided into from 9 to 13 cut-toothed divisions. The flowers are white, blooming between May and July. It grows in woodlands from Va. to Ill. south to N.C. and Ala. (Not illustrated)

APPENDAGED WATERLEAF *(Hydrophyllum appendiculatum)*

This is a bristly-hairy plant 1 to 2 feet high. Its stem leaves are palmately 5-lobed and coarsely toothed and the lower ones are divided. The name comes from the tiny reflexed appendages between the narrow and bristly-hairy sepals of its flowers; which have white to purplish, bell-shaped corollas. It grows in rich, moist woodlands; blooming in May or June. RANGE: Ont. to Minn. south Tenn. and Kan.

CANADA WATERLEAF *(Hydrophyllum canadense)*

The Canada Waterleaf is a nearly smooth plant 1 to 2 feet high which has roundish leaves 2 to 10 inches across. The leaves are palmately 5- to 9-lobed and have coarse, sharp teeth. Its flowers resemble those of the other waterleafs but the sepals are quite smooth, and the corollas are usually white. It grows in rich, moist woodlands; blooming from May to July. RANGE: Mass. to Ont. south to Ga., n. Ala. and Mo.

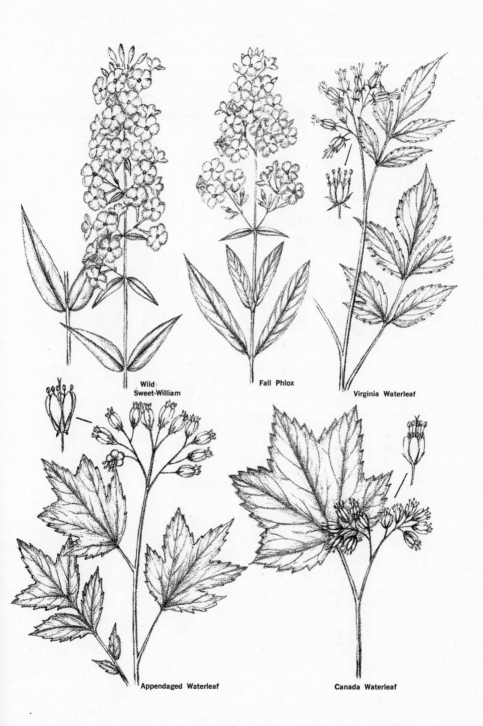

Wild
Sweet-William

Fall Phlox

Virginia Waterleaf

Appendaged Waterleaf

Canada Waterleaf

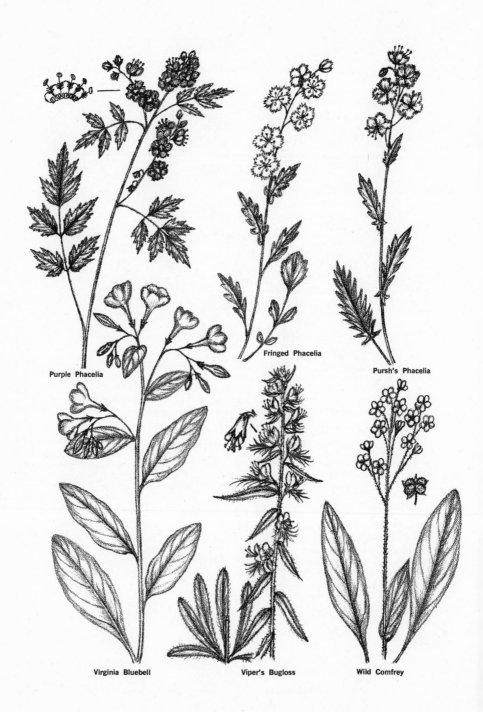

Purple Phacelia

Fringed Phacelia

Pursh's Phacelia

Virginia Bluebell

Viper's Bugloss

Wild Comfrey

PURPLE PHACELIA *(Phacelia bipinnatifida)*

This phacelia has a hairy, branching stem 1 to 2 feet tall; with long-stalked leaves pinnately divided into 3 to 7 sharply toothed or deeply cut segments. The numerous bell-shaped, violet-blue flowers are about ½ inch across, and have projecting stamens with hairy filaments. It grows in moist woods or on rocky slopes and stream banks, blooming between April and May. Also called Loose-flowered Phacelia.

RANGE: Va. to Ill. and Iowa south to Ga., Ala. and Ark.

FRINGED PHACELIA *(Phacelia fimbriata)*

The stems of this phacelia are weak, seldom over 6 inches tall, and have some spreading hairs. Its leaves are cut into 5 to 9 unequal, rather blunt-tipped segments. The lower ones are 2 to 4 inches long and slender-stalked but those along the stem are much smaller and stalkless. Its flowers are white to pale lilac, about ½ inch across, with lilac-colored anthers and the corolla lobes strongly fringed. It grows in rich woods and along streams in the mountains, blooming in April and May.

RANGE: w. Va. south to w. N.C. and e. Tenn.

PURSH'S PHACELIA *(Phacelia purshii)*

This is a finely hairy plant with usually branching stems 6 to 18 inches tall. The leaves are 1½ to 3 inches long and cut into 9 to 15 usually pointed segments, the lower ones being stalked. Its flowers are lavender-blue with a broad white "eye", about ½ inch across, and have the corolla lobes short-fringed. It grows in rich moist woods and meadows, blooming May or June.

RANGE: Pa. to Ill. and Wis. south to n. Ga., Ala., Tenn. and Okla.

SMALL-FLOWERED PHACELIA *(Phacelia dubia)*

The flowers of this species are lilac-blue to white, the corolla lobes are unfringed, and the stamen stalks are hairy. Its stem is 6 to 16 inches tall and has scattered entire or few-cleft small leaves, but the basal ones are 1 to 2 inches long and divided into 3 to 7 segments. It grows in rich woods and rocky slopes or cliffs, blooming from April to June. RANGE: Del. to N.Y. and Ohio south to Ga. and Miss. (Not illustrated)

BORAGE FAMILY (Boraginaceae)

Members of this family have flowers with 5 sepals, united at the base; 5 petals united to form a tube; 5 stamens, with filaments attached to the corolla tube; and a pistil with a deeply 4-lobed ovary, which matures as a group of 4 seed-like nutlets. The flower clusters are usually spirally coiled, straightening out as the flower buds open.

VIRGINIA BLUEBELL *(Mertensia virginica)*

Also known as the Virginia Cowslip and Roanoke-bells, this is one of our most beautiful wild flowers of spring. It is a smooth and pale green plant 1 to 2 feet high, with elliptic or egg-shaped leaves 2 to 5 inches long. The nodding, trumpet-shaped flowers are about an inch long, pink when in the bud but becoming a bright lavender-blue or bright blue when fully open. It grows in rich moist woods, on rocky slopes, or along streams; blooming between March and May.

RANGE: Ont. to Minn. south to Va., Ala., Ark. and Kan.

VIPER'S BUGLOSS *(Echium vulgare)*

Blueweed is another name for this bristly-hairy European immigrant which is now thoroughly at home here in America. Between June and September, its bright blue, ¾-inch long flowers with their long red stamens are very conspicuous in old fields, waste places, and by the wayside. The plant grows from 1 to 2½ feet tall and has many narrowly oblong or lance-shaped leaves 1 to 6 inches long, the ones on the upper part of the stem being small and stalkless.

WILD COMFREY *(Cynoglossum virginianum)*

The Wild Comfrey is a hairy plant with a simple stem 1½ to 2½ feet tall, the few leaves on the upper part being small and with clasping bases. The basal leaves are 4 to 12 inches long, oval-shaped, and taper into stalks. Its flowers are about ⅜ inch across and pale lilac to white, blooming between April and June. It grows in rather rich open woods and thickets. RANGE: Conn. to Ill. and Mo. south to Fla. and Tex.

VERBENA FAMILY (Verbenaceae)

Members of this family have flowers with 4 or 5 unequal sepals united into a tube; 4 or 5 petals united to form a slender tube with a flaring 4- or 5-lobed rim; usually 4 stamens, in pairs of different lengths; and a pistil with a more or less 4-lobed ovary, maturing as 4 seed-like nutlets. The leaves are nearly always opposite.

BLUE VERVAIN *(Verbena hastata)*

The Blue Vervain has an erect, 4-sided, rough-hairy stem 3 to 5 feet tall, which usually branches above. On it are pairs of narrowly egg-shaped to lance-shaped leaves 1½ to 5 inches long, which are roughish-hairy and have coarsely toothed margins. The small violet-blue flowers, hardly more than ⅛ inch across, are arranged in several long and very slender clusters at the tip of the stem and its branches. It is usually common in moist fields, meadows, and along streams; blooming between June and September.
RANGE: N.B. to B.C. south to Fla., Tex. and Calif.

WHITE VERVAIN *(Verbena urticifolia)*

This plant is similar to the preceding one but it has more lax end clusters of small white flowers. It grows in fields, thickets, and the borders of woods from Que. to Ont. and S.D. south to Fla. and Tex. (Not illustrated)

MOSS VERBENA *(Verbena tenuisecta)*

The Moss Verbena is a native of South America now naturalized in the Southeast. It is a prostrate or sprawling, hairy little plant with pairs of very finely dissected leaves; and flat-topped clusters of showy rose-purple, pink, or white flowers with 5-lobed corollas about ¼ inch across. It is commonly seen blooming in the sands along highways in the coastal plain between June and September, from e. N.C. south to Fla. and west to La.

LARGE-FLOWERED VERBENA *(Verbena canadensis)*

This is a smooth or hairy-stemmed plant 8 to 20 inches high, with ascending branches. The leaves are 1 to 3 inches long and are coarsely toothed, deeply cut, or 3-lobed. Its flowers are about ½ inch across, flesh-colored to reddish-purple, and the 5 corolla lobes are notched at the tip. The flower cluster tends to be somewhat flat-topped. This verbena grows in dry sandy or rocky thickets, fields, and on prairies; blooming between April and October. RANGE: Va. to Ill., Iowa, Kan. and Colo. south to Fla. and Tex.

CAROLINA VERBENA *(Verbena caroliniana)*

The Carolina Verbena is a slender stemmed, roughish-hairy plant 1 to 2½ feet tall; with widely spaced pairs of narrowly elliptic or lance-shaped leaves above and spoon-shaped ones toward the base. They are ¾ to about 3½ inches long. Its flowers are almost ¼ inch across, pink purplish, or white; and arranged in a long and narrow cluster, blooming between May and September. It grows in open sandy woods and thickets, chiefly in the coastal plain. RANGE: N.C. south to Fla. and west to La.

HOARY VERBENA *(Verbena stricta)*

This is densely pale-hairy plant with a quite roundish, simple or sparingly branched stem 1 to 4 feet tall. The leaves are stalkless or nearly so, sharply-toothed, and 2 to 4 inches long. Its flowers are deep blue or purple, a bit over ¼ inch across; and in dense, narrow, blunt-tipped, and practically stalkless clusters. It grows in dry open places from N.Y. and Ont. to Mont. south to Tenn., Ark., Okla., Tex. and N. Mex. Introduced in the Northeast. It flowers June to September. (Not illustrated)

FOG-FRUIT *(Lippia lanceolata)*

The Fog-fruit is a smooth or sparingly hairy plant with slender, trailing stems; and pairs of elliptic or lance-shaped, coarsely toothed leaves 1 to 3 inches long. The flowers are very small, pink, bluish, or white, and in scaly-bracted heads on long stalks from the leaf axils. It grows in wet places and on streambanks, flowering between May and September. RANGE: N.J. to Ont., Minn. and Neb. south to Fla. and La.

CAPEWEED *(Lippia nodiflora)*

This is a similar but downy plant growing in low grounds. Its leaves are ½ to 2½ inches long and broadest with a few sharp teeth toward the rounded tip. The small flowers are bluish to nearly white. RANGE: Va. to Mo. and Okla. s. to Fla. and Tex. (Not illustrated)

Blue Vervain

Moss Verbena

Large-flowered Verbena

Carolina Verbena

Fog-fruit

Plants belonging to the Mint Family have opposite leaves and usually, but not always, 4-sided stems. Many of them also have a distinctive and aromatic odor when crushed or bruised. Their flowers have a bilateral symmetry with 4 or 5 united sepals, 4 or 5 petals united to form a tube, and usually with a 2-lipped corolla; 4 stamens, in 2 pairs of different length, or sometimes only a single pair; and a pistil which has a decidedly 4-lobed ovary, which matures as 4 seed-like nutlets.

Key To Genera Of The Mint Family

1. Flowers with but 2 anther-bearing stamens.
   2. Lower lip of the corolla fringed. Flowers in a large, open, branched end cluster which overtops the leaves.　　　　　HORSE-BALM *(Collinsonia)*
   2. Lower lip of the corolla not fringed. Flowers in dense heads or narrow end clusters.
      3. Corolla large, usually an inch or more long.
         4. Flowers in terminal heads or with several head-like clusters in the axils of the upper leaves; calyx regular and 5-toothed.　　MONARDAS *(Monarda)*
         4. Flowers in elongate and often interrupted terminal clusters; calyx distinctly 2-lipped.　　　　　SAGES *(Salvia)*
      3. Corolla less than ½ inch long; calyx 2-lipped, with bristle-pointed teeth.　　　　　WOOD-MINTS *(Blephilia)*
1. Flowers with 4 anther bearing stamens.
   2. Lower lip of the corolla fringed. Flowers in a large, open, branched end cluster which overtops the leaves.　　　　　STONEROOT *(Collinsonia)*
   2. Lower lip of the corolla not fringed.
      3. Calyx with a cap-like hump on the upper side.　　SKULLCAPS *(Scutellaria)*
      3. Calyx otherwise.
         4. Stamens very long, describing an arch or curve extending well beyond the corolla.　　　　　BLUE-CURLS *(Trichostema)*
         4. Stamens otherwise.
            5. Flowers in the axils of large rounded bracts and in a dense cylindrical end cluster. Leaves untoothed.　　　　　HEAL-ALL *(Prunella)*
            5. Flowers not in a dense cylindrical cluster. Leaves usually toothed.
               6. Plants prostrate or creeping.
                  7. Flowers few, in a 1-sided end cluster.　　MEEHANIA *(Meehania)*
                  7. Flowers few and in the axils of the regular leaves.　　　　　GROUND-IVY *(Glechoma)*
               6. Plants more or less erect.
                  7. Corolla apparently without an upper lip, split on the upper side and the lower lip seemingly 5-lobed. GERMANDER *(Teucrium)*
                  7. Corolla nearly regular or distinctly 2-lipped.
                     8. Calyx deeply 4-toothed. Leaves heart-shaped.　　　　　SYNANDRA *(Synandra)*

229a

8. Calyx 5-toothed.

   9. Corolla large, ¾ inch or more long; flowers in a long and narrow end cluster. FALSE DRAGONHEAD *(Dracocephalum)*

   9. Corolla usually less than ½ inch long; flowers in dense axillary or end clusters.

      10. Corolla nearly regular with more or less erect lobes; flowers in axillary clusters or narrow and interrupted end clusters.   MINTS *(Mentha)*

      10. Corolla decidedly 2-lipped; flowers in axillary or sometimes flattened end clusters. MOUNTAIN-MINTS *(Pycnanthemum)*

BLUE-CURLS *(Trichostema dichotomum)*

This is a minutely downy or sometimes sticky-hairy plant with a slender and branching stem from 6 inches to 2 feet high; and lance-shaped or oblong, untoothed leaves from 1 to 3 inches long. Its violet-blue flowers are very distinctive as the long blue or violet filaments of the stamens describe an arch which extends well beyond the corolla. It grows in dry sandy open woods, fields, and on slopes; blooming between August and October. Another name often given it is Bastard-pennyroyal.

RANGE: S. Me. to Mich. and Mo. south to Fla. and Tex.

LARGER SKULLCAP *(Scutellaria integrifolia)*

Skullcaps get their name from a peculiar little cap-like projection on the upper side of the calyx. A dozen or more species of them occur in the eastern United States north of Florida, and this species is one of the more showy ones. It is a somewhat hoary-downy or hairy plant with an erect, simple or branched stem from 6 inches to 2 feet high. The leaves of the upper part of the stem are narrow, untoothed, 1 to 2 inches long, and stalkless or very short-stalked. Those toward the base are slender-stalked, egg-shaped to roundish, and have toothed margins. Its purplish-blue flowers are often whitish underneath and almost an inch long. Also known as the Hyssop Skullcap, it grows in open woods, thickets, and clearings; blooming between May and July.

RANGE: Mass. to Ky. and Mo. south to Fla. and Tex.

SHOWY SKULLCAP *(Scutellaria serrata)*

The Showy Skullcap has a simple or branched stem 1 to 2 feet tall, which is quite smooth or sometimes minutely downy above. Its egg-shaped leaves are sharply toothed, stalked, and 2 to 4 inches in length. The flowers are violet-blue, about an inch long, and bloom in May or June. It grows in rather dry but rich open woods, thickets, and clearings. RANGE: N.J. and s. N.Y. to Tenn. and Mo. south to S.C. and Ala.

LYRE-LEAF SAGE *(Salvia lyrata)*

The Lyre-leaf Sage is a somewhat hairy plant with a simple or sparingly branched and erect stem 1 to 2 feet tall, on which are pairs of small bract-like leaves and a terminal flower cluster. The basal leaves are stalked, 3 to 8 inches long, and vary from ones with merely wavy-toothed margins to others which are pinnately lobed, usually with a large terminal segment. Its bright blue flowers are about an inch long and occur in several whorls along the upper part of the stem, blooming between April and June. It grows in rather dry but rich open woods, pinelands, and along roadsides.

RANGE: Conn. to Ill., Mo. and Okla. south to Fla. and Tex.

BLUE SAGE *(Salvia azurea)*

The Blue Sage is a pale and minutely downy plant 1 to 4 feet tall with leaves narrowly oblong to lance-shaped or narrower, 1½ to 4 inches long, and with wavy or shallowly toothed margins. It has azure blue to white flowers about ¾ inch long. It grows in coastal plain pinelands and sandhills from N.C. south to Fla. and west to Tex. (Not illustrated)

RED SAGE *(Salvia coccinea)*

This, our only native sage with red or scarlet flowers is a softly-hairy, leafy-stemmed plant from 1 to about 2 feet tall. It has egg-shaped and bluntly toothed leaves 1 to 2½ inches long which are on slender stalks. The flowers are ¾ to about an inch long. It grows in sandy hammocks, waste places, and along roadsides in the coastal plain from S.C. south to Fla. and west to Tex. and Mex. (Not illustrated)

SELF-HEAL *(Prunella vulgaris)*

This plant which is also known as Heal-all or Carpenter's-weed, is common everywhere in open places. It is a low plant commonly with several branches and may be but a few inches to nearly 2 feet high. The egg-shaped to lance-shaped leaves are 1 to 4 inches long, slender-stalked, and often have some low teeth on the margin. Its small, bluish to lavender or whitish flowers are in cylindrical-shaped heads; in the axils of large, greenish or purplish-tinged, bristly-fringed bracts and bloom between May and October. The narrow-leaved variety found from Nfd. to Alaska south to se. N.Y., w. N.C., Tenn., Kan., N. Mex., Ariz. and Calif. is believed to be a native plant. The broad-leaved form has evidently been introduced from Europe.

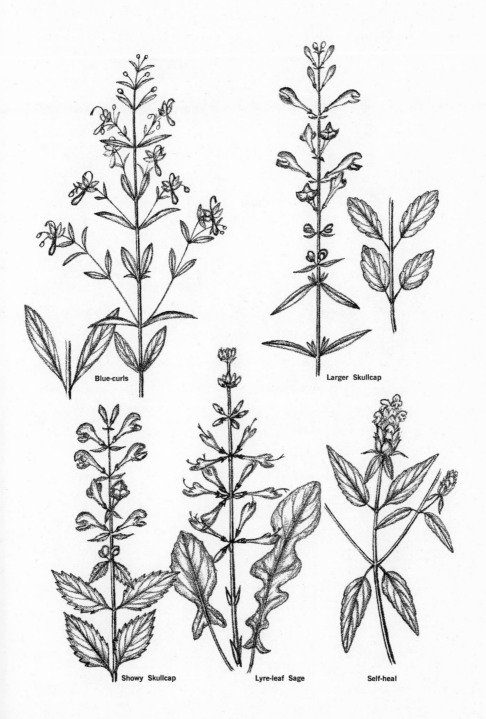

Blue-curls

Larger Skullcap

Showy Skullcap

Lyre-leaf Sage

Self-heal

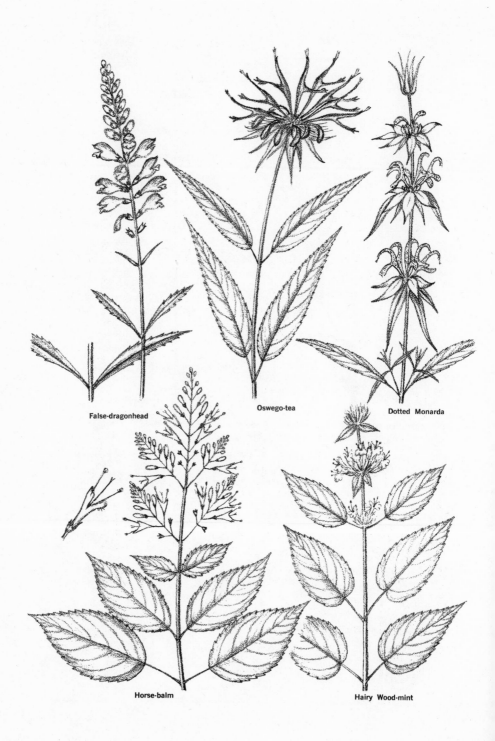

False-dragonhead

Oswego-tea

Dotted Monarda

Horse-balm

Hairy Wood-mint

FALSE DRAGONHEAD *(Dracocephalum virginianum)*

This plant has a smooth, erect, often branching stem 1 to 4 feet tall; with sharply-toothed lance-shaped leaves 1½ to 5 inches long. The pale purple or rose flowers are about an inch long, and borne in showy terminal spikes. The corolla is swollen at the throat, the upper lip being domed and the lower one spreading and 3-lobed. It is often called the Obedient-plant as the flowers tend to stay put when bent from their normal position. It grows in wet meadows, bogs, and along streams; blooming July to October. RANGE: Que. to Minn. south to Fla. and La.

FEW-FLOWERED DRAGONHEAD *(Dracocephalum purpureum)*

This species has fewer flowers in a looser spike and usually fewer than 10 pairs of bluntly-toothed leaves below the stem branches. It grows in river swamps and marshes from se. Va. south to Fla. and west to Miss., blooming May to July. (Not illustrated)

OSWEGO-TEA *(Monarda didyma)*

Often called the Bee-balm, this plant is well known for its bright red or scarlet flowers which are borne in showy heads at the summit of the stem or its branches. They are 1½ or 2 inches long and have a narrow, ascending upper lip and a somewhat drooping and broader lower one with 3 short lobes. It grows from 2 to 3 feet tall and has lance- to egg-shaped, sharply-toothed, stalked leaves 3 to 6 inches in length. It is often common in rich moist woods and bottomlands, blooming July to September.
RANGE: N.Y. to Mich. south to n. Ga. and Miss.

BASIL-BALM *(Monarda clinopodia)*

This plant is similar to the preceding but it has smaller whitish to pink, dark-spotted flowers, below which are white or partly white leafy bracts. It grows in woods from N.Y. to Ill. south to Md., n. Ga. and Tenn.; blooming between late May and Sept. (Not illus.)

WILD BERGAMOT *(Monarda fistulosa)*

This species has lilac to pinkish flowers with a hairy tuft near the tip of the upper lip, and leafy bracts which are often pinkish at the base. It grows in open woods and meadows from Me. to Sask. south to Ga. and Tex., blooming from June to September (Not illustrated)

DOTTED MONARDA *(Monarda punctata)*

Also known as Horsemint, this species has a stem 2 to 3 feet tall; with narrowly lance-shaped, shallowly toothed leaves which are pointed at both ends. The upper ones and the bracts of the flower cluster are lilac-pink to whitish. Th inch-long yellow flowers are spotted with purple and have a very slender, arching upper lip. It grows in open sandy woods and fields, blooming between late July and September.
RANGE: N.J. to Minn. south to Fla., Tex. and Ariz.

HORSE-BALM *(Collinsonia canadensis)*

Richweed and Stoneroot are other names for this nearly smooth plant with a branching stem 2 to 5 feet tall. Its long-stalked, coarsely-toothed, egg-shaped leaves are 6 to 10 inches long, and have a lemon-like odor when crushed. The flowers are light yellow, about ½ inch long, and have 2 stamens which protrude well beyond the corolla. It grows in rich moist woods, blooming between July and September.
RANGE: Mass. to Ont. and Wis. south to Fla., Miss. and Ark.

STONEROOT *(Collinsonia verticillata)*

Stoneroot has a slender, finely downy, often purplish stem 4 to 20 inches tall; with an apparent whorl of 4 thin, coarsely-toothed leaves at the summit below the flower cluster. The tawny or purplish flowers have 4 protruding stamens and a fringed lower lip. It grows in rich woods from s. Va. to Tenn. south to Ga., blooming late April to June. (Not illustrated)

HAIRY WOOD-MINT *(Blephilia hirsuta)*

This wood-mint has a downy or hairy stem 1½ to 3 feet tall, and sharply toothed, long-stalked leaves 2 to 4 inches long. The small white or pale lavender flowers are purple-spotted. It grows in moist and rocky woods, blooming between June and August.
RANGE: Que to Minn. south to w. N.C. Tenn., Mo. and Tex.

MOUNTAIN-MINT *(Pycnanthemum incanum)*

A number of species of mountain-mints occur in the eastern United States, some of them in the coastal region. This wide-spread species is apt to attract attention by the conspicuously whitened leaves or bracts associated with the flower clusters. It is a more or less downy plant with a branching stem 1½ to 3 feet tall. The egg-shaped to broadly lance-shaped leaves are 1½ to 3 inches long, with rather widely spaced marginal teeth. Its flowers, about ¼ inch long, are whitish to rose-pink or purple and have small purple spots. It grows in dry open woods, thickets and field; blooming between June and August.

RANGE: N.H. to Ill. south to Ga. and Miss.

FIELD BASIL *(Satureja vulgaris)*

This mint has a slender, simple or branched, more or less hairy stem 6 inches to 2 feet tall. The leaves are egg-shaped to elliptic, short-stalked, 1 to 2½ inches long, and some-times toothed on the margin. Its small flowers are lilac-pink to whitish and in dense clusters in the axils of the upper leaves. It grows in woods, thickets and fields; blooming between June and September.

RANGE: Nfd. to Man. south to N.C., Tenn., Ind., Wis. and Minn.

AMERICAN WILD MINT *(Mentha arvensis)*

The true mints, including the familiar Peppermint and Spearmint, are members of the genus *Mentha.* Although several species of them are found in eastern North America, only this species of world-wide distribution is a native plant. The others are immigrants from Europe. It is a smooth to somewhat downy plant with a slender, simple or branched stem 6 inches to 2 feet tall. The leaves are narrowly elliptic or lance-shaped, stalkless, sharply toothed on the margin, and 1½ to 3 inches long. The flowers are small, lilac-pink to purplish, and clustered in the axils of the leaves. It grows in woods, thickets and fields; blooming between July and October.

RANGE: Nfd. to Alaska south to Md., W. Va., Mo., N. Mex., and Calif.

AMERICAN GERMANDER *(Teucrium canadense)*

Also called the Wood-sage, this plant has an erect, simple or branched, finely hairy stem 1 to 3 feet tall. The leaves are lance-shaped or narrowly egg-shaped, coarsely toothed, short-stalked, grayish-downy beneath, and 1½ to 5 inches long. Its purplish-pink to cream-colored flowers are about ⅔ inch long, the lower lip with a large central lobe. They are arranged in long, narrow terminal clusters. It grows in moist woods and thickets and in marshes, blooming between June and September.

RANGE: N.S. to Minn. and Neb. south to Fla. and Tex.

GROUND-IVY *(Glechoma hederacea)*

This little native of Europe is widely naturalized in North America and is often abundant in moist woods, thickets, yards, waste places and along roadsides. Sometimes called Gill-over-the ground, it is a smooth or minutely downy plant with extensively creeping stems and short ascending branches. The leaves are roundish, heart-shaped at the base, ½ to 1½ inches wide, and coarsely and bluntly toothed. Its lavender to purplish-blue Flowers are about ½ inch long, in small axillary clusters, and bloom between late March and July.

MEEHANIA *(Meehania cordata)*

Meehania is a native plant most likely to be confused with the Ground-ivy for it also has trailing stems and similar but usually larger heart-shaped leaves. Its somewhat larger flowers are in end clusters, each with a small egg-shaped bract at the base. It grows in rich wooded coves and slopes from Pa. to Ill. South to w. N.C. and Tenn., blooming in May or June (Not illustrated)

HENBIT *(Lamium amplexicaule)*

Henbit is a European plant widely naturalized in fields, lawns and waste places; bloom-ing between March and June. The whorls of purplish flowers are subtended by pairs of stalkless leaves, but the lower leaves are roundish, coarsely and bluntly toothed, and long-stalked. (Not illustrated)

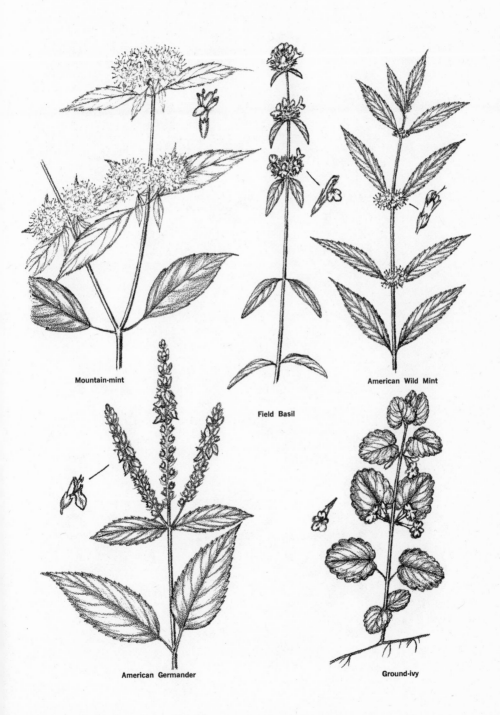

Mountain-mint

Field Basil

American Wild Mint

American Germander

Ground-ivy

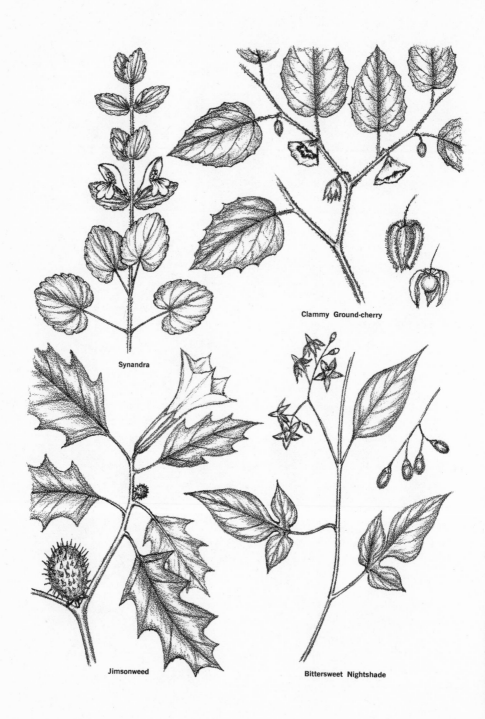

Clammy Ground-cherry

Synandra

Jimsonweed

Bittersweet Nightshade

SYNANDRA *(Synandra hispidula)*

This plant has a rather slender, hairy, ascending or erect stem 1 to 2½ feet high. The leaves on the upper part of it are egg-shaped to lance-shaped and stalkless. Those toward the base are egg-shaped to roundish, long-stalked, 2 to 4 inches long, and are bluntly toothed. Its flowers are 1 to 1½ inches long, yellowish-white with purple lines on the lower lip, and solitary in the axils of the upper leaves. It grows on damp wooded slopes and stream banks, blooming in May or June.

RANGE: Va. and W.Va. to Ill. south to w. N.C. and Tenn.

NIGHTSHADE FAMILY (Solanaceae)

Members of this family usually have alternate leaves, and flowers with 5 more or less united sepals; 5 petals which are united into a star-like, bell-shaped, or trumpet-shaped corolla; 5 stamens which are inserted on the corolla tube; and pistil which usually has a 2-chambered ovary. The fruits are either berries or capsules containing a number of small seeds.

CLAMMY GROUND-CHERRY *(Physalis heterophylla)*

There are a number of species of ground-cherries in our region, this being one of the more common ones. It is a sticky-hairy plant with often branching stems 1½ to 3 feet high, sometimes with long, spreading, and jointed hairs. Its leaves are egg-shaped, usually broadly rounded or heart-shaped at the base, more or less wavy-toothed on the margin, and 2 to 4 inches long. The flowers are shaped like a broad open bell about ¾ inch across, and are yellowish with a purplish-brown center. They are followed by small, round, yellow berries enclosed in the bag-like calyx. It grows in open woods and clearings, blooming between May and September.

RANGE: N.B. to Sask. south to Ga., Okla. and Tex.

VIRGINIA GROUND-CHERRY *(Physalis virginiana)*

This is another common species, with egg-shaped leaves which are pointed at both ends. It has red berries and the calyx which surrounds them has a deep depression at the stem end. Conn. to s. Ont. and s. Man. south to Fla. and Tex. (Not illustrated)

JIMSONWEED *(Datura stramonium)*

Also known as the Thorn-apple and Stramonium, this is a smoothish plant with a stout, forking, widely branched, often purple-tinged stem 1 to 5 feet tall. The rather thin, egg-shaped, irregularly toothed leaves are 3 to 8 inches long. It has trumpet-shaped white, lavender or violet flowers 3 to 4 inches long, with 5 pointed lobes on the corolla rim. The flowers are followed by erect spiny capsules. It is a native of Asia now widely naturalized in fields and waste places, blooming from July to September.

BITTERSWEET NIGHTSHADE *(Solanum dulcamara)*

This widely naturalized native of Europe is a somewhat woody vine which often has flowers, green berries, and bright red ripe ones present at the same time. The leaves, 2 to 4 inches long, are egg-shaped and often have a pair of ear-like lobes at the base. Its flowers, about ½ inch across, have 5 pointed violet or purple corolla lobes and a cone-shaped group of yellow stamens. It blooms between May and September.

HORSE-NETTLE *(Solanum carolinense)*

This species is a weedy native plant with slender yellowish prickles on its stem and midribs of its leaves. It is an erect plant 1 to 2 feet high; with lavender or whitish, 5-lobed flowers nearly an inch wide; followed by round yellow berries about ¾ inch in diameter. It grows in dry fields, waste places and along roadsides; blooming between May and July. Vt. to Ont., Iowa and Neb. south to Fla. and Tex. (Not illustrated)

BLACK NIGHTSHADE *(Solanum americanum)*

Black Nightshade is a smooth bushy plant up to 2 feet tall; with long-stalked, egg-shaped leaves of a thin texture and from 1 to 4 inches long. Its white or purple tinged flowers are borne in 2- to 4-flowered umbels and are followed by lustrous black berries ¼ to ⅜ inch across. It grows in dry open woods, fields and along roadsides from Me. to N.D. south to n. Fla. and e. Tex. (Not illustrated)

FIGWORT FAMILY (Scrophulariaceae)

Members of this family have flowers with 4 or 5 more or less united sepals; 4 or 5 petals, more or less united and most often forming a 2-lipped corolla; from 2 to 5 (usually 4) stamens attached to the corolla tube, 1 or 2 of them often without an anther; and a pistil consisting of 2 united carpels. The fruit is a 2-chambered pod containing numerous small seeds.

MOTH MULLEIN (*Verbascum blattaria*)

The Moth Mullein usually has a simple, smooth, slender stem 2 to 4 feet tall. Its leaves are egg-shaped to lance-shaped, toothed or sometimes cleft; those along the upper part of the stem being broad-based, stalkless or somewhat clasping, and ½ to 2½ inches long. The flowers are about an inch across, white or yellow, and have the filaments of the stamens bearded with violet hairs. They are rather widely spaced along the upper portion of the stem, blooming between June and September. The plant is a native of Europe but it is now common in fields, waste places, and along roadsides here in America.

COMMON MULLEIN (*Verbascum thapsus*)

During the first year this plant produces a large rosette of big, grayish-green, flannel-like leaves which are often conspicuous in fields, waste places, and by the wayside. The second year it sends up a wand-like leafy stem from 2 to 7 feet tall, which ends in a dense and cylindrical flower cluster. Stem and leaves alike are densely woolly-hairy; the leaves being elliptical, pointed at both ends, 4 to 12 inches long, and tapering into winged stalks. The flowers are about ¾ inch across, the 5-lobed yellow corolla being almost regular. It blooms between June and September, only a few flowers being open at any time. A native of Europe, it is widely naturalized in America.

YELLOW TOADFLAX (*Linaria vulgaris*)

Butter-and-eggs is another name often given this plant, which was originally introduced into this country from Europe as a garden flower. It now grows in fields, waste places, and along roadsides almost everywhere. Usually it has several, smooth, very leafy stems from 1 to 2 feet high, which end in a long cluster of flowers. The scattered leaves are very narrow, stalkless, and ½ to 1½ inches long. The attractive flowers are about an inch long, bright yellow, and have a prominent orange protuberance or palate on the lower lip; as well as a long, slender, and curved spur. The flowering season is between May and October.

BLUE TOADFLAX (*Linaria canadensis*)

The Blue Toadflax is a smooth plant with very slender ascending stems 8 inches to about 2 feet tall; with numerous, scattered, very narrow leaves ½ to 1½ inches long. Usually there are trailing offshoots at the base of the plant. The flowers are ¼ to ½ inch long, blue-violet with a white palate, and have a rather short spur. It grows in dry sandy or clayey fields and along roadsides, blooming between April and September. In the Southeast it is very abundant and often colors old fields blue in the early spring. Another name for it is Old-field Toadflax.

RANGE: N.S. to B.C. south to Fla., Tex. and Calif.

BLUE-EYED MARY (*Collinsia verna*)

The Blue-eyed Mary has slender, weak, sometimes minutely downy stems from 6 inches to 2 feet tall. The upper leaves are lance-shaped to egg-shaped, stalkless, partly clasping at the base, toothed on the margin, and ½ to 2 inches long. The lower ones are egg-shaped to roundish and have slender stalks. Its attractive flowers are ½ inch or more long, the 2-lobed upper lip being white and the 3-lobed lower one violet-blue. They are on slender stalks arising from the leaf axils, apparently often in whorls of from 4 to 6. It grows in rich, moist, open woodlands and thickets; blooming between April and June.

RANGE: N.Y. to Wis. and Iowa south to W.Va., Ky., Ark. and Kan.

238

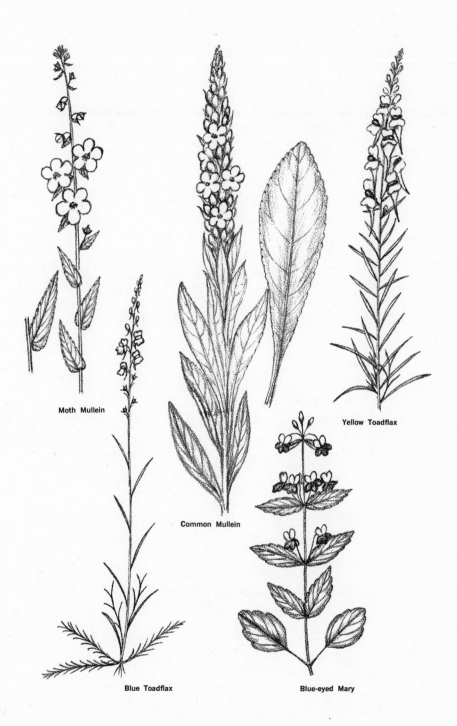

Moth Mullein

Common Mullein

Yellow Toadflax

Blue Toadflax

Blue-eyed Mary

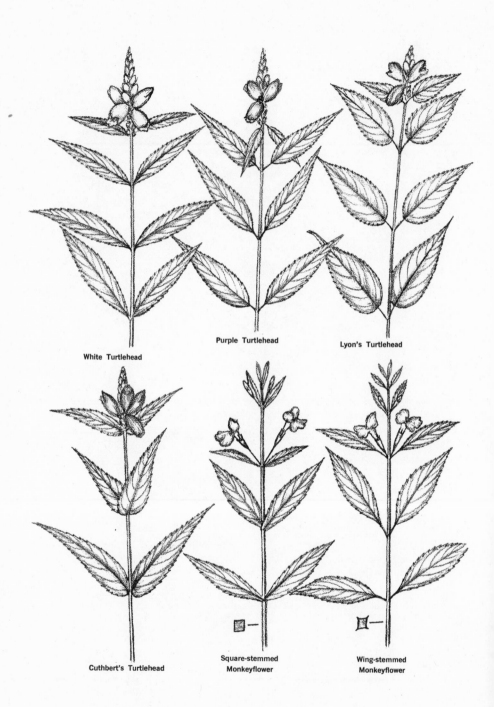

White Turtlehead

Purple Turtlehead

Lyon's Turtlehead

Cuthbert's Turtlehead

Square-stemmed
Monkeyflower

Wing-stemmed
Monkeyflower

WHITE TURTLEHEAD *(Chelone glabra)*

The turtleheads get their name from a fancied resemblance of their flowers to the head of a turtle. Those of this species are about an inch long and usually white, though they are quite often tinged with pink or purple near the tip. It is a smooth plant with a slender erect stem 1 to 3 feet tall; and the opposite leaves are lance-shaped, sharply toothed, stalkless or nearly so, and from 3 to 6 inches long. The flowers of this, and other species, are arranged in narrow but dense end clusters; blooming between August and October. It grows in swamps, along streams, and in other wet places.

RANGE: Nfd. to Ont. and Minn. south to Ga., Ala. and Mo.

PURPLE TURTLEHEAD *(Chelone obliqua)*

This is also a smooth plant 1 to 2 feet tall; with sharply toothed and rather broadly lance-shaped leaves 2 to 6 inches long. They taper at the base into slender stalks ¼ to ½ inch long. The flowers are about an inch long, deep pink to rose-purple and the lower lip is bearded with yellow hairs. It grows in wet woods and swamps; blooming between August and October.

RANGE: Md. to Tenn. south to Ga. and Miss.; Ind. to s. Minn. south to ark.

LYON'S TURTLEHEAD *(Chelone lyoni)*

This turtlehead can be distinguished by its egg-shaped leaves which are 3 to 7 inches long, rounded at the base, taper-pointed at the tip, sharply toothed, and have slender stalks up to 1½ inches long. Its flowers are about an inch long, deep pink to rose-purple; the corolla having a sharp ridge on its back and a lower lip bearded with deep yellow hairs. It grows in wet woods and along streams in the southern mountains; blooming between July and September.

RANGE: Va. south to w. N.C., nw. S.C. and e. Tenn.

CUTHBERT'S TURTLEHEAD *(Chelone cuthbertii)*

Cuthbert's Turtlehead may be distinguished by its sharply toothed, lance-shaped leaves which are rounded to somewhat heart-shaped at the base and completely stalkless. Its flowers are a deep violet-purple, the corolla having broad darker lines on the inside of the lower lip. It grows in wet woods and thickets; blooming in July to September.

RANGE: Uplands of N.C. into the coastal plain of se. Va.

SQUARE-STEMMED MONKEYFLOWER *(Mimulus ringens)*

The monkeyflowers received their name from the fancied resemblance of their 2-lipped corollas to a grinning face. This species is a smooth plant with a branching 4-sided or square stem 1 to 3 feet tall. The lance-shaped to narrowly oblong leaves are 2 to 4 inches long, sharply toothed, and stalkless. Its flowers are about an inch long and have slender stalks usually 1 to 2 inches in length; the corolla being a light violet-blue. It grows in wet meadows, swampy places, and along streams; blooming between June and September.

RANGE: N.S. to Man. south to Ga., La., Tex. and Colo.

WING-STEMMED MONKEYFLOWER *(Mimulus alatus)*

This species is similar to the preceding one but the 4-sided stems are more or less winged on the angles. Its leaves have very evident stalks and its pale blue-violet or pinkish flowers have stalks which are shorter, or no longer than the leaf stalks. It grows in similar situations, blooming between July and October.

RANGE: Conn. to s. Ont., Iowa and Neb. south to Fla. and Tex.

MUSKFLOWER *(Mimulus moschatus)*

The Muskflower is really a monkeyflower with yellow flowers. It has a weak, hairy or somewhat sticky-hairy stem which lies partly flat on the ground, rooting at the lower nodes, but sometimes ascending to a height of about a foot. The leaves are paired, short-stalked, egg-shaped, sometimes toothed, and 1 to 2 inches long. They may be rounded or somewhat heart-shaped at the base. The corolla is rather open, yellow, often striped with red in the throat, about ¾ inch long, and there are 2 densely hairy lines below the lower lip. It grows in the wet margins of ponds and streams, blooming between June and September.

RANGE: Nfd. to Ont. south locally to Mass., N.C., W.Va. and Mich. (Not illustrated)

HAIRY BEARD-TONGUE *(Penstemon hirsutus)*

Beard-tongues are so-called because their flowers have 5 stamens, the fourth one lacking an anther but having a hairy, or bearded, filament. This species has a slender, grayish-downy stem 1 to 3 feet tall, often with gland-tipped hairs in the flower cluster. It has pairs of lance-shaped, elliptic, or narrowly top-shaped leaves 2 to 4 inches long, with sharply toothed margins; the upper ones being stalkless, the lower ones with stalks. The flowers are about an inch long, the slender, dull purple or violet corolla having whitish lobes, and its throat closed by an upward arching lower lip. It grows in dry, rocky, open woods and in fields; blooming between May and July.

RANGE: Que. to Ont. and Wis. south to Va. and Tenn.

SMOOTH BEARD-TONGUE *(Penstemon laevigatus)*

The Smooth Beard-tongue has slender stems 1½ to 3 feet tall which are smooth except in the terminal flower cluster, where they are glandular-hairy. Its leaves are quite firm, lance-shaped to narrowly egg-shaped, 3 to 6 inches long, their margins usually with inconspicuous teeth above the middle. Those on the upper part of the stem are stalkless and slightly clasping; the lower ones tapering into somewhat winged stalks. Its flowers are about an inch long, light violet-purple to white; the corolla expanded above the middle and with an open throat. It grows in dry open woods, fields, and along roadsides; blooming during May and June. RANGE: N.J. and Pa. south to Fla. and Miss.

GRAY BEARD-TONGUE *(Penstemon canescens)*

This species has a slender, gray-downy stem from 1 to 3 feet tall. The egg-shaped to broadly lance-shaped leaves are 2 to 4 inches long; the upper ones are stalkless with rounded to heart-shaped bases and have sharply toothed margins; the lower ones are broader and stalked. The flowers are about an inch long, pale to rather deep violet-purple; the corolla being abruptly swollen about the middle, and with grooves and darker lines in the open throat. It grows in dry woods and on rocky slopes, chiefly in the mountains; blooming from May and July.

RANGE: Pa. to Ind. south to se. Va., n. Ga. and n. Ala.

SOUTHERN BEARD-TONGUE *(Penstemon australis)*

This is chiefly a coastal plain plant, growing in sandy pinelands and dry oak woods; and blooming in May or June. It is distinguished by its flowers which have a creamy corolla with a reddish-purple lower lip. The stems are downy and the upper leaves are nearly or quite toothless. Se. Va. south to Fla. and west to Ala. (Not illustrated)

INDIAN-PAINTBRUSH *(Castilleja coccinea)*

Also known as the Scarlet Painted-cup, this is a somewhat hairy, simple-stemmed plant 8 to 15 inches tall; with the upper stem leaves, or bracts, deeply 3- to 5-cleft and tipped with brilliant red (sometimes pink or white). The flowers are not very conspicuous, about an inch long, greenish-yellow, and in the axils of the colored bracts. It grows in moist meadows, thickets, along roadsides and on prairies; flowering between April and July. A parasite on the roots of other plants.

RANGE: N.H. to Man. south to Fla., La. and Okla.

CULVER'S-ROOT *(Veronicastrum virginicum)*

Culver's-root has a smooth, slender stem 2 to 6 feet tall; with lance-shaped, toothed, short-stalked leaves 3 to 6 inches long, arranged in whorls of from 3 to 9. Its small flowers have a tubular, white or purplish corolla; and are crowded in dense, long, narrow end clusters. It grows in rich moist woods, thickets, and meadows; blooming between June and September. RANGE: Mass. to Man. south to Fla. and Tex.

COMMON WOOD-BETONY *(Pedicularis canadensis)*

This is a hairy plant with a cluster of simple stems 6 to 18 inches high. The lance-shaped leaves are so deeply cut into toothed lobes that they appear almost fern-like, the larger ones being 3 to 5 inches long. Its flowers are about ¾ inch long, the corolla yellow and reddish and with a long and arching upper lip, and are borne in short, densely-bracted end clusters. It grows in open woods, thickets, and clearings; blooming between April and June. Another name is Lousewort.

RANGE: Me. to Que. and Man. south to Fla. and Tex.

242

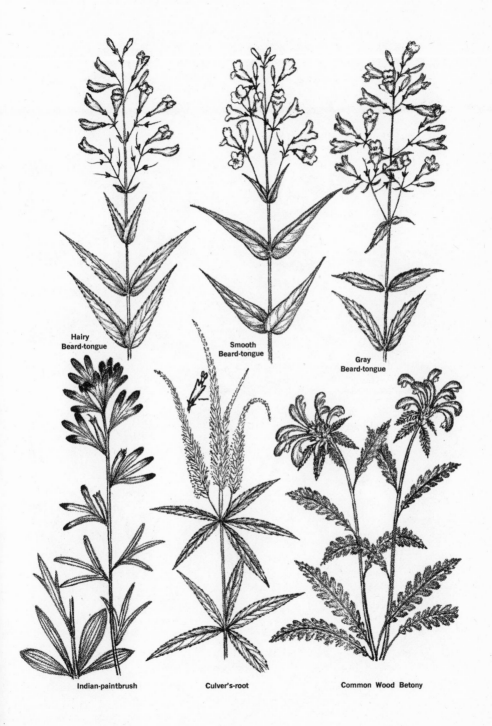

**Hairy
Beard-tongue**

**Smooth
Beard-tongue**

**Gray
Beard-tongue**

Indian-paintbrush

Culver's-root

Common Wood Betony

Smooth False Foxglove

Fern-leaf
False Foxglove

Flax-leaf Gerardia

Large Purple Gerardia

Slender Gerardia

SMOOTH FALSE FOXGLOVE (*Aureolaria flava*)

The yellow-flowered false foxgloves are parasitic on the roots of oak trees. This species is characterized by usually branched and often purplish stems 3 to 6 feet tall, which are more or less whitened with a bloom. Its leaves are elliptic to lance-shaped; the lower ones 4 to 6 inches long and pinnately cleft, the upper ones smaller and either toothed or untoothed. The flowers have a slightly bilateral, trumpet-shaped corolla 1½ to 2 inches long, with roundish lobes. It grows in dry to moist woods, blooming between July and September. RANGE: Me. to Minn. south to Fla. and La.

DOWNY FALSE FOXGLOVE (*Aureolaria virginica*)

This species resembles the preceding one but it has a simple or sparingly branced stem 2 to 4 feet tall, which is grayish-downy. It grows in dry open woods and thickets, blooming between May and August. RANGE: N.H. to Mich. south to Fla. and La. (Not illustrated)

ENTIRE-LEAF FALSE FOXGLOVE (*Aureolaria laevigata*)

This species has a simple or sparingly branched smooth, green stem 1 to 3 feet tall; and even the lower leaves are commonly untoothed. The flowers are somewhat smaller, with corollas just a little over an inch long. It grows in dry to moist woods and thickets, chiefly in the mountains, blooming in August and September.
RANGE: Pa. and Ohio south to Tenn. and Ga. (Not illustrated)

FERN-LEAF FALSE FOXGLOVE (*Aureolaria pedicularia*)

This is a more or less sticky-hairy plant with a much-branched and very leafy stem 1 to 4 feet high. The leaves are all deeply cut, sharply-toothed, and almost fern-like; from 1 to about 3 inches long. The flowers have a trumpet-shaped corolla about 1¼ inches long, which is yellow but commonly purple-tinged. It grows in dry woods and thickets, blooming in September or October. RANGE: Me. to Minn. south to Ga., Ky. and Ill.

COMB-LEAF FALSE FOXGLOVE (*Aureolaria pectinata*)

While similar to the preceding species, this one is usually 1 to 2 feet tall; with leaves even more sharply cut and very often purple-tinged. It grows in sandy woods, blooming from May to September. RANGE: Va. to Ky. and Mo. s. to Fla. and La. (Not illustrated)

LARGE PURPLE GERARDIA (*Agalinis purpurea*)

A number of species of *Agalinis* with pink or purplish flowers occur in the eastern United States, but few of them have such large flowers as the present species. Those of the Large Purple Gerardia average about an inch in length; and are rose-purple, with darker spots within the throat. It is a smooth or slightly roughish plant with a slender branching stem 1 to 2½ feet high; the very narrow leaves being 1 to 1½ inches long, often with smaller ones clustered in their axils. It grows in moist fields, thickets, and boggy places; blooming between August and October.
RANGE: Me. to Minn. and Neb. south to Fla. and Tex.

FLAX-LEAF GERARDIA (*Agalinis linifolia*)

This species also has large flowers, an inch or more long; rose-purple with deeper purple spots on the lower side. It has a smooth, slender, simple or sparingly branched stem 1 to 3 feet tall; with pairs of nearly erect, very narrow but thickish leaves 1 to 2 inches long. It grows in wet pinelands and about the margins of ponds in the coastal plain, blooming during August and September.
RANGE: Del. south to Fla. and west to La.

SLENDER GERARDIA (*Agalinis tenuifolia*)

The Slender Gerardia is a smooth plant with a slender and much-branched stem 6 inches to 2 feet tall; the numerous pairs of very narrow but flattened leaves being ½ to 1¼ inches long. Its flowers are light rose-purple or rarely white, smooth and spotted within the throat, about ⅔ inch long, and are on slender stalks arising in the axils of the upper leaves. It grows in dry to moist woods, thickets, and fields; blooming between August and October. RANGE: Me. to Minn. south to Ga. and La.

THREAD-LEAF GERARDIA (*Agalinis setacea*)

This is similar to the preceding species but its leaves are thread-like (not flattened), and its small flowers are downy. It grows in dry sandy woods, pinelands, and openings from se. N.Y. south to Ga. and Ala. (Not illustrated)

245

BIGNONIA FAMILY (Bignoniaceae)

Members of this family are mostly woody plants with opposite leaves, and flowers with a bilateral symmetry. Their flowers usually have 5 sepals, more or less united; 5 petals, united to form a tubular and often somewhat 2-lipped corolla; 4 or 5 stamens; and a solitary pistil consisting of 2 united carpels. The fruit is a capsule, usually with numerous winged seeds.

CROSS-VINE *(Anisostichus capreolata)*

The pith in the stems of this high-climbing woody vine is shaped like a Maltese-cross, hence its common name. Its paired leaves are divided into 2 egg-shaped or oblong leaflets which are heart-shaped at the base, 3 to 7 inches long, and have the leaf stalk extended beyond them as a branched tendril. Often there is a pair of small leaves at the base of the leaf stalk which resemble stipules. The flowers are long-stalked, trumpet-shaped, red on the outside and orange or yellow within, and about 2 inches long; with a cup-like calyx. They are borne in axillary clusters, blooming during April and May. It grows in rich moist woods and in swamps.

RANGE: Md. and W.Va. to Ohio, Ill. and Mo. south to Fla. and Tex.

TRUMPET-CREEPER *(Campsis radicans)*

The Trumpet-creeper climbs by means of rows of aerial rootlets on its stems. Its paired leaves are divided into from 7 to 11 egg-shaped leaflets which are coarsely and sharply toothed and from 1½ to 3 inches long. The bright orange or reddish-orange, trumpet-shaped flowers are about 3 inches long; and borne in terminal clusters between June and September. It grows in moist woods, thickets, and along fencerows. Although often cultivated as an ornamental vine, it produces a dermatitis similar to that of Poison-ivy in some persons; giving rise to another common name, Cow-itch.

RANGE: N.J. to W.Va., Ill. and Iowa south to Fla. and Tex.

BROOM-RAPE FAMILY (Orobanchaceae)

All members of this family are parasitic plants, without green color and with only scale-like leaves. Their flowers have 4 or 5 partly united sepals; 4 or 5 united petals, the corolla usually irregular or 2-lipped; 4 stamens which are attached to the corolla tube; and a solitary pistil consisting of usually 2 united carpels, with the ovary 1-chambered. The fruits are capsules.

SQUAWROOT *(Conopholis americana)*

This peculiar plant is usually found in the woods, at the bases of oak trees. It forms large rounded knobs on the roots of the trees from which it receives its nourishment; and produces groups of stout, brownish or yellowish, scaly stems 3 to 10 inches high. They look very much like slender pine cones. The tubular flowers on these stems are yellowish, about ½ inch long, and are in the axils of the scales; blooming between April and July. Another name for it is Cancer-root. RANGE: N.S. to Wis. south to Fla. and Miss.

BEECH-DROPS *(Epifagus virginiana)*

In woods, under the beech trees, one often sees this parasitic plant with slender, purplish or yellowish-brown stems and ascending branches. They are 6 to 15 inches high and have scales instead of leaves; and they arise from a thick, scaly base. It produces its flowers between September and November; the upper ones being largest, about ½ inch long, whitish with a band of purplish-brown on the upper side, but they are sterile. The smaller flowers produce the seeds. RANGE: N.S. to Ont. south to Fla. and La.

ONE-FLOWERED BROOM-RAPE *(Orobanche uniflora)*

This plant has a scaly stem which creeps beneath the surface, around the roots of the plants on which it is parasitic. It sends up whitish, naked flower stalks 3 to 8 inches high; each one bearing a solitary creamy-white to lilac-colored flower about ¾ inch long. The tubular corolla has 2 bearded, yellow folds in the throat and it is minutely downy on the outside. It grows in rich, moist woodlands and thickets where it is parasitic on the roots of various plants; blooming between April and June. Other names for it are Pale Broom-rape and Naked Broom-rape.

RANGE: N.B. to Que. and Mont. south to Fla. and Tex.

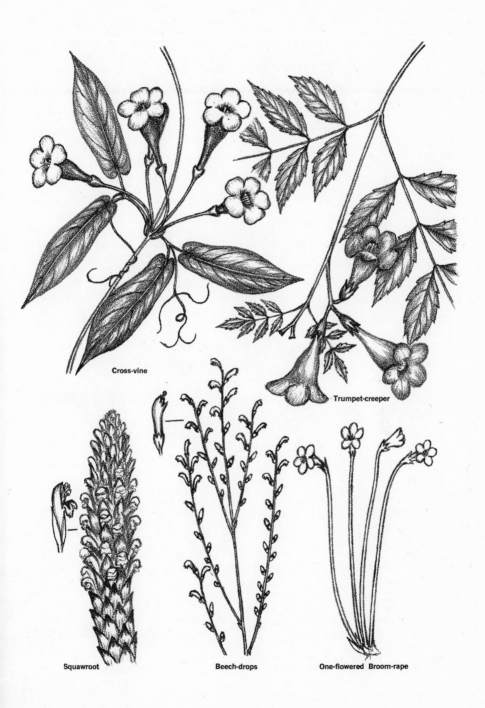

Cross-vine

Trumpet-creeper

Squawroot

Beech-drops

One-flowered Broom-rape

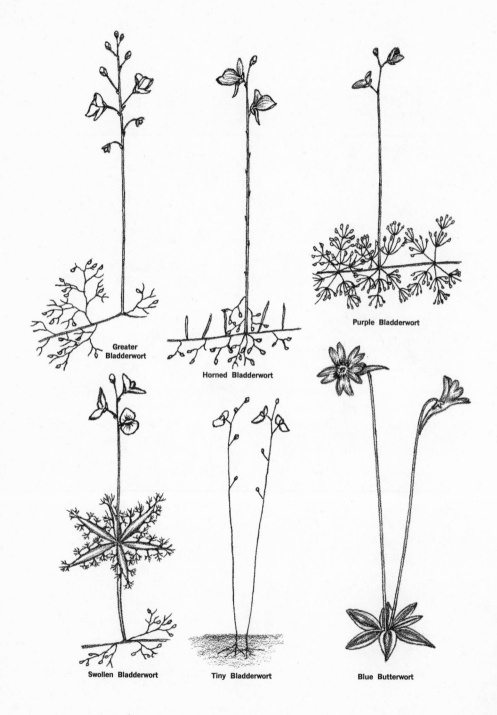

Greater
Bladderwort

Horned Bladderwort

Purple Bladderwort

Swollen Bladderwort

Tiny Bladderwort

Blue Butterwort

BLADDERWORT FAMILY (Lentibulariaceae)

Members of the Bladderwort Family are aquatic plants, or plants of wet soils which get part of their nourishment by trapping insects or small aquatic animals. Their flowers have a bilateral symmetry, the corolla tube being spurred and very often 2-lipped; and they are borne on naked or minutely scaly stalks. There are always 2 stamens and a single 1-celled pistil.

The aquatic bladderworts have very finely dissected leaves, some or all of them bearing small bladders which serve as traps in catching tiny water animals. The older bladders often appear blackish because they are full of the indigestible remains of such animals. Besides the following, quite a few other species occur in the shallower waters of lakes, ponds, and slow-moving streams.

GREATER BLADDERWORT *(Utricularia vulgaris)*

This species has stems 1 to 3 feet long which float horizontally beneath the surface of the water; sending up stout stalks 4 inches to 2 feet high which bear from 6 to 20 or more yellow flowers ¾ inch or more long, between May and September.
RANGE: Lab. to Alaska south to Va., Ohio, Mo. and Tex.

HORNED BLADDERWORT *(Utricularia cornuta)*

This bladderwort grows in bogs or on the wet sandy or muddy shores of lakes and ponds, the main portion of the plant being hidden. It sends up slender, brownish, wiry stalks 1 to 12 inches high; bearing from 1 to 5 yellow flowers about ¾ inch long between June and September. RANGE: Nfd. to Ont. and Minn. south to Fla. and Tex.

PURPLE BLADDERWORT *(Utricularia purpurea)*

The leaves of this bladderwort are in whorls along the 1- to 3-foot free-floating stems, and have bladders at the tips of the hair-like divisions. Between May and September it has erect stalks 2 to 6 inches high which bear from 2 to 5 deep pink to lavender-purple flowers. RANGE: N.S. to Que. and Wis. south to Fla. and La.

SWOLLEN BLADDERWORT *(Utricularia inflata)*

This species can be distinguished by the whorl of 3 to 10 float-like inflated leaves at the bases of its flower stalks. The latter are 5 to 12 inches high and bear from 3 to 5 or more yellow flowers ½ to ¾ inch across, between May and November.
RANGE: N.S. to N.Y. and Ind. south to Fla. and Tex.

TINY BLADDERWORT *(Utricularia subulata)*

This bladderwort grows in wet sandy places; sending up extremely fine, wiry, usually zig-zag and reddish-purple stems 3 to about 8 inches high. Between March and August, each one has from 1 to 12 yellow flowers about ⅓ inch across.
RANGE: N.S. south to Fla., west to Tex. and north to Ark.

BLUE BUTTERWORT *(Pinguicula caerulea)*

Butterworts got their name from the fact that the European species have been used as rennin in curdling milk. They have basal rosettes of shiny, sticky, pale green leaves. Insects stick to them as to flypaper, and the edges of the leaves roll up as their bodies are digested. This one has leaves ½ to 2 inches long. Its flowers are pale violet, almost an inch across, the corolla having 5 deeply notched lobes and a spur. They are solitary on sticky-hairy stalks 4 to 10 inches tall. It grows in wet coastal plain pinelands, blooming during April and May. RANGE: N.C. south to Fla.

YELLOW BUTTERWORT *(Pinguicula lutea)*

This species is similar to the preceding but it has golden-yellow flowers with the lobes shallowly 2- or 3-notched. It grows in similar situations from N.C. south to Fla. and west to La.; blooming during April and May. (Not illustrated)

SMALL BUTTERWORT *(Pinguicula pumila)*

This is a smaller species with white, pale blue, or rarely yellow flowers about ½ inch across; and leaves ½ to 1 inch long.. It grows in wet coastal plain pinelands from S.C. to Fla. and Tex.; blooming in April and May. (Not illustrated)

249

ACANTHUS FAMILY (Acanthaceae)

Members of this family have flowers with usually 5 partly united sepals; 5 more or less united petals forming a nearly regular to 2-lipped corolla; 2 or 4 stamens, in pairs of different length, and attached to the corolla tube; and a pistil consisting of 2 united carpels, the ovary being 2-celled and commonly with 2 ovules in each cell. The fruit is a capsule; the seeds being borne on small, hooked projections.

WATER-WILLOW *(Justicia americana)*

The Water-willow grows in slowly moving streams, the shallower waters of lakes and ponds, and more rarely in swamps. It is a smooth plant with numerous thick, cord-like runners; and it has slender, erect, grooved and angled stems 1 to 3 feet high. It leaves are paired, stalkless or nearly so, lance-shaped (often narrowly so) and 3 to 6 inches long. The attractive 2-lipped, pale violet flowers are about ¾ inch long; in dense and long-stalked clusters arising from the leaf axils. The flowering season is between June and October.

RANGE: Vt. and Que. to Ont., Wis. and Kan. south to Ga. and Tex.

HAIRY RUELLIA *(Ruellia ciliosa)*

The Hairy Ruellia is a somewhat variable plant. It has a more or less hairy, simple or branched stem 6 inches to 2½ feet tall. The egg-shaped, lance-shaped, or elliptic leaves have short stalks and are 1½ to 4 inches long ;usually being rather crowded toward the tips of the stems. The lavender or lilac-blue flowers are 1 to 2 inches long, the united sepals being prolonged into bristle-like and usually hairy-fringed tips. They are nearly stalkless and several usually occur together in the leaf axils. It grows in dry sandy woods and clearings, blooming between May and September.

RANGE: N.J. to Ind. south to Fla. and Tex.

SMOOTH RUELLIA *(Ruellia strepens)*

This is a smooth or sparingly hairy plant with a simple or branched stem 1 to 3 feet tall. The egg-shaped leaves are 3 to 6 inches long and taper into slender stalks. The flowers are pale blue-violet, 1½ to 2 inches long, and the calyx lobes are merely taper-pointed at the tip. It grows in rich, open woods and thickets; blooming between May and September.

RANGE: N.J. to Ill., Mo. and Kan. south to Fla. and Tex.

DYSCHORISTE *(Dyschoriste oblongifolia)*

Dyschoriste has a slender, erect, downy or hairy stem from 6 to 15 inches tall. On it are pairs of ascending or erect, oblong to oval or top-shaped, stalkless leaves ½ to 1¼ inches long. The flowers are blue, sometimes mottled with purple, about an inch long, and are usually solitary in the axils of the upper leaves. It grows in dry, sandy coastal plain pinelands or on sandhills; blooming during April and May.

RANGE: se. S.C. south to Fla.

LOPSEED FAMILY (Phrymaceae)

Members of this family have flowers with 5 united sepals; 5 petals united to form a 2-lipped bilateral corolla; 4 stamens attached to the corolla tube, in 2 pairs of different length; and a solitary pistil which matures as a 1-seeded fruit, enclosed in the persistent calyx. The family contains only the one genus, of which we have the following species.

LOPSEED *(Phryma leptostachya)*

This is a smooth or somewhat minutely downy plant with a branching stem 1½ to 3 feet tall. Its leaves are in widely-spaced pairs; egg-shaped, coarsely toothed, 2 to 6 inches long, and all but the upper ones are long-stalked. The white to lavender flowers are about ⅓ inch long and are arranged in pairs in a very long and slender cluster, blooming between June and August. After the flower fades, the calyx bends abruptly downward against the stalk and the fruits develop within it, hence the common name given to the plant. It grows in rich woodlands and in thickets.

RANGE: N.B. to Man. south to Fla. and Tex.

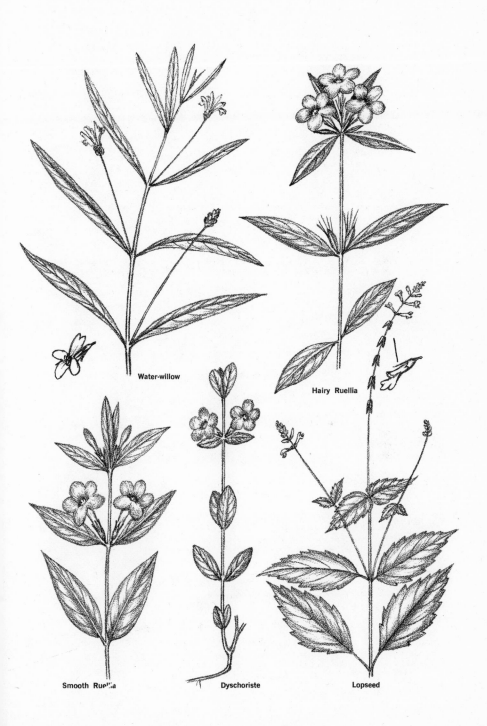

Water-willow

Hairy Ruellia

Smooth Ruellia

Dyschoriste

Lopseed

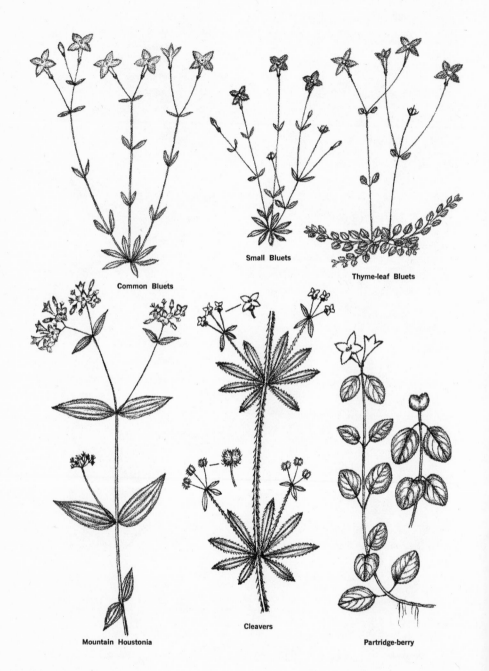

Common Bluets

Small Bluets

Thyme-leaf Bluets

Mountain Houstonia

Cleavers

Partridge-berry

MADDER FAMILY (Rubiaceae)

This is a large family of plants with opposite, untoothed leaves; and flowers with usually 4 sepals more or less united with the ovary, 4 united petals, and 4 stamens which are attached to the corolla tube.

COMMON BLUETS *(Houstonia caerulea)*
Often called Innocence or Quakerladies, this is a smooth little plant with thread-like tufted stems 3 to 6 inches high. It has narrowly top-shaped leaves about ½ inch long in a basal rosette, and pairs of smaller ones on the flower stems. Its bright pale blue to whitish flowers have a yellow "eye". It is common in open woods, meadows and clearings; blooming between April and June.
RANGE: N.S. to Ont. and Wis. south to Ga., Ala. and Mo.

SMALL BLUETS *(Houstonia pusilla)*
This bluet has thread-like stems 1 to 4 inches high. The oval or egg-shaped basal leaves are less than ½ inch long; and the deep violet-blue or purplish flowers with a dark yellow "eye" are about ¼ inch across. Often called the Star-violet, it grows in sandy or rocky open places; blooming in March or April.
RANGE: Va. to Ill., Mo. and Okla. south to Fla. and Tex.

LEAST BLUETS *(Houstonia minima)*
This species is very similar to the preceding and is best distinguished by its calyx lobes, which are nearly as long as the corolla tube. It grows in open woods and dry open places from Ill. to Iowa and Kan. south to Ark. and Tex.; blooming in April. (Not illustrated)

THYME-LEAF BLUETS *(Houstonia serpyllifolia)*
This is a delicate little plant with creeping, leafy stems 4 to 10 inches long. The deep blue flowers resemble those of the Common Bluet. It grows in wet places, often along mountain streams; blooming between April and July.
RANGE: Pa. and W.Va. south to n. Ga. and e. Tenn.

Houstonia procumbens is a coastal plain species which also has prostrate and creeping stems but its flowers are white. It grows on beach dunes and in sandy pinelands from se. S.C. south to Fla. and west to La.; blooming in March or April. (Not illustrated)

MOUNTAIN HOUSTONIA *(Houstonia purpurea)*
This plant has a simple or branched stem 4 to 18 inches tall; with pairs of egg-shaped to lance-shaped, 3- to 5-ribbed leaves ½ to 1 inch long. The small whitish to pale purple flowers are arranged in terminal clusters. It grows in open woods and on rocky slopes; blooming between May and July. Also called the Tall Houstonia.
RANGE: Del. to Iowa south to Fla., La. and Okla.

LONG-LEAF HOUSTONIA *(Houstonia longifolia)*
This species has narrow leaves ⅛ to ¼ inch wide; and calyx lobes longer than the corolla tube. Me. to Sask. south to Ga., Ky. and Okla. (Not illustrated)

CLEAVERS *(Galium aparine)*
Bedstraws or goose-grasses are slender plants with weak, mostly reclining, 4-sided stems; leaves arranged in whorls; and small, white to yellowish, 4-parted flowers in axillary or terminal clusters. A number of species occur in the eastern United States. This common one has narrow leaves 1 to 3 inches long, with rough margins and midribs, and arranged in whorls of from 6 to 8. The angles of its stems are bristly-prickly, the flowers white, and the fruits bristly. It grows in woods, meadows, and roadsides; blooming between April and July. RANGE: Nfd. to Alaska south to Fla. and Tex.

PARTRIDGE-BERRY *(Mitchella repens)*
Also known as Twinberry, this is a smooth plant with trailing slender stems 6 to 12 inches long; with pairs of lustrous, evergreen, roundish and stalked leaves usually ½ to ¾ inch long. The white or pinkish, fringed flowers are in pairs and have their bases united. They are followed by bright red, double berries about ⅓ inch across; which often persist until the next flowering time between May and July.
RANGE: Nfd. to Ont. and Minn. south to Fla. and Tex.

HONEYSUCKLE FAMILY (Caprifoliaceae)

Members of this family are mostly shrubs or woody vines with opposite leaves. Their flowers have 4 or 5 sepals which are united with the 3- to 5-celled ovary of the pistil; 4 or 5 more or less united petals which form a nearly radial to strongly bilateral or 2-lipped corolla; and 4 or 5 stamens which are attached to the corolla tube.

GLAUCOUS HONEYSUCKLE *(Lonicera dioica)*

This is a somewhat woody, climbing plant with smooth stems 3 to 10 feet long. The greenish-yellow and often purplish-tinged flowers are about ⅔ inch long. They are in a dense end cluster and the pair of leaves immediately below them are joined together at the base. The other leaves are oval or egg-shaped, stalkless or short-stalked, 1½ to 3½ inches long, and are pale or whitened beneath. The fruits are salmon-colored berries. It grows in rocky woods, thickets, and on slopes; blooming during May or June.

RANGE: Me. and Ont. to Man. south to Ga. and Mo.

TRUMPET HONEYSUCKLE *(Lonicera sempervirens)*

Also known as the Coral Honeysuckle, this native species is quite often cultivated. It is a climbing vine with pairs of oval to narrowly elliptic leaves 1½ to 3 inches long, which are dark green above and strongly whitened beneath. The flowers are slenderly trumpet-shaped with 5 short lobes at the summit, 1½ to 2 inches long, bright red on the outside and yellowish within. They are arranged in several whorls on a terminal stalk often several inches long, and bloom between April and September. It grows in the borders of woods, thickets, and in fencerows and is much more common southward.

RANGE: Me. to N.Y., Iowa and Neb. south to Fla. and Tex.

YELLOW HONEYSUCKLE *(Lonicera flava)*

This is one of the most attractive of our native climbing honeysuckles. It is a rather woody and twining plant somewhat like the Glaucous Honeysuckle, but its leaves are paler and grayish beneath. In April or May it has clusters of fragrant, bright yellow to orange-yellow flowers about an inch long, which are shaped somewhat like those of the familiar Japanese Honeysuckle. It grows naturally in rocky woods and on bluffs and is very desirable as a cultivated flowering vine.

RANGE: N.C. to Mo. south to Ga., Ala., Ark. and Okla.

JAPANESE HONEYSUCKLE *(Lonicera japonica)*

The Japanese Honeysuckle is a high-climbing and trailing vine with densely hairy stems and branchlets. It has pairs of egg-shaped to oval, short-stalked leaves 1 to 3 inches long which are downy beneath. The flowers are tubular and 2-lipped, the upper lip having 3 lobes and the lower one having 2. They are white at first but turn yellow, about 1¼ inches long, and are extremely fragrant. This Asiatic species has been widely cultivated in America and in many places—particularly in the South—it has escaped to become a very troublesome forest weed. It blooms between May and August and the flowers are followed by black berries.

TWINFLOWER *(Linnaea borealis* var. *americana)*

The Twinflower is a slender-stemmed, trailing or creeping plant which grows in cold woods and bogs in the northern portions of both the Old and the New Worlds. Between June and August it sends up 3- to 10-inch stalks bearing pairs of stalked, roundish or oval, obscurely toothed leaves ⅓ to ⅔ of an inch wide. At their tips they have a pair of nodding, bell-shaped, pink flowers about ⅓ of an inch long. The genus was named for the immortal Linnaeus who was especially fond of this dainty little plant.

RANGE: Lab. to Alaska south to Md., W.Va., the Great Lakes region, S.D., Colo., Utah and Calif.

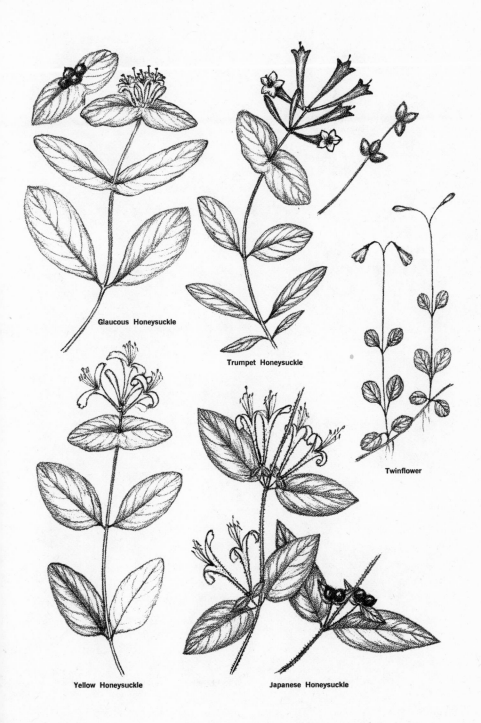

Glaucous Honeysuckle

Trumpet Honeysuckle

Twinflower

Yellow Honeysuckle

Japanese Honeysuckle

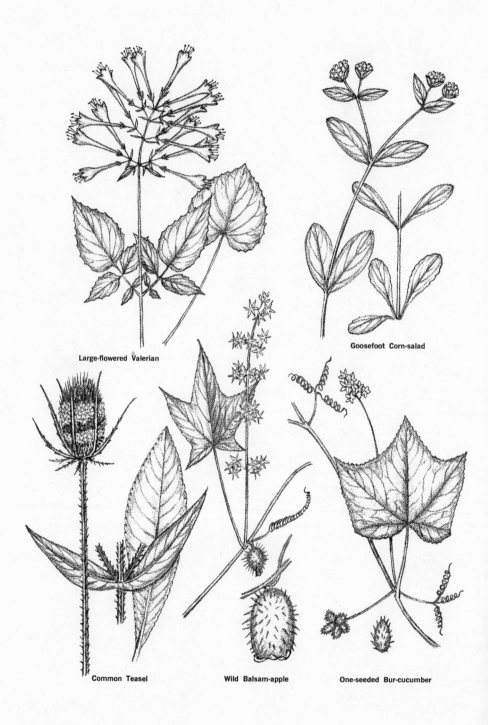

Large-flowered Valerian

Goosefoot Corn-salad

Common Teasel

Wild Balsam-apple

One-seeded Bur-cucumber

VALERIAN FAMILY (Valerianaceae)

Members of this family have a calyx united with the 1- to 3-chambered ovary of the pistil, the lobes often not evident or represented by plume-like bristles; a corolla of usually 5 united petals; and usually 3 stamens which are attached to the corolla tube. Each pistil usually produces only 1 seed.

LARGE-FLOWERED VALERIAN *(Valeriana pauciflora)*

Also known as the American Wild Valerian, this is a smooth plant with many spreading rootstocks and a slender stem 1 to 2½ feet high. The leaves on the stem are paired and divided into 3 to 7 thin leaflets, the terminal one being much the larger. The basal leaves are more or less heart-shaped, long-stalked, and sometimes have an additional pair of small leaflets. Its flowers have pale pink corolla tubes about ⅔ inch long, 5-lobed at the summit; and 5 stamens which extend well beyond the corolla. The calyx has feathery bristles which unroll as the fruits develop. It grows in rich moist woods and in stream bottoms, blooming in May or June. RANGE: Pa. to Ill. south to Va. and Tenn.

GOOSEFOOT CORN-SALAD *(Valerianella chenopodifolia)*

This is a smooth plant from 1 to 2 feet tall, with forking branches. It has pairs of lance-shaped to oblong, stalkless leaves 1 to 3 inches long on the stems. The lower and basal ones are broader toward the tip and often somewhat wavy-toothed on the margin. Its small white flowers are densely crowded in head-like clusters about ⅔ inch broad, with leafy bracts at the base. It grows in moist open woods, meadows, and in stream bottoms, blooming in May or June. RANGE: N.Y. and Pa. to s. Ont. and Ind.

TEASEL FAMILY (Dipsacaceae)

Members of this family have flowers with a calyx united with the ovary of the pistil; a corolla of 2 to 5 united petals; and 2 to 4 stamens attached to the corolla tube. The fruits are small, dry, and 1-seeded.

COMMON TEASEL *(Dipsacus sylvestris)*

This native of Europe is widely naturalized in waste places, old fields, and along roadsides in eastern North America. It has a stout prickly stem 3 to 6 feet tall. The pairs of lance-shaped or oblong leaves are 6 to 12 inches long, the upper ones clasping the stem at the base. The flowers are very small, with a tubular lilac or pinkish-purple corolla; and are crowded in an egg-shaped or cylindrical head, intermixed with prickly bristles. It blooms between July and October.

GOURD FAMILY (Cucurbitaceae)

Members of this family are usually tendril-bearing vines with alternate leaves. The stamens and the pistils are always in separate flowers, sometimes on separate plants. The flowers have 4 to 6 usually partly united sepals; and a like number of more or less united petals. The 3 stamens are joined together by their contorted anthers. The pistil is united with the calyx tube.

WILD BALSAM-APPLE *(Echinocystis lobata)*

This tendril-climber grows in rich soils, usually along streams, climbing about over bushes and other vegetation. It has rather thin, roughish leaves which are deeply and sharply 5-lobed as well as toothed on the margin. The stamen-bearing flowers are greenish-white and grouped in long and narrow clusters. The pistil-bearing ones are solitary and develop into an egg-shaped, green, prickly fruit about 2 inches long. It blooms from June to October. Other names given it are Wild Cucumber or Prickly Cucumber. RANGE: N.B. to Sask. south to Fla. and Tex.

ONE-SEEDED BUR-CUCUMBER *(Sicyos angulatus)*

Stems of this tendril-climber are angled and sticky-hairy, and its tendrils are branched. Its leaves are 5-angled or rather shallowly 5-lobed, toothed on the margin, and rough on both sides. The stamen-bearing flowers are whitish and clustered at the ends of long stalks. The pistil-bearing ones are also clustered but are on much shorter stalks. They develop into yellowish, dry, egg-shaped, prickly, 1-seeded fruits about ½ inch long. It grows along streams and in low moist woods and thickets; blooming between July and September. RANGE: Me. to Que. and Minn. south to Fla. and Tex.

Harebell

Tall Bellflower

Southern Harebell

Venus' Looking-glass

Small Venus' Looking-glass

BLUEBELL FAMILY (Campanulaceae)

Members of the Bluebell Family have flowers with 5 sepals which are united with the ovary of the pistil; 5 partly united petals forming a 5-lobed corolla; and 5 stamens which are usually free from the corolla and all separate. The plants have a milky juice and alternate leaves.

HAREBELL *(Campanula rotundifolia)*

Also called the Bluebells-of-Scotland, the Harebell is found in the northern parts of both the Old and New World and is frequently cultivated. It has a slender, weak, and much-branched stem 6 to 18 inches high. The stem leaves are all very narrow but the basal ones are roundish, rather heart-shaped, ¼ to 1 inch wide, and long-stalked. Its hanging flowers are bell-shaped, purplish-blue, and about ¾ inch long; blooming between June and September. It grows on moist rocky slopes, cliffs, and meadows.
RANGE: Nfd. to Alaska south to N.J., W.Va., Ohio, Ill., Mo., Neb., Tex. and Calif.

TALL BELLFLOWER *(Campanula americana)*

The Tall or American Bellflower usually has a simple, more or less hairy stem, from 2 to about 6 feet tall; along which are scattered lance-shaped to narrowly egg-shaped, toothed leaves 3 to 6 inches long, most of them tapering at the base into short stalks. Its flowers are star-shaped rather than bell-like, with 5 long and pointed lobes. They are about an inch across, light violet-blue, and are in the axils of leaf-like bracts; forming a long and slender end cluster. It grows in rich moist woods and thickets, blooming between June and August. RANGE: Ont. to Minn. south to Fla., Ala. and Mo.

SOUTHERN HAREBELL *(Campanula divaricata)*

This is a smooth plant with a slender and much-branched stem 1 to 3 feet high, which grows on dry rocky slopes and in open woods in the mountains. The leaves are lance-shaped to narrowly egg-shaped, pointed at both ends, coarsely and sharply toothed, and usually 1 to 3 inches long. The light lavender-blue flowers are bell-shaped, about ¼ inch long, and nod on slender stalks. They are usually very numerous and arranged in a rather large but loose cluster, blooming between June and September. It is sometimes called the Panicled Bellflower. RANGE: Md., W.Va. and Ky. south to Ga. and Ala.

MARSH BELLFLOWER *(Campanula aparinoides)*

This species has a weak and somewhat 3-sided, branching stem which is minutely rough-ish-bristly on the angles. The narrow leaves are 1 to 2½ inches long and are roughish on the margins and midribs. Whitish to pale blue, open bell-shaped flowers ½ inch or less long are produced on slender stalks between June and August. The plant grows in wet meadows, swales, and on shores and stream banks. It is also known as the Slender or Bedstraw Bellflower. Me. to Minn. south to Ga., Ky., Iowa, Neb. and Colo. (Not illustrated)

VENUS' LOOKING-GLASS *(Specularia perfoliata)*

The Venus' Looking-glass is a common plant of dry open woods, thickets, and fields. It is a more or less hairy plant with a simple stem, or sometimes branched toward the base, and 6 to 18 inches high. The numerous leaves are roundish or egg-shaped, toothed on the margin, ¼ to 1 inch wide, and clasp the stem by a heart-shaped base. The flowers in the axils of the lower leaves never open, remaining bud-like but producing seeds. The ones along the upper part of the stem are violet or violet-blue, about ½ inch across, and are star-shaped with 5 long corolla lobes; blooming between April and August. RANGE: Me. to Ont. and B.C. south to Fla. and Tex.

SMALL VENUS' LOOKING-GLASSS *(Specularia biflora)*

Although quite similar to the preceding species, the leaves of this plant are untoothed or inconspicuously toothed and are stalkless but do not clasp the stems. It produces only 1 or 2 showy flowers toward the tip of the 6- to 18-inch stem, all of the others remaining closed and bud-like. It grows in dry open woods and fields, blooming between April and June.
RANGE: Va. to Ky., Kan. and Ore. south to Fla., Tex. and s. Calif.

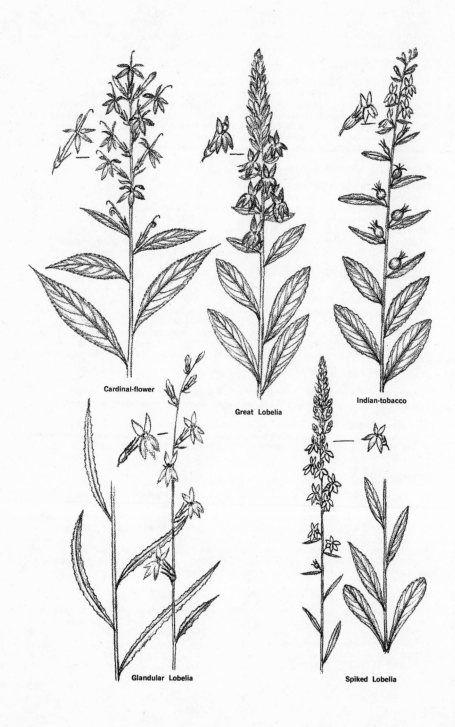

Cardinal-flower

Great Lobelia

Indian-tobacco

Glandular Lobelia

Spiked Lobelia

LOBELIA FAMILY (Lobeliaceae)

Members of this family have a milky juice, alternate leaves, and flowers with a bilateral symmetry. The flowers have 5 sepals united with the ovary of the pistil; 5 petals which are united below into a tube which is open along the upper side, the free ends of the petals forming 2 lips; and 5 stamens which have their anthers united in a ring about the style of the pistil.

CARDINAL-FLOWER *(Lobelia cardinalis)*

Also known as the Red Lobelia, this plant always attracts one's attention by its terminal clusters of brilliant red flowers. Each flower is about 1½ inches long and the tube of stamens projects upward through the cleft in the corolla. It usually has a simple stem from 1 to 3 feet tall. The numerous leaves are 2 to 6 inches long, lance-shaped to narrowly egg-shaped, and are toothed on the margin. It grows in moist meadows, thickets, swamps, and along the banks of streams; blooming between July and October.
RANGE: N.B. to Ont. and Minn. south to Fla. and Tex.

GREAT LOBELIA *(Lobelia siphilitica)*

Sometimes the Great Lobelia is called the Blue Cardinal-flower. It has a nearly smooth, erect, rather stout, and simple stem from 1 to 3 feet tall. The many leaves are lance-shaped to egg-shaped, stalkless, untoothed or irregularly toothed on the margin, and from 2 to 6 inches long. Its bright blue flowers are about an inch long and often have white marks on the lower corolla lobes. They are borne in the axils of crowded leaf-like bracts toward the summit of the stem; blooming between July and October. It grows in wet or swampy places.
RANGE: Me. to Minn. south to Va., nw. S.C., n. Ala., La. and Tex.

DOWNY LOBELIA *(Lobelia puberula)*

This pretty lobelia is similar to the Great Lobelia but it has densely downy stems and leaves; and somewhat smaller bright blue flowers. It grows in wet woods and swampy places from N.J. to W.Va., Ill. and Okla. south to Fla. and Tex.; blooming between August and October. (Not illustrated)

INDIAN-TOBACCO *(Lobelia inflata)*

The Indian-tobacco is easily recognized by its small pale violet-blue to whitish flowers, the oval-shaped bases of which become swollen and bladder-like as the fruits form. It is a somewhat hairy and usually much-branched plant 1 to 3 feet high. The numerous leaves are lance-shaped, egg-shaped, or oval and are often broadest above the middle. They are stalkless, toothed on the margin, and from 1 to 2½ inches long. The flowers are numerous and in slender clusters at the tips of the branches; blooming between July and October. It grows in open woods, thickets, and fields.
RANGE: Lab. to Sask. south to Ga., Miss., Ark. and Kan.

GLANDULAR LOBELIA *(Lobelia glandulosa)*

Also known as the Swamp Lobelia, this plant grows in the wetter coastal plain pinelands and swamps in the Southeast. It is a smoothish plant with a slender stem 1 to 4 feet tall, which is chiefly leafy on the lower part. Its leaves are all very narrow, rather stiff and thickish, and are wavy-toothed with hard-tipped teeth on the margin. The lower ones are often 6 inches long but they are greatly reduced in size upward along the stem. The flowers are lavender with a white "eye", which is surrounded by an area of deeper violet-blue. They are about an inch long and the calyx teeth have prominent gland-tipped teeth on their margins. It blooms during September and October. RANGE: se. Va. south to Fla.

SPIKED LOBELIA *(Lobelia spicata)*

This lobelia usually has a simple stem 1 to 3 feet high which is densely downy toward the base but rather smooth above. The lower leaves are mostly top-shaped and 1 to 3½ inches long. Those upward along the stem are smaller and lance-shaped or narrower. Its pale bluish or whitish flowers are about ⅓ inch long and in a rather dense but long and narrow terminal cluster. It grows in open woods, thickets, fields and along roadsides; blooming between June and August. RANGE: N.B. to Minn. south to Ga., La. and Kan.

COMPOSITE FAMILY (Compositae)

This is the largest of all plant families. The various members of the family have small flowers in a dense cluster or *head*, seated on the expanded end of the flower stalk which is called the *receptacle*. The group of flowers is surrounded by 1 or more series of *bracts*, collectively known as the *involucre*. In some composites, such as the asters, daisies, and sunflowers the heads contain two kinds of flowers. The ones in the central part, or *disk*, of the head are known as the *disk flowers*. These flowers have a radial symmetry. The calyx is united with the ovary of the pistil; the sepals often being represented by a tuft of hairs, bristles, or scales on its summit. Collectively they are called the *pappus*. The corolla is tubular, usually with 5 lobes at the summit and it is apparently situated on the top of the ovary. Within the corolla there are 5 stamens, their anthers united into a ring which surrounds the style of the pistil with the 2-branched stigma emerging from the top. The flowers around the border of the head, which look like petals, are the *ray flowers*. These flowers have a bilateral symmetry, the 5 petals all being united into a flattened or strap-shaped corolla.

In some composites, such as the dandelions and the Chicory, all of the flowers in the heads are ray flowers. In others, such as the ironweeds and thistles, the heads are made up entirely of disk flowers. In many composites the disk flowers are mixed with what is called the *chaff*. It may be seen on the receptacle when some of the disk flowers are pulled off.

The fruits are dry, 1-celled, and 1-seeded bodies called *achenes* which are generally taken to be seeds. A sunflower "seed", for example, is such a fruit, or achene. In many composites the pappus remains on the mature fruits, as silky tufts of hairs, awns, etc.

KEY TO GENERA OF THE COMPOSITE FAMILY

GROUP I. HEADS CONTAINING ONLY FLOWERS WITH STRAP-SHAPED COR-
OLLAS (RAY-FLOWERS).

1. Flowers blue or bluish.

    2. Flowers an inch or more across.   CHICORY *(Chicorium)*

    2. Flowers ½ inch or less across.   LETTUCES *(Lactuca)*

1. Flowers other than blue or bluish in color.

    2. Flowers pinkish to cream-colored or greenish-white; the heads borne in drooping clusters.   RATTLESNAKE-ROOTS *(Prenanthes)*

    2. Flowers yellow to orange-red.

        3. Flower heads borne on leafless or nearly leafless stems, leaves mostly basal.

            4. Flower heads clustered at the summit of the stem.
                HAWKWEEDS *(Hieracium)*

            4. Flower heads solitary at the summit of the stem or its few branches.

                5. Involucre with a row of recurved bracts at the base. Pappus of fine white hairs on the stalk-like summit of the achene.
                    DANDELIONS *(Taraxacum)*

                5. Involucre without recurved bracts at the base. Pappus of a few hairs and scales seated on summit of the achene.
                    DWARF DANDELIONS *(Krigia)*

        3. Flower heads borne on leafy stems.

            4. Flower heads solitary on the stem branches; pappus of reddish-brown hairs.
                FALSE-DANDELION *(Pyrrhopappus)*

            4. Flower heads several to very numerous.

                5. Achenes with a beak or stalk with a pappus of fine hairs on the summit.   LETTUCES *(Lactuca)*

                5. Achenes with a tuft of bristly hairs seated directly on the summit.
                HAWKWEEDS *(Hieracium)*

GROUP II. HEADS CONTAINING ONLY TUBULAR FLOWERS.

1. Plant climbing or twining.   CLIMBING-HEMPWEED *(Mikania)*
1. Plants otherwise.

  2. Flowers white or whitish to cream-colored.

    3. Flower heads in a cone-shaped end cluster. Stem white-woolly and with green wings running down from the leaf bases.   BLACKROOT *(Pterocaulon)*

    3. Heads not in cone-shaped end clusters. Stems not winged.

      4. Involucre with a single row of erect bracts with edges meeting, and sometimes with a row of minute ones at the base.

        5. Involucre with 1 row of bracts. Flower heads nodding.
            INDIAN-PLANTAINS *(Cacalia)*

        5. Involucre with a row of small bracts at the base. Flower heads held erect.   FIREWEED *(Erechtites)*

      4. Involucre with 2 to several rows of overlapping bracts.

        5. Involucral bracts wholly whitish and dry. Plants more or less woolly or cobwebby.

          6. Leaves chiefly basal, or with a few small ones on the flower stalk.
             EVERLASTINGS *(Antennaria)*

          6. Leaves scattered along the stems.

            7. Involucral bracts pearly-white and spreading.
               PEARLY EVERLASTING *(Anaphalis)*

            7. Involucral bracts tawny-white to brownish and close-fitting.
               CUDWEEDS *(Gnaphalium)*

        5. Involucral bracts greenish or at least partly green.

          6. Leaves opposite.   THOROUGHWORTS *(Eupatorium)*

          6. Leaves alternate.   FALSE BONESET *(Kuhnia)*

  2. Flowers purple to lavender or pink.

    3. Leaves opposite or in whorls.
       JOE-PYE-WEEDS AND THOROUGHWORTS *(Eupatorium)*

    3. Leaves alternate.

      4. Pappus of 5 or 6 nearly equal scales.
         BARBARA'S-BUTTONS *(Marshallia)*

      4. Pappus of fine hairs or bristles.

        5. Heads in small groups surrounded by a few leaf-like bracts.
           ELEPHANT'S-FOOTS *(Elephantopus)*

        5. Heads otherwise.

          6. Heads solitary at the tip of the stem or its branches. Leaves and often the involucral bracts prickly.   THISTLES *(Carduus)*

          6. Heads clustered. Plants not spiny or prickly.

            7. Involucral bracts nearly all of the same length.
               TRILISAS *(Trilisa)*

            7. Involucral bracts in several rows, the outer ones being successively shorter.

              8. Heads arranged in a long and narrow end cluster. Leaves usually very numerous and becoming smaller upward.
                 BLAZING-STARS *(Liatris)*

              8. Heads in a more or less flat-topped or open cluster.

                9. Plants with a rank camphor-like odor.
                   MARSH-FLEABANES *(Pluchea)*

                9. Plants otherwise.

10. Leaves toothed or, if untoothed narrow and with the margin rolled inward on the lower side. Style branches long and slender. IRONWEEDS *(Vernonia)*

10. Leaves untoothed and narrow but flat. Style branches rather club-shaped. CARPHEPHORUS *(Carphephorus)*

GROUP III. HEADS WITH A CENTRAL DISK CONTAINING TUBULAR FLOWERS (DISK FLOWERS) AND MARGINAL FLOWERS WITH STRAP-SHAPED COROLLAS (RAY FLOWERS).

1. Stems with rather prominent wings extending downward from the leaf-bases.

2. Receptacle without chaffy scales. SNEEZEWEEDS *(Helenium)*

2. Receptacle with chaffy scales.

3. Involucral bracts few and nearly equal in length. Disk roundish, the flowers pointing in all directions. Rays yellow. WING-STEM *(Verbesina)*

3. Involucral bracts many and in 2 or more rows, the outer ones shorter. Rays yellow or white. CROWN-BEARDS *(Verbesina)*

1. Stems not winged or but very slightly so.

2. Heads with yellow ray flowers.

3. Leaves opposite or in whorls, or mostly opposite with some of the uppermost ones alternate.

4. Ray flowers sterile or without a pistil.

5. Involucre with several rows of overlapping green bracts. Plants usually more or less roughish or hairy. SUNFLOWERS *(Helianthus)*

5. Involucre with 2 rows of bracts; the outer ones green and spreading, the inner ones erect and usually not green.

6. Pappus of 2 or 4 barbed awns, the achenes maturing as "stick-tights". Flowers sometimes without rays. BUR-MARIGOLDS *(Bidens)*

6. Pappus of 2 short teeth or none. TICKSEEDS *(Coreopsis)*

4. Ray flowers fertile or with a pistil.

5. Disk flowers perfect but never producing achenes.

6. Plant low, its stems more or less prostrate. GOLDEN-STAR *(Chrysogonum)*

6. Plants 2 to several feet tall, the stems erect.

7. Achenes flattened and with a winged margin. Plants with a resinous juice. ROSINWEEDS *(Silphium)*

7. Achenes thick and scarcely flattened. Plants usually sticky-hairy. LEAF-CUPS *(Polymnia)*

5. Disk flowers perfect and forming achenes.

6. Involucre with 4 large leaf-like outer bracts united to form a 4-angled cup. PINELAND-GINSENG *(Tetragonotheca)*

6. Involucre otherwise.

7. Ray flowers persisting on the achenes and becoming papery. Herbaceous upland plant. OX-EYE *(Heliopsis)*

7. Ray flowers not persisting. Shrubby plant of coastal salt and brackish marshes. SEA OX-EYE *(Borrichia)*

3. Leaves alternate.

4. Pappus of hair-like bristles.

264

5. Heads 2 to 4 inches broad, the ray flowers very numerous and narrow.
   ELECAMPANE *(Inula)*

5. Heads smaller, mostly 1 inch or less broad.

   6. Involucral bracts apparently in 1 row.   RAGWORTS *(Senecio)*

   6. Involucral bracts in several rows, the outer successively shorter.

      7. Flower heads mostly less than ½ inch across, with short rays.
         GOLDENRODS *(Solidago)*

      7. Flower heads ½ inch or more across, with rather long and showy rays.

         8. Plant with a rank camphor-like odor.
            CAMPHORWEED *(Heterotheca)*

         8. Plants otherwise.   GOLDEN-ASTERS *(Heterotheca)*

4. Pappus, if any, of scales.

   5. Rays with a pistil.   SNEEZEWEEDS *(Helenium)*

   5. Rays neutral or without a pistil.

      6. Receptacle but slightly dome-shaped, deeply honeycombed.
         ENDORIMA *(Baludina)*

      6. Receptacle conical to cylindrical, merely chaffy.

         7. Disk roundish or conical.   CONEFLOWERS *(Rudbeckia)*

         7. Disk oblong or cylindrical.   CONEFLOWERS *(Ratibida)*

2. Heads with white to bluish, violet, or pink rays.

   3. Heads solitary on leafless stalks. Leaves basal.
      SUN-BONNETS *(Chaptalia)*

   3. Heads clustered. Plants more or less leafy-stemmed or with some small leaves on the flower stalks.

      4. Pappus of hair-like bristles.

         5. Involucral bracts in 1 or 2 rows and all of about the same length.
            FLEABANES *(Erigeron)*

         5. Involucral bracts in several rows, the outer successively shorter.

            6. Rays short.   GOLDENRODS *(Solidago)*

            6. Rays rather long and showy.

               7. Rays about 5. Involucral bracts firm and with green tips.
                  WHITE-TOPPED ASTER *(Aster)*

               7. Rays more numerous. Involucral bracts thin and usually green.
                  ASTERS *(Aster)*

      4. Pappus, if any, not of bristles.

         5. Heads 1½ inches or more broad, with 12 or more ray flowers.

            6. Heads with a rather flat yellow disk and 20 to 30 bright white rays.
               OX-EYE DAISY *(Chrysanthemum)*

            6. Heads with a cone-shaped dark disk and 12 to 20 purplish rays.
               PURPLE CONEFLOWER *(Echinacea)*

         5. Heads 1 inch or less across, with 4 to 8 white or pinkish rays.

            6. Plant with finely dissected leaves and a strong odor. Heads ¼ inch or less across, with 4 to 6 small rays.   YARROWS *(Achillea)*

            6. Plant with narrow but not dissected leaves. Heads ½ to 1 inch across, with 4 to 8 rather long and narrow rays. TICKSEEDS *(Coreopsis)*

NEW YORK IRONWEED *(Vernonia noveboracensis)*

The New York Ironweed has a smoothish stem 3 to 6 feet tall; and scattered, lance-shaped, rather finely toothed leaves from 3 to 10 inches long. The numerous heads of deep purple, tubular flowers are in a big flat-topped cluster. Each head contains from 30 to 50 flowers which have a ring of purple or purplish-tinged bristles at the base of the corolla tube. The bracts of the involucre are also purplish and their tips are prolonged into slender and spreading "tails". It grows in moist thickets and fields, and along the banks of streams; blooming between July and September.

RANGE: Mass. to W.Va. and Ohio south to Ga. and Miss.

BROAD-LEAF IRONWEED *(Vernonia glauca)*

Like the preceding species, this one has slender and loose, tail-like tips on its involucral bracts; but the bristles accompanying its flowers are cream- to straw-colored. The stems are usually whitened with a bloom, and its broader leaves are more sharply toothed. It grows in rich woodlands from N.J. and Pa. south to Ga. and Ala.; blooming between late June and September. (Not illustrated)

TALL IRONWEED *(Vernonia altissima)*

The Tall Ironweed differs from both of the preceding species in having involucral bracts which are merely pointed instead of tapering and loose at the tips. Its heads have but 15 to 30 flowers, and the leaves are broader than those of the New York Ironweed as well as downy beneath. The smoothish stems are from 3 to about 8 feet tall. It grows in rich moist thickets and stream bottoms, blooming between August and October.

RANGE: N.Y. to Ill. and Mo. south to Fla. and La.

MISSOURI IRONWEED *(Vernonia missurica)*

This species is similar to the Tall Ironweed but its stem and lower leaf surfaces are densely woolly-hairy. The heads contain from 35 to 55 flowers, and the purplish bracts of the involucre are cob-webby. It is usually only 3 to 5 feet tall and blooms between July and September. Rich low grounds and prairies from s. Ont. and Ohio to Iowa south to Ala., Miss., Ark., Okla. and Tex. (Not illustrated)

NARROW-LEAF IRONWEED *(Vernonia angustifolia)*

This little ironweed has a slender stem 1 to 3 feet tall with numerous and very narrow leaves 1½ to 5 inches long. The leaves are roughish above and the margins are rolled inward on the lower side. The heads of dark purple flowers have an involucre of small bracts with spreading green tips. It grows in sandy woods and pinelands in the coastal plain, blooming between late June and September.

RANGE: se. N.C. south to Fla. and west to Miss.

SMOOTH ELEPHANT'S-FOOT *(Elephantopus nudatus)*

This plant has a basal rosette of top-shaped leaves 2 to 10 inches long, which usually lie flat on the ground. It has a smooth or slightly hairy stem 1 to 2 feet tall which forks above but is leafless or nearly so. The branches end in clustered heads of tubular purple flowers which are surrounded by large leaf-like bracts. The tubular flowers are more deeply cleft on one side. It grows in sandy woods and openings; blooming between late July and September.

RANGE: Del. and Ark. south to Fla. and La.

WOOLLY ELEPHANT'S-FOOT *(Elephantopus tomentosus)*

This species very closely resembles the preceding one but it is densely hairy, its leaves being velvety to the touch. It grows in dry woodlands; blooming between late July and September. Md. to Ky. south to Fla. and Tex. (Not illustrated)

CAROLINA ELEPHANT'S-FOOT *(Elephantopus carolinianus)*

Unlike either of the preceding species, this one has leaves scattered along the stem rather than in a basal rosette. It has a somewhat roughish-hairy stem, sometimes nearly smooth above, which is 1 to 3 feet high. As in the other species, the heads of tubular flowers are in clusters surrounded by leaf-like bracts. It grows in dry open woods and thickets; blooming between August and October.

RANGE: N.J. to Ill. and Kan. south to Fla. and Tex.

266

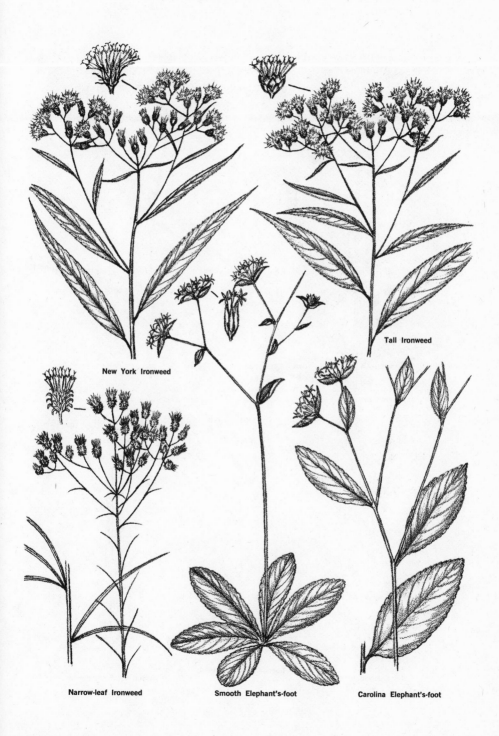

New York Ironweed

Tall Ironweed

Narrow-leaf Ironweed

Smooth Elephant's-foot

Carolina Elephant's-foot

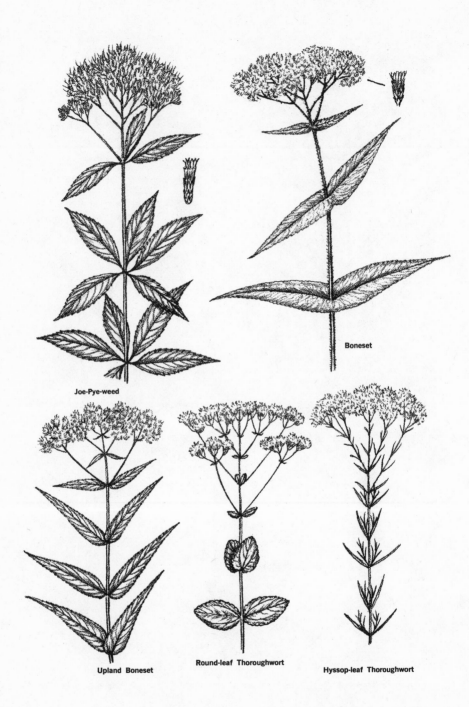

Joe-Pye-weed

Boneset

Upland Boneset

Round-leaf Thoroughwort

Hyssop-leaf Thoroughwort

JOE-PYE-WEED (*Eupatorium fistulosum*)

This species of Joe-Pye-Weed has a rather slender, smoothish, hollow, green to purplish-tinged and often somewhat whitened stem 3 to 10 feet tall. The lance-shaped leaves are in whorls of 4 to 7. They are bluntly toothed and 4 to 12 inches long. There are 5 to 8 tubular, purplish- to lilac-pink flowers in each head; and the heads are arranged in round-topped or dome-like clusters; blooming between July and September. It grows in moist meadows and thickets.
RANGE: Me. to Que., Ill., Iowa and Okla. south to Fla. and Tex.

JOE-PYE-WEED (*Eupatorium dubium*)

In general this species is similar to the preceding one; but the summit of the stem and the lower surfaces of the leaves are sprinkled with lustrous, sticky atoms. The leaves are usually in whorls of 3 or 4, often have 3 main veins, and are coarsely toothed. It grows in sandy swamps and thickets, chiefly in the coastal plain, from N.S. and sw. Me. to S.C. and Ala.; blooming between July and October.

GREEN-STEMMED JOE-PYE-WEED (*Eupatorium purpureum*)

This species has solid stems marked with purplish where the whorls of usually 3 or 4 leaves are attached. A vanilla-like odor is emitted when the plant is bruised. The heads have 3 to 7 creamy white to pale lilac flowers, and they are arranged in dome-like clusters; blooming between July and October. N.H. to Minn. and Neb. south to Fla., Tenn. and Okla. (Not illustrated)

SPOTTED JOE-PYE WEED (*Eupatorium maculatum*)

This species has a deep purple or purple-spotted stem often sticky-hairy above; with usually 4 or 5 sharply toothed leaves in each whorl. The heads have from 8 to 20 purplish flowers and they are arranged in a rather flat-topped cluster. It grows in moist places from Nfd. to B.C. south to nw. S.C., Ind., Neb., N.Mex. and Wash. (Not illustrated)

BONESET (*Eupatorium perfoliatum*)

The Boneset or Thoroughwort is a hairy plant with a stem 2 to 4 feet tall, usually branching above. The pairs of wrinkled-looking, lance-shaped, finely toothed leaves are 3 to 6 inches long; and are joined together at the base so that the stem appears to pass through them. The heads contain 10 to 20 small, white, tubular flowers; and they are arranged in flat-topped clusters. It grows in low moist thickets, open woods, and meadows; blooming between August and October. The plant was a favorite home remedy for colds and other afflictions. RANGE: Que. to Man. south to Fla. and Tex.

UPLAND BONESET (*Eupatorium sessilifolium*)

This is a rather smooth plant 2 to nearly 5 feet tall, usually branching above. It has pairs of lance-shaped, sharply toothed leaves 3 to 6 inches long, which are stalkless but not united at the base. The heads have about 5 tubular white flowers and are arranged in a flat-topped cluster. It grows in rather dry woods, thickets, and on hillsides; blooming between July and October. RANGE: Mass. to Minn. south to Ga., Ala. and Mo.

ROUND-LEAF THOROUGHWORT (*Eupatorium rotundifolium*)

The stem of this plant is hairy, rather slender, 1 to 3 feet tall, and usually branched above. The paired leaves are egg-shaped or roundish, stalkless, rather coarsely toothed, and from 1 to 2 inches long. They show 3 prominent veins from the base, are roughish above, and very veiny and downy beneath. The heads contain about 5 tubular white flowers and they are arranged in rather flat-topped clusters. It grows in dry to wet sandy or peaty soils in open woods, clearings, or savannahs; blooming between August and October. RANGE: se. N.Y., Tenn. and Ark. south to Fla. and Tex.

HYSSOP-LEAF THOROUGHWORT (*Eupatorium hyssopifolium*)

This is a more or less minutely rough-hairy plant with a slender stem 1 to 2 feet tall, which is rather bushy-branched above. It has narrow leaves ½ to 2 inches long which frequently have clusters of smaller leaves in their axils. The leaf margins are toothless or nearly so but often rolled inward on the lower side. The heads have about 5 tubular white flowers and they are arranged in a rather dense, flat-topped cluster. It grows in dry open woods, clearings, and old fields; blooming between July and October.
RANGE: Mass. to Ohio south to Fla. and Tex.

WHITE THOROUGHWORT *(Eupatorium album)*

The White Thoroughwort has a hairy and often roughish stem 1 to 3 feet high, which branches above. Its leaves are broadly lance-shaped to oblong, often broader above the middle, toothed on the margin, stalkless or nearly so, 1 to 4 inches long, and very veiny in appearance. The small tubular white flowers number 5 to 7 in each head, and the heads are arranged in flat-topped clusters which have opposite branches. It grows in dry and usually sandy open woods and clearings; blooming between late June and September.

RANGE: se. N.Y. to Md., Ky. and Ark. south to Fla. and La.

WHITE SNAKEROOT *(Eupatorium rugosum)*

The White Snakeroot usually has a smoothish and much-branched stem 1 to 4 feet high. The pairs of egg-shaped leaves are 3 to 6 inches long, sharply toothed on the margin, heart-shaped at the base, and have taper-pointed tips. They are rather thin in texture and have slender stalks usually 1 to 2½ inches long. The heads contain from 15 to 30 bright white, tubular flowers and they are arranged in rather dense flat-topped clusters; blooming between July and October. It grows in rich woods, thickets, and clearings. This plant is the principal cause of "milk sickness", which is transmitted to humans through the milk of cattle which have eaten it.

RANGE: N.B. to Sask. south to Va., n. Ga. and Tex.

SMALLER WHITE SNAKEROOT *(Eupatorium aromaticum)*

In a general way this plant resembles the preceding species. It is a somewhat more slender plant 1 to 2 feet tall, often with long ascending branches toward the summit. Its leaves are rather thickish, 1½ to 3 inches long, and they have stalks less than an inch in length. The tubular flowers are bright white but the flower heads are smaller. It grows in dry woods, thickets, pinelands, and clearings; blooming between late August and October.

RANGE: Mass. to N.J., W.Va. and Ohio south to Fla. and La.

PINK THOROUGHWORT *(Eupatorium incarnatum)*

This plant has a downy, loosely branched, and often reclining or straggling stem 2 to 4 feet long. Its leaves are rather triangular in outline, long-pointed at the tip, broadly pointed to somewhat heart-shaped at the base, ¾ to 2¼ inches long, and have slender stalks. The pinkish to lavender tubular flowers number about 20 in each head; and the heads are in rather loose and open clusters, mostly on stalks arising from the axils of the leaves. It grows in open sandy woods and in swampy places; blooming between September and November.

RANGE: Va. to Ohio, Ill. and Mo. south to Fla. and Ariz.

MISTFLOWER *(Eupatorium coelestinum)*

The Mistflower is also known as the Blue Boneset, and it is often cultivated under the name Hardy Ageratum. It is a somewhat downy plant with a branching stem from 1 to 3 feet high; and pairs of rather triangular, stalked, bluntly toothed leaves 1½ to 3 inches long. The bell-shaped heads contain a number of bright violet-blue, tubular flowers; and they are arranged in quite dense, flat-topped clusters. Its heads differ from all other species of *Eupatorium* in that they have a cone-shaped rather than a flat receptacle, and some botanists place it in a different genus. In general appearance and color the flowers resemble the cultivated ageratums. It grows in moist woods, thickets, and along the banks of streams; blooming between July and October.

RANGE: N.J. to Ill. and Kan. south to Fla. and Tex.

DOG-FENNEL *(Eupatorium capillifolium)*

This is a bushy plant 3 to almost 10 feet tall; with crowded, mostly alternate, finely dissected and feathery leaves. The small 3- to 5-flowered heads are very numerous and arranged in large, leafy, pyramid-shaped end clusters; blooming between September and November. It is very common and conspicuous in old fields, along roadsides, and in the borders of woods and clearings, especially in the South.

RANGE: Mass. to N.J., Va .and Tenn. south to Fla. and Tex. (Not illustrated)

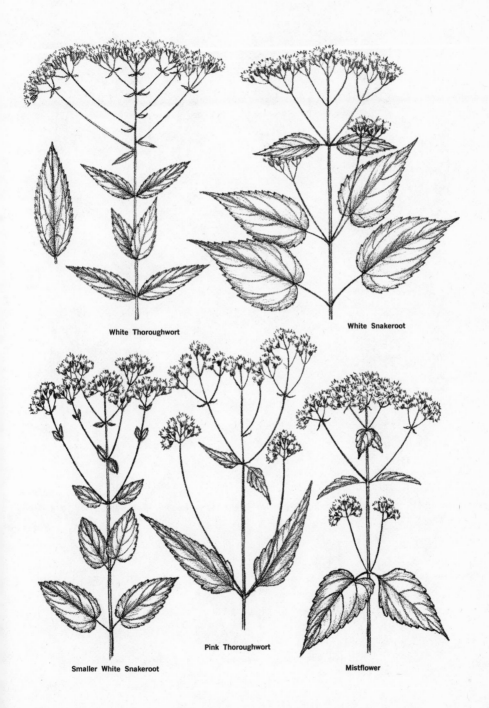

White Thoroughwort

White Snakeroot

Smaller White Snakeroot

Pink Thoroughwort

Mistflower

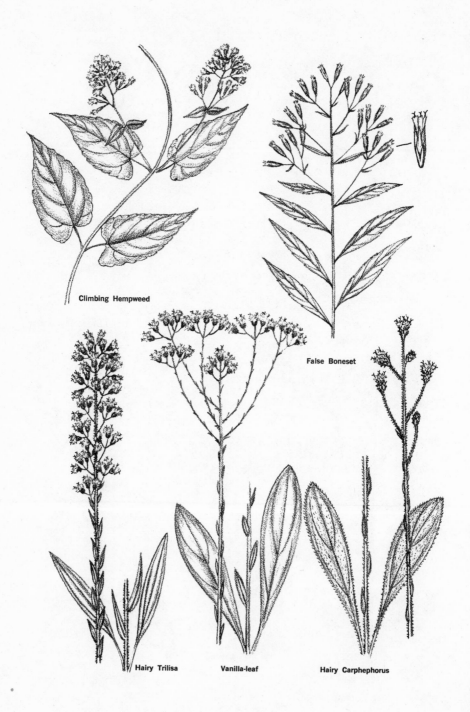

Climbing Hempweed

False Boneset

Hairy Trilisa

Vanilla-leaf

Hairy Carphephorus

CLIMBING HEMPWEED *(Mikania scandens)*

This plant is quite unusual among our composites as it is a climbing and twining vine, with smoothish stems from 5 to 15 feet long. Its leaves are somewhat triangular, heart-shaped at the base, taper-pointed at the tip, sometimes toothed, 2 to 4 inches long, and have long stalks. The whitish to pale purplish, tubular flowers number about 4 in each head; and they are clustered at the ends of long stalks arising from the leaf axils. It grows in swamps, moist thickets, and along the banks of streams; blooming between July and October.

RANGE: Me. to N.Y. and Ont. south to Fla. and Tex.

FALSE BONESET *(Kuhnia eupatorioides)*

The False Boneset is a resin-dotted and more or less hairy plant from 1 to 3 feet high, which is usually branched above. It has scattered, narrow or lance-shaped leaves which are untoothed or sparingly toothed and usually 1½ to 4 inches long. The heads contain from 10 to 25 tubular, creamy-white to purplish flowers. They are about ⅓ inch long and arranged in a rather loose terminal cluster. It grows in dry open woods, thickets, clearings, and on rocky slopes; blooming between June and October.

RANGE: N.J. to Ill. and Mo. south to Fla. and Tex.

HAIRY TRILISA *(Trilisa paniculata)*

This is a common and conspicuous plant in the low, wet coastal plain pinelands which blooms from August to October. It has a stiffly erect, sticky-hairy stem from 1 to 2 feet tall along which are numerous, scattered, small, lance-shaped leaves which tend to stand erect. The basal leaves are either lance-shaped or narrowly oblong and from 3 to 10 inches in length. Its numerous ¼ inch heads of tubular, rose purple flowers are arranged in a narrowly cylindrical cluster along the upper portion of the stem.

RANGE: N.C. south to Fla. and west to La.

VANILLA-LEAF *(Trilisa odoratissima)*

Unlike the preceding species, this is a smooth plant with an erect stem 2 to 3 feet tall, along which are scattered small leaves. The basal ones are smooth, thickish, usually broader above the middle but rather narrow, and from 4 to 10 inches long. When bruised they emit a characteristic vanilla-like odor. The numerous heads of small, tubular, rose-purple flowers are in a rather flat-topped terminal cluster. It grows in dry to wet coastal plain pinelands; blooming from August to October. Also known as Deer's-tongue, Hound's-tongue, and Carolina-vanilla; large quantities of its leaves are used in the flavoring of tobacco.

RANGE: N.C. south to Fla. and west to La.

HAIRY CARPHEPHORUS *(Carphephorus tomentosus)*

The Hairy Carphephorus has a simple, erect stem 1 to 2¼ feet tall which is quite hairy or woolly. On it are scattered, small, erect, lance-shaped leaves. The basal leaves are narrow and broadest toward the tip, and from 2 to about 6 inches long. Toward the summit of the stem it has several long-stalked heads, each one about ⅓ inch long and containing a number of rose-purple flowers. The heads are disposed in rather open but flat-topped terminal clusters. It grows in dry to moist coastal plain pinelands; blooming between August and October.

RANGE: se. Va. south to Fla.

CORYMBED CARPHEPHORUS *(Carphephorus corymbosus)*

This species also has rather downy stems 1 to 3 feet tall, but they are conspicuously leafy up to the flat-topped flower cluster which is rather dense. The bracts of the flower heads have blunt or roundish tips and thin, pale, dry margins. It grows in coastal plain pinelands from Ga. south to Fla. (Not illustrated)

Carphephorus bellidifolius often has clustered stems 1 to 2 feet tall which are smooth or nearly so, with scattered and spreading leaves. The ones on the lower part of the stem and at its base are narrowly top-shaped and 2 to about 6 inches long. The numerous flower heads have round-tipped bracts and are arranged in an open, slenderly branched cluster. It grows in dry coastal plain pinelands from se. Va. south to Fla.; blooming August to October. (Not illustrated)

273

Blazing-Stars

The Blazing-stars are also known as the Button-snakeroots and Gayfeathers. They are plants with usually simple, erect stems crowded with numerous and narrow leaves; and long and narrow clusters of stalkless or short-stalked heads of rose-purple, tubular flowers. The Blazing-stars are among the most gorgeous flowers of late summer and fall, blooming between July or August and September or October. In the coastal plain of the southeast, they occur in great abundance but some species are common in the mountain region. There are a number of species besides the ones included here, and they are often difficult to identify as to species.

LARGE BUTTON-SNAKEROOT *(Liatris scariosa)*

This beautiful blazing-star has flower heads which are bowl-shaped, up to an inch across, and contain from 25 to 60 flowers. Its stem is from 1 to 5 feet tall, finely downy at least above, and the leaves are hairy and often roughish. The basal ones vary from lance-shaped to slenderly top-shaped, up to a foot long, and ½ to 2 inches broad. It grows in dry woods and clearings chiefly in the mounain region.
RANGE: Pa. and W.Va. south to Ga. and Miss.

NORTHERN BUTTON-SNAKEROOT *(Liatris borealis)*

This species resembles the preceding one. It has similar large heads but the involucral bracts are dark reddish, with narrow and almost petal-like margins. The leaves are smoother and the lance-shaped basal ones are seldom over an inch broad. It grows in dry woods, thickets, or clearings from sw. Me. to N.Y. south to N.J. and cent. Pa. (Not illustrated)

DENSE BUTTON-SNAKEROOT *(Liatris spicata)*

This species has smoothish stems 1 to 6 feet tall with crowded, very narrow, smooth leaves gradually becoming larger toward the base. The lower ones are still narrow, ¾ inch or less across, but often 5 to 15 inches long. The upper portion of the stem has crowded heads of flowers which bloom progressively downward from the tip. Each head is usually about ⅓ inch across, containing between 5 and 15 flowers. It grows in wet open woods and fields. RANGE: Del. to W.Va., Ohio and Neb. south to Fla. and Tex.

SCALY BLAZING-STAR *(Liatris squarrosa)*

The large heads of this species have spreading or recurving, thickish, and stiff bracts; and they usually contain from 25 to 40 rather large flowers. The plant has rather stout stems 1 to 3 feet high; and numerous narrow, rigid, resin-dotted leaves. It grows in dry open woods and fields.
RANGE: Del. to W.Va., Ohio. and Neb. south to Fla. and Tex.

SANDHILL BLAZING-STAR *(Liatris secunda)*

This species and the similar *Liatris pauciflora* are unique blazing-stars of dry coastal plain pinelands and sand-hills in the Southeast. Both have narrowly cylindrical heads about ¾ inch long which are all turned to the upper side of the arching stems; the heads having relatively few but large flowers. The plants are 1 to 2½ feet high and have narrow leaves. *Liatris secunda* has downy stems while those of *Liatris pauciflora* are smooth. The former ranges from N.C. south to Fla. and west to Ala.; the latter, from Ga. south to Fla.

HANDSOME BLAZING-STAR *(Liatris elegans)*

The flower heads of this species have enlarged, petal-like, rose-colored or sometimes white tips. Another distinctive feature is the bending downward of the leaves along the upper part of the stem. It grows in dry sandy woods and pinelands in the coastal plain.
RANGE: S.C. south to Fla. and west to Tex.

GRASS-LEAF BUTTON-SNAKEROOT *(Liatris graminifolia)*

This species usually has somewhat hairy stems 1 to 3 feet tall, with numerous and very narrow leaves becoming smaller upward. The lower leaves often have hairy-fringed margins or leaf stalks, the widest being less than ½ inch broad. The narrowly top-shaped heads contain 5 to 15 flowers and are usually arranged in a long and slender, but sometimes branched cluster. It grows in open woods and pinelands.
RANGE: N.J. south to Fla. and Ala.

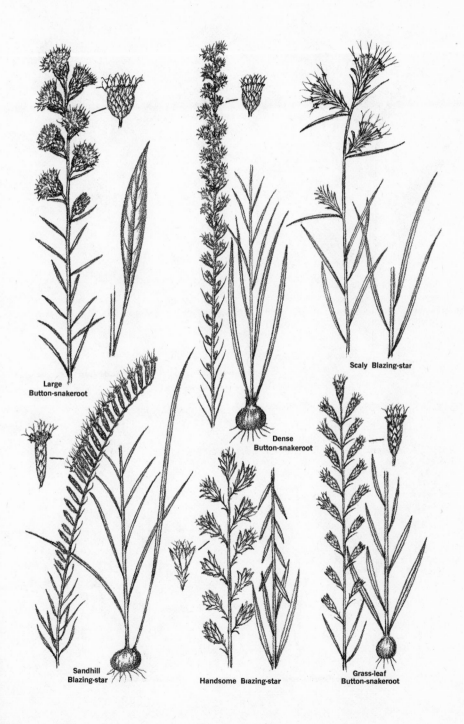

Large Button-snakeroot

Dense Button-snakeroot

Scaly Blazing-star

Sandhill Blazing-star

Handsome Blazing-star

Grass-leaf Button-snakeroot

Blackroot

Camphorweed

Maryland Golden-aster

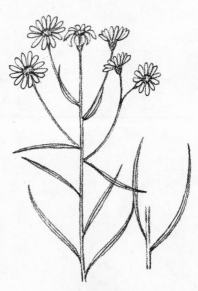

Grass-leaf Golden-aster

Narrow-leaf Golden-aster

BLACKROOT *(Pterocaulon pycnostachyum)*

The Blackroot is one of the unique and striking plants found in the more moist parts of the coastal plain pinelands. Usually 1 to 2 feet tall, it has a simple stem with scattered, wavy-margined, narrowly elliptic or lance-shaped leaves from 2 to 4 inches long. It is terminated in a dense but narrowly cone-shaped cluster of creamy-white heads of tubular flowers. The undersides of the leaves, the stem, and the flower cluster are densely coated with a felted whitish wool; the upper surfaces of the leaves, and the narrow wings which run down the stem from their bases, being a bright green. It gets its name from the thick black root. The flowering season is in May and June.
RANGE: N.C. south to Fla. and west to Miss.

CAMPHORWEED *(Heterotheca subaxillaris)*

The original home of this plant was in the West; but in recent years it has become a common weed in fields and along roadsides, especially in the Southeast. It has a branching, hairy stem from 1 to 3 feet high; with scattered egg-shaped to oblong, sharply-toothed leaves that are mostly 2 to 3 inches long. Those along the stem and its branches have heart-shaped and clasping bases. The basal ones have stalks but they rarely persist until flowering time which is between July and October. The crushed foliage has a camphor-like odor. RANGE: Del., N.J. to Ill. and Kan. south to Fla. and Ariz.

MARYLAND GOLDEN-ASTER *(Heterotheca mariana)*

This is a stout-stemmed, loosely hairy and often cobwebby plant from 1 to 2½ feet high; with scattered, oblong to lance-shaped, mostly bright green and stalkless leaves 1 to 2 inches long. The lower leaves are larger, broadest above the middle, and taper at the base into stalks. It has bright yellow, aster-like heads of flowers nearly an inch across; the bowl-shaped involucre having numerous but minute glands. It grows in open woods and fields, blooming between August and October.
RANGE: N.Y. to Ohio south to Fla. and Tex.

COTTONY GOLDEN-ASTER *(Heterotheca gossypina)*

This is one of the most attractive species of golden-asters; and, in a general way, it resembles the preceding species. Its stems, leaves, and even the involucres of the flower heads are permanently coated with a whitish and rather cobwebby wool. The flower heads are an inch or a little more across and have a number of bright golden-yellow rays. It grows in the dry coastal plain pinelands and on sandhills from N.C. south to Fla. and Ala., blooming during September or October. (Not illustrated)

GRASS-LEAF GOLDEN-ASTER *(Heterotheca nervosa)*

Also known as Silk-grass and Silver-grass, this is a silvery-silky plant with a slender stem 1 to 3 feet tall which branches above and has numerous, narrow, and erect leaves. Its basal leaves are narrow, soft, 4 to 12 inches long and grass-like. The numerous bright-yellow, aster-like flower heads are about ½ inch across and are on the ascending branches. They have a narrowly top-shaped involucre which is cobwebby, at least toward the base. It grows in dry, sandy or rocky, open woods and in fields; blooming between July and October. RANGE: Del. and W.Va., Ky., Ark. and Okla. south to Fla. and Tex.

GRASS-LEAF GOLDEN-ASTER *(Heterotheca graminifolia)*

This species is quite similar to the preceding one, but it is a tufted plant; and the branches of the flower cluster and the involucres of the flower heads have minute stalked glands. It grows in dry oak woods and pinelands, chiefly in the piedmont, from Va. south to Fla. and west to La. (Not illustrated)

NARROW-LEAF GOLDEN-ASTER *(Heterotheca falcata)*

This golden-aster usually has several stiff, cottony stems 4 to 12 inches high which branch above. Its numerous scattered leaves are narrow, stiff, spreading, often curved, and from 1 to 4 inches long. The relatively few aster-like flower heads are bright yellow, about ⅓ inch across, and tend to form a flat-topped cluster. It grows in dry sandy soils in the coastal region, blooming between July and October. RANGE: Mass. south to N.J.

Goldenrods

Anybody can tell a goldenrod from other kinds of flowers, but to distinguish the various species is quite another matter. That is a task which quite often perplexes even the trained botanist, for there are numerous similar species and they often hybridize. Only a few of the better marked ones are presented here. The heads contain both tubular (or disk) and strap-shaped (or ray) flowers.

BLUE-STEMMED GOLDENROD *(Solidago caesia)*

The Blue-stemmed or Wreath Goldenrod has slender, smooth, roundish stems 1 to 3 feet high, which are commonly purplish and usually coated with a whitish bloom. It has narrowly oblong or lance-shaped leaves which are stalkless, narrowed at both ends, sharply toothed, and 2 to 5 inches long. Its heads of flowers are in the axils of the leaves, blooming during September and October. It grows chiefly on wooded slopes or banks.

RANGE: N.S. to Ont. and Wis. south to Fla. and Tex.

BROAD-LEAF GOLDENROD *(Solidago flexicaulis)*

This is a well-marked goldenrod with a slender, zig-zag, somewhat angled green stem 1 to 3 feet high. The broad, egg-shaped, sharply toothed leaves are 2 to 7 inches long and are pointed at the tip and abruptly narrowed into winged stalks. Its heads of flowers are also clustered in the axils of the leaves, blooming between late August and October. It grows in rich woods and in ravines. Some know it as the Zig-zag Goldenrod.

RANGE: N.S. to N.D. south to Ga., Tenn. and Kan.

WHITE GOLDENROD *(Solidago bicolor)*

Silver-rod is another name often given to this pale-flowered goldenrod, the short outer rays of the heads being white or cream-colored. It is a grayish-downy plant up to 2 feet tall. The basal leaves are stalked, top-shaped, shallowly toothed, and 2 to 4 inches long. Those of the stem gradually decrease in size upward and are stalkless. It grows in dry open woods, thickets, and on slopes; blooming during September and October.

RANGE: N.B. to Ont. south to Ga. and Ark.

SLENDER GOLDENROD *(Solidago erecta)*

This species has a slender stem 2 or 3 feet tall which may be minutely hairy above. The lower leaves are usually broadest above the middle, shallowly toothed, and taper into winged stalks. The middle and upper ones are narrow, smaller, and stalkless. Its flower heads are arranged in a long narrow, end cluster; blooming between August and October. It may be found in dry to moist woods and thickets.

RANGE: N.J. to Ind. south to Ga. and Miss.

MOUNTAIN GOLDENROD *(Solidago roanensis)*

As its name indicates, this is a common goldenrod in the mountain woods and thickets. It has smoothish stems 1 to 3 feet tall. Its leaves are rather thin, 1 to 6 inches long, the lower ones being narrowly egg-shaped, sparingly toothed, and tapering into stalks; the upper ones lance-shaped, less toothed, and stalkless. The flower heads are in a slender but sometimes branched terminal cluster; blooming from August to October.

RANGE: Md. to Ky. south to n. Ga. and n. Ala.

CLUSTER GOLDENROD *(Solidago glomerata)*

This is the goldenrod whose large basal leaves are so conspicuous at high altitudes in the mts. of N.C. and Tenn. They are rather thin, long-stalked and sharply toothed. The flower heads are large, about ½ inch high, and clustered toward the summit of the 2- to 4-foot tall stems. Blooming August to October. (Not illustrated)

SEASIDE GOLDENROD *(Solidago sempervirens)*

True to its name, this goldenrod is found in coastal marshes and on the sea beaches. It has a smoothish, stout stem 2 to 8 feet tall; with numerous thickish, rather fleshy, smooth and untoothed leaves, the lowermost ones sometimes a foot long. The large flower heads are in a branched terminal cluster, blooming between August and November.

RANGE: Nfd. south to Fla.

278

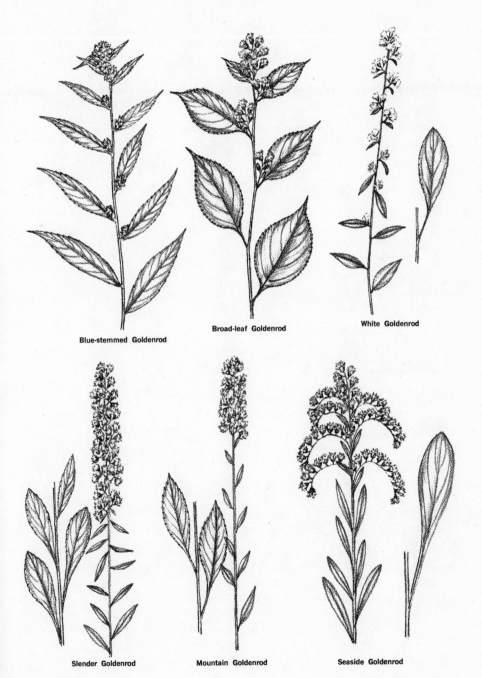

Blue-stemmed Goldenrod

Broad-leaf Goldenrod

White Goldenrod

Slender Goldenrod

Mountain Goldenrod

Seaside Goldenrod

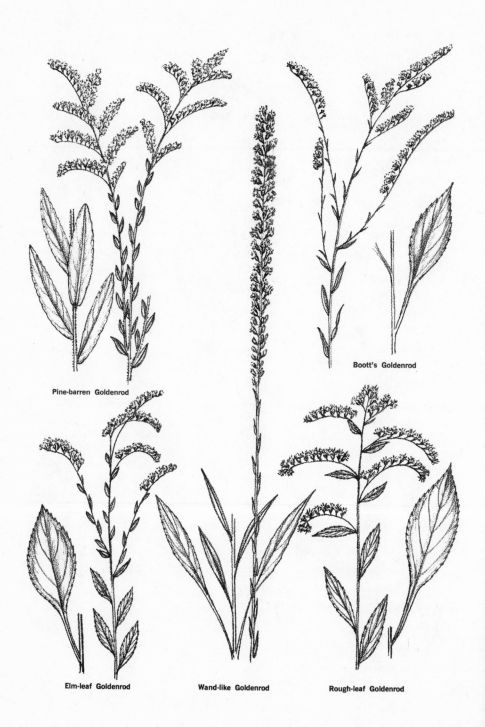

Pine-barren Goldenrod

Boott's Goldenrod

Elm-leaf Goldenrod

Wand-like Goldenrod

Rough-leaf Goldenrod

PINE-BARREN GOLDENROD *(Solidago fistulosa)*

This goldenrod has a rather stout, simple or branched stem 2 to 6 feet tall; with numerous, ascending, broadly lance-shaped or oblong leaves which are stalkless and have clasping bases. The lower ones are 1 to 4 inches long, broad at base, and sparingly toothed; the upper ones smaller and untoothed. Its small heads of flowers are in a terminal cluster which has several arching or spreading branches. It grows in low, moist, coastal plain pinelands; blooming between August and October or later.
RANGE: N.J. south to Fla.

BOOTT'S GOLDENROD *(Solidago boottii)*

Boott's Goldenrod has a smoothish, slender stem 2 to 5 feet tall; usually with long ascending branches at the summit, along which many small flower heads are arranged in more or less 1-sided clusters. The leaves are rather firm; the lower ones 3 to 6 inches long, broadly lance-shaped or egg-shaped, sharply toothed, and tapered into hairy-fringed stalks. The upper ones are much smaller, stalkless, and often untoothed. It grows in dry sandy or rocky woods and fields; blooming between July and October.
RANGE: Va. to Ky. south to Fla. and Tex.

ELM-LEAF GOLDENROD *(Solidago ulmifolia)*

This species has a slender, usually somewhat downy stem 2 to 4 feet tall which branches toward the summit. The leaves are thinnish, elliptic or lance-shaped, coarsely and irregularly toothed, and hairy beneath. The lower ones are 3 to 5 inches long and abruptly narrowed into winged stalks; the upper ones much smaller, stalkless or nearly so, and almost untoothed. The flower cluster has a few arching or ascending branches. It grows in rocky woods and along streams, blooming between August and October.
RANGE: Mass. to Minn. south to Ga., Miss., Okla. and Tex.

WAND-LIKE GOLDENROD *(Solidago stricta)*

This unique goldenrod is a smooth plant with a simple, slender, wand-like stem 2 to 8 feet tall; along which are numerous small, narrow, erect leaves. The basal leaves are lance-shaped or broadest near the tip, inconspicuously toothed, stalked and 3 to 8 inches long. It grows in wet coastal plain pinelands, meadows and savannahs; blooming in September or October.
RANGE: N.J. south to Fla. and west to Tex.

ROUGH-LEAF GOLDENROD *(Solidago patula)*

This species has a smooth, reddish, 4-angled and usually narrowly winged stem 2 to 6 feet tall. Its leaves are harshly rough above but smooth and veiny beneath and have sharply toothed margins. The basal ones are 1 to 4 inches long, elliptic or oval, and narrowed into winged stalks. Those along the stem are much smaller, lance-shaped and stalkless. The flower cluster has several spreading or recurved branches. It grows in wet meadows, bogs, and swamps; blooming between August and October.
RANGE: Vt. to Ont. and Mich. south to Ga., La. and Mo.

DOWNY GOLDENROD *(Solidago puberula)*

This species has minutely downy, often purplish stems 1½ to 3 feet tall; with numerous narrow leaves, the lower ones 2 to 4 inches long and sharply toothed. The flower heads are grouped in a rather narrow end cluster, the lower ones on short branches from the axils of the upper leaves. It grows in sandy or rocky open woods and fields from Que. south to Ga. and Tenn.; blooming between September and November. (Not illustrated)

DOWNY RAGGED GOLDENROD *(Solidago petiolaris)*

Downy Ragged Goldenrod has a slender stem 1 to 3 feet tall which is downy or roughish above. The numerous leaves are stalkless or nearly so, rather firm, minutely rough-hairy on both surfaces, usually untoothed, and ½ to 3 inches long. The flower heads have bracts with pointed green tips and are in a narrow end cluster. It grows in dry woods and open places from N.C. to Mo. and Neb. south to Fla. and Tex. (Not illustrated)

EARLY GOLDENROD *(Solidago juncea)*

The Early Goldenrod is a quite smooth plant with a rather stout and light green stem from 1 to 4 feet high; branching toward the summit into several ascending, spreading, or recurved flower-bearing branches. Its leaves are quite firm; the lower and basal ones 4 to 12 inches long, broadly lance-shaped to oval, sharply toothed, and tapering into winged and usually hairy-fringed stalks. The upper ones are gradually reduced in size upwards becoming lance-shaped stalkless, and untoothed. It grows in dry and rocky open places, blooming from June to October. RANGE: N.B. to Sask. south to N.C., Tenn. and Mo.

LATE GOLDENROD *(Solidago gigantea)*

This species has a stout, smooth stem from 2 to 8 feet tall which is usually whitened with a bloom. The leaves are lance-shaped or narrowly oblong, stalkless, sharply toothed at least above the middle, 3 to 6 inches long, conspicuously 3-veined, and somewhat hairy on the veins beneath. The small flower heads are arranged along the spreading or recurved branches of the terminal flower cluster, blooming between July and October. It often forms extensive colonies in the borders of damp woods and thickets.
RANGE: N.B. to B.C. south to Fla. and Tex.

WRINKLED-LEAF GOLDENROD *(Solidago rugosa)*

This is a common but variable goldenrod with a usually stout stem 2 to 6 feet high, crowded with leaves and often with lines running down from the leaf bases. The leaves, like the stem, may be either smooth or hairy but they present a very wrinkled appearance above and are very veiny beneath. They are 1 to 4 inches long, lance-shaped to oval, sharply toothed, and are often rough above. The flower cluster has a number of spreading or recurved branches. It grows in dry to moist open woods, clearings, and thickets; blooming between August and October.
RANGE: Nfd. to Ont. and Mich. south to Fla. and Tex.

TALL GOLDENROD *(Solidago altissima)*

The Tall or Canada Goldenrod has a stout grayish-downy or sometimes roughish stem 2 to 8 feet tall; with numerous, crowded, lance-shaped, sharply toothed, stalkless or short-stalked leaves 3 to 6 inches long. They are thickish, 3-veined, and rough on the upper surface. Involucres of the flower heads vary from less than ⅛ inch to ¼ inch in height; and the numerous heads are arranged in a large pyramid-shaped terminal cluster, with many spreading or recurved branches. It grows in old fields, meadows and thickets; blooming in September and October. RANGE: Nfd. to Sask. south to Fla. and Tex.

SWEET GOLDENROD *(Solidago odora)*

The crushed leaves of this goldenrod have an anise-like odor. It has a slender smooth or slightly downy stem 2 to 4 feet tall; and numerous narrowly lance-shaped leaves 2 to 4 inches long which are stalkless, untoothed, and marked with tiny translucent dots. The flower heads are in a loose, 1-sided, plume-like cluster. It grows in dry open woods, fields, and thickets; blooming between July and October. Also called the Anise-scented Goldenrod. RANGE: N.H. to Ohio, Ky., Mo. and Okla. south to Fla. and Tex.

BUSHY GOLDENROD *(Solidago graminifolia)*

This is a bushy-branched plant 2 to 4 feet tall, with numerous narrowly lance-shaped leaves 1 to 5 inches long which show 3 prominent veins. The small flower heads are in flat-topped end clusters. It grows in wet fields and stream bottoms, blooming between July and October. Also called Fragrant or Flat-topped Goldenrod.
RANGE: Nfd. to Sask. south to N.C. and Mo.

SLENDER FRAGRANT GOLDENROD *(Solidago tenuifolia)*

This species has narrow leaves which show but 1 prominent vein and often has small leaves in the axils of the larger ones. It grows in sandy soils from N.S. to Mich. south to Ga. and Ind. (Not illustrated)

SMALL-HEADED FRAGRANT GOLDENROD *(Solidago microcephala)*

This plant has flower heads less than ⅛ inch high and clusters of small leaves in the leaf axils. In old fields and savannahs; Va. south to Fla, and west to Tex. (Not illustrated)

282

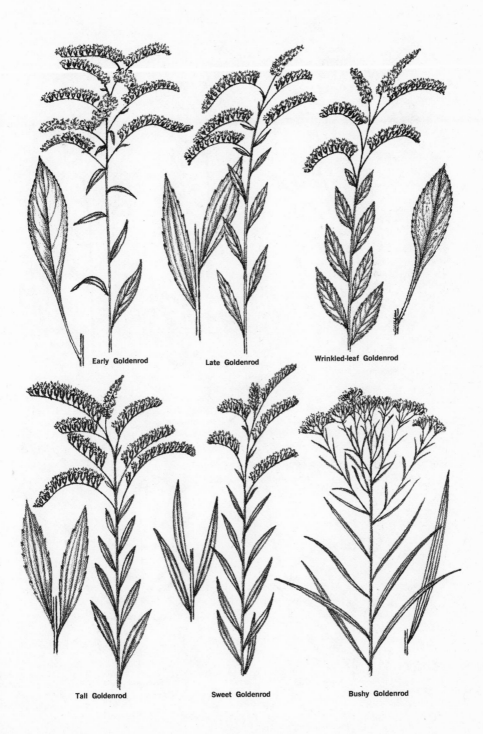

Early Goldenrod

Late Goldenrod

Wrinkled-leaf Goldenrod

Tall Goldenrod

Sweet Goldenrod

Bushy Goldenrod

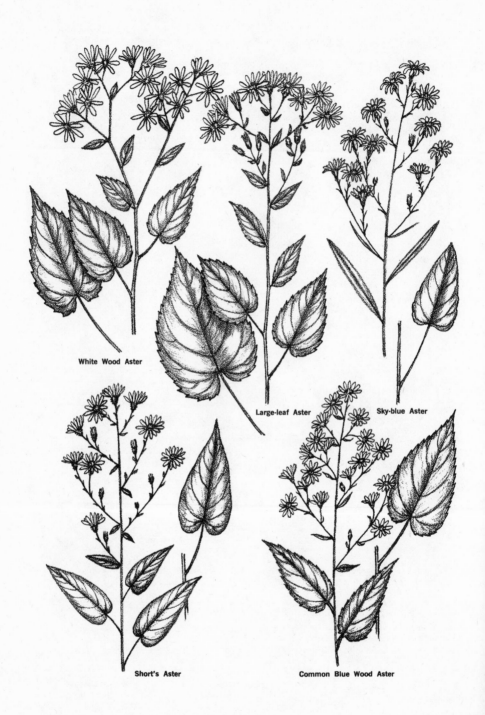

White Wood Aster

Large-leaf Aster

Sky-blue Aster

Short's Aster

Common Blue Wood Aster

Wild Asters

Wild asters bloom chiefly in the late summer and fall, when they are among the most conspicuous wild flowers. The heads have a disk of tubular flowers in the center which are yellow, often changing to red or purple; and white, lavender, blue, pink or purple ray flowers about the margin. Some species of our native asters have contributed to the garden forms commonly called "hardy asters" or Michaelmas-daisies. There are more than 75 species in eastern North America and their identification is not always an easy matter.

WHITE WOOD ASTER *(Aster divaricatus)*

This aster grows in dry open woods and clearings, blooming from August to October. It has a slender, often zig-zag, smoothish stem 1½ to 2½ feet tall. The thin heart-shaped leaves are smooth or sparingly hairy, mostly stalked, and at least the lower ones are very coarsely but sharply toothed. The flower heads are almost an inch across. They have from 6 to 10 white rays and the disk flowers soon become brownish.
RANGE: Me. to Ohio south to Ga., Ala. and Tenn.

LARGE-LEAF ASTER *(Aster macrophyllus)*

Very large, thickish, rough, sharply toothed, and heart-shaped basal leaves characterize this aster of the open woodlands. The flower heads have white to lavender or bluish rays, and the branches of the flower cluster have small stalked glands. It blooms from July to September. RANGE: Que. to Minn. south to Md., n. Ga., n. Ala., Ohio and Ill.

SCHREBER'S ASTER *(Aster schreberi)*

This aster also has basal tufts of large heart-shaped leaves but they are rather thin and smooth or barely roughish. The flower heads have a narrowly cylindrical involucre and about 10 white rays. It grows in moist open woods or thickets from N.Y. to Ill. south to w. Va. and Ky; blooming between July and September. (Not illustrated)

SKY-BLUE ASTER *(Aster azureus)*

The leaves of this aster are thickish, rough on both surfaces, and often untoothed. The lower ones are egg-shaped to lance-shaped, heart-shaped at the base, 2 to 6 inches long, and have slender stalks; the upper ones being smaller, narrow, and almost stalkless. The 1- to 4-foot stems are stiffly erect, branched above, and also roughish. Its flower heads are about ½ inch across and they have from 10 to 20 deep blue or violet-blue rays; and they may be seen between August and October. It grows in dry open woods, thickets, and on prairies. RANGE: Que. to Minn. south to Ga. and Tex.

SHORT'S ASTER *(Aster shortii)*

This aster has a smooth or roughish slender stem 2 to 4 feet tall. On it are numerous broadly lance-shaped or egg-shaped leaves with heart-shaped bases. They are 2 to 6 inches long and all but the uppermost ones have slender stalks. The attractive flower heads are about ½ inch across, with from 10 to 15 violet pale rays. It grows in open woods and on rocky banks, blooming between August and October.
RANGE: Pa. to Wis. south to Ga., Ala. and Tenn.

COMMON BLUE WOOD ASTER *(Aster cordifolius)*

This is a common but quite variable woodland aster. It usually has smoothish and branching stems 1 to 5 feet high. Most or all of the lower leaves are heart-shaped, coarsely toothed, 2 to 5 inches long, and have slender stalks. The ones on the stem above are smaller, shorter stalked, less toothed, and often taper at the base. It usually has numerous flower heads about ⅓ inch across, with 10 to 20 whitish, pinkish, or pale blue-violet rays; and often a reddish disk. It flowers between August and October.
RANGE: N.S. to Que. and Wis. south to Ga., Ala., Mo. and Kan.

LOWRIE'S ASTER *(Aster lowrieanus)*

Lowrie's Aster is somewhat similar to the preceding species but its leaves are very smooth, in fact they have an almost greasy feeling. They are also less prominently toothed and those of the stem have broadly winged stalks. It grows in open woods and thickets from Conn. to Ont. south to Md., w. N.C. and n. Ga.; blooming between August and October. (Not illustrated)

ARROW-LEAF ASTER *(Aster sagittifolius)*

This aster has a stiffly erect, smooth or sparingly hairy stem 2 to 5 feet tall, which branches only in the flower cluster. The lower leaves are egg-shaped with heart-shaped bases, sharply toothed, 3 to 6 inches long, and have broadly winged stalks. The upper ones are smaller, narrower, and stalkless or nearly so. Its heads of flowers are about ¾ inch across and have 10 to 15 pale blue, pinkish, or whitish rays. It grows in dry open woods, thickets, and open places; blooming between August and October.

RANGE: Vt. to Minn. south to Ga. and Tex.

WAVY-LEAF ASTER *(Aster undulatus)*

The Wavy-leaf Aster has a stiffly erect stem which is usually somewhat minutely roughish-hairy, branched above, and from 1 to 3½ feet tall. Its lower leaves are lance-shaped or egg-shaped, heart-shaped at the base, and 2 to 6 inches long. They are wavy on the margin, or sometimes with some low and blunt teeth, and have winged leaf-stalks which broaden at the clasping base. The ones upward along the stem are smaller and stalkless or nearly so. All of the leaves are roughish on the upper surface and downy underneath. The flower heads are about ½ inch across and have from 8 to 15 pale violet or bluish rays. It grows in dry open woods and thickets; blooming between August and November.

RANGE: N.S. to Ont. and Minn. south to Fla., La. and Ark.

LATE PURPLE ASTER *(Aster patens)*

The stems of this aster are slender, roughish-hairy, 1 to 3 feet tall, and are branched above. Its leaves are oblong or oval, mostly 1 to 2 inches long, untoothed, rather thickish and somewhat rigid, and roughish or hairy. They clasp the stem by their heart-shaped bases. The uppermost leaves in the flower cluster are small and often almost bract-like. It has beautiful flower heads about ⅔ inch across, with from 20 to 30 deep violet or bluish-purple rays, produced between August and October. This species also grows in dry open woods, thickets, and fields.

RANGE: Me. to Minn. south to Fla. and Tex.

CROOKED-STEMMED ASTER *(Aster prenanthoides)*

Usually this aster has a stout, somewhat zig-zag, branched stem 1 to 2 feet high, which may be smooth or have finely hairy lines. The leaves are lance-shaped to narrowly egg-shaped, taper-pointed at the tip, sharply toothed, and abruptly contracted into a broad and untoothed stalk-like portion expanding into 2 "ears" at the clasping base. The middle and lower ones are 3 to 8 inches long, usually roughish above but smooth beneath. Its flower heads are almost an inch across and have from 20 to 30 pale blue-violet rays. It grows in rich woods, damp thickets, and along streams; blooming between August and October.

RANGE: Mass. to Minn. south to Va., Ky. and Iowa.

PURPLE-STEMMED ASTER *(Aster puniceus)*

This is another common but variable aster. It usually has a stout stem which is reddish- or purplish-tinged, often rough-hairy, much-branched, and from 3 to 8 feet high. The leaves are more or less lance-shaped, sharply toothed, tapering gradually both to the tip and to the somewhat "eared" and clasping base. Those on the main part of the stem are 3 to 6 inches long, and they may be quite smooth or roughish-hairy. The flower heads are almost an inch across and have from 20 to 40 lilac, blue-violet, pinkish, or even whitish rays. It grows quite abundantly in moist meadows, thickets, and in swampy places; blooming between August and October. Also known as the Red-stalked Aster and Early Purple Aster.

RANGE: Nfd. to Man. south to Ga., Ala., Tenn. and Iowa.

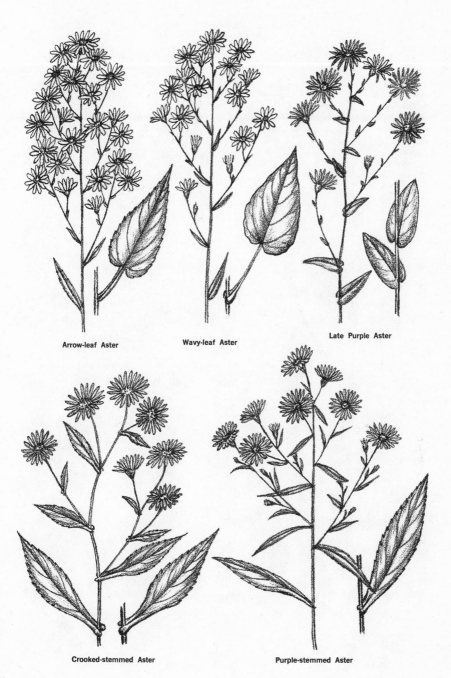

Arrow-leaf Aster

Wavy-leaf Aster

Late Purple Aster

Crooked-stemmed Aster

Purple-stemmed Aster

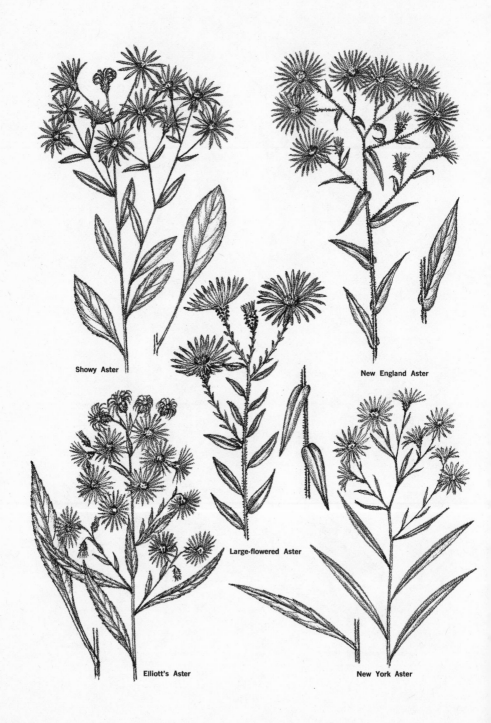

Showy Aster

New England Aster

Large-flowered Aster

Elliott's Aster

New York Aster

SHOWY ASTER *(Aster spectabilis)*

Although this aster is also known as the Seaside Purple Aster, and is usually found in sandy pinelands near the coast, it sometimes occurs in the mountains. As a rule it has several slightly roughish and somewhat glandular stems 1 to 2 feet high, which are sometimes branched above. Its leaves are thickish and firm; the lower and basal ones being oval, pointed, sparingly and inconspicuously toothed, 3 to 5 inches long, and tapering into slender stalks. Those along the stem become smaller and narrower upwards, and are stalkless and untoothed or nearly so. The flower heads are large, almost 1½ inches across, and have from 15 to 30 bright violet rays. It flowers between August and October.

RANGE: Mass. south to e. S.C.; also in mts. of w. N.C.

LARGE-FLOWERED ASTER *(Aster grandiflorus)*

This is the largest and showiest of our purple-flowered wild asters, with flower heads often 2 inches across which have numerous violet-purple rays. It is a rough-hairy plant 1 to 2½ feet high with long and slender, ascending, very leafy branches. The leaves are rigid, untoothed, narrow to oblong, stalkless and with somewhat clasping bases. On the main stem and branches they are up to 2 inches long and generally turned downward; but the uppermost ones are very small or bract-like, merging into the bracts of the cup-shaped involucre with their spreading green tips. It grows in dry oak woods and pinelands in the coastal plain and outer piedmont, blooming during September or October.

RANGE: Va. south to Fla.

NEW ENGLAND ASTER *(Aster novae-angliae)*

This is a very attractive wild aster which is sometimes cultivated. It is a hairy plant 2 to 8 feet high with a rather stout stem which is branched above and very leafy. The leaves are lance-shaped, untoothed, mostly 2 to 4 inches long, and clasp the stem by their heart-shaped or "eared" bases. The numerous flower heads are about 1½ inches across and have about 40 or 50 narrow violet-purple rays. Both the stalks of the heads and the involucres are covered with minute and sticky glands, and the involucral bracts have rather long, spreading tips. It grows in moist thickets, fields, swamps, and along roadsides; blooming between August and October.

RANGE: Que. to Alb. south to Md., w. N.C., e. Tenn., Kan. and Colo.

ELLIOTT'S ASTER *(Aster elliottii)*

Elliott's Aster grows in the coastal marshes of the Southeast, where it blooms from late September to November. It has a stout and stiffly erect stem which is smooth or sparingly hairy, 2 to 5 feet tall, and branches above. Its leaves are roughish on the upper surface but smooth beneath, the margins being sharply toothed. The upper ones are lance-shaped and stalkless but those on the lower portion of the stem are much larger, 4 to 8 inches long, more elliptic, and taper at the base into winged stalks. The flower heads are about an inch across, with numerous pale violet-purple rays and bracts with tapering and spreading tips.

RANGE: se. Va. south to Fla. and west to La.

NEW YORK ASTER *(Aster novi-belgii)*

The New York Aster is a rather smooth plant with a slender and branching stem from 1 to 3 feet high, sometimes being slightly downy above. Its leaves are all narrowly lance-shaped, often slightly fleshy, untoothed or with a few quite inconspicuous teeth on the margin, 2 to 6 inches long, and the upper ones more or less clasping at the base. The flower heads are about an inch across, usually numerous; with 15 to 25 blue-violet, or sometimes pinkish or whitish rays, and involucral bracts with slender and spreading tips. It grows in damp thickets, meadows, and on shores; blooming between August and November.

RANGE: Nfd. to Que. south to Ga.

EASTERN SILVERY ASTER *(Aster concolor)*

Also called the Lilac-flowered Aster, this species has a slender and usually minutely downy stem 1 to 2½ feet tall, which is simple or with a few almost erect branches. The numerous leaves are minutely silvery-silky, stalkless, and untoothed; the lower ones being elliptic to lance-shaped and 1½ to 2 inches long. Those upward on the stem are very much smaller or even bract-like. The pretty flower heads are about ¾ inch across, with from 10 to 15 lilac to violet-purple rays, and arranged in a long and narrow cluster. It grows in dry and sandy open woods and pinelands, chiefly in the coastal plain. Its flowering season is during September and October.
RANGE: Mass. and Ky. south to Fla. and La.

BUSHY ASTER *(Aster dumosus)*

This is a slender-stemmed and usually minutely downy plant 1 to 3 feet high, with spreading or ascending branches. Its heads of flowers are about ½ inch across, with 15 to 25 pale lavender or bluish rays. They terminate slender branchlets 2 to 4 inches long, on which are crowded, small, bract-like leaves. The larger leaves are quite narrow and from 1 to 3 inches long. Also known as the Rice-button Aster, it grows in dry to moist sandy fields and thickets; blooming between late August and October.
RANGE: Me. to Ont. and Mich. south to Fla. and Tex.

WALTER'S ASTER *(Aster squarrosus)*

This is a unique species of aster with a slender, almost smooth, loosely branched stem 1 to 2 feet tall. It has numerous rigid leaves which are stalkless, reflexed, and mostly less than ⅓ inch long. The upper ones, and those crowding the flower stalks, are very small and scale-like. The flower heads which terminate the branches are little more than ½ inch across and have from 10 to 15 lilac rays. It grows only in the dry coastal plain pinelands, blooming between August and October.
RANGE: N.C. south to Fla.

WHITE OLD-FIELD ASTER *(Aster pilosus)*

Sometimes this aster is pilose—meaning hairy—but just as often, it is smooth. It grows in dry thickets, clearings, and along roadsides; and it is often very abundant in abandoned fields. It grows from 2 to about 5 feet tall and has several slender branches which are ascending or stiffly spreading. Its leaves are all narrow or lance-shaped, stalkless, stiffish, slightly if at all toothed, and 1 to 3 inches long. The numerous flower heads are about ¾ inch across, with 15 to 25 white or sometimes pale purplish rays, and grow along the upper side of the branches; blooming between August and November.
RANGE: Me. to Minn. and Kan. south to Ga., Ala. and Ark.

CALICO ASTER *(Aster lateriflorus)*

The Calico or Starved Aster differs from the preceding species in having thinner and flexible leaves which are usually broader, 2 to 6 inches long, sharply toothed as a rule, and quite roughish. Its flower heads are about ½ inch across, with from 10 to 20 white rays and purplish disk flowers. The bracts of the involucre have a prominent green midrib. The heads are usually very numerous and borne in a branching flower cluster; blooming between August and November. It grows in dry to moist open woods, thickets, fields, and along roadsides.
RANGE: Que. to Minn. south to Ga. and Tex.

SMOOTH ASTER *(Aster laevis)*

This is a smooth plant with a rather stout and whitened stem 2 to 4 feet tall, which is often more or less branched. Its leaves are thick, lance-shaped to elliptic or egg-shaped, 1 to 3 inches long, and mostly untoothed. The ones on the upper part of the stem are stalkless but the lower and basal ones taper into winged stalks. Its flower heads are almost an inch across and have 15 to 30 violet or bluish rays; blooming between August and October. It grows on the borders of woods and in thickets or dry fields.
RANGE: Me. to Sask. south to Ga., La. and Kan.

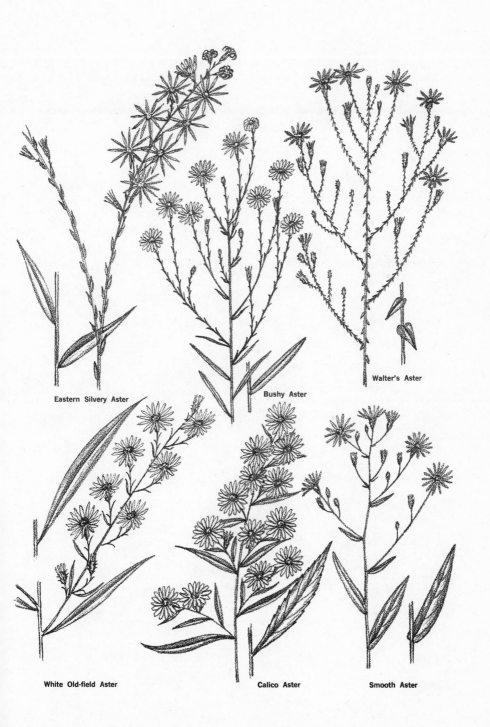

Eastern Silvery Aster

Bushy Aster

Walter's Aster

White Old-field Aster

Calico Aster

Smooth Aster

Stiff Aster

Mountain Aster

Cornel-leaf Aster

Flat-topped White Aster

White-topped Aster

STIFF ASTER *(Aster linariifolius)*

Savory-leaf Aster and Pine-starwort are other names given to this aster. It has a tuft of stiff, roughish, minutely hairy stems 6 inches to 2 feet high which are branched above. On them are numerous and rather closely crowded, very narrow, stiff, rough-margined leaves. The larger ones are ¾ to 1½ inches long, the upper ones being reduced to rigid bracts. The flower heads are solitary at the ends of the erect or ascending branches; each one about an inch across, with from 10 to 15 bright lavender rays. It grows in dry sandy or rocky open places, blooming between September and November.

RANGE: N.B. to Que. and Minn. south to Fla. and Tex.

MOUNTAIN ASTER *(Aster acuminatus)*

The Mountain or Whorled Aster has a somewhat zig-zag and minutely downy stem 1 to 3 feet high, branching toward the summit. Its leaves are thin, broadly lance-shaped or elliptic, 3 to 6 inches long, pointed at both ends, and rather coarsely toothed. Those on the upper part of the stem are often so close together that they appear to be whorled. The flower heads are about 1¼ inches across and have 12 to 18 narrow white or purplish-tinged rays. It grows in dry to moist woods and clearings, blooming between July and November.

RANGE: Nfd. to Que. south to N.J., Pa., n. Ga. and Tenn

CORNEL-LEAF ASTER *(Aster infirmus)*

This aster has a somewhat zig-zag, slender stem 1½ to 3 feet tall which is sparingly branched at the summit. Its leaves are elliptic or quite often broadest above the middle, untoothed, stalkless or nearly so, smooth above but slightly roughish-hairy on the veins beneath and from 2 to 5 inches long. The flower heads are about an inch across, with from 8 to 15 white or cream-colored rays, and arranged in an open terminal cluster. It grows in dry and usually rocky woods, thickets, and on slopes; blooming between late June and September.

RANGE: Mass. to Ohio south to Ga., Ala. and Tenn.

FLAT-TOPPED WHITE ASTER *(Aster umbellatus)*

This is a rather smooth plant with leafy stems from 1 to 8 feet tall. The leaves are lance-shaped to very narrowly egg-shaped, untoothed, pointed at both ends, up to about 6 inches long, and stalkless or very short-stalked. They are roughish on the upper surface and sometimes downy beneath. Its heads of flowers are ½ to about an inch across, with from 2 to 15 white rays; and are arranged in a broad, flat-topped cluster. It grows in both moist or dry open woodlands, thickets, and meadows; blooming between July and October.

RANGE: Nfd. to Ont. and Minn. south to Ga., Ky., Iowa and Neb.

CAROLINA ASTER *(Aster carolinianus)*

The Carolina or Climbing Aster is a unique species in that it has woody trailing, arching, or climbing stems. Its flower heads are solitary or sometimes clustered at the ends of conspicuously leafy branches. They are fairly large and have numerous pale purplish or pinkish ray flowers. The involucre is bowl-shaped and its bracts have prominent dark green and spreading tips. Its leaves are lance-shaped or elliptic, untoothed, minutely hairy, 1½ to 4 inches long, and have clasping bases. It grows in and about the coastal plain swamps from S.C. south to Fla.; blooming in late September and October or later. (Not illustrated)

WHITE-TOPPED ASTER *(Aster paternus)*

This plant usually has a somewhat downy and slightly angled stem from 1 to 2 feet high which is branched toward the summit. Its leaves are thin, veiny in appearance, and usually somewhat toothed. The lower ones are narrowly top-shaped, 2 to 4 inches long, and taper into winged stalks. The upper ones are smaller and stalkless or very nearly so. Its flower heads are about ½ inch across and have 5 white rays. They are arranged in a flat-topped cluster and bloom between June and September. It grows in dry woods, thickets, and clearings.

RANGE: N.H. to Ohio south to Ga. and La.

Fleabanes

Fleabanes differ from the asters in that their flower heads are on naked stalks; and the involucral bracts are narrow and in a single row, or sometimes in a row of long ones with very short ones at the base. As in the asters, the heads have a central disk of tubular flowers and a marginal row of strap-like ray flowers.

ROBIN'S-PLANTAIN *(Erigeron pulchellus)*

Between April and July, the attractive flowers of this fleabane may be seen on the wooded slopes and banks, or even along roadsides. The heads are an inch to 1½ inches broad and have about 50 narrow lavender or violet rays. They are usually arranged in a loose cluster of between 2 and 6 heads. The whole plant is quite hairy, with a simple stem from 1 to 2 feet high. The basal leaves are narrowly top-shaped or spoon-shaped, toothed, and 1 to 3 inches long. Those of the stem are few and widely spaced, smaller, lance-shaped, and untoothed or very nearly so.
RANGE: Que. to Ont. and Minn. south to Fla., La. and Kan.

PHILADELPHIA FLEABANE *(Erigeron philadelphicus)*

The Philadelphia Fleabane has a slender and downy stem 1 to 3 feet tall; along which are scattered, mostly untoothed, stalkless and somewhat clasping leaves. The lower and basal leaves are much larger, 1 to 3 inches long, narrowly top-shaped, toothed, and taper into winged stalks. The flower heads are ½ to an inch across and have 100 or more very narrow, rose-purple or pinkish rays. They may be relatively few or quite numerous. It grows in rich woods and fields or on springy slopes, blooming between April and July.
RANGE: Nfd. to B.C. south to Fla. and Tex.

OAK-LEAF FLEABANE *(Erigeron quercifolius)*

This fleabane resembles the preceding one but it is usually a smaller plant from 6 inches to 1½ feet tall. The lower and basal leaves are quite distinctly lobed, hence the name of Oak-leaf. Its flower heads are about ½ inch across and have a number of narrow bluish or violet rays. It grows in fields and along roadsides, generally in sandy soils of the coastal plain; blooming April to June.
RANGE: Va. and Tenn. south to Fla. and Tex.

EARLY FLEABANE *(Erigeron vernus)*

The Early Fleabane has a basal rosette of thickish, top-shaped, untoothed or indistinctly toothed leaves 2 to 4 inches long. Its slender stem is simple or loosely branched, usually quite smooth, 1 to 2½ feet tall, and has but a few very small and bract-like leaves. The flower heads are about ½ inch across and have from 20 to 30 lilac or whitish rays. There are usually from 2 to 12 together in a loose cluster. This fleabane grows in the wet coastal plain pinelands or in shallow ponds, blooming late March to June.
RANGE: se. Va. south to Florida and west to La.

NARROW-LEAF DAISY FLEABANE *(Erigeron strigosus)*

This is a branching plant from 1 to 3 feet high; the stems, and sometimes the leaves, with minute and closely pressed hairs. The leaves are firm and all but the lowest and basal ones are untoothed or nearly so. Those on the main part of the stem are quite narrow and rather scattered. The lowest and basal ones are narrowly top-shaped and taper at the base into stalks. Its flower heads are numerous, about ½ inch across, and have about 40 narrow, white or purplish-tinged rays. It grows in dry fields, pastures, waste places, and along roadsides; flowering between late April and October.
RANGE: N.S. to B.C. south to Fla., Tex. and Calif.

DAISY FLEABANE *(Erigeron annuus)*

Also known as the White-top and Sweet-scabious, this species is quite similar to the preceding one. It differs in having spreading hairs, leaves which are sharply toothed, the lower ones being broader and egg-shaped; and is also a somewhat taller plant, sometimes 4 or 5 feet high. Common everywhere in fields and waste places, it blooms between late March and August.
RANGE: N.S. to Man. south to Ga., Ala. and Miss.

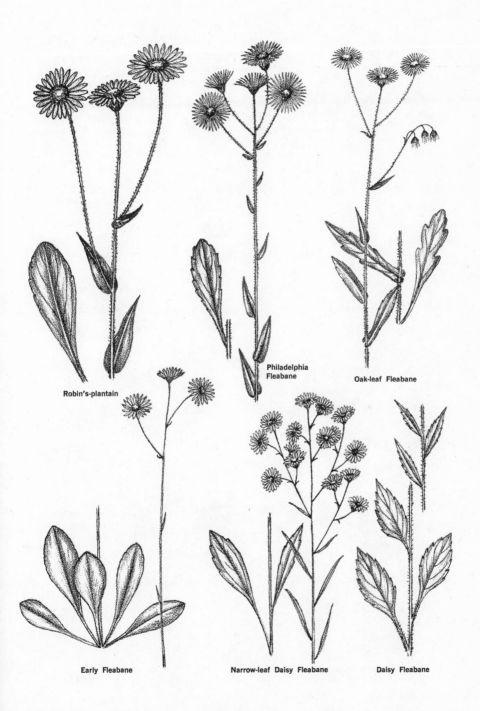

Robin's-plantain

Philadelphia
Fleabane

Oak-leaf Fleabane

Early Fleabane

Narrow-leaf Daisy Fleabane

Daisy Fleabane

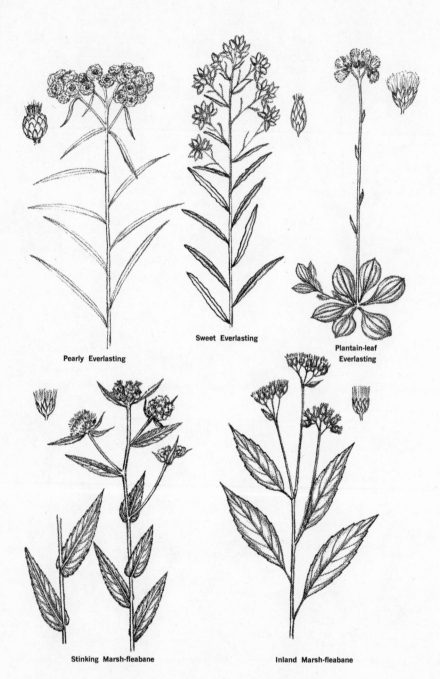

Pearly Everlasting

Sweet Everlasting

Plantain-leaf
Everlasting

Stinking Marsh-fleabane

Inland Marsh-fleabane

PEARLY EVERLASTING *(Anaphalis margaritacea)*

This plant gets its common name from the pearly-white involucral bracts of its flower heads. It is a snowy-white, woolly plant with an erect leafy stem 1 to 3 feet tall which branches toward the summit. Its leaves are all very narrow, white-woolly beneath and often also above, 1 to 4 inches long, with the margins rolled inward beneath. The flower heads are close to ½ inch across and contain many tubular flowers. It grows in dry fields and pastures, blooming between July and September.

RANGE: Nfd. to Alaska south to W. Va., Ohio, Wis., S.D., Colo. and Calif.

SWEET EVERLASTING *(Gnaphalium obtusifolium)*

This plant has pleasantly fragrant, wavy-margined, narrow leaves which are smooth and green above but white-woolly beneath, and 1 to 3 inches long. It is a whitish-cobwebby plant from 1 to 3 feet tall, often with a branched stem. The bracts of the involucres are pale yellowish. It grows abundantly in dry fields, clearings, and along roadsides; blooming August to October.

RANGE: Nfd. to Alaska south to W. Va., Ohio, Wis., N. Mex., and Calif.

PURPLISH CUDWEED *(Gnaphalium purpureum)*

This species is similar to the preceding but its leaves are noticably broader toward their tips. The flower heads are stalkless or nearly so and form a more slender end cluster, and their involucral bracts are brownish or purplish. It grows in open places from Me. to Pa., Ky., and Kan. south to Fla. and Tex.; blooming from March to June or later. (Not illustrated)

PLANTAIN-LEAF EVERLASTING *(Antennaria plantaginifolia)*

Members of this genus are often called Pussy-toes or Cat's-foot. All are small, woolly or cobwebby plants with chiefly basal leaves; and stems 6 to 12 inches tall bearing the heads of flowers. The Plantain-leaf Everlasting is one of the more common of the several species found in eastern North America. It has roundish to top-shaped basal leaves with 3 or 5 prominent veins, cobwebby above, silvery-hairy beneath, and 1½ to 3 inches long. It is sometimes called Ladies'-tobacco and grows in dry open woods or thickets, blooming between late March and June.

RANGE: Me. to Minn. south to Fla., Ala. and Mo.

STINKING MARSH-FLEABANE *(Pluchea foetida)*

Marsh-fleabanes are often called Camphorweeds or Stinkweeds because of their strong camphor-like odor. This species has a minutely downy and sticky stem 1½ to 3 feet tall which may be branched at the summit. The oblong to lance-shaped leaves are sharply toothed, 2 to 4 inches long, and are stalkless with clasping bases. The flower heads are about ¼ inch high and contain a number of small creamy-white, tubular flowers. It grows in marshes, ditches, and savannahs of the coastal plain; blooming July to October.

RANGE: N.J. south to Fla. and west to Ala.

Pluchea rosea is similar to the preceding but it has heads of pinkish flowers. It is found in similar situations in the coastal plain from N.C. south to Fla. and west to Miss.; blooming in June or July. (Not illustrated)

INLAND MARSH-FLEABANE *(Pluchea camphorata)*

This is a rather smooth plant from 2½ to 4 feet tall; with narrowly egg-shaped to oval, sharply toothed leaves, 4 to 10 inches long, on slender stalks up to about an inch in length. The lateral branches terminated by flower clusters are shorter than the terminal one; and the heads of purplish flowers are about ¼ inch tall. It grows in wet woods, marshes, meadows and ditches; blooming between August and October.

RANGE: Del. to Ohio, Ill., Mo. and Kan. south to Fla. and Tex.

SALT-MARSH-FLEABANE *(Pluchea purpurascens)*

This is a species of salt or brackish marshes. It is a tall plant with rather short-stalked leaves which are lance-shaped to egg-shaped, sometims toothed, and quite firm or fleshy in texture. The lateral branches terminated by clusters of flowers are as long as the terminal one, giving a flat-topped appearance. The flowers are pink or purplish; blooming between August and October. S. Me. s. to Fla. west to Tex. and Mex. (Not illustrated)

ELCAMPANE *(Inula helenium)*

Elcampane is a stout plant which usually has several simple, densely woolly stems from 2 to 6 feet high. Its leaves are roughish-hairy above and densely woolly beneath, and toothed on the margin. The basal ones are from 10 to 20 inches long and from 4 to 8 inches wide, and are narrowed at the base into long stalks. Those on the stem above are much smaller, stalkless, and often clasp the stem by a heart-shaped base. The relatively few flower heads are 2 to 4 inches across and have numerous, narrow, yellow rays from 1 to 1½ inches long. This plant has been introduced from Europe but it is now widely naturalized; growing in fields and along roadsides and fencerows from N.S. to Ont. and Minn. south to N.C. and Mo. It blooms between July and September.

CUP-PLANT *(Silphium perfoliatum)*

Indian-cup is another name often given to this plant which usually has a smooth square stem 4 to 8 feet tall, with branches toward the summit. It has pairs of egg-shaped or somewhat triangular leaves which are rough on both surfaces. The lower ones are abruptly contracted into a winged stalk and are coarsely toothed. The upper ones are untoothed and their bases are united, forming a cup about the stem. Its flower heads are numerous, 2 to 3 inches across, and have from 20 to 30 yellow rays. It grows in rich open woods, thickets, along riverbanks, and on prairies; blooming between July and September. RANGE: Ont. to S.D. south to Ga., Miss., Mo. and Okla.

ROSINWEED *(Silphium compositum)*

The Rosinweed has a smooth, whitened, wand-like stem from 3 to 9 feet tall; along which there are very small and widely scattered leaves. Its basal leaves are large, from 4 to 8 inches broad, long-stalked, and deeply cut-lobed or divided; or in the variety *reniforme*, simply roundish egg-shaped with a heart-shaped base and toothed margins. The flower heads are about 1½ inches across and have 10 or fewer yellow rays. They are quite numerous and arranged in a large but loosely forked terminal cluster; blooming June to September. It grows in dry sandy or rocky open woods and clearings. RANGE: Va. to e. Tenn. south to Ga.

WHORLED ROSINWEED *(Silphium trifoliatum)*

This species of rosinweed has lance-shaped or narrowly egg-shaped, short-stalked leaves 3 to 7 inches long, which are almost always arranged in whorls of 3 or 4. They are roughish above and smooth to hairy beneath, toothed to nearly untoothed on the margin. The flower heads are 1½ to 2 inches across and have from 15 to 20 yellow rays. The plant has a smooth, sometimes whitened, slender stem from 3 to 7 feet tall which branches toward the summit. It grows in woods, thickets, and on prairies; blooming between June and September. RANGE: Pa. to Ind. south to S.C. and Ala.

TOOTHED ROSINWEED *(Silphium dentatum)*

The Toothed Rosinweed somewhat resembles the preceding species but its leaves are mostly opposite, or the upper ones may be alternate, and the margins are usually coarsely toothed. It grows in sandy woodlands and thickets from N.C. and Ky. south to Ga. and Ala.; blooming in August and September. (Not illustrated)

LARGE-FLOWERED LEAF-CUP *(Polymnia uvedalia)*

Also known as the Bear's-foot, this is a roughish-hairy, very odorous, stout-stemmed and branching plant from 3 to 9 feet high. Its paired leaves are broadly egg-shaped, angled, and coarsely angular-toothed. The upper ones are stalkless or nearly so, but the lower ones are abruptly narrowed into a winged stalk. Its flower heads are 1½ to 3 inches across with from 10 to 15 bright yellow rays. The cup-shaped involucre has very large and hairy-fringed outer bracts. It grows in rich woods and thickets, blooming between July and October. RANGE: N.Y. to Ill. south to Fla. and Tex.

SMALL-FLOWERED LEAF-CUP *(Polymnia canadensis)*

This species is a more slender, somewhat sticky-hairy plant from 2 to 5 feet tall. The leaves are pinnately 3- to 5-lobed, stalked, and 4 to 10 inches long. Its flower heads are small and have 5 whitish or pale yellow rays which are shorter than the involucre, or they may even lack rays. It grows in moist woods and ravines from w. Vt. to Ont. south to Ga., Tenn., La. and Okla; blooming between July and October. (Not illustrated)

Elcampane

Cup-plant

Rosinweed

Whorled Rosinweed

Large-flowered Leaf-cup

Golden-star

Pineland-ginseng

Ox-eye

Small Yellow Crownbeard

Wing-stem

GOLDEN-STAR *(Chrysogonum virginianum)*

In early spring, when the Golden-star begins to bloom, it appears to be a stemless, low, hairy plant; but it later becomes from 3 to 12 inches high through the growth of branches. It has pairs of oblong or egg-shaped leaves which are 1 to 3 inches long, bluntly toothed, and rather long-stalked. The attractive flower heads are about 1¼ inches across, with usually 5 broad and bright yellow rays. It grows in sandy or rocky woodlands and on banks, blooming between late March and June.
RANGE: Pa. and W. Va. south to Fla. and La.

PINELAND-GINSENG *(Tetragonotheca helianthoides)*

This is a sticky-hairy plant which usually has a simple stem from 1 to 2½ feet tall. It has pairs of egg-shaped or oblong leaves 2 to 6 inches long, which are toothed and have stalkless but narrowed and often somewhat clasping bases. The heads of flowers are 1½ to 3 inches across and have from 6 to 10 pale yellow rays. An unusual feature is its double involucre in which the 4 large and leaf-like outer bracts are united to form a 4-sided cup. It grows in sandy open woods and thickets; blooming from April to July and sometimes again in the fall. RANGE: N.C. south to Fla. and west to Miss.

OX-EYE *(Heliopsis helianthoides)*

The Ox-eye is a sunflower-like plant with a smoothish stem 3 to 5 feet tall which may be simple or branched above. Its leaves are paired, egg-shaped or broadly lance-shaped, sharply toothed, slender-stalked, often more or less rough on the upper surface, and from 3 to 6 inches long. The heads of flowers are about 2 inches across and have 10 yellow rays which, unlike the rays of the true sunflowers, have pistils. It grows in open woods, thickets, and on dry banks; blooming between May and October. Also called False Sunflower. RANGE: N.Y. to Ont. and Minn. south to Ga. and Tex.

SMALL YELLOW CROWNBEARD *(Verbesina occidentalis)*

This plant has a narrowly 4-winged and usually smooth stem from 3 to 7 feet tall, with branches above which are also winged and often downy. It has pairs of egg-shaped to lance-shaped leaves which are toothed, pointed at both ends, stalked, and 4 to 10 inches long. The numerous flower heads are about an inch across, with from 1 to 5 yellow rays. They are arranged in a large and rather flat-topped terminal cluster, blooming between August and October. It grows in rich woods, thickets, and openings.
RANGE: Pa to Ill. south to Fla. and Miss.

SMALL WHITE CROWNBEARD *(Verbesina virginica)*

This Crownbeard differs from the preceding species in having scattered rather than paired leaves, and smaller flowers with from 3 to 5 white rays. It grows in dry open woods, thickets and clearings from Pa. to Ky., Mo. and Kan. south to Fla. and Tex.; blooming July to October. (Not illustrated)

SUNFLOWER CROWNBEARD *(Verbesina helianthoides)*

This species has alternate leaves, and relatively few heads of flowers which are 2 to 3 inches across with a bowl-shaped involucre and from 8 to 15 yellow rays. It has a rough-hairy stem up to about 3 feet high which is rather broadly 4-winged. The leaves are egg-shaped to lance-shaped, stalkless, toothed, 2 to 4 inches long, rough above but softly hairy beneath. It grows in dry open woods and on prairies from Ohio to Ill. and Iowa south to Ga. and Tex.; blooming between June and October. (Not illustrated)

WING-STEM *(Verbesina alternifolia)*

The Wing-stem, or Yellow Ironweed, has a stem from 4 to 9 feet tall which is winged along the upper portion, usually branched above, and often somewhat hairy. The leaves are scattered, or the lower ones may be opposite or in whorls of 3. They are mostly broadly lance-shaped, toothed, pointed at both ends, 4 to 12 inches long, and stalkless or short-stalked. The flower heads are numerous, 1 to 2 inches across, and the 2 to 10 yellow rays often differ quite a bit in size. It grows in the borders of moist woods and thickets, blooming during August or September.
RANGE: N.Y. to Ont. and Iowa south to Fla. and La.

TALL CONEFLOWER *(Rudbeckia laciniata)*

The Tall Coneflower has a smooth, whitened, and branching stem from 2 to 9 feet high. Its lower leaves are stalked, usually divided into 5 to 7 deeply cut or 3-lobed leaflets, and often a foot wide. Those upward along the stem are often similar but stalkless; or sometimes 3- to 5-parted, or merely toothed. The long-stalked flower heads are quite numerous, 2½ to 4 inches across; with 6 to 10 bright yellow rays and a greenish-yellow, dome-shaped disk. It grows in rich, moist, open woods and thickets; blooming between July and October. A form with more numerous ray flowers is cultivated as the Golden-glow.

RANGE: Que. to Mont. south to Fla., Tex. and Ariz.

THIN-LEAF CONEFLOWER *(Rudbeckia triloba)*

This coneflower usually has a somewhat roughish-hairy and branching stem from 1 to 5 feet high. The leaves are thin and rough on both sides; the lower ones being 2 to 4 inches long, stalked, mostly 3-lobed or 3-parted, and sharply toothed. Those along the upper part of the stem are short-stalked or stalkless and may even be untoothed. The flower heads are often very numerous, almost 2 inches across, and have from 8 to 12 bright yellow or orange-yellow rays and an egg-shaped dark purplish-brown disk. It grows in open woods, thickets, fields, and on rocky slopes; blooming between July and October.

RANGE: N.Y. to Minn. south to Ga., Tenn., Ark. and Okla.

SHOWY CONEFLOWER *(Rudbeckia speciosa)*

The Showy Coneflower has a rather sparsely hairy stem from 1 to 3 feet tall which is loosely branched above. Its leaves are quite firm, 2 to 5 inches long, broadly lance-shaped, coarsely toothed or somewhat cut, and taper into winged stalks. The flower heads are about 2½ inches across; with from 12 to 20 bright yellow and usually orange-based rays and a somewhat flattened, globular, purple-brown disk. It grows in moist woods, bottomlands, and swamps; blooming between July and October.

RANGE: N.Y. to Mich. and Mo. south to Ga., Ala. and Ark.

BLACK-EYED SUSAN *(Rudbeckia hirta)*

Often called the Yellow Daisy, this is one of our best known wild flowers. It grows very commonly in fields, on banks, and along the roadsides; blooming between May and September. A roughish-hairy plant, it has simple or few-branched stems from 1 to 3 feet tall; and lance-shaped or narrowly top-shaped leaves which are 2 to 7 inches long, with untoothed or indistinctly toothed margins. The larger, lower ones taper into rather long stalks. Its flower heads are 2 to 4 inches broad and have from 10 to 20 bright orange-yellow rays; and an egg-shaped disk which is dark purplish-brown.

RANGE: Ont. to Man. south to Fla. and Tex.

GRAY-HEADED CONEFLOWER *(Ratibida pinnata)*

This is a minutely roughish-hairy, hoary plant with a simple or branched stem 1½ to about 4 feet high. The leaves are pinnately divided into from 3 to 7 segments which are sometimes toothed. Its flowers are quite large; with from 4 to 7 drooping yellow rays 1 to 3 inches long, and an oblong grayish disk which may become brown. It grows in dry open woods and on prairies from n. N.Y. and Ont. to Minn. and Neb. south to Ga. and Okla.; blooming between June and September. (Not illustrated)

PURPLE CONEFLOWER *(Echinacea purpurea)*

The Purple Coneflower has flower heads 2½ to 5 inches across; with from 12 to 20 purple and drooping rays and a cone-shaped, purplish disk. It has a simple or branched, often bristly hairy stem 3 to 5 feet tall. The leaves are roughish above and sharply toothed; the basal ones egg-shaped, 3 to 8 inches long, 5-veined, and stalked. The upper ones are lance-shaped, stalkless and much smaller. It grows in dry open woods and on prairies; blooming between June and September.

RANGE: Va. to Mich., Ill. and Iowa south to Ga. and La.

SMOOTH-LEAF PURPLE CONEFLOWER *(Echinacea laevigata)*

This species is similar to the preceding one but it has smooth and whitened leaves. It grows in woods and fields from Pa. south to Ga. (Not illustrated)

Tall Coneflower

Thin-leaf Coneflower

Showy Coneflower

Black-eyed Susan

Purple Coneflower

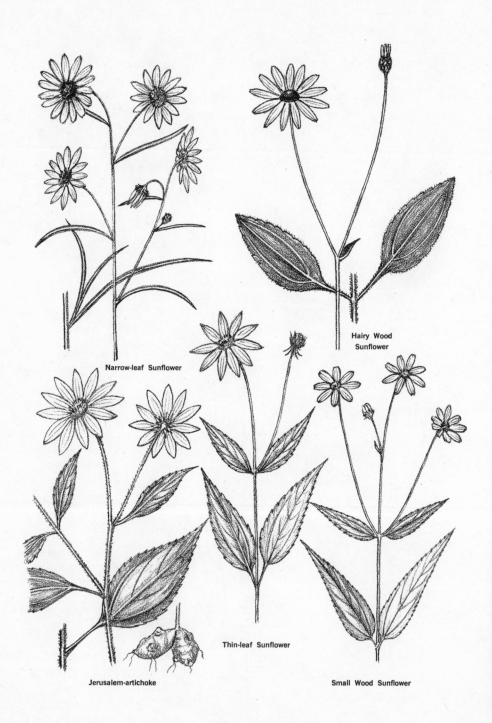

Narrow-leaf Sunflower

Hairy Wood
Sunflower

Thin-leaf Sunflower

Jerusalem-artichoke

Small Wood Sunflower

Sunflowers

Sunflowers are mostly tall plants, usually with opposite leaves, and with showy flower heads with a prominent disk and marginal ray flowers. The latter are neutral, containing no sexual organs and producing no seeds. The involucre has several rows of overlapping bracts which are green and more or less leaf-like. Close to 40 species have been described from eastern North America.

NARROW-LEAF SUNFLOWER *(Helianthus angustifolius)*

This sunflower of the wet pinelands and swampy thickets has a slender stem 2 to 6 feet tall. It may be simple or branched above and is more or less rough, at least on the lower part. Its leaves are all very narrow, stiff, rough, untoothed, stalkless, 2 to 7 inches long, and often have clusters of smaller leaves in their axils. The flower heads are 2 to 3 inches across, with a dark purplish-brown disk and from 12 to 20 bright yellow rays. It blooms between July and October.

RANGE: se. N.Y. to s. Ind. and Mo. south to Fla. and Tex.

HAIRY WOOD SUNFLOWER *(Helianthus atrorubens)*

Often called the Purple-disked Sunflower, this species is widely distributed from the coastal plain pinelands to open woods and thickets in the mountains. Its stem is 2 to 5 feet tall and is densely hairy below, but less so in the branching portion above. The leaves are mostly on the lower part of the stem and are egg-shaped to oval, usually abruptly narrowed into a long and winged stalk. They are 4 to 10 inches long, rough above, more or less hairy beneath, and rather shallowly toothed. The flower heads are about 2 inches across, with from 10 to 20 bright yellow rays and a purplish-brown disk; blooming between late July and October.

RANGE: Va. to Ky. south to Fla. and La.

JERUSALEM-ARTICHOKE *(Helianthus tuberosus)*

In spite of its common name, this is a native American sunflower. Its thick and fleshy rootstocks bear edible tubers which were once much used by the Indians, and still sometimes cultivated. It has a very roughish-hairy stem 6 to 10 feet tall which is branched above. Its leaves are thick and hard, very rough-hairy above, downy beneath, and prominently 3-veined. Those along the main part of the stem are 4 to 8 inches long, egg-shaped, coarsely toothed, and contracted into broadly winged stalks. The flower heads are quite numerous, 2 to 3 inches across, with from 12 to 20 bright yellow rays and a yellowish disk. It grows in moist thickets and open places, blooming between July and October.

RANGE: Ont. to Sask. south to Ga., Tenn. and Ark.; and more widely naturalized.

THIN-LEAF SUNFLOWER *(Helianthus decapetalus)*

Also known as the Ten-petalled Sunflower, this species has a smoothish stem 1 to 5 feet tall which is branched and may be slightly roughish above. Its thin textured leaves are smooth or but slightly roughish above and are rather indistinctly 3-veined. The larger and lower ones are egg-shaped, 3 to 8 inches long, sharply toothed, and slender stalked. Those of the upper part of the stem are smaller, lance-shaped, and taper into short stalks. The flower heads are 2 to 3 inches across, with from 8 to 15 light yellow rays and a yellowish disk. It grows in open woods, thickets, and often along streams; blooming between August and October.

RANGE: Me. to Que., Minn. and Neb. south to Ga., Ky. and Mo.

SMALL WOOD SUNFLOWER *(Helianthus microcephalus)*

This woodland sunflower has a slender, smooth stem from 3 to 6 feet high which is branched above. Its leaves are lance-shaped to narrowly egg-shaped, thin, roughish above, pale and downy beneath, sharply toothed, stalked, and from 3 to 7 inches long. The flower heads are numerous, about an inch across, and have 5 to 10 yellow rays and a yellowish disk. It usually grows in moist places, blooming from August to October.

RANGE: Pa. to Ill. south to Fla., Miss. and Mo.

WOODLAND SUNFLOWER *(Helianthus divaricatus)*

The Woodland Sunflower is also known as the Rough Sunflower. It has a smooth, slender, often whitened stem from 2 to 7 feet tall which is usually branched above. Its leaves are lance-shaped to narrowly egg-shaped, broad at the base, stalkless or nearly so, toothed, 3 to 8 inches long, more or less hairy beneath, and rough-hairy on the upper surface. The flower heads are about 2 inches across, with 8 to 15 yellow rays and a yellowish disk. It grows in dry open woods, thickets, and clearings; blooming between June and September.

RANGE: Me. to Que. and Sask. south to Ga., Tenn. and Ark.

PALE-LEAF WOOD SUNFLOWER *(Helianthus strumosus)*

This species has a smooth or slightly roughish stem from 3 to 7 feet tall, which is usually branched above. Its leaves are egg-shaped or broadly lance-shaped, distinctly stalked, shallowly toothed or almost toothless, thick and firm, very rough above, pale to whitish and downy beneath, and from 3 to 8 inches long. The flower heads are 2½ to 4 inches across, with 5 to 15 yellow rays and a yellowish disk. It grows in dry open woods, thickets, and clearings; blooming between July and September.

RANGE: Que. to N.D. south to Ga., Ala., Ark. and Okla.

TALL SUNFLOWER *(Helianthus giganteus)*

The Tall Sunflower has a roughish stem which is usually 5 to 12 feet tall, and often much-branched above. Its leaves are mostly scattered, lance-shaped, stalkless or short-stalked, shallowly or inconspicuously toothed, green and roughish on both sides, and 2 to 6 inches long. The numerous flower heads are 1½ to 2½ inches across, with from 10 to 20 rather pale lemon-yellow rays and a relatively large yellowish disk. It grows in swamps and wet thickets or meadows, blooming between July and October.

RANGE: Que. to Sask. south to Fla., La. and Colo.

VARIED-LEAF SUNFLOWER *(Helianthus heterophyllus)*

This sunflower has a slender and roughish stem from 3 to 4 feet high, which is usually simple or very rarely with a few long and ascending branches. Its lower leaves have egg-shaped to elliptic or narrowly top-shaped blades which taper into stalks, and may be as much as 8 inches long. The ones on the stem above are very narrow, stalkless, and smaller. All are rather coarse in texture, rough-hairy, and untoothed. The long-stalked flower heads are 3 or 4 inches across, with about 20 bright yellow rays and a dark purplish-brown disk. It grows in wet coastal plain pinelands and the borders of swamps and marshes; blooming between August and October.

RANGE: N.C. south to Fla. and west to La.

HAIRY SUNFLOWER *(Helianthus mollis)*

The Hairy Sunflower has a stout, densely grayish- or whitish-hairy, and more or less roughish stem from 2 to 4 feet tall which is simple or has a few ascending branches above. The leaves are egg-shaped to broadly lance-shaped, stalkless, toothed, grayish and rough above, pale and downy beneath. They are 2 to 5 inches long and more or less clasp the stem by a rounded to somewhat heart-shaped base. The flower heads are 2 to 3 inches across, and have from 15 to 25 yellow rays and a yellowish disk. It grows in dry open woods and fields, blooming between July and September.

RANGE: Ohio and Mich. to Iowa south to Ga. and Tex.

STIFF-HAIRED SUNFLOWER *(Helianthus hirsutus)*

In a general way this sunflower resembles the Woodland Sunflower but its stem has stiffish and spreading hairs and is often roughish. The narrow leaves are very rough-hairy above and somewhat so beneath, usually prominently 3-veined, short-stalked, and sharply toothed. It grows in dry open woods and thickets from w. Pa. to Minn. south to Fla. and Tex.; blooming between July and October. (Not illustrated)

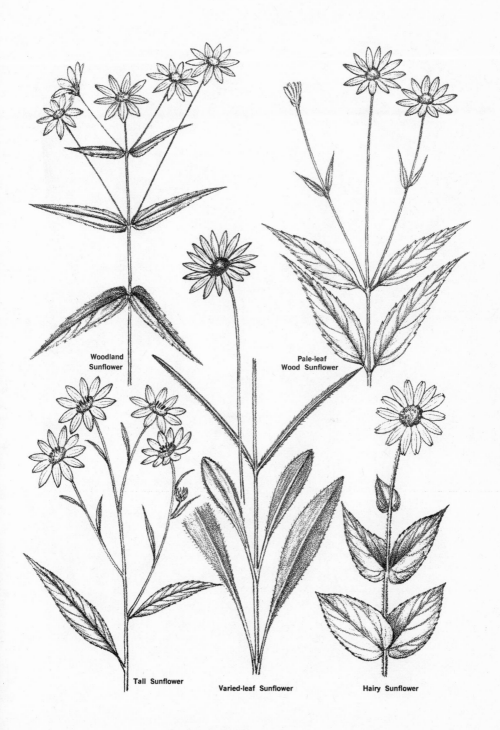

Woodland
Sunflower

Pale-leaf
Wood Sunflower

Tall Sunflower

Varied-leaf Sunflower

Hairy Sunflower

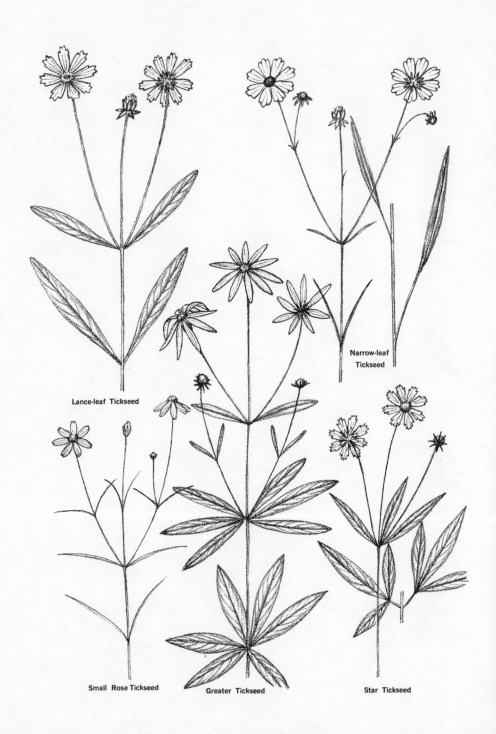

Lance-leaf Tickseed

Narrow-leaf Tickseed

Small Rose Tickseed

Greater Tickseed

Star Tickseed

Tickseeds

Tickseeds usually have opposite leaves and showy flower heads with a disk and about 8 marginal rays. The involucre is made up of two series of bracts: the outer ones green, leaf-like, and somewhat spreading; the inner ones broader, closely pressed, more or less erect, and usually not green in color.

LANCE-LEAF TICKSEED *(Coreopsis lanceolata)*

This plant has a slender, smoothish or hairy stem from 1 to 2 feet tall. Its leaves are lance-shaped to inversely lance-shaped, occasionally with 1 or 2 small lobes near the base. They are untoothed, 2 to 6 inches long, and the lower ones are stalked. The long-stalked flower heads are 1½ to 2½ inches across, with 6 to 10 bright yellow rays which are rather deeply lobed at the summit and a yellowish disk. The outer involucral bracts are lance-shaped, green and spreading; the inner ones egg-shaped and brownish or reddish tinged. It grows in dry, sandy or rocky, open woods, thickets, or clearings; blooming between April and July.

RANGE: Va. to Ont., Mich., Wis. and Mo. south to Fla. and N.Mex.

NARROW-LEAF TICKSEED *(Coreopsis angustifolia)*

This species has a slender and smoothish stem 1½ to 2½ feet tall. Its lower leaves are scattered, inversely lance-shaped, untoothed, 3 to 5 inches long, and taper into stalks. The upper ones are much smaller, very narrow, and usually paired. The flower heads are 1½ to 2 inches across and have 6 to 10 deep yellow rays which are lobed at the summit, and a dark brown disk. The outer involucral bracts are egg-shaped and greenish; the inner ones larger and mostly red. It grows in low, wet, coastal plain pinelands; blooming between August and October.

RANGE: N.C. south to Fla. and west to Tex.

SMALL ROSE TICKSEED *(Coreopsis rosea)*

The flower heads of this tickseed are ½ to 1 inch across and have from 4 to 8 pink, rose-colored, or occasionally white rays and a yellowish disk. It has slender, branching, smooth stems 6 inches to 2 feet tall. The leaves are very narrow, untoothed, 1 to 2½ inches long, and often have tufts of smaller leaves in their axils. It grows in moist to wet open places along the Atlantic Coast; blooming between July and September. Also called Pink Tickseed.

RANGE: N.S. south to Ga.

GREATER TICKSEED *(Coreopsis major)*

The Greater, or Wood Tickseed has a slender and more or less downy stem 2 to 3 feet tall. Its leaves are stalkless and all except a few of the uppermost ones are divided into 3 lance-shaped or narrowly egg-shaped, untoothed segments 2 to 4 inches long and from ¼ to an inch broad, the plant thus appearing to have whorls of 6 leaves. The flower heads are slender-stalked, 1 to 2 inches across, with 6 to 10 yellow rays and a yellowish disk. The outer involucral bracts are narrow and about as long as the inner ones. It grows in open woods, thickets, and clearings; blooming between May and August.

RANGE: Va. to Ohio south to Fla. and Miss.

WHORLED TICKSEED *(Coreopsis verticillata)*

This species is quite similar to the preceding one but its leaves are divided into very narrow segments less than ⅛ inch broad, and they are often branched. It grows in dry open woods and clearings from Md. to Ky. and Ark. south to Fla. and Ala. (Not illustrated)

STAR TICKSEED *(Coreopsis pubescens)*

The Star Tickseed has a slender and downy stem 2 to 4 feet tall, which may have a few branches. The upper leaves are short-stalked or stalkless, lance-shaped, or sometimes cut into 3 to 5 segments, and 2 to 3 inches long. The lower ones are top-shaped and taper into slender stalks. Its flower heads are about 1¼ inches across, with 8 to 10 yellow rays which are lobed at the summit and a yellowish disk. The spreading narrow outer bracts of the involucre are star-like and about as long as the inner ones. It grows in dry open woods and on slopes or cliffs, blooming between July and September.

RANGE: Va. to s. Ill. and Mo. south to Fla. and La.

TALL TICKSEED *(Coreopsis tripteris)*

The Tall Tickseed has a smooth stem 4 to 8 feet tall which is branched above. The principal leaves are 2 to 5 inches long, definitely stalked, and divided into from 3 to 5 lance-shaped, untoothed segments. The uppermost leaves are not divided but are lance-shaped, smaller, and stalkless. Its slender-stalked flower heads are 1 to 1½ inches across, with 6 to 10 yellow rays and a yellowish disk. The outer involucral bracts are only ⅛ inch or less long and very much shorter than the inner ones. It grows in moist open woods and thickets, blooming between July and September. The heads have an anise-like odor.

RANGE: Ont. to Wis. south to Ga., La. and Kan.

Beggar-Ticks, Bur-Marigolds, and Tickseed Sunflowers

As in the tickseeds, the flower heads have involucral bracts in 2 series, the outer ones being quite large and usually leaf-like. The heads have many flowers, often with 3 to 8 rays, but some species have only disk flowers. The seed-like fruits have 2 to 4 barbed awns. They are usually called "beggar-ticks" or "stick-tights" as they commonly stick to one's clothing in trips afield in late summer and fall. The plants have opposite leaves.

SMALLER BUR-MARIGOLD *(Bidens cernua)*

This is a variable plant, sometimes with simple and slender stems only a few inches high, stalked and narrow leaves, and heads of flowers about ½ inch across. Again it may have a rather stout stem 3 feet tall, with lance-shaped or narrowly oblong leaves 3 to 6 inches long which are stalkless or nearly so, and with flower heads about an inch across. The flower heads commonly nod and they may have 6 to 10 yellow rays or none at all. It grows in swamps and other wet places, blooming between July and October. Also called the Nodding Bur-marigold.

RANGE: Que. and N.S. to B.C. south to Md., w.N.C., Tenn., Mo. and Colo.

LARGER BUR-MARIGOLD *(Bidens laevis)*

Also known as the Smooth Bur-marigold, this species is a smooth plant with a branching stem 1 to 3 feet high; and lance-shaped, toothed leaves 3 to 8 inches long. Its flower heads are much more showy than those of the preceding species, 1 to 1½ inches across, with 8 to 10 rather large and bright yellow rays. It grows in swamps, wet meadows, or along streams; blooming between September and November.

RANGE: N.H. to W.Va. and Ind. south to Fla. and Mex.

TICKSEED-SUNFLOWER *(Bidens coronata)*

This is a rather smooth plant with a much-branched stem from 1 to 5 feet high. Its leaves are mostly 3 to 5 inches long and pinnately divided into from 3 to 7 narrow or lance-shaped segments which are sharply cut or toothed; the lower ones being distinctly stalked. The flower heads are 1 to 2 inches across and have from 15 to 25 rather short yellow rays and a large, deeper yellow disk. The involucre has from 6 to 8 outer bracts. It grows in wet places and blooms between August and October.

RANGE: Conn. to Ont. and Neb. south to Fla. and Ala.

WESTERN TICKSEED-SUNFLOWER *(Bidens aristosa)*

This species rather closely resembles the preceding one. It is best distinguished by the 8 to 12 spreading outer involucral bracts which are no longer than the inner ones. It grows in low wet grounds from Me. to Minn. south to S.C., Ala., La. and Tex.; blooming between August and October. (Not illustrated)

SEA OX-EYE *(Borrichia frutescens)*

This is the shrubby and more or less fleshy or leathery composite, with yellow heads of flowers, that is so conspicuous on the borders of salt or brackish marshes in the Southeast. It has a sparingly branched stem 1 to 4 feet high; and pairs of lance-shaped to top-shaped leaves from 1 to 3 inches long, which sometimes have a few teeth toward the base. Its flower heads are about an inch across, with 15 to 25 rather short yellow rays and a large dusky-yellow disk. All parts of the plant are covered with minute silky-white hairs, giving it a rather dusty appearance. It blooms between May and September.

RANGE: se. Va. south to Fla. and west to Tex.

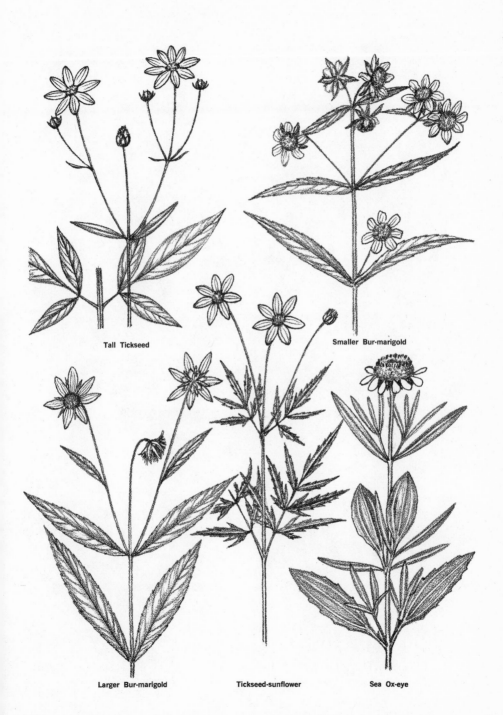

Tall Tickseed

Smaller Bur-marigold

Larger Bur-marigold

Tickseed-sunflower

Sea Ox-eye

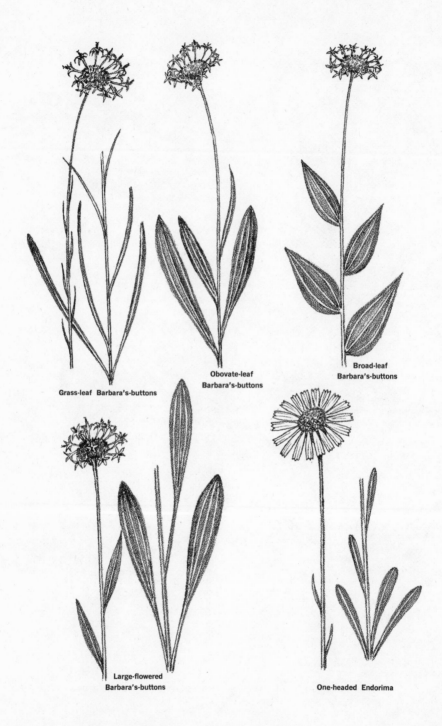

Grass-leaf Barbara's-buttons

Obovate-leaf
Barbara's-buttons

Broad-leaf
Barbara's-buttons

Large-flowered
Barbara's-buttons

One-headed Endorima

GRASS-LEAF BARBARA'S-BUTTONS *(Marshallia graminifolia)*

This is a smooth plant with a simple or sparingly branched and slender stem 1 to 2 feet tall; along which are scattered, narrow leaves. The leaves toward the base are larger, up to 4½ inches long, and mostly broadest near or somewhat above the middle. Its flower heads are long-stalked, about 1 inch across, and made up of a number of pink flowers having a slender tube with 5 flaring lobes at the summit and bluish anthers. This very attractive wildflower grows in moist to wet coastal plain pinelands and savannahs, blooming between July and September.

RANGE: N.C. south to Fla. and west to La.

OBOVATE-LEAF BARBARA'S-BUTTONS *(Marshallia obovata)*

Unlike the preceding species, this one grows in old fields and open woods chiefly in the piedmont region. It is also a smooth plant, usually with a slender and simple stem from 6 inches to about 2 feet tall, which is leafy chiefly below the middle or only toward the base. Its leaves are mostly narrowly top-shaped and from 1 to 4½ inches long. The flower heads are about an inch across; made up of a number of whitish to pale pink flowers with slender tubes. It blooms during April and May.

RANGE: N.C. and Mo. south to Fla. and Ala.

BROAD-LEAF BARBARA'S-BUTTONS *(Marshallia trinervia)*

This is a smooth plant with a simple or sparingly branched stem 1 to 2 feet tall, leafy to or somewhat beyond the middle. Its leaves are thin, egg-shaped to broadly lance-shaped, conspicuously 3-ribbed, stalkless, untoothed and 2 to 3 inches long. The flower heads are about ¾ inch across and made up of a number of purplish flowers with slender tubes. It grows in damp woods and pinelands, blooming in May and June.

RANGE: Va. and Tenn. south to Ga. and Miss.

LARGE-FLOWERED BARBARA'S-BUTTONS *(Marshallia grandiflora)*

While most Barbara's-buttons are plants of the lowlands, this species grows in boggy places in the mountains. It is a smooth plant with a simple slender stem 1 to 2 feet tall, leafy to or beyond the middle. The lower leaves are narrowly top-shaped, 2 to 6 inches long, thickish, and taper into stalks which are often as long as the blades. The upper ones are much smaller, lance-shaped, stalkless and more or less clasping at the base. Its flower heads are an inch or more across and made up of a number of slender-tubed purplish flowers about ⅔ inch long. It blooms in May and June.

RANGE: Pa. to Ky. south to w. N.C.

ONE-HEADED ENDORIMA *(Baludina uniflora)*

This plant usually has a simple, rather stout, minutely downy stem 1 to 3 feet tall. On it are just a few scattered leaves for most of the leaves are basal. The leaves are thickish, narrow, stalkless, untoothed and 1 to 2 inches long; the lower ones usually being somewhat broader toward the tip. The long-stalked flower head is 2 to 2½ inches across; with from 20 to 30 yellow rays which are lobed at the tip, and a large yellowish disk. The receptacle has a peculiar honey-combed surface. It grows in moist coastal plain pinelands, blooming between July and September.

RANGE: N.C. south to Fla. and west to La.

PURPLE-DISKED ENDORIMA *(Baludina atropurpurea)*

This species is very similar to the preceding but its flower heads have purple disks. It is less common in the coastal plain of S.C. and Ga. (Not illustrated)

COMMON SNEEZEWEED *(Helenium autumnale)*

The conspicuously wing-angled stem of this plant is 2 to 6 feet tall and branches toward the summit. Its narrowly oblong to lance-shaped leaves are stalkless, usually toothed, and 2 to 5 inches long. The usually numerous flower heads are 1 to 2 inches across; with from 10 to 18 drooping bright yellow rays which are 3-lobed at the summit, and a large ball-shaped yellowish disk. It grows in swamps, wet meadows and thickets; blooming in September and October.

RANGE: Que. to Minn. and Neb. south to Fla., Tex. and Ariz.

PURPLE-HEAD SNEEZEWEED *(Helenium nudiflorum)*

This species has a narrowly wing-angled, more or less downy stem 1 to 3 feet tall, with stiffly ascending branches above. Its leaves are lance-shaped or narrower, mostly un-toothed, 1½ to 3 inches long, and the lower ones taper into winged stalks. The flower heads are slightly more than an inch across; with from 10 to 15 drooping yellow rays 3-lobed at the summit, and a large ball-shaped purplish-brown disk. It grows in moist mea-dows, fields, or along roadsides; blooming between June and October.

RANGE: Ky. to Kan. south to Ga. and Tex.; spreading as a weed into the N.E.

BITTERWEED *(Helenium amarum)*

This yellow-flowered composite is common in fields and along roadsides in the Southeast and is gradually spreading northward. It is a smooth or minutely downy plant with a slender, much-branched stem 6 inches to 2 feet tall; with very numerous narrow leaves ½ to 1½ inches long, which often have clusters of small leaves in the axils of the larger ones. The numerous flower heads are about an inch across; with 4 to 8 drooping yellow rays 3-lobed at the summit, and a large ball-shaped yellowish disk. Also called Fine-leaf Sneezeweed or Yellow Dog-fennel. It blooms between June and November.

RANGE: Va. to s. Ill., Mo. and Kan. south to Fla., Tex. and Mex.

SAVANNAH SNEEZEWEED *(Helenium vernale)*

This species has a simple, erect stem 1 to 2 feet tall. The lower and basal leaves are long and narrow, from 2 to 6 inches in length, and have sparingly wavy-toothed mar-gins; but on the stem they are rapidly reduced in size upward. The solitary flower head is about 2 inches across; with 15 to 25 spreading bright yellow rays 3-lobed at the sum-mit, and a large yellowish disk which is flattened and dome-shaped. It grows in wet coastal plain pinelands and savannahs, blooming in April or May.

RANGE: S.C. south to Fla. west to Miss.

SHORT-LEAF SNEEZEWEED *(Helenium brevifolium)*

This species is distinguished from the preceding by the purplish-brown disks of its flower heads, and also by its leaves whose bases run for some distance down the stem. It grows in wet pinelands, chiefly in the coastal plain, from se. Va. south to Fla. and west to Miss.; blooming in May or June. (Not illustrated)

COMMON YARROW *(Achillea millefolium)*

Often called Milfoil, this European plant is now widely naturalized in old fields, waste places and along roadsides. It is a smoothish to cobwebby plant with a very strong and distinctive odor, with a simple or branched stem 1 to 2 feet tall. The narrowly oblong to lance-shaped leaves are finely dissected into numerous and very slender segments, the lower ones often as much as 10 inches long and tapered at the base into stalks. The nu-merous small flower heads are arranged in a dense, flat-topped, terminal cluster. Each head has 4 to 6 small white or occasionally pink or purplish rays. It blooms from late April to September or October.

314

Common Sneezeweed

Purple-head Sneezeweed

Bitterweed

Savannah Sneezeweed

Common Yarrow

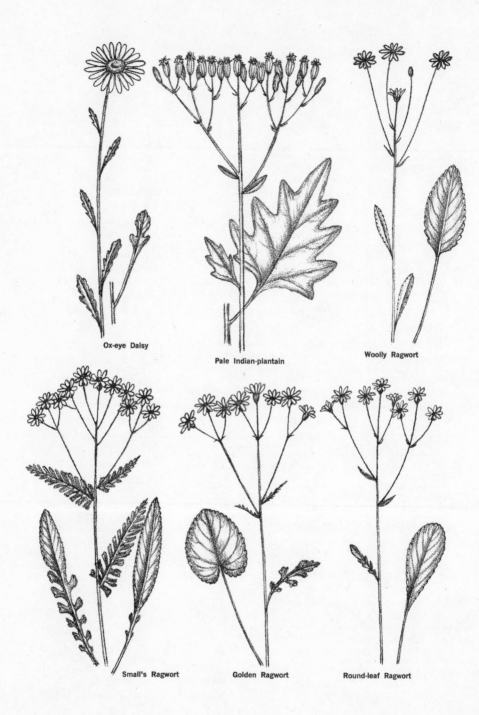

Ox-eye Daisy

Pale Indian-plantain

Woolly Ragwort

Small's Ragwort

Golden Ragwort

Round-leaf Ragwort

OX-EYE DAISY *(Chrysanthemum leucanthemum)*

This common and well-known plant, often called the White or Field Daisy, is a native of Europe which is now widely naturalized in fields, meadows, waste places and along roadsides. It is a smooth or slightly hairy plant with a simple or sparingly branched stem 1 to 3 feet tall. The basal leaves are top-shaped or spoon-shaped, toothed or often lobed, and rather long-stalked. Those along the stem are narrow, stalkless, toothed or often cut-lobed, and 1 to 3 inches long. The flower heads are 1 to 2 inches across, with 20 to 30 bright white rays and a somewhat flattened yellow disk. It blooms from April to July or August.

PALE INDIAN-PLANTAIN *(Cacalia atriplicifolia)*

This striking plant has a smooth, round, whitened stem 3 to 6 feet tall. The leaves are somewhat triangular or fan-shaped with a broad base and angular lobes. They are thin, pale green above, whitened beneath, and up to 6 inches across. It numerous heads have a cylindrical involucre about ⅓ inch high and contain several tubular white flowers; and they are arranged in a large, loose, more or less flat-topped cluster. It grows in dry open woods and thickets, blooming between June and September.
RANGE: N.Y. to Minn. south to Ga., Tenn. and Okla.

Cacalia lanceolata is a similar plant which grows in low wet pinelands and savannahs of the coastal plain from N.C. south to Fla. and west to La. It has narrowly egg-shaped or lance-shaped leaves which are untoothed or very sparingly toothed, and it blooms between August and October. (Not illustrated)

WOOLLY RAGWORT *(Senecio tomentosus)*

This ragwort usually has a tuft of several whitish-woolly stems 1 to 2½ feet high. The stem leaves are small, narrow, and scattered; but the basal ones are oblong to lance-shaped, stalked, toothed, white-woolly beneath and often cobwebby above, and 2 to 6 inches long. The flower heads are about ¾ inch across, with 10 to 15 yellow rays and a small yellow disk. It grows in moist sandy or rocky open woods and thickets, blooming between April and June. RANGE: N.J. to Ark. south to Fla. and La.

SMALL'S RAGWORT *(Senecio smallii)*

This species has several stems 1½ to 2½ feet tall which are loosely woolly toward the base. The basal leaves are lance-shaped or narrowly oblong, bluntly toothed and 3 to 6 inches long. Those upward along the stem become progressively smaller and deeply cut into many segments. The numerous flower heads are about ½ inch across, with 8 to 10 bright yellow rays. It grows in open woods, fields and roadsides; blooming from May to early July. RANGE: N.J. to Pa. and Ky. south to Fla. and Ala.

GOLDEN RAGWORT *(Senecio aureus)*

Also called Squaw-weed, this is a rather smooth plant with usually several slender stems 6 inches to 2½ feet tall. The basal leaves are oblong-heart-shaped, bluntly-toothed, slender-stalked, often purplish beneath and 1 to 6 inches long. Those upward along the stem are small, narrow, and more or less deeply cut. The many flower heads are about ¾ inch across, with 8 to 12 bright yellow rays. It grows in rich moist woods, wet meadows, swamps and bogs; blooming late March to July.
RANGE: Nfd. to Que. and Wis. south to Fla., Tenn. and Mo.

ROUND-LEAF RAGWORT *(Senecio obovatus)*

This species has a rather smooth and slender stem 1 to 1½ feet tall. The basal leaves are usually more top-shaped than round, bluntly toothed, and 1 to 3½ inches long. Those upward along the stem are small, narrow, and more or less cut. The flower heads are about ⅔ inch across with 8 to 12 bright yellow rays. It grows on wooded slopes and in ravines, blooming between April and June.
RANGE: N.H. to Ont. and Mich. south to Fla. and Tex.

BUTTERWEED *(Senecio glabellus)*

This species is an annual plant with a succulent, hollow stem 1 to 3 feet tall. Its stem leaves have an end lobe but slightly larger than the others, and the basal ones are pinnately divided into more or less toothed segments. The flowers have 7 to 10 yellow rays. It grows in wet places from N.C. to sw. Ohio, s. Ill and Mo. south to Fla. and Tex.; blooming between March and June. (Not illustrated)

317

Thistles

The flower heads of thistles contain a large number of slender tubular flowers which have a deeply 5-lobed rim. There are no ray flowers. The feathery pappus becomes the "thistledown", a sort of parachute attached to the top of the seed-like fruits or achenes. The plants have alternate prickly leaves, and most species also have prickly involucral bracts. During the first year the plant forms a rosette of leaves. After blooming the second year, the plant dies.

YELLOW THISTLE *(Carduus spinosissimus)*

This thistle has a very stout, leafy, branching stem 2 to 5 feet tall which is somewhat woolly when young. Its leaves are 2 to 5 inches long, green on both sides, and cut into triangular lobes which have many yellowish prickles. The flower heads are 2 to 4 inches across, with numerous pale yellow to purple flowers. The involucre is surrounded by narrow, spiny, bract-like leaves but the true bracts of the involucre have soft and unarmed tips. It grows in sandy fields, savannahs, roadsides and waste places; blooming between late March and June.

RANGE: Me. to Pa. south to Fla. and Tex.

COMMON THISTLE *(Carduus lanceolatus)*

Often called the Bull Thistle, this native of Europe is now widely naturalized in fields, pastures, and along roadsides. It has a stout, branching, leafy stem 3 to 6 feet tall which is more or less wooly and has prickly wings running down from the leaf bases. Its leaves are green above, pale or with a web-like wool beneath, 3 to 6 inches long, and pinnately cut into a number of spiny segments. The flower heads are 1½ to 2 inches across, with numerous purple flowers; and all of the involucral bracts are tipped with a prickle. It blooms between June and October.

SWAMP THISTLE *(Carduus muticus)*

This is a rather slender plant with a smoothish or somewhat woolly stem 3 to 8 feet tall. Its leaves are rather thin, green above, pale and more or less webby beneath, and pinnately cut into broad prickly segments. The flower heads are about 1½ inches across, with numerous purple flowers; and the involucral bracts lack prickles but are usually webby and stickly. It grows in wet woods or swamps, blooming between July and October.

RANGE: Nfd. to Sask. south to N.C., Tenn. and n. La.

TALL THISTLE *(Carduus altissimus)*

Often called the Roadside Thistle, this species has a fairly stout, branching, woolly, and leafy stem 3 to 10 feet tall. Its leaves are undivided but have shallowly lobed or bristly-toothed margins, and they are densely felted with white wool beneath. The flower heads are about 2 inches across, with numerous rose-purple flowers; while the outer involucral bracts have a dark glandular spot and also a weak prickle. It grows in open woods, fields, pastures and thickets; blooming from August to late fall.

RANGE: N.Y. to Mich. and Minn. south to Fla. and Tex.

PASTURE THISTLE *(Carduus pumilus)*

This species is also called the Fragrant or Bull Thistle. It has a stout stem 1 to 3 feet tall; with leaves which are pinnately cut into shallow, very spiny lobes and green on both sides. The flower heads are 2 to 3 inches across, with numerous purple flowers; but only the lower bracts of the broadly egg-shaped involucre are prickly. It grows in woods and fields from Me. to Ohio south to n. S.C., blooming between late May and August. (Not illustrated)

SANDHILL THISTLE *(Carduus repandus)*

This small thistle grows in the dry coastal plain pinelands and sandhills. It has a simple or few-branched stem 6 inches to 1½ feet high, with narrow leaves 1½ to 3 inches long which are wavy-lobed and very prickly. Its flower heads are about an inch across and contain purple flowers. The outer involucral bracts are prickly and have a pale sticky band down the center. It blooms from May to July.

RANGE: N.C. south to Fla.

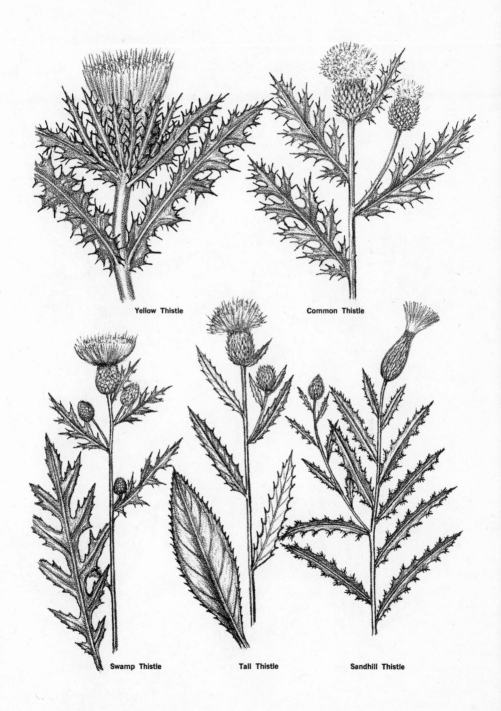

Yellow Thistle

Common Thistle

Swamp Thistle

Tall Thistle

Sandhill Thistle

Sun-bonnets

Fireweed

Dwarf Dandelion

Cynthia

Potato Dandelion

SUN-BONNETS *(Chaptalia tomentosa)*

This little daisy-like composite is one of the first flowers to appear in the spring in the coastal plain pinelands. The plant has a basal rosette of leaves which are bright green and smooth above but densely white-woolly beneath, the new ones not being fully grown at the time the plant blooms. Its flower heads are almost an inch across when fully expanded, and they have a number of marginal rays which are white or creamy-white on the upper surface and violet-tinged on the back. Each head nods at the summit of a slender, naked, woolly-coated stem from 4 to 12 inches tall. It grows in moist places, blooming between late February and May.

RANGE: N.C. south to Fla. and west to Tex.

FIREWEED *(Erechtites hieracifolia)*

This is a smooth or somewhat hairy, rank-odored plant with a grooved and usually branched stem from 1 to 8 feet tall. Its leaves are thin, lance-shaped or oblong, with ragged teeth and sometimes deeply cut, and from 2 to 8 inches long. The numerous flower heads have a cylindrical involucre about ⅔ of an inch high and contain a number of tubular whitish flowers. The pappus is of silky whitish hairs. It grows in moist thickets, clearings, and open woods and it is often abundant on recently burned-over areas; blooming between July and October.

RANGE: Nfd. to Ont. and Minn. south to Fla. and Tex.

The Chicory Tribe

The remaining composites have heads made up entirely of flowers with strap-shaped corollas (rays), which are usually 5-toothed at the summit. Most of them have a bitter and milky juice. Some botanists consider them as belonging to a separate plant family, the Chicory Family.

DWARF DANDELION *(Krigia virginica)*

The Dwarf Dandelion has bright yellow heads of dandelion-like flowers about ½ inch across, on slender stalks from 2 to about 10 inches tall. Its leaves are almost always in a basal cluster or rosette. Most of them are between 2 and 4 inches long and they are variously toothed or lobed, or more rarely entire. It grows in dry open woods, fields, and along roadsides; blooming between late March and July.

RANGE: Me. to Ont., Wis. and Iowa south to Fla. and Tex.

CYNTHIA *(Krigia biflora)*

Cynthia is a smooth and somewhat whitened plant with a stem from 1 to 2 feet tall, usually with a single clasping leaf below the middle. The stem forks above the leaf and each branch ends in a head of orange-yellow flowers from 1 to 1½ inches across. Its clustered basal leaves are 2 to 6 inches long and may be either wavy-toothed or lobed, or quite entire. It grows in moist open woods, fields, and meadows; blooming between May and October. Also known as the Virginia Goat's-beard.

RANGE: Ont. to Man. south to Ga., Ky., Mo. and Colo.

MOUNTAIN CYNTHIA *(Krigia montana)*

This plant is also called the Blue Ridge Dandelion as it grows on rocky slopes and cliffs in the mountains from w. N.C. and e. Tenn. south to n. Ga. It has a branched stem from 5 to 15 inches high, usually with a reclining base, and bearing several scattered leaves. The leaves are quite narrow and vary from being untoothed to irregularly cut-toothed. Its flower heads are bright yellow, dandelion-like, almost an inch across, and bloom between May and September. (Not illustrated)

POTATO-DANDELION *(Krigia dandelion)*

The Potato-dandelion derives its name from tuber-bearing roots. It is a smooth and somewhat whitened plant with a cluster of basal leaves; and a slender and leafless stalk from 6 to 18 inches high which bears a single, bright yellow, dandelion-like flower head about an inch across. The leaves are 3 to 6 inches long and untoothed to sparingly toothed or lobed. It grows on the borders of woods, prairies, and in meadows; blooming between April and June.

RANGE: N.J. to Ky., Ill. and Kan. south to Fla. and Tex.

FALSE DANDELION (*Pyrrhopappus carolinianus*)

The False-dandelion is a smoothish plant with a leafy and branching stem 1 to 3 feet high. Its leaves are variable; the larger and lower ones 3 to 8 inches long and pinnately lobed, cleft or toothed. Those along the upper part of the stem are quite small, lance-shaped, and have clasping bases. Its flower heads are dandelion-like, about 1½ inches across, and usually a pale yellow; but a form which occurs locally in n. Fla. and Ala. has cream-colored rays which are tipped with rose. The pappus is very soft and tawny or reddish in color. It grows in dry fields, clearings, and along roadsides; blooming between April and June.

RANGE: Del. to s. Ind. and Kan. south to Fla. and Tex.

COMMON DANDELION (*Taraxacum officinale*)

The familiar and weedy dandelion occurs abundantly in open or grassy places throughout much of North America but, in spite of its widespread distribution, it is an immigrant from Europe. It is a stemless plant with a basal rosette of narrow leaves which are variously and pinnately lobed and cut-toothed. The bright golden-yellow heads of flowers are about 1½ inches across and are borne on hollow and leafless stalks from 2 to 10 inches long. The involucre has an outer circle of small bracts which curve outward and backward, and an inner circle of long ones. It blooms abundantly between late February and June and occasionally much later or in winter. Many people enjoy the leaves as spring greens.

CHICORY (*Chicorium intybus*)

The Chicory, or Succory, is a common but quite pretty weed which also came from Europe. It is now common in fields and along roadsides throughout much of eastern North America except in the Deep South. It is an erect plant often 3 feet or more high, and on its upright and rigid branches it produces a procession of flower heads a bit more than an inch across, their numerous rays being a most beautiful bright blue color. Its flowering season often extends from late May to October. The lower leaves are 3 to 6 inches long, variously toothed, cut, or lobed, and taper into long stalks. Those upward along the stem are smaller and have clasping bases. Some of its varieties are cultivated either as a leafy vegetable or for the roots which are used as a substitute or adulterant for coffee. Endive is a closely related species, *Chicorium endivus*.

GRASS-LEAF LETTUCE (*Lactuca graminifolia*)

This is a quite unique species of wild lettuce with a remotely leafy stem from 1 to 3 feet tall. Its leaves are all very long and narrow, the larger ones toward the base sometimes as much as 15 inches in length and often with a few coarse teeth or spreading lobes. The bright purplish-blue heads of flowers are about ½ inch across. It grows in dry, open, sandy woods and fields chiefly in the coastal plain; blooming between April and July.

RANGE: S.C. south to Fla. and west to Tex.

WILD LETTUCE (*Lactuca canadensis*)

This is a variable but smooth and somewhat whitened plant with a leafy stem from 3 to 10 feet tall, which branches above into a large cluster of innumerable flower heads. The leaves are 2 to 8 inches long and may be untoothed to deeply lobed; those of the stem being stalkless or having clasping bases. Its flower heads are little more than ¼ inch across and contain a number of yellow-rayed flowers. The Wild Lettuce is commonly seen in moist thickets, clearings, and the borders of woods; blooming between June and October. It is also known as the Tall Lettuce.

RANGE: N.S. to B.C. south to Fla. and Tex.

PRICKLY LETTUCE (*Lactuca scariola*)

The Prickly Lettuce is a widespread and common weed introduced from Europe. It is now found in fields, waste places and along roads quite generally in eastern North America. Although it quite closely resembles the preceding species, it may be readily distinguished by the row of bristly prickles along the midrib on the undersides of its leaves, which quite frequently are turned vertically. Its yellow flower heads are also small and produced between July and October. (Not illustrated)

322

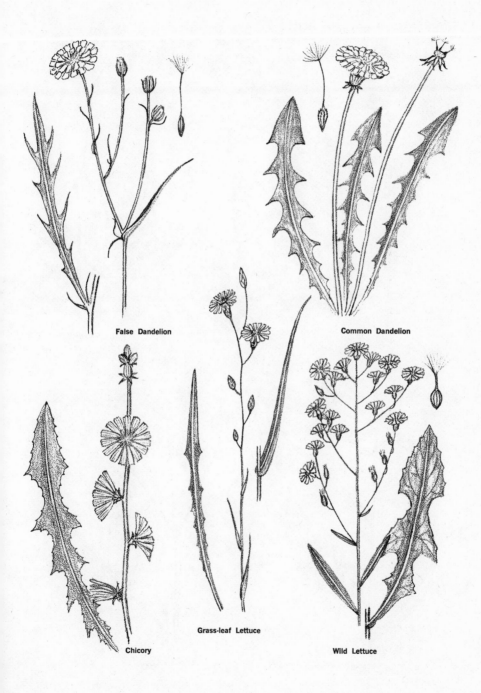

False Dandelion

Common Dandelion

Chicory

Grass-leaf Lettuce

Wild Lettuce

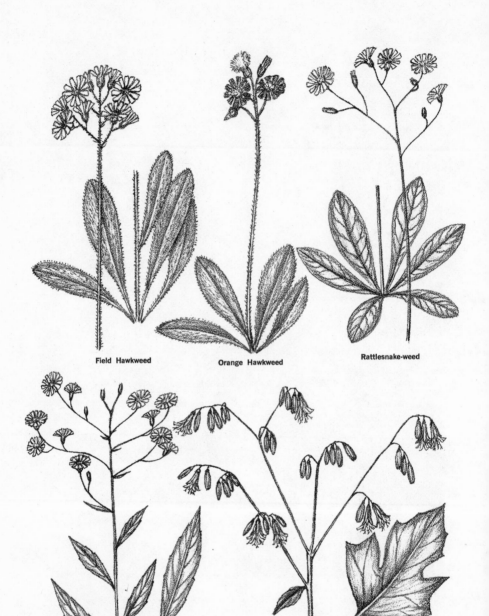

Field Hawkweed

Orange Hawkweed

Rattlesnake-weed

Panicled Hawkweed

White-lettuce

FIELD HAWKWEED *(Hieracium pratense)*

Our most common and weedy species of hawkweeds, such as this one, are naturalized immigrants from Europe. The Field Hawkweed, or King-devil, is a hairy plant with a cluster of basal leaves and a simple stem 1 to 2 feet high, which has but 1 or 2 small leaves. The basal leaves are oblong or narrowly top-shaped, 2 to 5 inches long, mostly untoothed, and tapered into winged stalks. The flower heads are borne in a more or less compact terminal cluster and contain a number of yellow-rayed flowers. It is often common in fields, clearings, and along roadsides as far south as w. N.C. and n. Ga.; blooming between May and August. Some of the hairs on the upper part of the stem are blackish.

ORANGE HAWKWEED *(Hieracium aurantiacum)*

Also known as the Devil's-paintbrush, this plant is quite similar to the preceding species, but it has heads of bright orange-red flowers. A very pretty but often extremely troublesome weed, it is also a native of Europe. It and the preceding species often occur together, blooming at the same time.

RATTLESNAKE-WEED *(Hieracium venosum)*

This native species is often common in dry open woods and clearings, and is sometimes called Poor Robin's-plantain. It is quite a smooth plant with a basal rosette of elliptic to narrowly top-shaped leaves from 1 to 4 inches long. They are beautifully veined or mottled with purple above and are pale to purplish and somewhat hairy beneath. The heads of bright yellow flowers are little more than ½ inch across and are in a loose cluster at the summit of a leafless or few-leaved stalk usually 1 to 2 feet high. It blooms between May and September. RANGE: Me. to Ont. south to Fla. and La.

PANICLED HAWKWEED *(Hieracium paniculatum)*

This hawkweed has a stem from 1 to 3 feet tall, smooth except toward the base, and leafy up to the open and slenderly-branched cluster of flower heads. The leaves are rather thin, mostly lance-shaped, sparingly toothed, whitish beneath, and from 2 to 6 inches long. Its numerous flower heads are about ½ inch across, containing a number of yellow-rayed flowers. It grows in dry open woods, blooming between July and October.
RANGE: N.S. to Ont. and Mich. south to Ga. and Tenn.

ROUGH HAWKWEED *(Hieracium scabrum)*

This species has a slender, roughish stem with leaves mostly below the middle; and yellow-rayed flower heads in a rather flat-topped cluster. It grows in dry open woods from Mass. to Mich. and Kan. south to Ga. and Tex.; blooming from July to October. (Not illustrated)

WHITE-LETTUCE *(Prenanthes alba)*

Also called Rattlesnake-root, this is a smooth whitened plant, usually with a purplish stem 2 to 5 feet tall. Its leaves are variable but commonly egg-shaped, heart-shaped or triangular; and coarsely toothed, lobed or divided. Most of them are stalked and the lower ones may be as much as 8 inches long. The usually numerous flower heads are in an open cluster. They contain 8 or more whitish flowers with a cinnamon-brown pappus, and the purplish involucre is whitened with a bloom. It grows on wooded slopes and roadbanks; blooming from August to October.
RANGE: Me. to Que. and Sask. south to N.C., Tenn. and Mo.

TALL WHITE-LETTUCE *(Prenanthes altissima)*

This species is similar but the flower heads have 5 or 6 greenish flowers with a creamy-white pappus. It grows in woods from Que. to Man. south to Ga. and Ala, blooming July to October. (Not illustrated)

LION'S-FOOT *(Prenanthes serpentaria)*

Lion's-foot usually has a purplish stem, and thickish leaves variously lobed. The flower heads have 8 to 12 pinkish or creamy flowers and a creamy pappus. Woods and roadbanks from Mass. to Ohio south to Fla. and Miss.; blooming Aug. to Oct. (Not illustrated)

SLENDER RATTLESNAKE-ROOT *(Prenanthes autumnalis)*

This plant has pink-rayed heads in a spike-like cluster. It grows in wet coastal plain pinelands and savannahs from N.J. south to Fla. and west to Miss.; blooming September to November. (Not illustrated)

325

BOOKS TO READ
FOR FURTHER INFORMATION

Fernald, M. L.   Gray's Manual of Botany, 8th ed. American Book Co., N.Y. 1950. (T)

Gleason, H. A.   Illustrated Flora of the Northeastern United States and Canada (New Britton & Brown), 3 vols. N.Y. Botanical Garden. 1952. (T)

Grimm, W. C.   Recognizing Native Shrubs. Stackpole Co., Harrisburg, Pa. 1966.

House, H. D.   Wild Flowers. Macmillan Co., N.Y. 1961.

Lemmon, R. S. & Johnson, C. C.   Wildflowers of North America. Hanover House, N.Y. 1961.

Massey, A. B.   Virginia Flora. Virginia Agricultural Experiment Station, Technical Bulletin 155. Blacksburg, Va. 1961. (T)

Peterson, R. T. & McKenny, M.   Field Guide to Wildflowers. Houghton Mifflin Co., Boston, Mass. 1968.

Radford, A. E.; Ahles, H. E. & Bell, C. R.   Guide to the Vascular Flora of the Carolinas. Book Exchange, University of North Carolina, Chapel Hill, N.C. 1964 (T)

Rickett, H. W.   The New Field Book of American Wild Flowers. G. P. Putnam's Sons, N.Y. 1963.

Rickett, H. W.   Wildflowers of America. Crown Publishers, N.Y. 1953.

Strausbaugh, P. D. & Core, E. L.   Flora of West Virginia. West Virginia University Bulletin, Series 52. Morgantown, W. Va. 1952-1964. (T)

Stupka, A.   Wildflowers in Color. Harper & Row, N.Y. 1965.

Wherry, E. T.   Wild Flower Guide, Eastern and Midland United States. Doubleday & Co., N.Y. 1954.

Books marked (T) are technical and require some knowledge of botanical terminology.

INDEX

327

Meadow-beauty, Virginia, 182
Meadow-beauty, Yellow, 182
Meadow-parsnip, 195
Meadow-parsnip, Hairy-jointed, 195
Meadow-parsnip, Purple, 195
Meadow-rue, Early, 108
Meadow-rue, Mountain, 108
Meadow-rue, Purple, 108
Meadow-rue, Skunk, 108
Meadow-rue, Tall, 108
Meadow-rue, Waxy-leaf, 108
Medeola virginiana, 56
Meehania, 234
Meehania cordata, 234
Melanthium hybridum, 45
Melanthium virginicum, 45
Melastomaceae, 182
Melilotus alba, 146
Melilotus officinalis, 146
Mentha arvensis, 234
Menyanthes trifoliata var. *minor*, 211
Mertensia virginica, 227
Mikania scandens, 273
Milk-pea, 149
Milk-pea, Elliott's, 149
Milkweed, Blunt-leaf, 215
Milkweed, Common, 215
Milkweed Family, 212
Milkweed, Few-flowered, 212
Milkweed, Four-leaf, 215
Milkweed, Green, 216
Milkweed, Lance-leaf, 212
Milkweed, Poke, 216
Milkweed, Purple, 216
Milkweed, Red, 215
Milkweed, Sandhill, 216
Milkweed, Swamp, 215
Milkweed, Tall, 216
Milkweed, Thin-leaf, 215
Milkweed, White, 216
Milkweed, Whorled, 215
Milkweed, Yellow, 212
Milkwort, Cross-leaf, 162
Milkwort Family, 161
Milkwort, Field, 162
Milkwort, Fringed, 161
Milkwort, Low Pine-barren, 161
Milkwort, Orange, 162
Milkwort, Pink, 162
Milkwort, Purple, 162
Milkwort, Racemed, 162
Milkwort, Tall Pine-barren, 161
Milkwort, Yellow, 162
Milkwort, Whorled, 162
Millfoil, 314
Mimosa Family, 136

Mimosoideae, 136
Mimulus alatus, 241
Mimulus moschatus, 241
Mimulus ringens, 241
Mint, American Wild, 234
Mint Family, 229
Mistflower, 270
Mitchella repens, 253
Mitella diphylla, 128
Mitella nuda, 128
Miterwort, False, 128
Miterwort, Naked, 125
Miterwort, Two-leaf, 128
Moccasin-flower, 70
Monarda clinopodia, 233
Monarda didyma, 233
Monarda, Dotted, 233
Monarda fistulosa, 233
Monarda punctata, 233
Moneses uniflora, 199
Monkey-flower, Square-stemmed, 241
Monkey-flower, Wing-stemmed, 241
Monkshood, New York, 107
Monkshood, Trailing, 107
Monkshood, Wild, 107
Monotropa hypopithys, 200
Monotropa uniflora, 200
Morning-glory, Arrow-leaf, 219
Morning-glory Family, 219
Morning-glory, Wild, 219
Moss-pink, 223
Mountain-fringe, 112
Mountain-lettuce, 124
Mountain-mint, 234
Mountain-moss, 123
Mountain-tea, 200
Mullein, Common, 238
Mullein, Moth, 238
Muskflower, 241
Musquash-root, 196
Mustard Family, 115

Nelumbo lutea, 90
Nemastylis floridana, 67
Nemastylis geminiflora, 67
Never-wet, 36
Nightshade, Bittersweet, 237
Nightshade, Black, 237
Nightshade Family, 237
Nothoscordum bivalve, 49
Nuphar advena, 90
Nuphar sagittifolium, 90
Nymphaeaceae, 90
Nymphaea mexicana, 90
Nymphaea odorata, 90
Nymphaea tetragona, 90

Nymphaea tuberosa, 90
Nymphoides aquatica, 211
Nymphoides cordata, 211

Obedient-plant, 233
Obolaria virginica, 211
Oconee-bells, 200
Oenothera biennis, 185
Oenothera fruticosa, 186
Oenothera humifusa, 185
Oenothera laciniata, 185
Oenothera perennis, 186
Oenothera speciosa, 186
Onagraceae, 185
Onion Family, 40
Onion, Nodding Wild, 49
Opuntia compressa, 181
Orange-plume, 73
Orangeroot, 107
Orchid, Cranefly, 81
Orchid, Crested Yellow, 73
Orchid Family, 68
Orchid, Fringless Purple, 74
Orchid, Green-fly, 70
Orchid, Green Fringed, 73
Orchid, Hooker's, 74
Orchid, Large Purple Fringed, 73
Orchid, Ragged, 73
Orchid, Rose, 77
Orchid, Rosebud, 77
Orchid, Round-leaf, 74
Orchid, Small Green Wood, 74
Orchid, Small Purple Fringed, 73
Orchid, Small Southern Yellow, 74
Orchid, Snowy, 74
Orchid, White Fringed, 73
Orchid, White Rein, 74
Orchid, Yellow Fringed, 73
Orchidaceae, 68
Orchis, Showy, 73
Orchis spectabilis, 73
Orobanchaceae, 246
Orobanche uniflora, 246
Orontium aquaticum, 36
Orpine, American, 123
Orpine Family, 123
Oswego-tea, 233
Osmorhiza claytoni, 195
Osmorhiza longistylis, 195
Oxalidaceae, 158
Oxalis acetosella, 158
Oxalis grandis, 158
Oxalis stricta, 158
Oxalis violacea, 158
Ox-eye, 301
Ox-eye, Sea, 310

Painted-cup, Scarlet, 242
Painted-leaf, 165
Panax quinquefolium, 189
Panax trifolium, 189
Pansy, Field, 178
Papaveraceae, 111
Papilionoideae, 136
Papoose-root, 108
Parnassia asarifolia, 128
Parnassia glauca, 128
Parnassia grandifolia, 128
Parsley Family, 190
Partridge-berry, 253
Partridge-pea, 138
Pasque-flower, 98
Passiflora incarnata, 181
Passiflora lutea, 181
Passifloraceae, 181
Passion-flower Family, 181
Passion-flower, Purple, 181
Passion-flower, Yellow, 181
Pea Family, 136
Pedicularis canadensis, 242
Peltandra virginica, 36
Peltandra sagittaefolia, 36
Pencil-flower, 157
Pencil-flower, Decumbent, 157
Pennyroyal, Bastard-, 230
Pennywort, 211
Penstemon australis, 242
Penstemon canescens, 242
Penstemon hirsutus, 242
Penstemon laevigatus, 242
Penthorum sedoides, 123
Pepper-and-salt, 123, 192
Peppermint, 234
Pepperroot, 115
Phacelia bipinnatifida, 227
Phacelia dubia, 227
Phacelia fimbriata, 227
Phacelia, Fringed, 227
Phacelia, Loose-flowered, 227
Phacelia, Purple, 227
Phacelia purshii, 227
Phacelia, Pursh's, 227
Phacelia, Small-flowered, 227
Phaseolus polystachios, 153
Phlox amoena, 220
Phlox amplifolia, 224
Phlox, Broad-leaf, 224
Phlox buckleyi, 220
Phlox, Carolina, 223
Phlox carolina, 223
Phlox, Creeping, 223
Phlox divaricata, 220

341